D0712288

Suppressing Terrorist Financing and Money Laundering

Jae-myong Koh

Suppressing Terrorist Financing and Money Laundering

 Springer

Dr. Jae-myong Koh
Rm# 1407 Ministry of Foreign
Affairs and Trade, 95-1
Doryum-dong, Jongro-gu
Seoul
Korea 110-787
macario27@msn.com

ISBN-10   3-540-32518-2 Springer Berlin Heidelberg New York
ISBN-13   978-3-540-32518-5 Springer Berlin Heidelberg New York

Cataloging-in-Publication Data
Library of Congress Control Number: 2006922259

Springer is a part of Springer Science+Business Media

springer.com

© Springer Berlin · Heidelberg 2006
Printed in Germany

Softcover-Design: Erich Kirchner, Heidelberg

SPIN 11675914   64/3153-5 4 3 2 1 0 – Printed on acid-free paper

For my father:
Kwang-woong KOH (1941-)

Preface

When watching the collapse of the Twin Towers on CNN 11 September 2001, the international community was awakened to the urgent needs of open discussion to identify the emerging threat and the way to cope with it. Given the unprecedented heinous nature of the incident, the moves that the international community made were quick and included countermeasures in various dimensions. One of the major countermeasures highlighted as a result was to target the financial infrastructure of terrorist organisations. In this campaign, diverse organisations have participated, including the Security Council, Financial Action Task Force (FATF), IMF, World Bank, etc. At the same time, various methodologies have also been introduced at both the international and national level. Such a consensus and mobilisation of resources to one end in the international community may be considered phenomenal in the history of public international law, and without doubt merits an in-depth analysis for both academic and practical purposes.

In this context, this book examines the evolution and implementation of international standards on countering the financing of terrorism. There are two dimensions to be taken into account to understand the structure of this book. The first is concerned with a sequential perspective. Given that 9/11 has provided a critical momentum in this area, chapter 2 deals with the international position prior to 9/11, whereas chapters 3, 4 and 5 analyse development following 9/11. The second is related to a hard law and soft law perspective. Chapters 2 and 3 look into the development of hard law in this area, while chapters 4 and 5 focus on international standards and their monitoring and enforcement from a soft law perspective.

Chapter 1, as a preliminary, presents an overview of terrorism in general and current terrorist financing problems in the world. This chapter points out that religious terrorism has emerged as a major driving force behind the international terrorist movement, and places emphasis on a financial war on terrorism. Particularly, it clarifies the elusive relationship between terrorist financing and money laundering.

Chapter 2 examines the manner in which the international community dealt with terrorism prior to the 9/11 attack. The practices of the UN General Assembly and the Security Council are analysed for this purpose. Of particular note is the full commentary on the 1999 International Convention for the Suppression of the Financing of Terrorism, given that an analysis of the overall text of the convention is scarcely to be found in the existing literature.

Chapter 3 analyses the way in which the Security Council has been involved in a counter-terrorist financing campaign since 9/11. To this end, this chapter analyses two distinctive approaches. One is a structural approach which comprises long-term measures to build up a counter-terrorism infrastructure at both the international and national level, as with Resolution 1373 (2001). The other is an operational approach which refers to immediate measures taken in the context of an imminent or actual crisis or danger caused by some terrorists. In other words, this approach could be said to be a crackdown on particular terrorists, and Resolution 1390 (2002) plays a pivotal role in this operational campaign.

Chapter 4 examines the current developing international standards set by specialist bodies such as the Financial Action Task Force (FATF), the Basel Committee on Banking Supervision, the Wolfsberg Group of Banks, and the Egmont Group, etc. Particularly, the commentary on the Nine Special Recommendations on Terrorist Financing and the 2003 revised FATF Forty Recommendations is provided in a comparison with the 1996 version of FATF Forty Recommendations. In the course of this, a parallel development of hard law and soft law is also highlighted by way of contrast with earlier chapters. In so doing, attention is given to the non-binding nature as well as detailed contents of the standards, which is typical of the soft law phenomena.

Chapter 5 analyses the monitoring and enforcement of these international standards by the specialist bodies. Firstly, the overall work of the FATF is examined as well as some controversial issues such as the Non-Cooperative Countries and Territories (NCCT) initiative. Furthermore, the involvement of the IMF, World Bank, and FATF-style regional bodies are dealt with in detail, which is seldom found in the existing literature. Lastly, in-depth analysis of the soft law nature of the involvement of specialist bodies is made, and the transformation process from soft law into hard law is highlighted as well.

Chapter 6 examines the overall impact of 9/11 on the anti-money laundering and counter-terrorist financing campaign. Finally, suggestions are made to utilise the issue of the suppression of the financing of terrorism as a Trojan horse in providing further support to anti-money laundering campaigns and to extend the operational approach of the Security Council to other criminal finances.

Acknowledgements

This book is based on a Ph.D thesis, submitted at the Faculty of Law, University of Edinburgh in November 2005. My utmost thanks go to Professor William.C. Gilmore. Throughout my Ph.D work, I realised that as a mentor, he set the standards for me in every aspect: immense academic knowledge, rich hands-on field experience, humane generosity and meticulous care. To him, I am deeply indebted.

I would also like to express my gratitude to Professor Choon-ho Park, the judge of the International Tribunal for the Law of the Sea, for his constant guidance in my study of international law since my undergraduate days, and Professor Alan E. Boyle who also kindly offered insightful comments on my thesis in relation to soft law.

I would like to take this opportunity to thank all those in the United Nations, the IMF and the World Bank who kindly gave interviews, sharing their time and expertise. In particular, Ambassador Curtis A.Ward of New York, Mr. Ross S. Delston and Mr. Joseph Halligan of Washington, Mr. Jong-youn Choo, the then Counsellor of the Permanent Mission of Korea to the UN. Moreover, I thank all those in the Library of Congress, and the Law Library of the University of Columbia for their assistance in respect of my research. I would also like to acknowledge the financial support received from the School of Law of the University of Edinburgh in relation to my research trips.

I extend my special thanks to all those in the Korean governments. In particular, Mr. Il-suek Jang, Head of Planning & Administrative Office of the Korean FIU, who kindly arranged interviews with officers of the Korean FIU during my research trip to Seoul.

I also feel grateful to Mr. John Stevenson and Mr. Seung-hwan Jin for their suggestions and assistance in the development of my book. Last but not least, I appreciate wholeheartedly the unconditional love and support of my family thus far.

The views contained in this work are mine alone and are not intended to represent the perceptions of any institution or government with which I am associated. I am solely responsible for the outcome. The text seeks to represent the position as of 1 July 2005 although I have incorporated changes of a more recent vintage where possible.

Seoul, February 2006   Jae-myong KOH

Table of Contents

Dedication V

Preface.. VII

Acknowledgements.. IX

Table of Contents.. XI

List of Abbreviations..XVII

1 Terrorism and its Financing..1
  1.1 Introduction..1
  1.2 Terrorism in the 21st Century 2
    1.2.1 An overview of general trends in modern terrorism...............................2
      1.2.1.1 The types of terrorist groups 2
      1.2.1.2 The trend in the late 1960s and 1970s..3
      1.2.1.3 The trend since the 1980s 5
    1.2.2 The importance of financing for modern terrorism 10
      1.2.2.1 Context...10
      1.2.2.2 Various needs for financing 12
  1.3 Terrorist Financing and Money Laundering 19
    1.3.1 The sources of terrorist financing...19
      1.3.1.1 Criminal activities..19
      1.3.1.2 Donations 21
      1.3.1.3 Legitimate businesses 22
    1.3.2 The role of money laundering in terrorist financing............................24
      1.3.2.1 Context...24
      1.3.2.2 The relationship of money laundering and terrorist financing....26
      1.3.2.3 Some cases of money laundering in terrorist financing 28
  4 Conclusion 30

2 The Common Perception on Terrorist Financing prior to 9/11 31
  2.1 Introduction..31
  2.2 The Orthodox Stance on International Terrorism 32
    2.2.1 UN General Assembly and anti-terrorism conventions......................32

2.2.2 Security Council and the *Lockerbie* Incident 35
2.3 The Emergence of Counter-Terrorist Financing Strategy........................38
   2.3.1 The prototypes..38
      2.3.1.1 Context..38
      2.3.1.2 Public sector 42
      2.3.1.3 Private sector 49
      2.3.1.4 A bridging mechanism: the FIU 54
      2.3.1.5 International cooperation 56
   2.3.2 UN General Assembly and the 1999 Convention 60
      2.3.2.1 Context..60
      2.3.2.2 Nature and scope..61
      2.3.2.3 Public sector 62
      2.3.2.4 Private sector 71
      2.3.2.5 A bridging mechanism..75
      2.3.2.6 International cooperation 76
   2.3.3 Security Council and the *Afghanistan* situation 78
2.4 Conclusion..79

3 The Role of the Security Council since 9/11 81
3.1 Introduction 81
3.2 Structural Approach: Resolution 1373...82
   3.2.1 Background 82
   3.2.2 The nature of Resolution 1373 83
   3.2.3 The general framework of the resolution 86
   3.2.4 The monitoring mechanism...89
      3.2.4.1 The operating procedure of the CTC 89
      3.2.4.2 The monitoring priorities of the CTC 90
      3.2.4.3 The various activities of the CTC 91
      3.2.4.4 The current progress and revitalisation of the CTC....94
   3.2.5 The criticism..95
3.3 Operational Approach: Resolution 1390 97
   3.3.1 The context..97
   3.3.2 The nature of Resolution 1390 98
   3.3.3 The general framework of the resolution 99
   3.3.4 The enforcement body and the monitoring mechanism 100
      3.3.4.1 The operating procedure of the Sanctions Committee............100
      3.3.4.2 The activities of the Sanctions Committee 101
      3.3.4.3 The Monitoring Group...102
   3.3.5 The criticism..103
3.4 Lessons for Future Campaign against Terrorist Financing.......106
   3.4.1 General...106
   3.4.2 The definition of terrorism 108
   3.4.3 The establishment of a fair and objective mechanism for listing
      and de-listing...110

3.4.4 The avoidance of duplication 115
3.4.5 The sustaining of momentum 117
3.5 Conclusion 117

4 Standards set by Specialist Bodies since 9/11 119
4.1 Introduction 119
    4.1.1 The definition of soft law 120
    4.1.2 The utility of soft law 122
4.2 The Major International Standard Setter: the FATF 124
    4.2.1 Context 124
    4.2.2 The general framework of the Nine Special Recommendations
        on Terrorist Financing and the 2003 Forty Recommendations 126
        4.2.2.1 Major changes 126
        4.2.2.2 The criminal justice measures in the public sector 128
        4.2.2.3 The prevention of money laundering in the private sector 131
        4.2.2.4 The FIU: a bridging body between relevant sectors 141
        4.2.2.5 International cooperation 142
4.3 Other Standard Setters 143
    4.3.1 Context 143
    4.3.2 Basel Committee on Banking Supervision 143
        4.3.2.1 Prevention of Criminal Use of the Banking System for the
            Purpose of Money-Laundering (1988) 144
        4.3.2.2 Core Principles for Effective Banking Supervision (1997) 144
        4.3.2.3 Core Principles Methodology (1999) 145
        4.3.2.4 Customer due diligence for banks (2001) 146
    4.3.3 Wolfsberg Group of Banks 147
        4.3.3.1 Anti-Money Laundering Principles for Private Banking
            (2000) 148
        4.3.3.2 Statement on the Suppression of the Financing of Terrorism
            (2002) 149
        4.3.3.3 Anti-Money Laundering Principles for Correspondent
            Banking (2002) 149
        4.3.3.4 Monitoring Screening and Searching Wolfsberg
            Statement (2003) 150
    4.3.4 International Association of Insurance Supervisors 150
        4.3.4.1 Anti-Money Laundering Guidance Notes for Insurance
            Supervisors and Insurance Entities (2002) 151
        4.3.4.2 Insurance Core Principles and Methodology (2003) 151
    4.3.5 International Organization of Securities Commissions 152
        4.3.5.1 Resolution on Money Laundering (1992) 152
        4.3.5.2 Principles on Client Identification and Beneficial
            Ownership for the Securities Industry (2004) 153
    4.3.6 Egmont Group of Financial Intelligence Units 153
4.4 Soft law phenomena: non-binding but detailed provisions 154

5 Monitoring and Enforcing Standards by Specialist Bodies...................**157**
  5.1 Introduction 157
  5.2 FATF 157
    5.2.1 The monitoring of standards 157
      5.2.1.1 Context.. 157
      5.2.1.2 Self-assessment... 158
      5.2.1.3 Mutual evaluation 159
      5.2.1.4 NCCT... 161
    5.2.2 The enforcement of standards 162
      5.2.2.1 FATF member countries.. 162
      5.2.2.2 Non-FATF member countries....................................... 164
    5.2.3 Other supporting activities 167
  5.3 IMF / World Bank 168
    5.3.1 Context... 168
    5.3.2 The monitoring of standards 170
    5.3.3 Other supporting activities 175
  5.4 FATF-Style Regional Bodies (FSRBs).. 177
    5.4.1 The development of FSRBs 177
    5.4.2 The nature and scope of the FSRBs work 178
      5.4.2.1 The background to the APG 178
      5.4.2.2 The structure and functions of the APG 179
      5.4.2.3 The monitoring of standards by the APG 182
      5.4.2.4 The enforcement of standards by the APG 184
      5.4.2.5 Other supporting activities.. 185
    5.4.3 The FSRBs strategy: developments and prospects............. 187
  5.5 The soft law phenomena 188
    5.5.1 The soft enforcement and the blurring boundary between
        monitoring and enforcement 188
    5.5.2 Future developments: transformation from soft law into hard law .. 193
  5.6 Conclusion 197

6 The Financing of Terrorism: a Trojan Horse..**199**
  6.1 Context 199
  6.2 Further Support for the AML Campaign 199
    6.2.1 The impact of 9/11 on the AML campaign 199
    6.2.2 Issues concerning duplication 201
      6.2.2.1 Assessment 201
      6.2.2.2 Technical assistance.. 203
      6.2.2.3 Research.. 205
      6.2.2.4 Sanctions.. 205
    6.2.3 Securing further involvement of influential actors........... 206
    6.2.4 Introducing intrusive legal tools....................................... 208
  6.3 Extending the Operational Approach to Criminal Finances 209
  6.4 Food for Further Research 212

References **215**

  Books and Articles...215

  Documents 225

     <APG> 225

     <FATF> 225

     <IMF/World Bank> 226

     <UN> 228

Index **233**

List of Abbreviations

AML	Anti-Money Laundering
APG	Asia/Pacific Group on Money Laundering
BCBS	Basel Committee on Banking Supervision
CAS	Country Assistance Strategy
CDD	Customer Due Diligence
CFATF	Caribbean Financial Action Task Force
CFT	Combating the Financing of Terrorism
CTC	Counter-Terrorism Committee
CTED	Counter-Terrorism Committee Executive Directorate
ESAAMLG	Eastern and Southern Africa Anti-Money Laundering Group
FATF	Financial Action Task Force on Money Laundering
FSA	Financial Sector Assessment
FSAP	Financial Sector Assessment Programme
FSRBs	FATF-Style Regional Bodies
FSSA	Financial System Stability Assessment
GAFISUD	Financial Action Task Force on Money Laundering in South America
IAIS	International Association of Insurance Supervisors
ICSFT	International Convention for the Suppression of the Financing of Terrorism
IMF	International Monetary Fund
IOSCO	International Organisation of Securities Commissions
KYC	Know Your Customer
MONEYVAL	Council of Europe Select Committee of Experts on the Evaluation of Anti-Money Laundering Measures
NCCT	Non-Cooperative Countries and Territories
OFC	Offshore Financial Centre
OGBS	Offshore Group of Banking Supervisors
ROSC	Report on Observance of Standards and Codes
TA	Technical Assistance
WMD	Weapons of Mass Destruction

1 Terrorism and its Financing

1.1 Introduction

"Terrorists want a lot of people watching and a lot of people listening and *not* a lot of people dead"(emphasis added). This is a famous remark made by Brian Jenkins in 1975[1], and there was for decades widespread acceptance of his observation.[2] However, the September 11th 2001 attack on the US has shaken this general acceptance to its foundations. Nowadays there is a growing concern that terrorists might use even weapons of mass destruction (WMD) thus annihilating as many innocent people as possible.

Nevertheless, some may ignore this concern simply by saying, "I am not living in the Western Hemisphere". Then the scenario of "Pandora's Box"[3] about which Western intelligence agencies have serious concerns, may be helpful in awakening indifferent readers to the devastating and universal impact of this new kind of terrorism. With this scenario, terrorists could for example load a portable nuclear suitcase bomb[4], or a dirty bomb made with nuclear material wrapped around conventional explosives onto a cargo ship and detonate it in a major port.[5] Unfortu-

---

[1] Jenkins BM (1975) "International Terrorism: A New Mode of Conflict". In: Carlton D, Schaerf C (eds) *International Terrorism and World Security*, p.15.

[2] Hoffman B "Re-Thinking Terrorism in Light of a War on Terrorism", Testimony before the Subcommittee on Terrorism and Homeland Security, House Permanent Select Committee on Intelligence, US House of Representatives, 26 September 2001.

[3] Felsted A, Odell M, "Agencies fear extent of al-Qaeda's sea network", *Financial Times*, 21 February 2002.

[4] Al-Qaida reportedly obtained several nuclear suitcase bombs in the autumn of 1998 (see Reeve S (1999) *The New Jackals: Ramzi Yousef, Osama bin Laden and the future of Terrorism*, pp.214-216). This allegation seems to be supported by the remarks of General Aleksandr Ivanovich Lebed, the former security czar of Russia. He told a visiting US congressional delegation in May 1997 that of 132 "suitcase bomb" in the former Soviet arsenal, he had been able to locate only 48, leaving 84 unaccounted for. Other senior Russian officials also told the congressional delegations that tactical nuclear weapons were missing (see, Stern J (1999) *The Ultimate Terrorist*, p.90).

[5] Felsted A, Odell M, *supra* note 3.

nately, this is not a remote possibility. For instance, roughly 6 million containers enter US ports annually and only 2 percent of them are checked.[6] If this scenario happens, needless to say, there would be huge casualties, and to make matters worse, government authorities might have to check all containers physically, thus seriously depressing international trade.[7]

Facing such overwhelming challenges, it is worthwhile to examine the question of why terrorism has recently changed so much in character and scope, and what the implications for the future are. In this vein, this chapter points out that among several kinds of terrorism, religious terrorism has emerged as a major driving force behind the international terrorist movement. Then, as countermeasures, analysis is given to the appropriateness of waging a financial war on terrorism and the roles of anti-money laundering regimes in this campaign.

1.2 Terrorism in the 21st Century

1.2.1 An overview of general trends in modern terrorism

1.2.1.1 The types of terrorist groups

In the 20th century, terrorist activities with various causes were observed, but three are of significance and direct relevance to the present analysis[8]: ethno-nationalist/separatist terrorism, ideological terrorism, and religious terrorism.

---

[6] "An Overview of International Terrorist Organizations", Hearing before the Subcomittee on International Terrorism, Nonproliferation and Human Rights of the Committee on International Relations, House of Representatives, 108th Congress, 1st Session, 26 March 2003, Serial No.108-10, p.36.
    Currently, 35 million containers are estimated to be in use around the world (Felsted A, Odell M, *supra* note 3).

[7] The US was concerned about this scenario that it brought up the issue at the G8 summit in June 2002 (For the result, see "G8 Recommendations on Counter-Terrorism" (visited on 7 July 2004) <http://www.iaea.org/NewsCenter/Features/RadSources/G8_Recomend.html>).

[8] Thus far, there is no clear-cut categorisation of terrorism phenomenon in literature but a common thread can be drawn without difficulty. See, e.g., Hoffman B (1999) *Inside Terrorism*; Wilkinson P (2001) *Terrorism Versus Democracy: The Liberal State Response*, pp.19-21; Russell CA, Banker Jr LJ, Miller BH (1979) "Out-Inventing the Terrorist". In: Alexander Y, Carlton D, Wilkinson P (eds) *Terrorism: Theory and Practice*, pp.31-32; Dinse J, Johnson S (1993) "Ideologies of Revolutionary Terrorism: Some Enduring and Emerging Themes". In: Han HH (ed) *Terrorism & Political Violence: Limits & Possibilities of Legal Control*, pp.61-68; Comb C (2003) *Terrorism in the Twenty-First Century*, 3rd edn, pp.44-47.

The ethno-nationalist/separatist groups seek political self-determination as is the case with the IRA (Irish Republican Army), the ETA (Basque Homeland and Liberty), and the PLO (Palestinian Liberation Organisation) of the 1970s.[9] Secondly, the ideological terrorist groups attempt to change the entire political, social and economic system either to an extreme left, or extreme right model.[10] The Revolutionary Armed Forces of Columbia (FARC) and Red Brigades in Italy are cases in point.[11] Lastly, religious terrorist groups conduct terrorist activities for the realisation of their religious goals as illustrated by Al-Qaida's attack on the US or Dr. Goldstein's massacre in the Cave of the Patriarchs.[12] However, in reality, it is difficult to simply classify certain terrorist groups into one category given that a group might comprise several components at the same time as with the "Catholic" IRA or the "Islamic" Hamas.[13]

1.2.1.2 The trend in the late 1960s and 1970s

Among the three major types of terrorism, it was the ethno-nationalist/separatist groups that brought the advent of modern international terrorism in the late 1960s.[14] The Popular Front for the Liberation of Palestine (PFLP), one of the six groups then comprising the PLO, hijacked an El Al commercial flight en route from Rome to Tel Aviv, and diverted it to Algiers on 22 July 1968.[15] Importantly, this incident is different from many of the post-war anti-colonial terrorist campaigns.[16] For the first time, the transnational "third country operation" concept was

---

[9] Russell CA, Banker Jr LJ, Miller BH, *supra* note 8, p.31. However, it should be pointed out that although the PLO began as a terrorist group, it was later recognised as a legitimate political organisation by the international community. See, Adams J (1988) *The Financing of Terror*, p.145, 158.

[10] Wilkinson P, *supra* note 8, p.20.

[11] *Ibid.*, p.20.

[12] In 1994, Dr. Baruch Goldstein, an orthodox Jew and ardent disciple of Kahane, entered the Ibrahim Mosque located at the Cave, and opened fire on Muslim worshippers, killing 22 and wounding 150 (Ranstorp M (2002) "Terrorism in the Name of Religion". In: Howard RD, Sawyer RL (eds) *Terrorism and Counterterrorism: Understanding the New Security Environment*, p.121).

[13] Hoffman B, *supra* note 8, p.87; Ranstorp M, *supra* note 12, p.122; Russell CA, Banker Jr LJ, Miller BH, *supra* note 8, p.8.

[14] Hoffman B, *supra* note 8, p.67. There seems to a general consensus to this argument. See, e.g, Wilkinson P, *supra* note 8, p.28; Russell CA, Banker Jr LJ, Miller BH, *supra* note 8, p.5.

[15] Hoffman B, *supra* note 8, p.68. The negotiations extended over forty days, and both the hijackers and hostages went free later.

[16] For example, most hijacks before the late 1960s were generally aimed at facilitating refugee escapes to otherwise inaccessible countries such as Cuba.

applied in modern terrorism.[17] Terrorists began to travel regularly from one country to another to launch their attacks.[18] In addition, the terrorist operation was
aimed at promoting their political cause worldwide[19] and bringing about changes
in government policies.[20] In this sense, it ushered in the era of international terrorism in the full sense. It was followed by a wave of terrorist operations of a
similar nature.[21]

Along with the surge of ethno-nationalist/separatist terrorism, ideological terrorism, mostly revolutionary left-wing terrorism, began to flex its *international*
muscles in the late 1960's and early 1970's.[22] However, these kinds of terrorist
groups, such as the Red Army Faction and the Japanese Red Army, for the most
part originated within industrialised liberal democracies, and did not seem to constitute any serious long-term threat to Western states.[23] Perhaps, the unprecedented
economic prosperity allowed the youth of affluent and privileged homes the
"luxury of introspection and self-criticism" on socio-economic iniquities.[24] Yet,
these ideological sects were politically marginalised, especially after the demise of
the Cold War.[25] Nonetheless, some left-wing local terrorists groups, such as the

---

[17] Alexander Y, Carlton D, Wilkinson P, *supra* note 8, p.6.

[18] *Ibid.*, p.68.

[19] For example, Zehdi Labib Terzi, the PLO's chief observer at the UN, remarked in a
1976 interview, "The first several hijackings aroused the consciousness of the world and
awakened the media and world opinion much more- and more effectively-than 20 years
of pleading at the UN", quoted in Schmid AP, de Graaf J (1982) *Violence as Communication: Insurgent Terrorism and the Western News Media*, p.32.

[20] Hoffman B, *supra* note 8, pp.67-69. Consequently, the PLO could force the Israeli government to communicate directly with it, despite the Israeli government's previous policy pronouncements to the contrary.

[21] For example, the PLO's attack on the Israeli athletes' dormitory during the Munich
Olympic Games in 1972 earned it wider publicity given that estimated 900 million people saw the crisis on their TV screens. As a result, Yassir Arafat, the PLO's leader, was
invited to address the UN General Assembly and shortly afterwards the PLO was granted special observer status in the UN (*Ibid.*, pp.71-75).

[22] The revolutionary left-wing terrorists attempted to benchmark the success of the PLO.
Furthermore, an alliance had developed between these different movements in the form
of the training of the German Red Army Faction (RAF) by the PLO. Eventually, this
unprecedented cooperation led to the Lod airport massacre by the Japanese Red Army in
1972, and the seizure of the OPEC oil ministers' conference in Vienna 1975 by the
combined teams of German RAF and Palestinian Terrorists (*Ibid.*, pp.82-83).

[23] Wilkinson P, "Terrorist Movements". In: Alexander Y, Carlton D, Wilkinson P (eds),
supra note 8, pp.106-107.

[24] *Ibid.*, p.107; Hoffman B, *supra* note 8, p.80.

[25] For example, the Red Army Faction finally collapsed in 1992. See, Hoffman B, *supra*
note 8, p.84.

FARC, are still very active in the 21st century. However, it is doubtful whether they could be properly classified as "modern international" terrorist groups given their indigenous nature and the limited scope of their operations.[26] Moreover, they are criticised for the allegation that their criminal enterprises have assumed greater priority than their own ideological agendas.[27]

1.2.1.3 The trend since the 1980s

To make a long story short, the late 1960s and 1970s were characterised by the rise of "secular" ethno-nationalist/separatist and left-wing terrorist groups. In contrast, the early 1980s saw the dramatic emergence of "religiously" motivated terrorism, more precisely that involving extreme Islamist movements.[28]

What triggered this change was the success of the Iranian Revolution in 1979.[29] It was a great surprise to the world that a *theocratic* state should emerge in the *secularised* international political arena. The concern about theocracy was recently summarised by Francis Fukuyama as follows:[30]

> "If politics is based on religion, there will never be any civil peace because people cannot agree on fundamental religious values. Secularism is a relatively recent development in the West: the modern democratic state emerged out of the bloody religious conflicts in Europe during the sixteenth and seventeenth centuries in which different Christian groups slaughtered one another mercilessly. The separation of church and state became a necessary component of modernization precisely because of the need for civil peace."

---

[26] Berry LV, Curtis GE, Hudson RA, Kollars NA (2002) " A Global Overview of Narcotics-Funded Terrorist and Other Extremist Groups", Library of Congress, May, pp.50-57.

[27] For example, the FARC is alleged to pursue power and economic gains under the guise of promoting their Marxist agenda (*Ibid.*, p.2).

[28] Wilkinson P, *supra* note 8, p.34. According to Bruce Hoffman, there has been a dramatic increase in identifiable religious terrorist groups from none in 1968 to eleven in 1992. A decade later, if we look at the list of the terrorist organisations designated by the US government, more than half of the 37 designated groups include strong religious components (US Department of State, "Patterns of Global Terrorism-2003", 29 April 2004). For the use of the term "Islamists", see, Paz R, "Targeting Terrorist Financing in the Middle East", *International Policy Institution for Counter-Terrorism*, 23 October 2000.

[29] For the background to the Iranian Revolution, see, Han HH, "Autocracy of the Shah of Iran: Views of the Media Reporters". In: Han HH (ed), *supra* note 8, pp.167-185.

[30] Fukuyama F, "History and September 11". In: Booth K, Dunne T (2002) *World in Collision: Terror and the Future of Global Order*, p.30.

When the international community took secularism for granted, the Iranian Revolution seemed to turn the wheels of history backwards.[31] Following the success in Iran, the modern Islamist terrorist groups have aimed at exporting the Islamic revolution all over the world, especially from the Middle Eastern countries such as Saudi Arabia, Egypt, Turkey, etc.[32] Indeed, the same "domino theory" used in the Cold War is now deployed by analogy to the spread of militant Islam.[33]

In order to secure a "domino success", it is imperative for the Islamist terrorist groups to keep the Western powers from influencing the Middle East.[34] However, since they cannot overwhelm the Western states, more precisely the US, by military force, they instead employ terrorism as an alternative tactic to engage the enemy.[35] Nevertheless, it is extremely difficult to bring about a sufficient change in the policies of the Western states (e.g., to withdraw from the oil-rich Middle East). Thus, terrorist attacks need to be very powerful to "inflict so much pain on these states that their governments would find it impossible to tolerate the pubic outcry and be compelled to withdraw and stop the Islamist terrorism at home".[36] To this end, the attacks need to be carried out on a huge scale, even using weapons of

---

[31] From the point of view of the Islamists, legitimacy of a nation can be conferred only through the adoption of Islamic law(*Sharia*) with sovereignty resting with Allah. See, Capitanchik D "Terrorism and Islam". In: O'Sullivan N (ed) (1986) *Terrorism, Ideology, and Revolution*, pp.126-127.

[32] See, Bodansky Y (1999) *Bin Laden: The Man Who Declared War on America*, pp.53-55; Robbins JS (2002) "Bin Laden's War". In: Howard RD, Sawyer R L (eds), *supra* note 12, pp.354-355; Gunaratna R (2002) *Inside Al Qaeda: Global Network of Terror*, pp.88-89.

[33] According to Simon Reeve, if the fundamentalists take over in Egypt, the theory goes, the whole of North Africa and the Middle East will follow. Then Afghanistan, and the Muslim Central Asian states will fall consecutively (Reeve S, *supra* note 4, p.227).
In their revolutionary campaign, the Islamists emphasise their role as a vanguard of professional revolutionaries to awaken and lead the Muslim masses. In this context, we can find a surprising analogy with communist revolutionary terrorism theory. See, e.g., Dinse J, Johnson S "Ideologies of Revolutionary Terrorism: Some Enduring and Emerging Themes". In: Han HH (ed) (1993), *supra* note 8, pp.61-63; Napoleoni L (2003) *Modern Jihad: Tracing the Dollars Behind the Terror Networks*, p.155.

[34] Bodansky Y, *supra* note 32, p.177, p.190, p.349, and p.385. Furthermore, for the situation of the Central Asia, see, Olcott MB, "Narco-Terror: The Worldwide Connection Between Drugs and Terrorism", Testimony, United States Senate Committee on the Judiciary, 13 March 2002.

[35] Bodansky Y, *supra* note 32, p.203, pp.334-335; Richardson L (2002) "Global Rebels: Terrorist Organisations as Trans-National Actors". In: Howard RD, Sawyer RL (eds), *supra* note 12, p.99; Gearson J (2002) "The Nature of Modern Terrorism". In: Freedman L (ed) *Superterrorism: Policy Responses*, p.23.

[36] Bodansky Y, *supra* note 32, p.177.

mass destruction (WMD), but more importantly *with continuity*. The case of the Vietnam War would be a good scenario: a benchmark.[37] In this context, it seems that a significant change has taken place in the nature of terrorism, constituting a real threat to international peace and security indeed.[38] The concerns about this change are well exemplified by the US adoption in September 2002 of a new doctrine in the use of force, the core of which is recourse to pre-emptive strikes based on the right to self-defence.[39]

Given these scenarios, as the next logical step, there can be conceived an important question: "If the Western powers withdraw, could the Islamist groups succeed in winning support at grassroots level, thus transforming a political system into a theocracy, by either revolution or a peaceful referendum ?".[40] Unfortunately, many scholars are of the view that the Islamist trend has grown and will continue to expand because of its genuine grassroots and popular appeal.[41]

Among many complicated factors underlying its popular appeal, two common reasons can be observed: economic poverty, and loss of self-esteem. For the purpose of understanding the widespread economic poverty in the Middle East, let us consider for example Saudi Arabia which is the biggest oil-producing country in the region. Oil revenues that had earned the nation more than US$ 140 billion a year during the 1980s appeared to dwindle to just US$ 20 billion a year in the 1990s.[42] Moreover, GDP per capita is said to have fallen from US$ 15,000 per year a decade ago to as low as US$ 4,000 in 1998.[43] Consequently, unemployment and discontent is growing among the population.[44] Saudis who used to travel to smaller Gulf countries to party and shop are now being forced to take employment

---

[37] The US public opinion was then sick of endless war, and subsequent huge casualties and costs, thus urging to pull U.S. troops out of Vietnam.

[38] Murphy SD (2003) "Contemporary practice of the United States relating to international law: the U.S. Adoption of New Doctrine on Use of Force", *American Journal of International Law*, vol.97, p.207.

[39] *Ibid.*

[40] In Algeria, an Islamist party(the Islamic Salvation Front) scored a stunning victory in the June 1990 municipal elections, and in the June 1997 parliamentary elections. However, the Algerian military intervened, arresting the Islamist party's leaders and imprisoned them in desert camps. Thus, a cycle of violence and counterviolence was set in motion. See, Esposito JL (2002) *Unholy War : Terror in the name of Islam*, pp.102-103.

[41] See, e.g., Bodansky Y, *supra* note 32, p.133 and p.334; Esposito JL, *supra* note 40, pp.79-84, pp.93-95, and p.116; Wilkinson P, *supra* note 8, p.35; Capitanchik D, *supra* note 31, pp.127-129; Fukuyama F, *supra* note 30, p.33; Ranstorp M, *supra* note 12, p.129 and p.132; Reeve S, *supra* note 4, pp.228-230.

[42] Reeve S, *supra* note 4, p.230.

[43] *Ibid.*, p.230.

[44] *Ibid.*, p.230.

there, even in menial jobs, which is almost unprecedented for Saudi citizens.[45] Usama bin Laden did not overlook this point, utilising it as a rallying cause.[46] He claimed in 1997 that the US was stealing Muslim oil given that the price of Arab oil increased by no more than 8 dollars while the price of American wheat increased threefold over a period of 24 years.[47] Needless to say, this kind of revolutionary message exacerbates a sense of deprivation among Muslims.

However, more fundamentally, incompetent authoritarian regimes in the region are criticised for aggravating their problems. It is understandable in some sense that several Middle Eastern states were created by the West following the First World War[48] and thus have a relatively short experience of governance. Nonetheless, the governments within the region have not made good use of the opportunities for economic and political reform, thus failing to create a self-sustaining industrial society.[49]

Along with underlying economic poverty, Arab states have suffered a continuous loss of self-esteem. For instance, they saw a humiliating defeat of the combined forces of Egypt, Jordan, and Syria by US-backed Israel in the 1967 Six-Day war.[50] To the despair of Arab people, they are continuously reminded of the US's pro-Israel policy through the development of the Palestine issue.[51] The US military presence on the "holy soil" of Saudi Arabia since the first Gulf war in the early 1990s also inflamed anti-Western feeling.[52] To make matters worse, the US was not free from the suspicion of abusing the Iraq issue for domestic purposes as was the case in the US bombing campaign against Iraq and Afghanistan in 1998 when the US House of Representatives decided to seek to impeach President Clinton for his sex scandals.[53] Since the US and the UK invaded Iraq in 2003 in large measure

---

[45] *Ibid.*, p.230.

[46] *Ibid.,* p.230.

[47] *Ibid.*, p.230. For every barrel sold over the period, he further claimed that the US swindled US$ 135 and the total loss of income has been estimated at US$ 4 billion a day, thus entitling the 1.2 billion Muslims worldwide to claim US$ 30 million each in compensation from the US (Jacquard R (2002) *In the Name of Osama Bin Laden*, p.96). According to *The Economist*, this argument seems to make some sense, given that oil prices in the late 1970s equaled US$ 80 a barrel in today's money ("Pain at the pump", *The Economist,* 22 May 2004, pp.85-86).

[48] Esposito JL, *supra* note 40, pp.80-81.

[49] Fukuyama F, *supra* note 30, p.33. Fukuyama further pointed out that no Arab governments have decided on their own to voluntarily step down in favour of democratic rule, like the Spanish monarchy after the dictator Franco.

[50] Esposito JL, *supra* note 40, pp.83-84.

[51] *Ibid.*, pp.83-84.

[52] On the occasion of the 2nd Gulf war in 2003, the US finally withdrew its troops from Saudi Arabia.

[53] Bodansky Y, *supra* note 32, pp.351-355.

on the pretext of preventing the development of WMD, anti-Western feelings seems to have reached a peak. This may be explained, in part, by the fact that the war was fought without any substantial proof of Iraq's development of WMD.[54]

Indeed, where there is no way out to express their despair and no reason to expect any solutions from their own governments, the Muslim masses are thought by some to have no option but to admire and eulogise the Islamist terrorist groups[55] which dare to confront the Western states as well as local authoritarian secular regimes.[56] Moreover, where governments fail to meet the basic needs of their people, Islamist groups sometimes establish their own structures of health, education and welfare provision, in many cases better than governments have been able to deliver.[57]

In addition to increasing popularity, Islamist groups have become more and more emboldened by their continuous victories in Iran in 1979, Lebanon in 1983, Afghanistan in 1989, and Somalia in 1994 where they succeeded in evicting the "Imperialist powers".[58] These Islamist groups have further strengthened their powers since the mid 1990s. In this, the role of Usama bin Laden cannot be overlooked given his ability to use his financial resources and charismatic appeal to unite disparate groups throughout the Muslim world under a common cause to attack the West.[59]

---

[54] Duelfer C, "Comprehensive Report of the Special Adviser to the DCI on Iraq's WMD", (30 September 2004) <http://www.cia.gov/cia/reports/iraq_wmd_2004/>; The BBC News, "US gives up search for Iraq WMD", 12 January 2005.

[55] Retired lieutenant general Asad Durrani of Pakistan, quoted in Bodansky Y, *supra* note 32, p.334.

[56] Islamists continue to weaken or topple the secular regimes as with Pakistan or Egypt. In relation to Pakistan, Benazir Bhutto warned that Islamists try to infiltrate every class of society as follows:
"These Islamist groups are working to try and influence the placing of people within the military, within the intelligence services, within the election commission, and they are creeping towards power in every sphere of the country." (Reeve S, *supra* note 4, p.227).
In the case of Egypt, they employed a bolder tactic as illustrated by the assassination attempt on President Mubarak in 1995 who adopted a strict policy to repress Islamist challenges (Bodansky Y, *supra* note 32, pp.121-133).

[57] Wilkinson P, *supra* note 8, p.35.

[58] The eviction of the Soviet army from Afghanistan by Mujahideens (Islam's holy warriors) in some degree restored the injured self-esteem of the Muslim masses since the 1967 defeat in the Six-Day war. In Somlia, Islamists are said to have been behind the attacks on the US troops, thus forcing them to withdraw. For further details, see, Bodansky Y, *supra* note 32, p.55 and pp.78-90.

[59] Kressel NJ (2002) *Mass Hate: The Global Rise of Genocide and Terror*, p.xiii; Bodansky Y, *supra* note 32, p.404.

1.2.2 The importance of financing for modern terrorism

1.2.2.1 Context

A common criticism against the effectiveness of a financial war on terrorism is that terrorist operations do not necessarily cost much, and thus the targeting of the financial aspects of terrorist organisations might not be as effective in preventing terrorism as people expect.[60] This argument seems in some sense to hold water, especially given that some modern terrorist organisations tend to adopt a decentralised cell structure, thus eliminating the need for significant financing to maintain their entire organisations.[61]

However, it should be remembered that we are here aiming not at preventing a single terrorist attack but at staving off a transnational mega-trend in our time. Any terrorist groups that are engaged in a sustained and significant campaign, will require some degree of organisation, some training in the special skills of terror-

---

The differences between Sunni and Shi'a originated from the position on whether to recognise the legitimacy of the first three caliphs elected after the death of Prophet Muhammed. Sunnis recognise the legitimacy of the three caliphs but Shi'as reject them on the ground that they were not descendants of Muhammed and only when the fourth caliph, the cousin of Muhammed, succeeded the post, the legitimacy was restored. As a result, Shi'as are opposed to all Arab monarchies and secular regimes in that the leadership of the Muslim world should be appointed by divine ordinance. The success of Shi'a was illustrated by the Iran Revolution that overthrew the regime of the Shah (Capitanchik D, *supra* note 31, pp.118-128). See also, Adams J, *supra* note 9, p.91.

In particular, given that even within the Muslim world different sects have antagonised and competed with each other as illustrated by the rivalry between Sunni and Shi'a, Usama bin Laden's capacity to unite disparate groups in a common cause to attack the West is worthy of note. See, Richardson L (2002) "Global Rebels: Terrorist Organisations as Trans-National Actors". In: Howard RD, Sawyer RL (eds), *supra* note 12, pp.72-73; Reeve S, *supra* note 4, pp.224-225.

[60] Navias MS, "Financial Warfare as a Response to International Terrorism". In: Freedman L (ed) *supra* note 35, p.69; Gunaratna R, *supra* note 32, pp.64-65; US Department of States, "International Narcotics Control Strategy Report", March 2002, p.XII-5.

[61] The cell structure has many strong points. First of all, since cells do not know each other, even if a cell gets caught, other cells would not be affected and proceed with their work normally. Moreover, individual cells usually finance themselves, and thus financial needs are not so big as they are in a traditional hierarchical organisation. Furthermore, even a single cell might constitute an individual terrorist group. Therefore, sometimes, this cell structure is compared to the "Hydra". For further details, see, e.g., Gunaratna R, *supra* note 32, p.76; Arquilla J, Ronfeldt D, Zanini M (2002) "Networks, Netwar, and Information-Age Terrorism". In: Howard RD, Sawyer RL (eds) *supra* note 12, pp.102-103; Wilkinson P (1986) "Fighting the Hydra". In: O'Sullivan N (ed), *supra* note 31, p.210.

ism, as well as weapons, and other supplies.[62] Furthermore, given the grand goals of major terrorist groups, which include, for example, the reestablishment of a Caliphate from North Africa to Central and Southeast Asia, it goes without saying that global, long-term coordination among various groups and support for each other would be necessary to realise their aims.[63] This course of action would inevitably require constant and reliable funding sources.[64] A glimpse into the financial structure of Al-Qaida, the most successful terrorist organisation with the broadest cell network yet known,[65] confirms the old premise that "there is no successful organisation without successful financing".[66] Indeed, it has built the most complex, robust and resilient financial network yet seen, as acknowledged by Western intelligence agencies.[67] This success in financial management was possible with Al-Qaida's policy placing a high priority on sustained generation and investment of funds.[68] Usama bin Laden seems to clearly understand that money facilitates and speeds the growth and self-sufficiency of the jihad he has instigated.[69]

---

[62] Wilkinson P, *supra* note 8, p.62. See also, Bell RE (2003) "The Confiscation, Forfeiture and Disruption of Terrorist Finances", *Journal of Money Laundering Control*, vol.7, no.2, p.105.

[63] Robbins JS, *supra* note 32, pp.354-355; Gunaratna R, *supra* note 32, pp.88-89.

[64] The importance of financing of terrorism was also hinted by Usama bin Laden himself in an interview by *al-Quds a-Arabi*, a Arab newspaper:
"If we wanted small actions, the matter would have been easily carried out. But the nature of the battle calls for operations of a specific type that will make an impact on the enemy, and this, of course, calls for excellent preparation."(recited from Bodansky Y, *supra* note 32, p.326).

[65] Along with his doctrinal flexibility, bin Laden has attracted widespread support due to his anti-Western and anti-Israeli rhetoric. Moreover, he has advocated pan-Islamic unity rather than just pan-Arabism. See, Gunaratna R, *supra* note 32, pp.86-87.

[66] The best success story of an old-style terrorist group is the case of the PLO. Its survival and transition to mainstream politics were primarily due to its skillful handling of finances. Initially, the PLO depended on donations from other Arab countries but a prudent and clever handling of long-term investment transformed it into a financial colossus in the Middle East that cannot be ignored any more. See, Napoleoni L, *supra* note 33, p.63. As of 1999, the PLO was said to possess assets worthy of US$ 58 billion. See, Ehrenfeld R "Intifada Gives Cover to Arafat's Graft and Fraud", *Insight on the news*, 16 July 2001.

[67] Gunaratna R, *supra* note 32, p.61.

[68] *Ibid.*, p.61. Rohan Gunaratna explains that Al-Qaida's finance and business committee which consists of professional bankers, accountants, and financiers, manages the group's funds across continents.

[69] Anonymous (2003) *Through Our Enemy's Eyes: Osama bin Laden, Radical Islam, and the Future of America*, p.32.

1.2.2.2 Various needs for financing

Although currently published data is not conclusive, it helps us to understand the importance of financing in strengthening the overall capacity of modern terrorist groups. For the purpose of facilitating the understanding of various needs for financing, terrorist organisations can be classified into two simple categories depending on whether they have a specific constituency or not. While most of both *religious* terrorist groups and *secular* terrorist groups are tied to their specific constituencies such as Hamas of Palestine, the Islamic Movement of Uzbekistan (IMU), Abu Sayyaf of the Philippines, and the FARC of Colombia, some modern religious terrorist groups such as Al-Qaida, a transnational revolutionary movement, do not have any fixed constituencies. Despite this distinction, what both types of terrorist organisations have in common is that they need money, typically for spending on recruiting and training, the procurement of weaponry and the launching of operations. However, importantly, terrorist groups without any specific constituency tend to need financing for more strategic and broader causes.[70] With this basic difference in mind, let us proceed to examine the financing needs of modern terrorist groups.

Firstly, solid financing is necessary for the purpose of recruiting and training. Numerous cases can be identified to confirm the importance of this dimension. For instance, Al-Qaida was reported to have had 70,000 Islamist militants trained in its camps in Afghanistan prior to 9/11.[71] In the Philippines, the Abu Sayyaf group, one of the most violent Islamist separatist groups,[72] was once suffering financial difficulty, and its armed militants reduced to only 200.[73] However, after raising US$ 5.5million through kidnapping in 2000, the Abu Sayyaf's ranks expanded to at least 3,000.[74] According to Philippine intelligence sources, Abu Sayyaf paid US$ 1,100 to its militants. In a desperately poor area with high unemployment, Abu Sayyaf has become the single biggest employer.[75] In Uzbekistan,

---

[70] Since 1998, Al-Qaida consists of three major parts: a pyramidal structure to facilitate strategic and tactical direction; a global cell network; a base force for guerrilla warfare inside Afghanistan. Among these parts, the pyramidal structure is the brain of the entire organisation and is made up of four committees: a military committee, a finance and business committee, a *fatwa* and Islamic study committee; and, a media and publicity committee. See, Gunaratna R, *supra* note 32, p.57.

[71] "Bin Laden's martyrs for the cause", *Financial Times*, 28 November 2001.

[72] Unlike other terrorist groups in the Philippines, Abu Sayyaf clearly belongs to the world of Islamism. For a comparison of the Islamist terrorist groups in the Philippines, see, Yom SL (Fall 2001) "Abu Sayyaf in the Philippines: More Than Just Criminal", *CSIS Prospectus*, vol. 2, no. 3.

[73] Shahar, Y., "Libya and the Jolo Hostage: Seeking a new image, or polishing the old one?", *International Policy Institute for Counter-Terrorism*, 20 August 2000.

[74] *Ibid.*

[75] *Ibid.*

the IMU which aims at establishing an Islamic state there, is reported to be a major employer in the region, paying its men between US$ 100-500 a month.[76] Young men in the poverty-stricken local area have no choice but either to go to Russia to look for work or to join the IMU.[77] Indeed, this terrorist group seems to greatly benefit from its financial ability in promoting its cause. In Palestine, the more extreme examples can be noted in relation to recruitment of suicide bombers in the occupied territories who are reported to be given US$ 30,000 for their families. The money comes mostly from outside sponsors such as charitable organisations, groups of sympathisers or foreign regimes.[78] In Colombia, the FARC and M19 (Movimiento 19 Abril) were struggling to survive on an income from armed robbery and the kidnapping of local businessmen until 1980.[79] The number of their followers dropped to around 200, and recruitment was at a standstill since there was no cash for salaries, and the leaders of the two organisations predicted the end of their campaign.[80] However, in 1981, the FARC and M19 struck a deal with the Colombian drug mafia; they would provide armed protection against the army in exchange for a share in the coca profits.[81] By 1984, the FARC and M19 were said to earn US$ 150 million a year from the business of protecting drug traffickers.[82] A large percentage of the profits were spent on recruitment, so that by 1988 both groups commanded a combined militia of 10,000 people, large enough to be feared by the government.[83]

Secondly, terrorist groups attempt to get access to a stock of weaponry. For instance, Usama bin Laden has paid attention to "high-tech" conventional weaponry such as surface-to-air missiles (SAM). Since 1998, there has been something of a race between Usama bin Laden and the Pentagon, with the latter trying to recover all the Stinger missile launchers that had been distributed during the war in Afghanistan.[84] If the American military offered US$ 100,000 for a Stinger, Usama bin Laden was said to offer twice that.[85] The current black market price is said to

---

[76] Ahmed R (2002) *Jihad: The Rise of Militant Islam in Central Asia*, p.163.

[77] *Ibid.*

[78] Goldberg S, "The Man behind the Suicide Bombers", *Guardian*, 12 June 2002.

[79] Adams J, *supra* note 9, p.303

[80] *Ibid.*, p.303.

[81] The FARC levied a 10 per cent protection tax on all coca growers in areas under its control.

[82] *Ibid.*, p.303.

[83] Adams J, *supra* note 9, p.303. It is said to cost about US$ 75 million a year to equip a militia army of 10,000 troops with light arms (Block R, Doyle L, "Drug Profits Funds Weapons for Balkans", *Independent,* 10 December 1993).

[84] Jacquard R, *supra* note 47, p.127.

[85] *Ibid.*, p.127.

be about US$ 200,000.[86] Recent examples of the use of the SAMs was the firing on a US military aircraft taking off from the Prince Sultan military base in Saudi Arabia in December 2001,[87] and the attack on an Israeli chartered jet in Mombasa in November 2002. Moreover, governments believe that terrorist would love to get their hands on weapons of mass destruction (WMD). For example, there is evidence from Al-Qaida training manuals and other intelligence, that they have investigated the means of developing WMD.[88] In particular, Al-Qaida created a "WMD committee", which is known to have approached a number of Muslim scientists to assist the terrorist network with the creation and procurement of chemical, biological, radiological and nuclear weapons.[89] Needless to say, solid financing would be necessary for this intention to materialise.[90]

Thirdly, terrorist groups need to buy popular support to take solid root on their home ground. For example, the Palestine-based Hamas has cleverly mixed guerrilla warfare with political and social activism.[91] It has extensively engaged in community and charitable programmes, pouring money into a wide network of social services which support schools, orphanages, mosques, health care clinics,

---

[86] Napoleoni L, *supra* note 33, p.185. Coupled with the transportation capability of the Al-Qaida which is believed to operate a fleet of vessels, high-tech weaponry could be employed anywhere in the world. See, e.g., Felsted A, Odell M, "Agencies fear extent of al-Qaeda's sea network", *Financial Times*, 21 February 2002; Gunaratna R, *supra* note 32, p.xxxii.

[87] Gunaratna R, *supra* note 32, p.xxvi.

[88] UN, "Letter dated 7 July 2003 from the Chairman of the Security Council Committee established pursuant to resolution 1267 (1999) addressed to the President of the Security Council", S/2003/669, 8 July 2003, p.24.

[89] *Ibid.*, p.24.

[90] There is an allegation that in the autumn 1998, Usama bin Laden was reported to have acquired several tactical nuclear warheads, costing him US$30 million in cash and two tons of Afghan heroin that was worth US$70 million (Riyad Alam-al-Din, "Report Links Bin Laden, Nuclear Weapon", 13 November 1998, recited from Anonymous, *supra* note 69, p.191).

Furthermore, Usama bin Laden's representative reportedly bought three chemical and biological laboratories in the former Yugoslavia in early May 1998 (Olimpio G, "Islamic Cell Preparing Chemical Warfare, Toxins, Gases against West", *Corriere della Sera*, 8 July 1998, recited from Anonymous, *supra* note 69, p.188).

[91] Hamas calls for the destruction of Israel and its replacement by a Palestinian pan-Islamic state stretching from the Mediterranean Sea to the River of Jordan, while the PLO's goal is a secular state with equal rights for all citizens, Muslims and Christians (Napoleoni L, *supra* note 32, p.70 and p.96). Since 1994 when Goldstein opened fired on Muslim worshippers in the Mosque of the Patriarch in Hebron, Hamas introduced a new type of warfare, the suicide bombers (Esposito J, *supra* note 40, p.99).

soup kitchens and sports clubs in the poorest areas.[92] As a result, its popularity is particularly high in the shanty towns of the Gaza Strip.[93] As seen in this example, where poor Muslim migrant populations have suffered the lack of basic social welfare services for decades, Islamist parties and groups have filled the vacuum by establishing their own socio-economic and welfare organisations.[94] This interaction with Muslim communities has given these organisations an opportunity to politicise and radicalise the Muslim masses into supporting their aims and objectives.[95] A similar case can also be found in relation to ideological terrorist groups. For instance, in Colombia, the FARC has also carried out social and public works in its constituency. It has built and paved new roads and improved the communal areas of some towns. It has also provided people with security, a luxury they had lacked for a long time. As with many Palestinians helped by Hamas, the local Colombians might share a similar sentiment, and give support to the cause of the FARC.[96]

Fourthly, terrorist organisations without any specific constituency support and strengthen the capacity of other fledgling local terrorist groups with a similar cause through financial support.[97] This is said to be the case, for example, with Al-Qaida. It has reportedly provided considerable financial help to other Islamist groups in conflict areas all over the world,[98] thus establishing a universal jihad network.[99] In this context, Al-Qaida has been compared to a holding company and

---

[92] Esposito J, *supra* note 40, p.97

[93] *Ibid.*, p.97.

[94] Gunaratna R, *supra* note 32, p.239.

[95] *Ibid.*, p.239. In addition, these activities also served as a tool to attract recruits as well as attracting foreign donations for charity purposes. Indeed, interesting synergy effects can be observed between social services and recruiting and the flow of money. However, Islamist groups are not the only ones to appeal to the general public. For example, see the IRA's use of financing in buying votes in electoral campaigns (Adams J, *supra* note 9, pp.203-206).

[96] *Ibid.*, p.77.

[97] In addition to financial support, Al-Qaida dispatches cadres who were the vanguard fighters as well as the most accomplished trainers in their previous campaigns, to its associate groups. See, Gunaratna R, *supra* note 32, pp.55-56.

[98] *Ibid.*, p.235. Having the grand picture in mind, Al-Qaida has tried to orchestrate overall Islamist movements worldwide. For example, Usama bin Laden launched the Islamic Front in 1998, in which many clandestine organisations participated, such as the Egyptian Islamic Jihad, the Egyptian Armed Group, the Pakistan Scholars Society, the Partisans Movement in Kashmir, the Jihad Movement in Bangladesh, and the Afghan military wing of the "Advice and Reform" commission. See, Bodansky Y, *supra* note 32, pp.316-317.

[99] Shahar Y, "Tracing bin Laden's Money: Easier said than done", *International Policy Institute for Counter-Terrorism*, 21 September 2001; Reeve S, *supra* note 4, pp.184-185.

its associated Islamist groups as its subsidiaries, with Al-Qaida providing the venture capital.[100] In the Philippines, the Moro Islamic Liberation Front (MILF) was suffering from the shortage of weapons in 1998, and reportedly it was bin Laden who rectified the problem by funding the delivery of 3,000 high-powered weapons, and the procurement of an international satellite communication system to assist its fight for an independent Islamic state in Mindanao.[101] In June 2000, according to the Philippine military intelligence, Usama bin Laden had further transferred US$ 3 million to the MILF.[102] In Uzbekistan, Usama bin Laden reportedly offered US$ 20 million to the IMU in the spring of 2000 and also paid for three MI-8 transport helicopters as well, thus securing a solid partner in Central Asia where he did not have an operational base before.[103] Moreover, in September 2003, the Groupe Salafiste pour la Predication et Combat made a public announcement of its affiliation with Al-Qaida to allow it to seek bases in the poorly policed area of sub-Saharan Africa.[104] This strategic alliances with local groups seems to gain increasing importance for Al-Qaida because it has to rely more on associate local organisations for its operations due to the setback it has suffered since 9/11. Furthermore, it would earn Al-Qaida some influence as well, thus facilitating its search for a safe haven in various regions in case of emergency.[105]

Fifthly and in a similar context, terrorist groups without any constituency seek to buy influence over top-class power elites to establish a parasitic operational base in a targeted area. For instance, before 9/11, Usama bin Laden tried to extend his friendship with Mullah Mohamed Omar, the most powerful man in Af-

---

[100] Gunaratna R, *supra* note 32, pp.68-69.

[101] As a result, the MILF was said to expand its arsenal of firearms from 3,000 in 1997 to more than 11,000 in 2000, thus transforming itself into a threatening armed group in the region (Anonymous, *supra* note 69, pp.181-182). Muslims in the Philippines, called *Moros* constitute 5 % of the population and waged bloody wars for independence from the late 1960s. For the further history of the conflict, see, Iacovou C, "From MNLF to Abu Sayyaf: The Radicalization of Islam in the Philippines", *International Policy Institute for Counter-Terrorism*, 11 July 2000.

[102] "Information on Bin Laden's Plans to Set Up Base in Somalia", Al-Sharq Al-Awsat, recited from Anonymous, *supra* note 69, p.41.

[103] Rashid A, "They are only sleeping: Why militant Islamists in Central Asia aren't going to go away", *The New Yorker*, 14 January 2002. The price of a MI-8 helicopter is US$ 3.2 million (the price of a used MI-8 is approximately one third of the original price) (visited on 20 July 2004) <http://www.fas.org/man/dod-101/sys/ac/row/mi-8.htm>.

[104] UN, "Letter dated 14 February 2005 from the Chairman of the Security Council Committee established pursuant to resolution 1267(1999) concerning Al-Qaeda and the Taliban and associated individuals and entities addressed to the President of the Security Council", S/2005/83, 15 February 2005, p.7.

[105] Anonymous, *supra* note 69, p.182.

ghanistan at that time. Bin Laden sustained Omar financially[106] and he also secured Omar's friendship with gifts, which included an offer to take over the funding of an irrigation canal in Helmland province in 1997.[107] Moreover, in Pakistan, Usama bin Laden reportedly donated US$ 10 million to opposition politicians to bring about the approval of a vote of no confidence in Benazir Bhutto's government in the late 1990s.[108] During this period, Usama bin Laden was trying to destabilise the Bhutto government to ensure the election of politicians who would be more amenable to his presence in Afghanistan.[109] In Somalia which Al-Qaida also intended to use as a base from which to reach out elsewhere in Africa and to use it as a potential safe haven, it provided unspecified support to the United Front for the Liberation of Western Somalia (UF).[110] In return, Al-Qaida also had some of its fighters trained in UF camps, which the West watched far less closely than those in Sudan, Yemen, and Afghanistan.[111]

Sixthly, although decentralised terrorist groups like Al-Qaida do not need to support hierarchical structures, they still have to look after their fledgling cells which are loosely linked worldwide. In other words, the central command sometimes has to provide "seed money" to help cells settle down and sustain themselves, or "operational money" to launch a strategic attack on a considerable scale.[112] For instance, in 1994, Usama bin Laden dispatched Mohamed Sadeek to

---

[106] Al-Qaida paid US$ 10-20 million annually to its Taliban hosts prior to 9/11 (UN, "Letter dated 23 August 2004 from the Chairman of the Security Council Committee established pursuant to resolution 1267 (1999) concerning Al-Qaeda and Taliban and associated individuals and entities addressed to the President of the Security Council", S/2004/679, 25 August 2004, p.12).

[107] Reeve S, *supra* note 4, p.189.

[108] *Ibid.*, p.188.

[109] *Ibid.*, pp.188-189. After winning the General Election, Benazir Bhutto was nominated as the first female Prime Minister to lead a Muslim nation on 2 December 1988 but was dismissed on 6 August 1990 by President Ghulam Ishaq Khan. Following victory in the 1993 election, she was once again nominated as the Prime Minister but was dismissed by her own-nominated President Farooq Ahmad Khan Leghari in 1996 (visited on 20 July 2004)
< http://www.storyofpakistan.com/person.asp?perid=P024&Pg=3>.

[110] The political chaos and economic collapse after the civil war and UN intervention in the 1990s made the Somali groups eager for Usama bin Laden's financial and military support as they compete for supremacy in Somalia. See, Anonymous, *supra* note 69, pp.179-180.

[111] Sa'id al-Qaysi, "Report on U.S. Embassy Bombing Probe", *Al-Watan Al-Arabi,* 30 October 1998, recited from Anonymous, *supra* note 69, p.180.

[112] As of 2004, conservative intelligence estimates indicate that al-Qaeda is present over 60 countries and a rump leadership is still intact and over 18,000 potential terrorists at

Kenya to create a cell in the Al-Qaida network.[113] He was financed with Al-Qaida money to buy a seven-tonne boat and set up a fishing business.[114] Catches from the boat were used to support other Al-Qaida members who then began arriving in the country.[115] This cell was eventually employed in the US embassy bombing in Nairobi in 1998.[116] Moreover, the arrest in July 2004 of Ahmed Khalfan Ghailani revealed that as a follow-up to Usama bin Laden's February 2003 broadcast appealing to Muslims, Al-Qaida recruiters were sent to northern Nigeria to establish a presence there.[117] This must have cost seed money. Moreover, the "operational funding" for cells is also common expenditure for Al-Qaida, and some have likened it to the Ford Foundation, where researchers present projects and after careful consideration, some are funded while others are discarded.[118] For example, in mid 1999, Hambali and his group which are best known for the Bali bombing in 2002, once made a video that contained a plan to blow up a bus service used by U.S. soldiers in Singapore.[119] They showed Usama bin Laden the video in the hope of receiving funds for their terror activity in Southeast Asia.[120] The video was found in late 2001 in Kabul, in the house of Mohammad Atif, Usama bin Laden's military commander.[121] In 1999, Usama bin Laden and his network were said to be receiving hundreds of similar requests.[122] All in all, they must be presumed to be still engaged in this kind of funding assistance as long as there is no trustworthy counter evidence.

In conclusion, as illustrated by the cases of terrorist spending on a large scale for various purposes, it is clear that money plays an important role in facilitating terrorist activities worldwide.

---

large, with recruitment accelerating on account of Iraq. See, International Institute for Strategic Studies, *Strategic Survey 2003/2004*, pp.6-7.

[113] Reeve S, *supra* note 4, p.198.

[114] *Ibid.*, p.198.

[115] *Ibid.*, p.198.

[116] *Ibid.*, p.198.

[117] UN, S/2005/83, *supra* note 104, p.6.

[118] Gunaratna R, *supra* note 32, pp.68-69; Williamson H, Burns J, Fidler S, Huband M, "A catastrophic failure of intelligence", *Financial Times*, 29 November 2001.

[119] Burke J, "The Secret Mastermind behind the Bali Horror", *Observer*, 20 October 2002.

[120] *Ibid.*

[121] *Ibid.*

[122] *Ibid.*

1.3 Terrorist Financing and Money Laundering

1.3.1 The sources of terrorist financing

Given the constant need for a ready supply of cash, weaponry, ammunition, and other essential resources, modern terrorist groups turn to various financing activities which can fall into three categories: criminal activities, donations, and legitimate businesses.[123]

1.3.1.1 Criminal activities

Criminal activities are believed to be the single most important source for terrorist groups. For example, the narcotics trade has given various terrorist groups a new breath of life, making it possible for them to achieve self-sufficiency.[124] In Columbia, 60 to 90 per cent of the funding for paramilitaries and guerillas comes from drug trafficking.[125] Furthermore, Islamist groups in Central Asia, the Balkans, Kashimir, the Caucasus, India, Western China, and Southeast Asia, are also involved in narcotics since they need solid financing to run their wars. The IMU is known to control opium movement through Central Asian routes, including as much as 70 per cent of the opium trade entering Kyrgyzstan.[126] Al-Qaida has also been alleged to have used drug-trafficking to finance itself.[127] In fact, almost all

---

[123] For the categorisation, see, Greenberg MR, Wechsler W, Wolosky LS, "Terrorist Financing: Report of an Independent Task Force", Council on Foreign Relations, 25 November 2002, pp.6-7. For the analysis of bin Laden's case, see, e.g, Shahar Y, *supra* note 99.

[124] Napoleoni L, *supra* note 32, p.94.

[125] Berry LV, *supra* note 26, p.52. Particularly, the United Self Defence Forces of Columbia (AUC) has admitted earning up to 70 percent of its income from the drug trade (Berry LV, *supra* note 26, p.52).

[126] Smith RG, "Narco-Terror: The Worldwide Connection Between Drugs and Terrorism", Testimony, United States Senate Committee on the Judiciary, 13 March 2002; Berry LV, *supra* note 26, p.92. In 2001, the IMU reportedly set up laboratories in Tajikistan to refine heroine, which explained the arrival of large quantity of raw opium from Afghanistan to Central Asia (Ahmed R, *supra* note 76, pp.165-166).

[127] Although there is some reservation with regard to Al-Qaida's involvement in drug trafficking, it should be remembered that overall Islamist terrorist groups are already actively engaged in this field, and there are circumstantial cases for Al-Qaida's involvement in the drug trade as well as bartering drugs for weaponry and other costs. For example, three individuals were arrested in Hong Kong in November 2002 when they attempted to trade heroin and hashish for Stinger missiles which were needed for Al-

Islamist terrorist groups identified as being involved in narcotics trafficking reportedly have had contacts with Al-Qaida.[128] Furthermore, specific *fatwas* (theological decrees) from Islamist luminaries openly authorised Islamist terrorist groups to use drugs as another weapon to attack the West.[129] In this context, it is a matter of grave concern that Afghanistan which accounted for over 70 per cent (4,600 metric tonnes) of the world's supply of opium in the year 1999, recently resumed poppy cultivation despite the official renewal of the ban on poppy growth by the Karzai government. Although Afghanistan has not yet reached its peak of poppy production recorded in 1999, the country is estimated to have produced 4,200 metric tonnes of oven-dried opium in 2004, substantially recovering its original production capacity.[130] This is a huge quantity of opium worth US$ 2.8 billion.

Kidnapping is also another important funding source and has become an extremely lucrative business for some groups. The Abu Sayyaf case as mentioned above is a good example. Similarly in 1999, the IMU raised about US$ 5 million as ransom for the release of four Japanese geologists abducted in Kyrgyzstan.[131] The ETA (Basque Homeland and Liberty) is also a major actor in this field, reportedly generating US$ 15 million in 1997 alone.[132]

Besides, there are many other lucrative criminal enterprises. In 2001 alone, the IRA is said to have raised US$ 11 million through criminal activities.[133] Tobacco smuggling from Eastern Europe to England and the Irish Republic was the largest source of income. Evading duties, the IRA resold this tobacco, netting profits of up to US$ 640,000 per lorry.[134] Furthermore, Al-Qaida's financial network in Europe, which is dominated by Algerians, relies heavily on credit card fraud. Se-

Qaida. For details, see, US Department of State, "International Narcotic Control Strategy Report 2002", 1 March 2003, p.XII-26; UN Doc, S/2005/83, *supra* note 104, p.30.

[128] See, Berry LV, *supra* note 26, p.1, p.7, p.28, pp.43-44, and p.68; Hutchinson A, "Narco-Terror: The Worldwide Connection Between Drugs and Terrorism", Testimony before United States Senate Committee on the Judiciary, 13 March 2002; Ehrenfeld R (2003) *Funding Evil: How Terrorism Is Financed-and How to Stop It*, pp.51-57.

[129] Beers R, Taylors FX, "Narco-Terror: The Worldwide Connection Between Drugs and Terror", a hearing held by the U.S. Senate Judiciary Committee, Subcommittee on Technology, Terrorism and Government Information, 13 March 2002; Bodanksy Y, *supra* note 32, p.322.

[130] UNODC, *Afghanistan Opium Survey 2004*, November 2004, p.4.

[131] Napoleoni L, *supra* note 33, p.89.

[132] *Ibid.*, p.36.

[133] Clarke L, Leppard D, "Photos link more IRA Men to Colombia", *Sunday Times*, 28 April 2002.

[134] *Ibid.*

curity and intelligence agencies estimate that nearly US$ 1 million a month is raised in this fashion.[135]

Interestingly, a new trend can be noted with regard to terrorist groups' involvement in criminal activities. Some terrorist groups are now gradually turning into a big business as exemplified by the practices of the FARC and Abu Sayyaf.[136] Although these groups may originally have embarked on revolutionary terrorism from motives of political idealism, they seem to enjoy the unexpected fruits of their way of life.[137] In this regard, to tackle the symbiotic and synergetic link between terrorism and criminal activities seems to be an increasing challenge for the international community.

1.3.1.2 Donations

In the 1960s and 1970s, the IRA secured funding through donations from the US. The Irish Northern Aid (Noraid) was established in the 1960s for this purpose and within a decade, Noraid achieved a budget of US$ 7 million, funding more than 50 per cent of the IRA's cash needs.[138] In a similar context, Islamist terrorist groups also have recourse to donations.[139] In particular, Al-Qaida is believed to utilise a financial network which was developed to finance the mujahideen in the 1980s.[140] This network is said to include various sources ranging from wealthy Persian Gulf Arabs who could be solicited directly to give huge sums of money,[141] to the masses who would make regular charitable donations as part of their religious obligations.[142] In this context, it is of value to note the *zakat* which is a religious donation of at least 2.5 per cent of one's accumulated wealth held for a full year for

---

[135] Gunaratna R, *supra* note 32, p.65.

[136] Berry LV, *supra* note 26, p.2.

[137] Wilkinson P, "Terrorist movement". In: Alexander Y, Carlton D, Wilkinson P (eds), *supra* note 8, p.114.

[138] Adams J, *supra* note 9, p.172

[139] Greenberg MR, *supra* note 123, p.7.

[140] *Ibid.*

[141] For some cases of fund-raising tours of Al-Qaida to Saudi merchants, see, e.g., Huband M, "Bankrolling bin Laden", *Financial Times*, 28 November 2001.

The way Usama bin Laden utilised donations is worthy of note as illustrated by the words of the late leader of the anti-Taliban Northern Alliance, Ahmed Shah Masood:

"He did not have large savings. Even today when he is supplying the Taliban with everything they need, he does not have the flow of finance people ascribe to him. He knows where to find finance and how to persuade interested people to invest in him and his cause. You cannot take that away from bin Laden" (Yemelyarenko V, "Ahmed Shah Mas'ud: Afghan War Will End in Pakistan", *Izvestiya*, 2 December 2000, recited from Anonymous, *supra* note 69, p.37).

[142] APG, "Annual Typologies Report 2003-2004", p.31.

charitable purposes.[143] Interestingly, Islamic banks also apply *zakat* to every contract or transaction they handle. They deduct the appropriate amounts, equivalent to 2.5 per cent of assessed personal wealth, and transfer them to Islamic charitable organisations.[144] However, *zakat* transfers are generally off the balance sheets and therefore hardly traceable.[145] In addition, all records are destroyed as soon as transactions are complete.[146] Indeed, it could be turned into one of many tricks used to finance terrorist groups.[147] In 2003, the Chief Executive Officer of the Benevolence International Foundation was convicted of diverting more than US$ 315,000 of charitable donations to terrorist organisations by a US court.[148] Moreover, it was also revealed that the Holy Land Foundation for Relief and Development raised millions of dollars for the Hamas prior to its designation by the US government as a terrorist supporter.[149]

1.3.1.3 Legitimate businesses

Lastly, legitimate businesses are a versatile tool for terrorist financing. This area has been highlighted since 9/11, especially in connection with Usama bin Laden's firms scattered worldwide.[150] Government sources and other experts on terrorism indicated that a large portfolio of ostensibly legitimate businesses continues to be maintained on behalf of Usama bin Laden by a number of as yet unidentified intermediaries and associates across North Africa, Europe, the Middle East, and

---

[143] Buckmaster D (ed) (1996) *Islamic Banking: an overview*, 1996, p.98; Lewis MK, Algaud LM (2001) *Islamic Banking*, pp.27-30.

[144] Brisand and Dasquie, *La Verita' Negata*, p.71, recited from Napoleoni L, *supra* note 33, p.120.

[145] *Ibid.*; Greenberg MR, *supra* note 123, p.7.

[146] Brisand and Dasquie, *supra* note 144, p.120.

[147] However, there is also some criticism that the vast majority of Islamic charities is not radical and should not be stereotyped as terrorist supporting organisations. Furthermore, sometimes the collections of resources are misused without the knowledge of donors. See, the statement of Dr.Quintan Wiktorowicz at pp.15-18 and the statement of Kenneth W. Dam at pp.32-34 in "The Role of Charities and NGO's In the Financing of Terrorist Activities", Hearing before the Subcommittee on International Trade and Finance, US Senate Committee on Banking, Housing, and Urban Affairs, 107th Congress, 2nd Session.

[148] APG, "Annual Typologies Report 2003-04", p.29.

[149] *Ibid.*, p.29.

[150] In an interview in 1996, Usama bin Laden admitted that his economic and financial establishment was present in more than 13 countries-Albania, Pakistan, Malaysia, the Netherlands, UK, Romania, Russia, Turkey, Lebanon, Iraq and several Gulf states. See, Leppard D, Sheridan M, "London Bank Used for bin Laden Cash", *Sunday Times*, 16 September; Mintz J, "Bin Laden's Finances are Moving Target", *Washington Post*, 28 August 1998; Shahar Y, *supra* note 99.

Asia.[151] For example, Usama bin Laden is said to have invested in the wood and paper industries in Norway about US$ 40 million; and hospital equipment in Sweden to the tune of US$ 15 million.[152] He also invested in Qudarat Transport, a fleet of fishing boats.[153] In addition, real estate investments are believed to be scattered around the globe to offset losses and to maximise profits. The portfolio is said to include real estate in London, Paris and the French Riviera.[154] However, one of the most profitable businesses that Usama bin Laden cannily obtained is the Gum Arabic Company Limited, a Khartoum-based firm which has a virtual monopoly over most of the Sudan's exports of gum arabic, and comprises around 80 per cent of the world's supply.[155] Gum arabic comes from the sap of the Sudanese acacia tree.[156] It makes newspaper ink stick to printing presses, prevents sediment forming in soft drink at the bottom of a can, and forms a film around sweets and medical pills.[157] Even now the US State Department and the CIA remain unsure whether Usama bin Laden is still profiting from his investment.[158] While 30 per cent of the shares in Gum Arabic Company Limited are held by the Sudanese government, the other 70 per cent is held by individual shareholders and banks, any or all of whom may be acting as fronts for bin Laden.[159]

However, since 9/11 there is a belief that Usama bin Laden suffered serious losses to his legitimate businesses, due to strengthened international scrutiny and the defection of his accountant to the Saudi regime who knew quite a bit about Usama bin Laden's remaining small companies. This developing situation is said to have forced bin Laden to sell those companies with significant losses before being exposed.[160]

Nevertheless, even after 9/11 legitimate business still seems to be an important factor both for terrorist groups and for counter-terrorism policy makers. Above all, these companies operate to provide income to support Al-Qaida and to provide cover for money laundering, procurement of explosives, weapons and chemicals

---

[151] UN, "Letter dated 19 September 2002 from the Chairman of the Security Council Committee established pursuant to resolution 1267(1999) concerning Afghanistan addressed to the President of the Security Council", S/2002/1050, 20 September 2002, p.11.

[152] Jacquard R, *supra* note 47, p.128.

[153] *Ibid.*, p.128.

[154] *Ibid.*, p.128.

[155] Reeve S, *supra* note 4, pp.178-179.

[156] *Ibid.*, p.179.

[157] *Ibid.*, p.179.

[158] *Ibid.*, p.179.

[159] *Ibid.*, p.179.

[160] Interview with Dr. Saad al-Faqih. *Frontline Online* (visited on 20 July 2004)
< http://www.pbs.org/wgbh/pages/frontline/shows/binladen/interviews/al-fagih.html>.

and for the travel of Al-Qaida operatives.[161] For example, honey is a very popular and profitable trade item in the Middle East and is also considered a good product in which to conceal contraband. When drugs, arms, cash, etc. are literally buried in honey, the smell and consistency of the honey put off customs officers from examining the containers.[162] Moreover, legitimate businesses are worthy of added attention by law enforcement authorities since even a few remaining firms can provide a very good chance of tracing the money trail to catch a "big fish". For policy makers, the focus on legitimate businesses can be an efficient use of limited resources if it is supported by appropriate intelligence.

Although there is no accurate data on how terrorist groups make money from these respective sources, some empirical research might be worthy of note and give a rough picture of financial flows to international terrorism. Based on the statistical theory which takes into account some hidden variables, Friedrich Schneider estimated the wealth of Al-Qaida at up to US$ 5 billion, and its annual financial flow at US$ 20-25 million. The proportion of each financing source is calculated as follows.

Table 1. Sources of terrorist financing

Ways of financing of terror organisation (using the example of Al-Qaida)	
Drug business (mainly transporting drugs)	30-35%
Donations/tribute payments of governments or wealthy individuals or religious groups	25-30%
Classic criminal activities (blackmail, kidnapping, etc.)	10-15%
Illegal diamond trading	10-15%
Additional unknown financial means (legal+illegal)	5-25%

Source: Friedrich Schneider's own calculation[163]

1.3.2 The role of money laundering in terrorist financing

1.3.2.1 Context

Terrorist financing consists of two activities: money making and its distribution. Thus, naturally there are two corresponding strategies to suppress the financing of terrorism: one to combat the money making activities (criminal activities, legiti-

---

[161] Reeve S, *supra* note 4, p.178.

[162] Miller J, Gerth J, "Trade in Honey is Said to Provide Money and Cover for bin Laden", *New York Times*, 11 October 2001.

[163] Schneider F (2004) "Macroeconomics: The Financial Flows of Islamic Terrorism". In: Maschiandaro D (ed) *Global Financial Crime: Terrorism, Money Laundering and Off-shore Centres*, p.120.

mate businesses, and donations) and the other to tackle the distribution process. With regard to the first strategy, unfortunately nobody can guarantee that such an initiative will be efficient and effective in terms of cost-benefit analysis.[164] Although it partially overlaps with conventional policing strategy, especially in relation to criminal activities, the other methods such as donations and legitimate businesses entail more complicated challenges. Given that terrorist money could be accumulated under almost any circumstances such as donations at grassroots level, it would require enormous resources to establish a mechanism to take control of every aspect of the money-making activities in the private sector.

Given such constraints, it seems to be better to target terrorist funds at their transfer and distribution stages. It could be an efficient use of limited investigative resources.[165] For example, if investigators trace any significant distribution of funds based on either human intelligence or the amount of money, they can concentrate their limited resources on the major players, first catching them and as a result, eliminating the funding channels.[166] It could generate the positive cycle of following money, catching "big fish", eliminating the funding channels and shifting the investigation to others who are exposed through the links with those originally apprehended.[167] The possibility is already confirmed by the investigators' use of wire transfer data in identifying the accomplices and supporters of the 9/11 attack.[168]

---

[164] For example, *zakat* are collected across every walk of the Middle Eastern societies, and it is distributed to various sectors in need such as charities and social services. In this case, without hard evidence on the connection with terrorism, it would be extremely difficult for governments to interfere with every use of *zakat*, thus courting public anger. Moreover, it would be indeed beyond the capability of government authorities to place all those voluntary collection activities in the private sector under the strict government control.

[165] The 9/11 Commission Report, pp.381-383.

[166] *Ibid.*, p.383.

[167] *Ibid.*, p.382.

[168] "The Role of Charities and NGO's In the Financing of Terrorist Activities", *supra* note 147, p.18. See also the view of the 9/11 Commission on the use of terrorist financing in incapacitating the capability of Al-Qaida:
"Vigorous efforts to track terrorist financing must remain front and center in U.S. counterterrorism efforts. The government has recognized that information about terrorist money helps us to understand their networks, search them out, and disrupt their operations. Intelligence and law enforcement have targeted the relatively small number of financial facilitators-individuals al Qaeda relied on for their ability to raise and deliver money-at the core of al Qaeda's revenue stream. Their efforts have worked. The death or capture of several important facilitators has decreased the amount of money available to al Qaeda and has increased its costs and difficulty in raising and moving that money.

Fortunately the international community does not have to develop a new infrastructure for this purpose but can utilise the already existing one that was established in the context of combating the laundering of the proceeds of acquisitive crimes.[169] This is for the reason that in practice the "distribution process" is quite close to the concept of "money laundering".

1.3.2.2 The relationship of money laundering and terrorist financing

Originally, the term "money laundering" was used in the 1920s in the US. At the time, Mafia groups owned and used launderettes to gain a legitimate appearance for money derived from acquisitive crimes.[170] Later, although there were subtle differences, a three-stage definition was generally employed by scholars and policy makers. For example, the FATF described the process of money laundering as follows: firstly, cash enters into the domestic financial system either formally or informally; secondly, it is sent abroad to be integrated into the financial systems of regulatory havens; and, thirdly, it is repatriated in the form of transfers of legitimate appearance.[171] Thus, despite several variations of the definition of money laundering, it can be generally described as a *legitimisation-oriented* concept: from a dark side to a sunny side.

However, terrorist financing does not put an emphasis on legitimisation. Money has only to be distributed to final terrorist cells but it does not need to be legitimate. Rather, added weight must be given to the activity of brushing off or breaking the money trail. Especially, if the amount of money on the move is small, this approach is more appropriate. Thus, terrorist financing can be categorised as a *lead line cutting-oriented* concept: the dark or sunny side does not matter. To

---

Captures have additionally provided a windfall of intelligence that can be used to continue the cycle of disruption." (The 9/11 Commission Report, p.382).

[169] FATF, "Report on Money Laundering Typologies, 2000-2001", p.20.

[170] Stessens G (2000) *Money Laundering: A New International Law Enforcement Model*, p.82.

[171] For an overview of various definitions of money laundering, see, e.g., Mitsilegas V (2003) *Money Laundering Counter-Measures in the European Union: A New Paradigm of Security Governance versus Fundamental Legal Principles*, pp.25-30. Similarly, the UN defines money laundering as a dynamic three-stage process that requires: firstly, moving the funds from direct association with the crime; secondly, disguising the trail to foil pursuit; and, thirdly making the money available to the criminal once again, with its occupational and geographic origins hidden from the view. See, United Nations Office for Drug Control and Crime Prevention (1998) *Financial Havens, Banking Secrecy and Money Laundering*, p.4.

move funds clandestinely from source to recipient, terrorist group networks disguises the true identities of both parties.[172]

In sum, money laundering begins with brushing off the audit trail and ends by achieving legitimisation, while terrorist financing begins with money making and ends by distributing it. Despite the difference in their final goals, what money laundering and terrorist financing share in common is the concerns about how to erase money trails as represented by the overlapping middle bold line in the diagram below. Out of this similarity, the skills of the money launderer have become an indispensable tool for terrorists to hide the flow of their money as well as to keep sustainable financing sources intact.[173] Consequently, there is significant room for anti-money laundering counter-measures to attack terrorist financing.

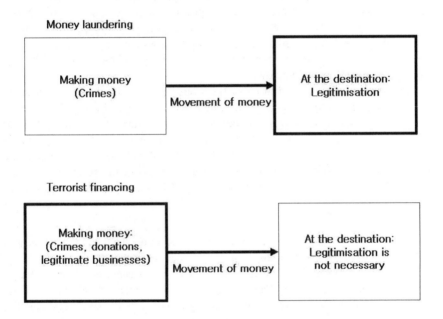

Fig.1. The relationship between money laundering and terrorist financing

However, as mentioned briefly above, this approach to share the anti-money laundering infrastructure is in some ways vulnerable to the criticism that terrorist money is not always criminal in origin and the amount of terrorist money might

---

[172] Gunaratna R, *supra* note 32, p.61; Thachuk KL (May 2002) "Terrorism's Financial Lifeline: Can It be Severed?", *Strategic Forum*, Institute for National Strategic Studies, National Defense University, no.191, p.3.

[173] Thachuk KL, *supra* note 172, p.3.

not be so conspicuous as to attract the attention of relevant authorities. Accordingly counter-terrorist financing efforts needs to rely on relevant intelligence more than general anti-money laundering measures.[174]

1.3.2.3 Some cases of money laundering in terrorist financing

In practice, numerous money laundering cases can be found in the use of terrorist financing as below. In the late 1970s, the Italian Red Brigades were always short of cash, and turned to kidnapping and bank robbery to raise funds. At one time, the Red Brigades discovered that the banknotes of their victim's ransom had all been stained with yellow ink and were thus unusable. Unwilling to give up the money, the kidnappers physically washed it. Three people spent days washing the banknotes one by one and drying them with a hair dryer in a damp Milan basement flat.[175] In contrast to such curious practices, current terrorist groups employ state of the art techniques, sometimes emulating or outdoing professional transnational criminal organisations. Some money laundering techniques shared by terrorist groups are illustrated below.[176]

First of all, Al-Qaida used to move the money it raised by the *hawala* system. This is an underground, unregulated system based on trust by which money is transferred from one location to another, without the actual physical movement of cash.[177] Following its move to Afghanistan in 1996, Al-Qaida had increased recourse to the *hawala* system because the banking system there was unreliable and formal banking was risky due to the scrutiny that Al-Qaida received after the August 1998 East African Embassy bombings.[178] It relied on the established *ha-*

---

[174] In this context, it should be noted that even if investigators focus on the movement of money in both terrorist financing cases and money laundering cases, a different approach needs to be employed. In other words, since money laundering derives from acquisitive crimes, the amount of money plays an important role in developing the suspicion of investigators. It is an operation that targets money itself, and catches some fish as a by-product. By comparison, terrorist financing does not necessarily involve money in bulk and needs to be supported by human intelligence. Thus, it is more likely that the operation targets money trails first, and catches the fish eventually. For a discussion of the need for intelligence, see, e.g., Navias MS (2002) "Financial Warfare as a Response to International Terrorism". In: Freedman L (ed), *supra* note 35, p.73.

[175] Napoleoni L, *supra* note 33, p.54.

[176] For an overview of Al-Qaida's use of money laundering techniques, see, Bell RE (2003) "The Confiscation, Forfeiture and Disruption of Terrorist Finances" *Journal of Money Laundering Control*, vol.7, no.2, pp.107-108; Lilley P (2003) *Dirty Dealing: The Untold Truth about Global Money Laundering, International Crime and Terrorism*, pp.141-142.

[177] UN, S/2005/83, *supra* note 104, p.24.

[178] The 9/11 Commission Report, p.171.

wala networks operating in Pakistan, in the United Arab Emirates, and throughout the Middle East.[179] Since 9/11, it is said that the dependence of Al-Qaida on the *hawala* system has become even greater.[180]

Secondly, wire transfer has long been regarded as one of most popular and convenient means of transferring money.[181] This refers to any financial transactions carried out for a person through a financial institution by electronic means.[182] The speed and efficiency with which funds can be moved across international boundaries by the wire transfer system appeals to financiers of terrorism as exemplified by the essential role played by this method in providing the 9/11 hijackers with necessary financial means to carry out their attack.[183] However, it was also wire transfers that provided the first and most concrete leads for investigators to outline the full scope of those involved in the attack, including the identities of the perpetrators, their logistical and financial support networks, and links to other terrorist groups and accomplices.[184] In this sense, the potential of the use of wire transfer data in identifying the link between known terrorist groups and individuals cannot be ignored.[185]

Thirdly, terrorist groups often employ the traditional and extremely basic money laundering method of cash smuggling. Al-Qaida employed this technique to provide Jemmah Islamiya (JI) with the funding for the Bali bombing that took place in October 2002.[186] JI's head of operations who was hiding in Thailand passed US$ 30,000 to the perpetrators of the bombings in two batches using several cash couriers.[187] The couriers took several weeks to complete the runs.[188] Al-Qaida also provided the funding for the J.W. Marriott Hotel bombing in Jakarta by this method of cash smuggling.[189] A total of US$ 30,000 was sent to Indonesia in April 2003 through a string of cash couriers.[190]

---

[179] *Ibid.*, p.171.

[180] UN, S/2002/1050, *supra* note 151, p.3.

[181] APG, "Annual Typologies Report 2003-2004", p.23.

[182] FATF, "Report on Money Laundering and Terrorist Financing Typologies 2003-2004", p.3.

[183] For details, see the statement of the FBI to the US Congress
<http://www.fbi.gov/congress/congress02/lormel021202.htm>.

[184] "The Role of Charities and NGO's in the Financing of Terrorist Activities", US Congress, *supra* note 147, p.18.

[185] APG, "Annual Typologies Report 2003-2004", p.23.

[186] Greenberg MR, *supra* note 123, p.11. The JI is a Southeast Asia-based terrorist network which aims to create an Islamic state in the area. See, US Department of State, "Patterns of Global Terrorism-2003; Appendix B", 29 April 2004.

[187] APG, "APG Annual Typologies Report 2003-04", June 2004, p.34.

[188] *Ibid.*, p.34.

[189] *Ibid.*, p.34.

[190] *Ibid.*, p.34.

Fourthly, precious metals and stones such as gold and diamonds are another method that terrorist groups use to generate and hide revenues. For example, gems are easy to hide and virtually untraceable, while generally maintaining their value.[191] Usama bin Laden's associates reportedly converted US$ 20 million into diamonds following the 1998 bombings of two U.S. Embassies in East Africa to put it out of reach of the asset freezing regime imposed on Al-Qaida.[192]

Fifthly, money laundering techniques provide terrorists with the opportunity to make money. For example, there have been claims that Al-Qaida financed itself through manipulation of the stock market based on its advanced knowledge of the 9/11 attack.[193] However, since the stock market was not an area strictly controlled under the anti-money laundering regime at the time, no trail could be found to prove that speculation.[194] This allegation may be true or not true. However, it clearly points to a future possibility that terrorists may utilise this loophole.

4 Conclusion

Terrorism has evolved greatly over the last few decades, and has now become a serious threat to international peace and security. One of the effective counter strategies will be to launch a financial war on terrorism since solid financing is essential for terrorist groups in order to promote their cause. For this purpose of targeting terrorist money, it has been noted that fortunately the international community can benefit from the already established anti-money laundering strategy, given the similarity of the two strategies. This book which has its roots in the international criminal law approach will primarily focus on this money laundering-related aspect of terrorist financing. In addition, efforts will also be extended to undertake some other activities at the money-making stage such as the abuse of charities.

---

[191] Thachuk K, *supra* note 172, p.4. Diamonds purchased illegally and below fair market value from rebels in Sierra Leone can be resold in Europe at a significant profit.

[192] UN, S/2005/83, *supra* note 104, p.29.

[193] For example, in the three days prior to 9/11, the volume of put options in the US surged 285 times the average trading level. A similar trend was reported in the insurance business with leading companies becoming the object of exceptional and unexpected speculation on the futures market (Napoleoni L, *supra* note 33, pp.163-165). For further details in relation to the allegation of Al-Qaida's involvement in the speculation in the stock market, see, Radlauer D, "Black Tuesday: The World's Largest Insider Trading Scam?", *International Policy Institute for Counter-Terrorism*, 19 September 2001.

For reference, stock options are contracts that give their owner the right (but not the obligation) to buy ("call" option) or sell ("put" option) stocks at a set price.

[194] Napoleoni L, *supra* note 33, p.165.

2 The Common Perception on Terrorist Financing prior to 9/11

2.1 Introduction

In Chapter One, the characteristics of modern terrorism were reviewed. It is clear from the analysis that "A successful terrorist group, like any criminal organization, is necessarily one that is able to build and maintain an effective financial infrastructure".[1] In this context, the current prominence of Al-Qaida, the broadest terrorist network yet known, would be nearly impossible without its clandestine and resilient financial infrastructure.[2]

However, there might be a criticism that the financial capability of a terrorist organisation is not so crucial to its operation as illustrated by the financial profile of the September 11th attack which, it has been estimated, cost less than US$ 500,000.[3] In respect of this criticism, it should be noted that although it would be very difficult ever to stop a single terrorist attack, what we can hope to do is to stop major attacks, and to stop the major movement of funds and thus cut off the long-term ability of terrorists to launch attacks.[4]

Given the significance of targeting terrorist financing, this chapter will examine the manner in which the international community dealt with this issue prior to 9/11. To this end, Section 2.2 will analyse the international position concerning terrorism in general. Then Section 2.3 will examine the text of the International Convention for the Suppression of the Financing of Terrorism (1999), and explain the origin of the 1267 Sanctions Committee of the Security Council. As the 1999 convention was heavily influenced by the general anti-money laundering strategy, in Section 2.3, a theoretical basis of the anti-money laundering framework will al-

---

[1] FATF, "Guidance for Financial Institutions in Detecting Terrorist Financing", 24 April 2002, p.3.

[2] For terrorist groups' various needs for financing, see, Chapter One, Section II.2.b. of this study.

[3] Gunaratna, R (2002) *Inside Al Qaeda,* p.64.

[4] Juan Zarate, the then US Deputy Assistant Secretary for Terrorist Financing, cited in BBC News, "Choking off al-Qaeda's cash lifeline", 2 October 2003 <http://newsvote. bbc.co.uk/mpapps/print/news.bbc.co.uk/1>.

so be provided as preliminary work for the main discussion on the development of counter-terrorist financing strategy.

During this period, despite the fledgling attempts to combat terrorist financing, it should be admitted that this was a neglected area, illustrated by the fact that only four countries before 9/11 had ratified the 1999 convention.[5]

2.2 The Orthodox Stance on International Terrorism

2.2.1 UN General Assembly and anti-terrorism conventions

The UN has been at the centre of the counter-terrorism campaign at the international level, especially since the 1970s. In this process, the General Assembly has played an essential role. Its involvement in international terrorist affairs can be said to have commenced with the adoption of Resolution 3034 in 1972, following the massacres at Lod airport in Israel,[6] and at the Olympic Games in Munich.[7] In the resolution, the General Assembly decided to establish an *ad hoc* Committee on Terrorism with a mandate to submit recommendations for the speedy elimination of international terrorism.[8] However, this *ad hoc* Committee did not make any substantial progress by reason of the divided attitudes between the West and the Third World.[9] The West was nervous that a definition of terrorism could be used to include 'state terrorism' which was defined by the Third World countries, for

---

[5] Gilmore WC, "International Initiative". In: Graham T(ed) (2003) *Butterworths International Guide to Money Laundering Law and Practice*, 2nd edn, p.137. The four countries are Botswana, Sri Lanka, the UK and Uzbekistan.

[6] On 30 May 1970, three members of the Japanese United Red Army opened fire at Lod Airport terminal near Tel Aviv, killing 27 and injuring 69. See, Sederberg PC (1989) *Terrorist Myths: illusion, rhetoric, and reality,* p.114.

[7] On 5 September 1972, eight Palestinian terrorists broke into the Olympic Village, killing eleven Israeli team members. See, Rosie G (1987) *The Directory of International Terrorism*, pp.179-180.

[8] UN, A/RES/3034, 18 December 1972, para. 9, 10. There was an unsuccessful attempt by the League of Nations to draft a universal definition. On 16 November 1937, the League of Nations adopted the Convention for the Prevention and Punishment of Terrorism, but it was a failure since the convention was signed by only twenty-four states and ratified by one, India. See, Cassese A (1989) *Terrorism, Politics and Law: The Achille Lauro Affair*, p.9.

[9] For the final recommendations of the *ad hoc* committee, see, UN, "Analytical Study Prepared by the Secretariat in accordance with General Assembly Resolution 32/147" (hereafter, "Analytical Study"), A/AC/160/4, 28 February 1979, para.51-58. In: Friedlander RA (1981) *Terrorism: Documents of International and Local Control*, vol.III.

instance as acts practised by states against the sovereignty of other states, particularly smaller states, through the use of force, economic blockade or threatening the security and sources of wealth of the smaller states; acts of imperialist or racist regimes against peoples struggling for their liberation; the insistence of colonialist states on remaining in the colonised regions, draining their resources; and, the collective expulsion of peaceable peoples from their homelands, scattering them over various parts of the world, etc.[10] By comparison, the Third World countries insisted that the acts performed by recognised national liberation movements in their struggle to obtain their goals of self-determination and independence should be excluded from any definition of international terrorism.[11] Consequently, it could not even draft a definition of terrorism.[12]

In 1996, the General Assembly once again established an *ad hoc* committee, one of whose mandates was to draw up a universal definition of terrorism and to draft a comprehensive convention.[13] This committee is still working on the issue,[14] but at the same time the old tradition of legal debate related to terrorism is also going on in and outside the UN as illustrated by the exclusion of terrorism from

---

[10] Higgins R "The general international law of terrorism". In: Higgins R, Flory M (eds) (1997) *Terrorism and International Law*, pp.14-16; UN, "Analytical Study", *supra* note 9, para.33-37; Zeidan S, "Desperately Seeking Definition: The International Community's Quest for Identifying the Specter of Terrorism", (2004) *Cornell International Law Journal*, vol.36, p.494.

[11] UN, "Analytical Study", *supra* note 9, para.27-32. The Organisation of the Islamic Conference (OIC) recently insisted on including the exception of the national liberation movement, see, Halberstam M (2003) "The Evolution of the United Nations Position on Terrorism: From Exempting National Liberation Movements to criminalizing Terrorism Wherever and by Whomever Committed", *Columbia Journal of Transnational Law*, vol. 41, p. 573.

[12] UN, "Report of the *Ad Hoc* Committee on International Terrorism", A/9028, 1973, para.26. In: Friedlander RA, *supra* note 9; UN, "Report of the *Ad Hoc* Committee on International Terrorism", A/32/37, 1977, para.10. In: Friedlander RA, *supra* note 9 ; UN, "Analytical Study", *supra* note 9, para. 16-39.

[13] UN, A/RES/51/210, 17 December 1996; UN, A/RES/53/108, 26 January 1999; UN, A/RES/545/110, 2 February 2000; UN, A/RES/56/88, 24 January 2002. The 1996 *ad hoc* committee has been mandated with several important tasks ever since its establishment, such as the elaboration of an international convention for the suppression of terrorist bombings, international convention for the suppression of the financing of terrorism, international convention for the suppression of acts of nuclear terrorism, and comprehensive convention on international terrorism.

[14] UN, "Report of the Ad Hoc Committee established by General Assembly resolution 51/210 of 17 December 1996: Sixth Session (28 January-1 February 2002)", A/57/37, 2002.

the jurisdiction of the International Criminal Court (ICC), the statute of which entered into force in 2002.[15]

In the meantime, what was possible despite the constraint of divided positions during this period was the conclusion of international conventions to prohibit certain types of act, for instance, the hijacking of aeroplanes or ships, hostage taking and attacks on internationally protected persons, rather than addressing terrorism as a whole.[16] Obviously, the UN and its specialised organisations have played a crucial role in preparing these instruments.[17] Some efforts have also been made at the regional level.[18] Interestingly, the majority of these crime-specific treaties are very similar in terms of their approach in that they criminalise certain types of

---

[15] Terrorism has not been included within the jurisdiction of the ICC since a majority of countries opposed inclusion by reason of the lack of definition, and terrorist acts were viewed as crimes of a different character for which effective systems of international cooperation were already in place. See, UN, "Report of the Ad Hoc Committee on the Establishment of an International Criminal Court", A/50/22, 1995, para.55, 83. In: Bassiouni MC (ed) (1998) *The Statute of the International Criminal Court: A Documentary History*, p.624, p.629; UN, "Report of the Preparatory Committee on the Establishment of an International Criminal Court", vol. I, A/51/22, 1996, para. 103, 107. In: Bassiouni MC (ed) (1998) *The Statute of the International Criminal Court: A Documentary History*, p.401.For further discussion, see, McKay F (2004) "U.S. Unilateralism and International Crimes: The International Criminal Court and Terrorism", *Cornell International Law Journal*, vol. 36, p.456; Morris M (2004) "Terrorism and Unilateralism: Criminal Jurisdiction and International Relations", *Cornell International Law Journal*, vol.36, pp.486-487; Kittichaisaree K (2001) *International Criminal Law*, p 227.

[16] Kittichaisaree K, *supra* note 15, p.228.

[17] Currently, there are 12 global conventions directly pertaining to the subject of international terrorism (visited on 1 June 2005) <http://untreaty.un.org/English/Terrorism.org>. For an overview of the contents of these conventions, see, McClean D (2002) *International Co-operation in Civil and Criminal Matters*, pp.289-294.

[18] Currently, there are seven regional anti-terrorism conventions : Organization of the Islamic Conference, Convention on Combating International Terrorism (1999); European Convention on the Suppression of Terrorism (1977); Organization for American States, Convention to Prevent and Punish the Acts of Terrorism Taking the Form of Crimes Against Persons and Related Extortion that are of International Significance (1971); African Union, Convention on the Prevention and Combating of Terrorism (1999); South Asian Association for Regional Cooperation, Regional Convention on Suppression of Terrorism (1988); Commonwealth of Independent States, Treaty on Cooperation among the States Members of the Commonwealth of Independent States in Combating Terrorism (1999) (visited on 1 June 2005) <http://untreaty.un.org/English/Terrorism.org>.

violent acts; provide the bases for jurisdiction; and, include basic provisions on extradition and other issues for international cooperation.[19]

Yet, the weakest point of this piecemeal approach was that these conventions focus on the *symptomatic treatment* of terrorist attacks. In other words, when certain acts of violence took place, a new convention attempted simply to criminalise these specific acts, but did not go further in any meaningful way to target the overall terrorist movements with a view to their destruction. Indeed, the international community had to wait until the late 1990s to see the emergence of a more fundamental solution: the International Convention for the Suppression of the Financing of Terrorism (1999). For the first time, an anti-terrorism convention was adopted with the insight to tackle the basic financial infrastructure of terrorist groups, thus weakening their long-term viability. This convention will be reviewed in Section 2.3.2.

2.2.2 Security Council and the *Lockerbie* Incident

While the General Assembly and other UN specialised organisations were struggling to deal with international terrorism, the Security Council appeared to stand behind them with its arms folded until the late 1980s.[20] It was on the occasion of the *Lockerbie* incident (1988) that the organ began to engage in the fight against international terrorism on a full scale, eventually flexing its muscles through recourse to its Chapter VII powers.[21]

On 21 December 1988, Pan Am Flight 103 exploded over Lockerbie, Scotland, killing 270 people. Following this incident, another aerial tragedy of UTA Flight 772 took place on 19 September 1989, causing 171 deaths. The results of the investigations by the victim states indicated the involvement of the Libyan government in both cases. Accordingly, the victim states made demands on the Libyan government to settle the case. In the *Lockerbie* incident, the UK and US govern-

---

[19] For an analysis of the patterns of international convention concerning international crimes, see, Clark RS (1998) "Offenses of International Concern: Multilateral State Treaty Practice in the Forty Years Since Nuremberg", *Nordic Journal of International Law*, vol.57, p.49. This article classifies a multitude of issues into four categories: (a) the question of jurisdiction; (b) the package of extradition-related issues; (c) the rights of the accused; (d) the "general part" of criminal law such as *mens rea*, complicity, and diplomatic immunity.

[20] Occasionally, the Security Council adopted resolutions to condemn terrorism, however, this organ confined its role to employing political rhetoric without taking any substantive measures. See, e.g., Resolution 286 (1970); Resolution 579 (1985); Resolution 635 (1989).

[21] Gilmore WC "International Financial Counterterrorism Initiatives". In: Fijnaut C, Wouters J, Naert F (eds) (2004) *Legal Instruments in the Fight against International Terrorism: A Transnational Dialogue*, p.194.

ments were interested parties, and demanded the Libyan government cooperate on several requests such as the surrendering of the accused and the paying of compensation.[22] In contrast to the UK and US approach, the French government which was an interested party in the UTA 772 Flight case, did not seek extradition of the six Libyan nationals but tried them *in absentia*. To this end, the French government called upon the Libyan government to cooperate and assist the French criminal proceedings by means of the production of all material evidence and the facilitation of access to all documentation by the French authorities.[23]

Although the victim countries in both cases made different requests vis-à-vis the Libyan government, they adopted the same strategy to bring the Libyan government into compliance with their demands. This means they involved the Security Council in their affairs. At first, the Security Council adopted Resolution 731 (1992),[24] urging the Libyan government to provide a full and immediate response to those requests by the victim states. However, given that the operative paragraphs of Resolution 731 were not adopted under Chapter VII authority, the Security Council could not evoke any response from the Libyan government.[25] Subse-

---

[22]   The British and American Governments demanded that the Government of Libya must: (i) surrender for trial all those charged with the crime; and accept complete responsibility for the actions of Libyan officials; (ii) disclose all it know of this crime, including the names of all those responsible, and allow full access to all witnesses, documents and other material evidence, including all the remaining timers; (iii) pay appropriate compensation (Joint US/UK Declaration of 27 November 1991, Annexed to UN Doc. A/46/826-S/23307 and A/46/827-S23308. In: Grant JP (2004) *The Lockerbie Trial: A Documentary History*, p.101). For an overview of the negotiation history on the *Lockerbie* case, see, Aust A (2000) "Lockerbie Case", *International and Comparative Law Quarterly*, vol.49, p.278.

[23]   France called upon Libya (i) to produce all the material evidence in its possession and to facilitate access to all documents that might be useful for establishing the truth; (ii) to facilitate the necessary contacts and meetings, inter alia, for the assembly of witnesses; (iii) to authorise the responsible Libyan officials to respond to any request made by the examining magistrate responsible for judicial information (French Communiqué of 12/20/91, UN Doc.A/46/825-S/23306. In: Grant JP, *supra* note 22, p.102).

[24]   UN, S/RES/731, 21 January 1992.

[25]   Libya instead instituted two parallel proceedings in the ICJ, against the UK and the US. However, with the adoption of Resolution 748, the ICJ dismissed Libya's request for provisional measures in 1992. For details with regard to the involvement of the ICJ in the *Lockerbie* case, see, e.g.,Vera GD (1994) "The Relationship between the International Court of Justice and the Security Council in the light of the *Lockerbie* case", *The American Journal of International Law*, vol.88, pp.644-647. In 1998, the ICJ rejected the objection to jurisdiction raised by the US which argued that there was no legal dispute between the parties under the Montreal Convention (Grant JP, *supra* note 22, p.512). Finally in 2003, Libya, the UK and the US agreed to discontinue the proceedings

quently, the Security Council passed Resolution 748 (1992)[26], but this time under the mandatory Chapter VII powers, imposing sanctions such as aviation restrictions and an arms embargo. Following this measure Resolution 883 (1993) was further adopted with a view to reinforcing the sanctions regime, which is particularly worthy of note in that it was made obligatory for all states to freeze Libyan public assets under their jurisdiction.[27] For the purpose of resolving the impasse among the parties concerned, various suggestions were made, including a Scottish trial of the accused Libyan officials in the Netherlands.[28] Accordingly, the Security Council adopted resolution 1192 (1998) which provided for the immediate suspension of sanctions if the accused Libyan officials arrived in the Netherlands for the purposes of trial as mentioned above.[29] In accordance with this resolution, when the two accused Libyan officials arrived in the Netherlands in 1999, the sanctions were suspended immediately.[30] The sanctions were finally lifted when Libya complied fully with the requests of the Security Council in 2003. [31]

In conclusion, the Security Council joined the counter-terrorism campaign late but it has brought the great potential of Chapter VII powers into the campaign. The *Lockerbie* incident laid the groundwork in this respect.

---

initiated by the Libyan Application filed on 3 March 1992 (Grant JP, *supra* note 22, p.553).

[26] UN, S/RES/748, 31 March 1992. In the resolution, the Security Council stated its view that the suppression of international terrorism is essential for the maintenance of international peace and security, and adopted countermeasures with its Chapter VII powers. In fact, this change was of note since no form of terrorism had previously been found to constitute a threat to international peace and security (Beveridge F (1992) "Current Developments: Public International Law; I. The Lockerbie Affair", *International and Comparative Law Quarterly*, vol.42, p.912).

[27] UN, S/RES/883, 11 November 1993. In para.3, the Security Council "decides that all States in which there are funds or other financial resources(including funds derived or generated from property) owned or controlled, directly or indirectly, by the Government or public authorities of Libya, or any Libyan undertaking, shall freeze such funds and financial resources and ensure that neither they nor any other funds and financial resources made available, by their nationals or by any persons within their territory, directly or indirectly, to or for the benefit of the Government or public authorities of Libya or any Libyan undertaking....".

[28] For the summary of the suggestions, see, Black R (1999) "Analysis: The Lockerbie Disaster", *The Edinburgh Law Review*, vol.3, p.88.

[29] UN, S/1999/378, 27 August 1998.

[30] UN, "Secretary-General's Letter of 4/5/99", S/1999/378, 5 April 1999. In: Grant JP, *supra* note 22, pp.171-173.

[31] UN, S/RES/1506, 12 September 2003. In the meantime, with regard to the UTA 772 Flight case, Libya already paid damages totalling US$ 30 million which the French Foreign Ministry acknowledged in 1999 (Aust A, *supra* note 22, p.296).

2.3 The Emergence of Counter-Terrorist Financing Strategy

2.3.1 The prototypes

2.3.1.1 Context

In Chapter One the sources and methods of terrorist financing were analysed. It was noted that the financing techniques of terrorists are in large part not distinct from the money laundering skills used by organised criminal groups to launder their criminal proceeds.[32] In both cases, what these two distinct groups have in common is the concerns about how to erase their money trails. In other words, both criminal groups and terrorist groups attempt to *hide or obscure the link* between the nature of the funds, and their eventual destination.[33]

As a result of this similarity, the strategy to target the financing of terrorism has been heavily influenced by the strategy to combat the dirty money of acquisitive crime such as drug trafficking and people smuggling. In this context, this study examines the development of anti-money laundering strategy as a preliminary work for the discussion on the development of counter-terrorist financing strategy. The anti-money laundering framework can be divided into four categories: (a) public sector; (b) private sector; (c) a bridging mechanism; (d) international cooperation.[34]

---

[32] With regard to the financing methods used by terrorists, there was a discussion within the FATF whether the same technique as criminal organisations employ to launder their monies is applicable to terrorist financing since terrorist groups have legitimate funding sources as well as illicit sources. Later, the FATF concluded that there is little difference in the methods used by terrorist groups or criminal organisations in attempting to hide or obscure the link between the source of the funds and their eventual destination or purpose. See, e.g., FATF, "Guidance for Financial Institutions in Detecting Terrorist Financing", 24 April 2002, p.5; FATF, "Report on Money Laundering Typologies: 2000-2001", 1 February 2001, pp.19-21; FATF, "Report on Money Laundering Typologies: 2001-2002", 1 February 2002, p.2; FATF, "Report on Money Laundering Typologies: 2002-2003", 14 February 2003, p.3.

However, it should be pointed out that there exists a distinction between these two crimes in that monies are the objective of typical organised crimes, whereas they are simply a *means* to achieve a goal with regard to terrorism. For a related discussion on this aspect, see, e.g., Kersten A (2002) "Financing of Terrorism—A Predicate Offence to Money Laundering?". In: Pieth M (ed) *Financing of Terrorism*, p.56.

[33] FATF, "Report on Money Laundering Typologies: 2002-2003", 14 February 2003, p.3.

[34] For backgrounds of this categorisation, see, Gilmore WC (2004) *Dirty Money: The evolution of international measures to counter money laundering and the financing of terrorism*, 3rd edn, pp.19-23 and pp.93-94; Albrecht H (1997) "The Money Trail, Developments in Criminal Law, and Research Needs: An Introduction", *European Journal of*

Firstly, in the public sector, for the purpose of coping with acquisitive crimes that have taken on new dimensions in the last quarter of the 20th century,[35] governments have strengthened their criminal law and criminal justice systems with a fresh perspective: a proceeds-oriented approach instead of a perpetrator-oriented approach.[36] The main rationale of this approach is to promote an effective campaign against organised crime through "financial devastation".[37] The intended effect is to incapacitate criminal organisations by undermining their financial infrastructure, eliminating their capacity to trade and reducing their attractiveness to recruits.[38] However, when government authorities pursued the huge proceeds of organised criminal groups, it was difficult for them to recover the proceeds since these criminal assets are hidden somewhere as legitimised property through money laundering. Accordingly, government authorities sought, to begin with, the *criminalisation of money laundering* and strengthened legal powers for *confiscation of criminal proceeds*.[39] Indeed, it is an *orthodox* approach of a sovereign state to control crime. It was the UN Convention against Illicit Traffic in Narcotic

---

Crime, Criminal Law and Criminal Justice, vol.5, pp.193-195; Mitsilegas V (2003) *Money Laundering Counter-Measures in the European Union: A New Paradigm of Security Governance versus Fundamental Legal Principles*, pp.8-14; UN (1998) "Commentary on the United Nations Convention Against Illicit Traffic in Narcotic Drugs and Psychotropic Substances 1988", pp.65-70.

In a similar context, it is worthy of note how the U.S. and Switzerland have developed their anti-money laundering legislation in a different way. See, Stessens G (2000) *Money Laundering: A New International Law Enforcement Model*, pp.109-112.

[35] For an overview of the threats posed by organised crime, see, e.g., Williams P, Savona, EU (eds) (1996) *The United Nations and Transnational Organised Crime*, pp.32-39.

[36] Verbruggen F (1997) "Proceeds-oriented Criminal Justice in Belgium: Backbone or Wishbone of a Modern Approach to Organised Crime?" *European Journal of Crime, Criminal Law and Criminal Justice*, vol.5, p. 314. In particular, given that members of modern criminal organisations are easily replaceable, this change of perspective seems more persuasive.

[37] Gilmore WC, *Dirty Money*, *supra* note 34, p.20. Of course, in addition to this new justification, traditional rationales of punishment is also applicable such as to make sure that "crime does not pay", and the subsequent deterrent effect.

[38] Levi M (1997) "Taking the Profit Out of Crime: The UK experience", *European Journal of Crime, Criminal Law and Criminal Justice*, vol.5, pp.228-229.

[39] Stessens G, *supra* note 34, pp. 3-6. The experience of the US law enforcement agencies provides a case in point. For details, see, Stessens G, *supra* note 34, pp. 96-100, and pp.108-112. For relevant discussions, see, Giovanoli M, "Switzerland. Some Recent Developments in Banking ". In: Cranston R (ed) (1993) *European Banking Law: The Banker-Customer Relationship*, pp.189-198; Grant, TD (1995) "Toward a Swiss Solution for an American Problem: An Alternative Approach for Banks in the War on Drugs", *Annual Review of Banking Law*, vol. 14, p. 225.

Drugs and Psychotropic Substances of 1988 (the 1988 Vienna Convention) that introduced these instruments into the international arena.[40]

Secondly, however, it should also be admitted that there is a limit to the capacity of a state in preventing crime in every corner of society.[41] Thus, modern governments have developed a new strategy of crime control. This is called the *responsibilisation* strategy by which a government delegates its responsibility for crime control to relevant private sector actors.[42] This strategy regards the private sector as a valuable counterpart to share the burden of policing society and at the same time, attempts to utilise the expertise and resources of the private sector to the maximum.[43] In particular, such a possibility should not be overlooked that agencies in the private sector could act more efficiently and effectively than the government field agencies in the relevant area.[44] It was the Forty Recommendations (1990) of the Financial Action Task Force on Money Laundering (FATF)[45]

---

[40] Prior to 1988, there existed two central pillars to combat drugs: the Single Convention on Narcotic Drugs (1961) and its Protocol (1972), and the Convention on Psychotropic Substances (1971). For the purpose of covering the various aspects of the drug problem as a whole, especially those not envisaged in existing instruments, the drafting of the Vienna Convention was then proposed with the adoption of a General Assembly Resolution in 1984 (UN, A/RES/39/141, 14 December 1984). As a result, a draft convention was prepared by the ECOSOC Commission on Narcotic Drugs, and later adopted at the UN Conference in Vienna on 19 December 1988 (Gilmore WC (1991) *Combating International Drugs Trafficking: The 1988 United Nations Convention Against Illicit Traffic in Narcotic Drugs and Psychotropic Substances*, p.1).

[41] Garland D (1996) "The Limits of the Sovereign State: Strategies of Crime Control in Contemporary Society", *The British Journal of Criminology*, vol.36, p.448.

[42] Garland D (1997) "The Punitive Society: Penology, Criminology and the History of the Present", *Edinburgh Law Review*, vol.1, pp.189-191; Mitsilegas V, *supra* note 34, p.12.

[43] For example, with adequate training provided, the staff of financial institutions can, in effect, be turned into field agents for a government. In some sense, a well-trained and motivated staff behind the counter could be in a better position to develop the suspicion of money laundering on the spot than relevant government authorities. In this vein, the practice of Switzerland is worthy of note. The Swiss reporting model tries to make the best use of the resources and expertise of the private sector. See, Noble RK, Golumbic CE (1998) "A New Anti-Crime Framework For the World: Merging The Objective and Subjective Models for Fighting Money Laundering", *New York University Journal of International Law and Politics*, vol.30, p.79; Grant TD, *supra* note 39, p.225.

[44] Noble RK, Golumbic CE, *supra* note 43, at section I.

[45] The FATF was established by the G-7 Economic Summit in Paris in July 1989 as an independent international body whose Secretariat is housed at the OECD. It is a temporary body and its mandate has been renewed four times (1989-1994,1994-1999,1999-2004, 2004-2012). See, FATF, "Annual Report 1989-1990", 7 February 1990, p.3; FATF, "Annual Report 1993-1994", 16 June 1994, p.3; FATF, "Annual Report 1997-

that fully brought forward this idea of responsibilisation into an international context,[46] the core of which is "to identify your customers, retain their records and report any suspicious transactions". However, it should also be pointed out that this responsibilisation strategy is not premised on the unilateral sacrifice of the private sector. To some extent the strategy can also be of mutual benefit, for instance, by reducing the reputational risk of the private sector, given that money laundering operations can put financial institutions at risk through the loss of credibility and investor confidence.[47]

Thirdly, with the emergence of the private sector as a counterpart to control crime, it seems apparent that there is necessarily an interaction between the public and private sectors. For instance, one of the major tools for the private sector to prevent money laundering is to report suspicious transactions to a relevant law enforcement agency. Thus, there could be generated a flow of substantial financial data from the private sector to the public sector. For the purpose of facilitating this interaction, *a new bridging mechanism* was created by policy makers. It is called a Financial Intelligence Unit (FIU). It acts as an intermediary between the two sec-

---

1998", 25 June 1998, p.9; FATF, "FATF mandate renewed for eight years", Press Release, 14 May 2004; Gilmore WC, *supra* note 34, p.92.

[46] Prior to the Forty Recommendations (1990), there were two important precursors of the responsibilisation strategy in anti-money laundering context: Recommendation No.R(80)10 on "Measures Against the Transfer and Safekeeping of Funds of Criminal Origin" adopted by the Committee of Ministers of the Council of Europe in June 1980 and the Statement on "Prevention of Criminal Use of the Banking System for the Purpose of Money Laundering" issued by the Basel Committee on Banking Supervision in December 1988. For details of the Basle Committee, see Chapter 4 of this book. For the summary of this statement, see, Drage J (1993) "Countering Money Laundering: The Response of the Financial Sector". In: Macqueen HL (ed) *Money Laundering*, 1993, p.65.

[47] Sherman T (1993) "International Efforts to Combat Money Laundering: The Role of the Financial Action Task Force". In: Macqueen HL (ed), *supra* note 46, p.16. For relevant discussions, see also BCBS, "Customer due diligence for banks", October 2001, pp.3-4; Clark A, Burrell P (2003) "The Money Laundering Threat". In: Clark A, Burrell P (eds) *A Practitioner's Guide to International Money Laundering Law and Regulation*, 1st edn, pp.7-8.

The Chiasso Affair, the worst financial scandal in Switzerland's history, is perhaps a case in point in this regard. In 1977, two Credit Suisse officials engaged in fraud and money laundering at one of the bank's Italian branches. The episode cost Credit Suisse US$ 830 million, caused a run on the branch, and led Swiss bankers to create their own code of conduct on the acceptance of suspicious funds (Bartlett BL (May 2002) "The Negative Effects of Money Laundering on Economic Development", For the Asian Development Bank Countering Money Laundering in The Asian and Pacific Region Regional Technical Assistance Project No.5967, p.16).

tors in effect providing a service of information-filtering, and encouraging a climate of mutual trust.[48] With pooled specialised expertise the FIU can select really suspicious cases that deserve investigation, and prevent the situation where all reported clients are subject to immediate police investigation.[49] This helps to relieve the concerns of the private sector thus encouraging it to provide proactive cooperation.[50] It was the Egmont Group established in 1996 that consolidated the concept of an FIU in the international arena.

Lastly, modern money laundering techniques commonly and increasingly include a transnational dimension.[51] Accordingly, for a successful anti-money-laundering strategy, the significance of international cooperation cannot be overlooked. In fact, most of the measures in relation to the international cooperation have long been discussed in the literature of public international law, mainly in relation to treaty practice on criminal matters. If there is any substantial change to the traditional perception, the FIU has also emerged as an important actor in this area of international cooperation for the anti-money laundering purposes.[52] Now, having this contextual background in mind, let us proceed to the theoretical basis of countermeasures in each category.

2.3.1.2 Public sector

Firstly, let us consider the criminalisation of money laundering. The decision to establish money laundering as an independent criminal offence rather than dealing with it as an ancillary offence under the traditional criminal law, provided considerable advantages to law enforcement agencies in hunting down criminal proceeds. Above all, in a practical sense, when the track of the original offence disappears or is hardly traceable, it is the offence of money laundering that helps law enforcement agencies to tackle suspicious assets either in the hands of a frontman or the real owner.[53] For the purpose of confiscating the targeted proceeds, the

---

[48] Stessens G, *supra* note 34, p.185.

[49] *Ibid.*, p.185.

[50] Furthermore, the FIU can also provide a feedback to the private sector on the cases that they reported, which would elicit more proactive reports from the private sector (FATF, "Annual Report 1997-1998:Annex E—Providing Feedback to Reporting Financial Institutions and Other Persons: Best Practice Guidelines", June 1998, pp.73-74).

[51] Peterson NH (1997) "Toward a European Security Model for the 21st Century", *NATO Review*, Nov.-Dec., p.4.

[52] In effect, the FIU constitutes a versatile coordinator that runs across all these three areas: public sector, private sector, and international cooperation. This aspect becomes clear in the 2003 revised Forty Recommendations of the FATF.

[53] Stessens G, *supra* note 34, pp.85-86; Verbruggen F, *supra* note 36, pp.318-319. Usually, the suspicion is developed from the reports of financial institution in that huge criminal

prosecution does not have to prove the guilt of the perpetrator of the initial money–making offence, the professional terminology of which is a "money laundering predicate offence" or simply a "predicate offence".[54] The confiscation of the targeted assets is possible by proving the charge of money laundering behaviour by the ownership.[55] Particularly, the law enforcement agencies do not have to trouble to establish the guilt of their predicate offence beyond reasonable doubt.[56]

Moreover, a justification can also be made given that money laundering can be defined as a "primary harm" crime rather than "ancillary harm" crime. This point of view considers that money laundering involves a "separate harm" from its predicate offence, constituting threats to a multitude of interests.[57] For example, money laundering could seriously undermine the soundness of the financial system and legitimate economy.[58] A good example of the devastating and far-reaching effect of money laundering is the Bank of Credit and Commerce International (BCCI) Affair revealed in 1988.[59]

In the international arena, the 1988 Vienna Convention for the first time established money laundering as "independent criminal offence" although it confined its application only to drug-related proceeds.[60] Article 3(1) imposes a "binding"

---

proceeds are most vulnerable at the stage when they first come into contact with legal economy (Gilmore WC, *supra* note 34, p.33).

[54] For the definition of "predicate offence", see the 1990 Council of Europe Convention on Laundering, Search, Seizure and Confiscation of the Proceeds from Crime, Article 1(e).

[55] Stessens G, *supra* note 34, p.85.

[56] Verbruggen F, *supra* note 36, p.318.

[57] Mitsilegas V, *supra* note 34, pp.105-106.

[58] *Ibid.*, pp.103-106; Alldridge P (2003) *Money Laundering Law: Forfeiture, Confiscation, Civil Recovery, Criminal Laundering and Taxation of the Proceeds of Crime*, p.27, pp.63-66. For a broader justification for the criminalisation of money laundering, see also Bosworth-Davies R (1997) *The Impact of International Money Laundering Legislation*, pp.5-6.

[59] It was a huge scandal involving money laundering, allegations of corruption, and bribery. Later the BCCI was convicted and was subject to forfeiture which amounted to US$ 15.3million, eventually being closed down in 1991 with an estimated 530,000 creditors left worldwide (Gilmore WC, *supra* note 34, p.34). For further details, see also Kerry J, Brown H (December 1992) "The BCCI Affair: A Report to the Committee on Foreign Relations United States Senate", 102nd Congress 2nd Session Senate.

[60] The scope of the predicate offence expanded beyond drug trafficking later to include other organised crime, for example the 1990 Council of Europe Convention on Laundering, Search, Seizure and Confiscation of the Proceeds from Crime defines predicate offence as any criminal offence as a result of which proceeds were generated in Article 1(e); the Council of European Communities Directive of 10 June 1991 on Prevention of the use of Financial System for the Purpose of Money Laundering, as amended in 2001, expands the list of predicate offences by reference to set thresholds of punishment; the

obligation on "all party states" to make it a criminal offence to convert or transfer property for the purpose of concealing or disguising its illicit origin. The contribution this bold initiative made to the fight against transnational organised crime was significant. It promoted the concept of money laundering both domestically and internationally, thus emphasising the significance of "financial warfare" on organised crime. Furthermore, with the "international" criminalisation of money laundering, law enforcement agencies could secure a solid basis for international criminal cooperation in respect of confiscation, mutual legal assistance and extradition,[61] especially by eliminating the obstacle of the double criminality rule.[62] Indeed, the 1988 Vienna Convention has worked as a major force in harmonising national laws and enforcement actions around the world.[63]

Secondly, it should be remembered that the overall strategy to fight dirty money is ultimately aimed at facilitating the "confiscation" of criminal proceeds. In other words, confiscation lies at the heart of this financial warfare on organised crime and is considered to be one of the most important legal tools.[64] Originally this concept of confiscation developed in various ways in different legal cultures, and three standards can be identified for its categorisation. (a)With regard to the form of confiscated property, two models of confiscation can be distinguished: object confiscation and value confiscation. The object confiscation is imposed on the concerned property itself, while the value confiscation is implemented through the obligation to pay a certain amount of money corresponding to the value of the concerned property.[65] (b) In respect of whether it is a means or end of crime, a

---

1996 revised Recommendation 4 of the FATF extends the predicate offence to any serious crimes generating a significant amount of proceeds; and, eventually, the 2003 version of the FATF Forty Recommendations lists twenty predicate offences.

[61] Gilmore WC, *Combating International Drugs Trafficking, supra* note 40, p.6.

[62] "Report of the United States Delegation to the United Nations Conference for the adoption of a Convention Against Illicit Traffic in Narcotic Drugs and Psychotropic Substances", reproduced in Gilmore WC (ed) (1992) *International Efforts to Combat Money Laundering*, p.120.

[63] Stewart DP (1990) "Internationalizing the War on Drugs: The UN Convention Against Illicit Traffic in Narcotic Drugs and Psychotropic Substances", *Denver Journal of International Law and Policy*, vol.18, p.388. 170 states are parties to the 1988 Vienna Convention (visited on 1 June 2005) <http://www.unodc.org/unodc/en/treaty_adherence.html#1988>.

[64] Stessens G, *supra* note 34, p.29.

[65] *Ibid.*, pp.31-35. According to Stessens, value confiscation is to be preferred to object confiscation in that it can be enforced on legitimate property, thus covering more diverse situations such as when (i) proceeds of crime are already consumed at the time of the judicial decision or cannot be traced any more; (ii) when the right of bona fide third parties might suffer because of the 'blind' application of object confiscation. See also, UN Commentary, *supra* note 34, p.119.

distinction can be made between confiscation of the proceeds (end) and confiscation of instrumentalities (means) of crime.[66] The instruments of crime can be diverse, for example, ranging from a knife used as a killer's weapon to a yacht on which lessees transported drugs.[67] (c) In relation to the necessity of a criminal conviction of the suspect for a confiscation order, two types can be distinguished: criminal confiscation and civil confiscation. The criminal confiscation operates *in personam* (against a specific person) and needs a criminal conviction, while the civil confiscation is an *in rem* (against a thing) procedure by nature and is not conditional upon a criminal conviction.[68] Civil confiscation is quite a powerful legal tool and is widely used in the U.S.[69] Recently it was also introduced in the UK as illustrated by the Anti-Terrorism, Crime and Security Act 2001[70] and the Proceeds of Crime Act 2002.[71]

---

[66] Confiscation of instrumentalities rests on such assumptions that the convicted person is unworthy to use property by using it for criminal purpose, or that the property itself is considered to be tainted, or that the society must be protected against the uncontrolled use of dangerous property (Stessens G, *supra* note 34, pp.43-45).

[67] *Calero-Toledo v. Pearson Yacht Leasing Co.*, 416 US 663 (1974).

[68] In civil confiscation, the state bears a lower burden of proof than in criminal confiscation. In other words, for criminal confiscation, the state should prove its case by criminal standard of proof ("beyond reasonable doubt"). However, for civil confiscation, the state has only to establish its case by civil standard of proof ("probable cause"). The evidence does not need to be sufficient to free the mind wholly from all reasonable doubt, and the burden of proof is reversed to the side of defendants (Palm CW (1991) "RICO Forfeiture and the Eighth Amendment: When is Everything too much?", *The University of Pittsburgh Law Review,* vol.53, at section II).

Moreover, criminal confiscation covers only property which was held by the criminal at the time of conviction. In contrast with this, civil confiscation relates back to the original date of the illegal use of property, no matter whether it is still owned by the defendant or not. This aspect of civil confiscation is called the 'relation-back' doctrine. Under this doctrine, when property is used to further an illegal activity, title immediately vests in the government, even though the government does not take actual possession until it eventually seizes the property (Jankowski MA (1990) "Tempering the Relation-Back Doctrine: A More Reasonable Approach to Civil Forfeiture in Drug Cases", *Virginia Law Review*, vol.76, p.165).

[69] Considering the US experience, however, civil confiscation entails fierce legal controversies surrounding the fundamental right to a fair trial such as the danger of double jeopardy, the undermining of presumption of innocence, the violation of the prohibition of self-incrimination, and, the encroachment of the rights of third parties (Stessens G, *supra* note 34, p.29).

[70] See, e.g., Section 1.

[71] See, e.g., Section 243-244.

What is common in these classifications is that the former model in each category generally serves as a basic approach, whereas the latter model further strengthens the legal powers of law enforcement agencies although sometimes it entails controversies.[72] The 1988 Vienna Convention includes all three basic models (object confiscation,[73] confiscation of proceeds,[74] and criminal confiscation[75]) and further provides for strengthened models in the first two categories (value confiscation,[76] confiscation of instrumentalities[77]). In fact, only civil confiscation is left out. Importantly, it should be noted that the Vienna Convention prudently introduces a "reversed burden of proof" in Article 5(7) on a non-mandatory basis. The reversed burden of proof is useful in confiscation proceedings because it will be very difficult for the prosecution to prove, beyond reasonable doubt, the criminal origin of proceeds, for example when they have been generated in violation of foreign criminal law,[78] or when suspicious assets are owned by legal persons that are domiciled in offshore finance centres.[79] In particular, it should also be considered that many predicate offences are without a victim to give evidence on the nature of the offences and the extent of the proceeds.[80] This reversed burden of proof can sometimes be introduced in criminal proceedings by way of establishing a separate *in rem* confiscation procedure following a conviction of perpetrators.[81]

---

[72] See, *supra* note 69.

[73] Article 5(1)(a).

[74] Article 5(1)(a).

[75] With regard to the third category, the Vienna Convention seems to mean only criminal confiscation because Article 3(4)(a) expressly refers to confiscation as a sanction to which the commissioner of the offence is liable. In other words, confiscation is a result of criminal conviction of an offender (See, UN Commentary, *supra* note 34, p.117).

[76] Article 5(1)(a). In contrast to the brief mentioning of value confiscation in the Vienna Convention, the "1990 Council of Europe Convention on Laundering, Search, Seizure and Confiscation of the Proceeds from Crime" goes further by providing a very detailed procedure for value confiscation. See, e.g., Article 7, para. 2(a); Article 13, para. 3 and 4; Article 14, para. 4; Article 16.

[77] Article 5(1)(b).

[78] Stessens G, *supra* note 34, p.67. For further justification for the reversal of the burden of proof, see also Smellie A (2004) "Prosecutorial Challenges in Freezing and Forfeiting Proceeds of Transnational Crime and the Use of International Asset Sharing to Promote International Cooperation", *Journal of Money Laundering Control*, vol. 8, no.2, p.107.

[79] Council of Europe (August 2004) *Combating organised crime*, p.44.

[80] Stessens G, *supra* note 34, p.67.

[81] *Ibid.*, pp.42-43. In relation to the separate *in rem* confiscation, Netherlands can be a case in point. See, Daams CA (2003) *Criminal Asset Forfeiture: One of the most effective weapons against (organised) crime?*, pp.104-105.

Furthermore, it is also included in civil confiscation proceedings since the burden of proof is already lowered to the level of balance of probabilities.[82]

Thirdly, issues concerning the "general part" of international criminal law need to be mentioned.[83] In this category, issues concerning the state of mind, inchoate (or incomplete) offences and complicity, and corporate criminal liability are of particular significance for the study. First, state of mind (*mens rea*) is an essential requirement in convicting a perpetrator of a money laundering offence. A useful categorisation can be found in the OAS Model Regulations that the accused (a) knows that the property constitutes proceeds of a criminal activity (b) should have known that...; (c) is intentionally ignorant that...."[84] The first type is a basic mental standard for obtaining a conviction, while the second constitutes a form of negligent money laundering.[85] The third type means that the accused was wilfully blind[86] when he or she "could have known" of the criminal nature of the money concerned by investigation or inquiry.[87] This state of mind falls between negligence and the knowledge standard of intent.[88] The Vienna Convention is conservative in this respect by adopting only the first type (knowing that the proceeds are the product of a predicate offence).[89] With regard to the "test" of state of mind, the Vienna Convention also stipulates that "knowledge, intent or purpose as an element of an offence may be inferred from objective factual circumstances".[90] Second, inchoate (or incomplete) offences and complicity also entails matters for consideration.[91] In fact, it should be admitted that these concepts vary and depend upon national legal systems, making it very difficult to draft a universal formula.[92]

---

[82] It is the reversed burden of proof that accounts for most of the criticism on civil confiscation such as the undermining of presumption of innocence and the danger of self-incrimination. For details, see *supra* note 69; Council of Europe (August 2004) *Combating organised crime*, pp.49-50.

[83] For an overview of the issues, Clark RS, *supra* note 19, p.72.

[84] The OAS Model Regulations Concerning Laundering Offenses Connected to Illicit Drug Trafficking and Other Serious Offenses, Article 2 (Schott PA (2003) *Reference Guide to Anti-Money Laundering and Combating the Financing of Terrorism*, p.V-8).

[85] Schott PA, *supra* note 84 , p.V-7and V- 8.

[86] Wilful blindness probably exists when a person deliberately shuts his eyes to the means of knowledge because he prefers to remain in ignorance (Gordon GH, *Criminal Law*, p.296).

[87] Schott PA, *supra* note 84, p.V-8.

[88] *Ibid.*, p.V-8.

[89] Article 3(1)(b).

[90] Article 3(3).

[91] Clark RS, *supra* note 19, p.78.

[92] Although the terminology employed in the international text needs a different interpretation dependent upon national legal systems, the relevant theory of the common law system might be of help in understanding the relevant text. To begin with, it should be

Accordingly, the Vienna Convention stipulates to cover as many types of activities as possible. It provides for inchoate offence such as incitement, conspiracy, and attempts.[93] It also enumerates different kinds of complicity as well.[94] The suspect can be regarded as an accomplice when joins in the association or conspiracy to commit a crime or when they encourage the commission of the crime by facilitating or counselling or when they participate in the criminal activity by being present thus aiding and abetting.[95] Third, the concept of corporate criminal liability needs to be considered.[96] This can be of particular utility for example, where com-

---

remembered that a distinction can be made between inchoate offence and complicity offence based on whether a specific crime is committed or not.

Then, the inchoate offence can be divided into two categories: conspiracy and attempt. A conspiracy is an agreement of two or more persons for a criminal purpose (Gordon GH, *Criminal Law*, p.228) and an attempt is the act of a person who has necessary intent to commit a crime but falls short of its commission (Garner BA (ed) *Blacks Law Dictionary*, p.123). The concept of conspiracy is sometimes more useful to the prosecution than attempt, constituting a "complete" crime in the absence of a specific crime or acts (attempt) that falls short of the specific crime. Furthermore, both concepts can be combined together as "attempted conspiracy", creating a new offence that is called "incitement". This means that merely to invite someone to commit a crime is a completed crime. Once the invitation has been given, there is a "complete" crime (Gordon GH, *Criminal law*, p. 243).

With regard to complicity, the old common law made a distinction between principals and accessories. A principal could be either of two degrees. A principal in the first degree is the actual perpetrator. A principle in the second degree is one who is present physically (standing watching) or constructively (outside at the wheel of the getaway car) who is said to "aid and abet". Accessories also come in two varieties, before the fact and after the fact. Accessories before the fact "procure", "counsel" or "command" others to commit the offence. An accessory after the fact "receive", "relieve", "comforts" or "assist" one of the other perpetrators, typically to effect an escape. Principals in the second degree and accessories are often referred to generically accomplices on which modern penal codes draw no distinctions for the purposes of trial, except that accessories after the fact are not guilty of the substantive offence and liable to less punishment than the others (Clark RS, *supra* note 19, p.78).

[93] The Vienna Convention, Article 3(1)(c) (iii) and (iv). With regard to "induce", the Commentary explains it as a form of incitement which involves the offering of money or money's worth (UN Commentary, *supra* note 34, p.75).

[94] Article 3(1)(c)(iv).

[95] UN Commentary, *supra* note 34, p.75.

[96] Most of the common law countries subject corporations to criminal liability, while in civil law countries corporations may not be covered by criminal laws. See, Schott PA, *supra* note 84, p.V-9; Council of Europe (1990) "Liability of enterprises for offences: Recommendation No.R(88) adopted by the Committee of Ministers of the Council of

plex management structures can render the identification of the real perpetrator difficult or impossible.[97] In such cases, the imposition of liability on the legal person may be the only choice if the activity in question is not to go unpunished.[98] Furthermore a sanction imposed on an institution rather than an individual can act as a catalyst for the management and supervisory structures to maintain due diligence so that similar conduct might be prevented in the future.[99] However, the Vienna Convention which is quite innovative in every other respect remained silent on this issue. Eventually, the concept of corporate criminal liability was introduced two years later in the 1990 FATF Forty Recommendations.[100]

In sum, the Vienna Convention was in effect the first international convention to emphasise the law enforcement aspect of the fight against acquisitive crime,[101] and has established both a framework for cooperation and a common minimum standard for implementation across national boundaries.[102] Particularly, it should be noted that the Vienna Convention for the first time criminalised money laundering at the international level with an explicit definition. However, the Vienna Convention still left much to be desired in that it is related only to initiatives in the public sector.[103] A more balanced strategy came to the fore with the establishment of the FATF which deals with initiatives both in the public and private sectors.[104]

2.3.1.3 Private sector

Major issues to be considered with regard to the private sector are three: (a) on whom is the responsibility imposed?; (b) what is the content of that responsibility?; (c) and, how to control and supervise the work of the private sector?

Firstly, let us consider the scope of the private sector placed under the *responsibilisation* regime. What should be noted here is that the boundary of this

---

Europe on 20 October 1988 and explanatory memorandum", pp.10-11. For further discussions on the basis for corporate criminal liability, see also, Savla S (2001) *Money Laundering and Financial Intermediaries*, pp.186-188; Wells C (2001) *Corporations and Criminal Responsibility*, 2nd edn, pp.63-83.

[97] UN Commentary, *supra* note 34, p.67.

[98] *Ibid.*, p.67.

[99] *Ibid.*, p.67. For example, in the UK, banks have been indirectly obliged to take on the responsibility for the prevention of money laundering due to the possibility of being prosecuted. See, FATF, "Annual Report 1989-1990", 7 February 1990, p.14.

[100] The 1990 Recommendation 7 stipulates that "where possible, corporations themselves-not only their employees-should be subject to criminal liability.

[101] McClean D (2002) *International Co-operation in Civil and Criminal Matters*, pp.172-174.

[102] *Ibid.*, p.3.

[103] UN Commentary, *supra* note 34, p.68.

[104] For a detailed discussion on this aspect, see, e.g., Gilmore WC, *supra* note 34, pp.92-94.

responsibilisation regime cannot be fixed once and for all but has a tendency to sprawl *horizontally* and *vertically*. This is mainly because of the fast development of money laundering techniques and its displacement effect.[105] In respect of the horizontal expansion, the industries which were initially placed under the anti-money laundering regime included financial institutions such as banks but nowa-days spreads farther to cover non-financial institutions such as real estate agencies and professions such as lawyers.[106] Wherever any loopholes are found which can be utilised by the money launderer, the responsibilisation regime needs to be imposed. On the other hand, vertical extension means that the responsibilisation regime should be applied not only to a headquarters operation but also to branches and major subsidiaries.[107] It is needless to say that the partial application of anti-money laundering regimes within the same institution will seriously undermine consistency and effectiveness.

In the international arena, the 1990 Forty Recommendations of the FATF can be said to realise the idea of responsibilisation on a full scale, maintaining a balanced approach by including initiatives in respect of the public and international sectors as well as the private sector. The 1990 Recommendation 9 clearly stipulated that the responsibility for fighting money laundering should apply not only to banks, but also to non-bank financial institutions. However, it should be noted that the scope of application was confined to "non-bank financial institutions" rather than "non-financial institutions". This position was not changed in the revised 1996 Recommendations. All in all, the scope of application was limited to "financial institutions of any kind". A significant change was eventually introduced in the revised 2003 Forty Recommendations which designate non-financial institutions in detail but not exhaustively.[108] Unlike the horizontal expansion, the progress in the vertical extension was fast. The idea was already incorporated in the Forty Recommendations from the revised 1996 version. The 1996 revised Rec-

---

[105] The displacement effect takes place, for example, when an increased compliance by financial institutions with anti-money laundering measures brings about a shift in the money laundering phenomenon to other sectors of the economy (FATF, "Annual Report 1996-1997", p.7).

[106] For instance, see the treatment of so-called "gate keepers" by the 2001 EU Directive Amending Council Directive 91/308/EEC on Prevention of the Use of the Financial System For the Purpose of Money Laundering, Article 2.a; the 2003 FATF Recommendation 12.

[107] Schott PA, *supra* note 84, p.VI-3.

[108] In Glossary of the 2003 revised Forty Recommendations, non-financial business and professions means; a) Casinos (which also includes internet casinos); b) Real estate agents; c) Dealers in precious metals; d) Dealers in precious stones; e) Lawyers, notaries, other independent legal professionals and accountants; f) Trust and company service providers. For the open attitude of the FATF concerning the scope of application, see Recommendation 20.

ommendation 20 stipulated that financial institutions should ensure that the principles of responsibilisation also be applied to branches and majority owned subsidiaries located abroad, especially in countries which did not or insufficiently applied these recommendations.[109] If local law and regulations prohibited such implementation, compulsory enforcement measures could be collectively employed by the FATF member countries.[110] Lastly in the context of discussion on the scope of the responsibilisation strategy, one classic case should not be overlooked. It is the responsibility imposed on an individual. When an individual personally carries a certain amount of cash across an international border, a number of countries require that person to provide identification, and report the amount of money to relevant authorities.[111] In effect, this obligation is quite similar in content to those imposed on financial institutions that will be explained below. Importantly, the 1990 Recommendation 23 addressed (in a permissive fashion) the reporting of the physical cross-border transportation of cash, and the attention of the FATF to this issue remains undiminished in spite of subsequent revisions of the text.[112]

Secondly, with regard to the content of responsibility, this can be reduced to three key measures: customer identification, record keeping, and the reporting of (suspicious) transactions.[113] First, it is clear that customer identification is the starting point of the responsibilisation strategy, given that the measure concerns the initial placement stage of money laundering and that *de facto* anonymity at this stage would be the optimal haven for money laundering criminality.[114] The core elements of this measure are (i) identifying and verifying the customer and any beneficial owners; (b) understanding the financial and personal circumstances of customers; and, (c) ongoing monitoring and updating the information obtained on a regular basis.[115] Although the logic is very simple, it is indeed a difficult task to implement in practice, given the various scopes and complicated nature of the private sector into which the dirty money might flow.[116] Each relevant industry in the

---

[109] Where the minimum regulatory standards of the home and host countries differ, branches and subsidiaries in the host jurisdiction should apply the higher standard of the two (BCBS, "Customer due diligence for banks", October 2001, para. 66, p.16).

[110] Recommendation 21. For further discussion, see Section 5.2.2 of Chapter Five of this study.

[111] See, e.g., Special Recommendation IX, issued on 22 October 2004 by the FATF.

[112] Similar provisions can be found in the 1996 Recommendation 23 and the 2003 Recommendation 19(a).

[113] Stessens G, *supra* note 34, p.159.

[114] *Ibid.*, p.146.

[115] Clark A, Russell M (2003) "Know Your Customer". In: Clark A, Burrell P (eds) *A Practitioner's Guide to International Money Laundering Law and Regulation*, 1st edn, p.93.

[116] There exist various methods to disguise the genuine ownership such as shell companies, trust, independent professionals such as lawyers, etc. For the details of the development

private sector needs to prepare their own set of rules for customer identification tailored to their service. Second, the obligation to keep the records on the identity of customers or transactions is of great value because a paper trail can be formed. This database could also facilitate the *post hoc* investigation by the government authorities seeking to follow the paper trail.[117] Lastly, there is an obligation to make a report on transactions. This obligation is the climax of the responsibilisation strategy. Generally there exist two types of reporting regime in international practice: threshold-based reporting and suspicion-based reporting.[118] The first type can be regarded as an objective model in that all transactions above a fixed amount (what is called the "threshold") must be reported.[119] In contrast, the second type can be considered as a subjective model since the decisions to report transactions in question are based on a subjective judgement by the financial institutions themselves.[120] In fact, the suspicion-based model seems to fit better into the responsibilisation strategy. However, it should be noted that both models have merits and demerits respectively and they could be complementary to each other if mixed wisely.[121] Furthermore, two rules relating to the reporting obligation need to

---

of techniques, see, e.g., FATF, "Report on Money Laundering Typologies 1999-2000", 3 February 2000, pp.8-10; FATF, "Annual Report 1997-1998: Annex C—1997-1998 Report on Money Laundering Typologies", June 1998, pp.52-53.

[117] Schott PA, *supra* note 84, p.VI-13, 14.

[118] Usually, the American practice is subsumed under the threshold-based model, while the Swiss practice belongs to the suspicion-based model. For a relevant discussion, see, Clark A, Russell M (2003) "Reporting Regime". In: Clark, A & Burrell, P (eds) *A Practitioner's Guide to International Money Laundering Law and Regulation*, 1st edn, pp.130-134; Grant TD, *supra* note 39.

[119] Stessens G, *supra* note 34, p.161. For example, in the U.S., the threshold is US$ 10,000.

[120] *Ibid.*, p.161.

[121] Noble RK, Golumbic CE, *supra* note 43. The threshold-based model has the following merits (i) it has psychological deterrent effect on money launderers; (ii) it ensures an extensive paper trail for investigators to follow; (iii) it promotes uniformity and consistency in enforcement. However, the demerits are (i) the model entails the increase in the data which financial institutions have to produce, thus overburdening both financial institutions and law enforcement authorities; (ii) it might discourage the private sector from making a proactive report for the private sector may easily conclude that their task is complete upon the mere submission of the reporting form; (iii) all in all, in terms of cost-benefit analysis, the efficiency is quite low. By way of comparison, the merits and demerits of the suspicion-based model correspond to those of the objective model in reverse. The suspicion-based model (i) markedly reduces the amount of data; (ii) promotes better efficiency, namely, the law enforcement can spot money laundering with less effort by utilising the expertise of the financial institutions. However, (i) the deterrent effect might be weaker; (ii) it fails to establish an extensive paper trail; (iii) no uniformity or consistency; (iv) the private sector might under-report suspicious transactions due to

be explained. One is the "safe harbour" provision which protects financial institutions and employees from criminal and civil liability when reporting suspicious transactions to competent authorities in good faith.[122] The other is the "no-tipping off" provision which prohibits the private sector from informing its customers of its reporting to the authorities.[123]

In the international arena, to begin with, the 1990 Forty Recommendations provided for the obligation of customer identification in general terms.[124] Later the 1996 revised Forty Recommendations inserted a paragraph on legal entities for the purpose of identifying beneficial owners but did not go further in any meaningful way.[125] Finally, significant progress has been made in the 2003 revised Recommendations, including the elaboration of detailed procedures for customer identification.[126] Next, the 1990 Recommendation 14 stipulated that financial institutions should maintain, for at least five years, all necessary records on transactions, both domestic and international. This requirement was not changed in the subsequent revised versions of the Forty Recommendations. Lastly, with regard to the reporting obligation, the FATF has always opted for the suspicion-based model.[127] However, it should be noted that the FATF also left the choice of the threshold-based reporting model open by encouraging countries to consider the introduction of that model as well.[128] In respect of the reporting obligation, the FATF has also introduced the rules of "safe harbour" and "no-tipping off" into its text.[129]

Thirdly, two mechanisms have been conceived for the purposes of monitoring and controlling the work of the private sector: *internal* control and training, and *exterior* supervision. Internal control and training are organised by the management of a private enterprise, while exterior control is conducted by an outsider;

---

lack of information or because of the desire to reduce costs and protect customer confidentiality.

[122] Schott PA, *supra* note 84, p.VI-12. For the justification for this provision, see, e.g., Clark N (1996) "The Impact of Recent Money Laundering Legislation on Financial Intermediaries". In: Rider B, Ashe M (eds) *Money Laundering Control*, pp.138-140.

[123] For an overview of this concept, see, Mitsilegas V, *supra* note 34, pp.143-146.

[124] Recommendations 12 and 13.

[125] Recommendation 10.

[126] See, Section 4.2.2.3 of Chapter Four of this book.

[127] The 1990 Recommendation 16; the 1996 Recommendation 15; the 2003 Recommendation 13.

[128] The 1990 Recommendation 24; the 1996 Recommendation 23; the 2003 Recommendation 19. For an example of an effective internal control mechanism, see, Hyland M (2003) "Corporate Culture". In: Clark A, Burrell P (eds) *A Practitioner's Guide to International Money Laundering Law and Regulation*, 1st edn, pp.57-66.

[129] For the safe harbour provision, see the 1990 Recommendation 16; the 1996 Recommendation 16; the 2003 Recommendation 14. As to the no-tipping off rule, see the 1990 Recommendation 17; the 1996 Recommendation 17; the 2003 Recommendation 14(b).

i.e., the supervisory authority in the relevant industry such as the central bank of a country. Internal controls and training are important because they allow the staff of an obligated institution to detect suspicious transactions more.[130] On the other hand, exterior supervision provides objective mechanism to monitor the development of the anti-money laundering framework within relevant industries.

The FATF requires financial institutions to develop programmes against money laundering such as internal policies, the designation of compliance officers at the management level, an ongoing employment training, and an auditing function to test the system.[131] Similarly, the role of supervisory authorities in establishing an effective anti-money laundering strategy has always been emphasised by the FATF. The 1990 Recommendation 26 required supervisory authorities to ensure that the supervised institutions have adequate programmes to guard against money laundering. Moreover, the 1990 Recommendation 29 warned against the possibility that the management level may be infiltrated by criminals, and thus it pointed out the importance of prudential supervision.[132] There was no change of treatment to this issue in the 1996 text.

2.3.1.4 A bridging mechanism: the FIU

According to the Egmont Group the FIU has three core functions: to act as a centralised repository of financial information; to undertake the analysis of the information; and, to facilitate the dissemination of the results.[133] FIUs can take various forms in different national situations, and they can be classified into three basic models: an administrative model; a law-enforcement model; and, a prosecutorial

---

[130] These internal compliance programmes are particularly important to avoid wilful blindness. Especially in the US the internal programmes are in some degree considered as a means of avoiding criminal liability than as a means of cooperating with the government (Stessens G, *supra* note 34, p.178). For a further discussion, see, Adams W (1993) "Effective Strategies for Banks in Avoiding Criminal, Civil, and Forfeiture Liability in Money Laundering Cases", *Alabama Law Review*, vol.44, pp.699-701.

[131] The 1990 Recommendation 20; the 1996 Recommendation 19; the 2003 Recommendation 15.

[132] The BCCI case is a good example. The investigation was originally initiated with the information provided by the US Federal Reserve (Stessens G, *supra* note 34, p.201).

[133] See the definition of the FIU in "Statement of purpose of the Egmont Group of Financial Intelligence Units", the Hague: the Egmont Group, 13 June 2001, p.2; Schott PA, *supra* note 84, p.VII-4-9. In addition, the FIU may have other functions such as monitoring compliance with AML/CFT requirements, blocking transactions and freezing accounts, training, conducting research, and, enhancing public awareness of AML/CFT issues. For details, see, IMF (2004) *Financial Intelligence Units: An Overview*, pp.71-82.

model.[134] In the administrative model, it is either attached to a supervisory authority such as the central bank or the ministry of finance, or exists as an independent administrative authority.[135] In the law-enforcement model, it is annexed to and forms part of a police force.[136] In the prosecutorial model, the FIU is affiliated with the prosecutor's office as a judicial authority.[137] In practice, it is not so easy to simplify the types of the FIU because many existing FIUs actually use a mixed model.[138]

Given the short history of the FIU, most international texts did not explicitly mention it before 9/11 as with the Vienna Convention or the Forty Recommendations of 1990 and 1996. In its recommendations, the FATF simply laid out a concept of the FIU implicitly by way of mentioning the role of competent authorities in coordinating all anti-money laundering strategies.[139]

At this point, one premise and two important principles should be mentioned which come to the fore wherever the "flow of information" matters. First, as a premise, the tap of information sources should be opened to generate the flow of information. In the anti-money laundering context, it is the lifting of the bank secrecy rule which is of paramount importance.[140] Then as a compensatory gesture

---

[134] Schott PA, *supra* note 84, p.VII-9; Clark A, Burrell M (2003) "Reporting Regimes". In: Clark A, Burrell P (eds) *A Practitioner's Guide to International Money Laundering Law and Regulation*, 1st edn, pp.121-129; Thony JF (1996) "Processing Financial Information in Money Laundering Matters: The Financial Information Unit", *European Journal of Crime, Criminal Law and Criminal Justice*, vol.4, no.3, pp.265-272.

[135] It can better enjoy the trust of the private sector, acting as a buffer between the private sector and law enforcement agencies, and can also better exchange information with other foreign FIUs. However, it is less independent and may be slow in law-enforcement measures. France is a case in point. See, Mitsilegas V, *supra* note 34, pp.161-163.

[136] There is no need to set up a new agency but it can build on an existing infrastructure, and it can enjoy the merits of a law enforcement agency. However, it may have difficulty in establishing mutual trust with the private sector, and be less independent. See, IMF (2004) *Financial Intelligence Unit*, pp.13-14. In this regard, see, the UK practice in Mitsilegas V, *supra* note 34, pp.163-168.

[137] It is independent and the judiciary's powers (e.g., seizing, freezing) are immediately available. However, it lacks the trust with the private sector, and is less efficient in exchanging information with foreign FIUs. See, IMF (2004) *Financial Intelligence Unit*, p.16. See also the practice of Luxembourg in Mitsilegas V, *supra* note 34, pp.168-169.

[138] Schott PA, *supra* note 84, p.VII-10.

[139] The 1990 Recommendations 26-29; the 1996 Recommendations 26-29.

[140] For the traditional justification for banking secrecy and the changing attitudes on this issue in the banking industry, see, Hinterseer K (2002) *Criminal Finance: The Political Economy of Money Laundering in a Comparative Legal Context*, pp.285-289; Campbell D (ed) (1992) *International Bank Secrecy*, pp.vii-x.

for the elimination of this bank secrecy rule, two principles follow.[141] One is the principle of confidentiality that is used as protection against abuse of private financial information.[142] The other is the principle of specialty, which limits the use of information reported by the private sector or requested by the FIU for any other purpose other than fighting money laundering.[143] They are necessary to promote the climate of trust between concerned parties regardless of whether it is the exchange of information between relevant sectors in domestic terms or with foreign counterparts in international terms.

In the international context, the Vienna Convention stipulates the lifting of the bank secrecy rule both in domestic and international terms.[144] With regard to the principles of confidentiality and specialty, the Vienna Convention provides for them only in terms of international cooperation.[145] In a similar context, the 1990 FATF Recommendations 16 and 37 indirectly provide for the lifting of the bank secrecy rule both in domestic and international terms and this position does not change much in the 1996 revised text.[146] The 1990 Recommendation 32 also implicitly provided for the need for strict safeguards with regard to privacy and data protection only in terms of international cooperation, and this provision remains in the 2003 revised text.[147]

2.3.1.5 International cooperation

This area has a long history of discussion in pubic international law, but for this study three major areas will be dealt with briefly: (a) how to decide upon questions of jurisdiction?; (b) what kinds of cooperation should be promoted?; and, (c) what are the principles relevant to international cooperation in this context?

Firstly, given the transnational nature of money laundering and predicate offences, the question of which state has primary jurisdiction is initially significant for international cooperation. Two standards can be identified in categorising jurisdiction: function and basis. In terms of function, legislative, judicial, and executive jurisdiction can be distinguished. In other words, jurisdiction to prescribe, adjudicate, and enforce can be differentiated.[148] On the other hand, according to the basis for jurisdiction, a distinction can be made between jurisdiction based on

---

[141] Stessens G, *supra* note 34, p.341, 347.

[142] Schott PA, *supra* note 84, p. VII-14.

[143] *Ibid.*, p.VII-15.

[144] Article 5(3); Article 7(5).

[145] Article 7(12) and (13).

[146] The 1990 Recommendations 16 and 37; the 1996 Recommendations 16 and 37. In the 2003 Recommendation 14(a), 36(d), 40(b), these provisions become more explicit.

[147] The 1996 Recommendation 32; the 2003 Recommendation 40.

[148] Oxman BH (1997) "Jurisdiction of States", *Encyclopaedia of Public International Law*, vol.3, p.55.

territory and jurisdiction based on persons.[149] If we go into details in this regard, a further distinction can be made. Firstly, with regard to territory there are the principles of objective territoriality and subjective territoriality.[150] The principle of objective territorial jurisdiction (or effects doctrine) is established when an offence is completed in its territory or its effect is felt in its territory. The subjective territorial jurisdiction is established when partial elements of a whole offence take place in its territory but the offence is consummated in a foreign territory.[151] Secondly, in respect of persons, two types can be distinguished: the principle of active and passive personality. The active personality principle allows a state to assert extraterritorial jurisdiction when one of its nationals commits an offence, whereas the passive personality principle provides a state with extraterritorial jurisdiction when its national is the victim of an offence.[152] In addition, the all-inclusive principle of universality can be noted. Under the principle, every country has extraterritorial jurisdiction over such offences that are regarded to be particularly offensive to the international community as a whole like piracy and war crimes.[153] Furthermore, there are variations such as the principle of the flag,[154] the principle of protection,[155] the representation principle,[156] etc.

In the international arena, nearly all international legal texts include provisions on these principles of jurisdiction. For example, the Vienna Convention requires all countries to adopt the objective territorial principle and the principle of the flag on a mandatory basis, and further encourages them to choose the active personality principle, and some tailor-made principles in the context of fighting drugs.[157] In

---

[149] It should be remembered that the categorisation by this standard is in respect of criminal jurisdiction rather than civil jurisdiction (Shaw M (1997) *International Law*, 4th edn, pp.457-458).

[150] See, Oxman BH (1997) "Jurisdiction of States", *Encyclopaedia of Public International Law*, vol.3, p.57; Camreon I (1994) *The Protective Principle of International Criminal Jurisdiction*, p.53; the Council of Europe (1990) *Extraterritorial criminal jurisdiction*, pp.8-9.

[151] The subjective territorial jurisdiction is an American terminology, and a similar concept can be found in Europe as "ubiquity theory"(Stessens G, *supra* note 34, p.218).

[152] See, the Council of Europe, *supra* note 150, pp.10-13.

[153] Shaw M, *supra* note 149, p.470.

[154] A country possesses jurisdiction over offences committed on board ships or aircraft flying its flag (the Council of Europe, *supra* note 150, pp.11-12).

[155] A country has jurisdiction over offences which are committed abroad with the intention of damaging its fundamental interests such as counterfeiting its currency or attacking its diplomatic missions (*Ibid.*, pp.13-14).

[156] A country possesses extraterritorial jurisdiction for another country which is more directly involved, provided certain conditions are met (*Ibid.*, p.14).

[157] Article 4. The tailor-made principles do not fit into any of traditional principles. Article 4.1.(b)(ii) appears to be a variant of the representation principle, whereas Article

practice since elements and participants of money laundering offences may involve more than one country, it would not be so easy to apply these rules in a clear-cut way. In this sense, the needs for international cooperation are greater than ever as indicated by the 1990 FATF Recommendation 39.

Secondly, with regard to the content of cooperation, it should be understood that it can include almost everything imaginable in relation to investigation, prosecution, judicial proceedings, and sanctions. Nowadays, with the increase in transnational criminality, relevant international instruments tend to make provisions on international criminal cooperation as detailed as possible.

In this regard, the Vienna Convention set the standards. By way of illustration, the Vienna Convention makes it mandatory to cooperate in the enforcement of a confiscation order. To this end, it provides for two alternative approaches: the traditional approach and the reformative approach. Under the former approach, the requested state should submit the foreign request to a competent domestic authority for the purpose of obtaining a confiscation order.[158] By the latter approach, the requested state directly enforces a foreign confiscation order and in this sense, it is quite reformative.[159] Other relevant provisions of the Vienna Convention are also much more detailed than previous multilateral treaties by way of including issues such as evidence-taking,[160] identifying proceeds,[161] extradition,[162] the transfer of proceedings,[163] provisional measures,[164] enforcement of confiscation orders,[165] asset sharing,[166] etc. In particular, while other criminal law conventions set out the general obligation to render assistance, Article 7 of the Vienna Convention deals with mutual legal assistance in such a detailed way that it could in itself be considered a mini-mutual legal assistance treaty or as a treaty within a treaty.[167]

Thirdly, let us proceed to some principles required for international cooperation. To begin with, the smooth flow of information is important at the interna-

---

4.1.(b)(iii) seems to be a variant of the protective principle. For a relevant discussion, see, Sproule DW, St.Denis P (1989) "The UN Drug Trafficking Convention: An Ambitious Step", *The Canadian Yearbook of International Law*, vol.27, pp.276-277; Shutte JJE (1991) "Extradition for Drug Offences: New Developments Under the 1988 U.N. Convention Against Illicit Traffic In Narcotic Drugs and Psychotropic Substances", *International Review of Penal Law*, vol.62, pp.135-136.

[158] Gilmore WC, *Combating International Drugs Trafficking*, *supra* note 40, p.16.
[159] *Ibid.*, p.16.
[160] Article 7(2).
[161] Article 7(2).
[162] Article 4(2), 6.
[163] Article 8.
[164] Article 5(4)(b).
[165] Article 5.
[166] Article 5(5)(a).
[167] Sproule DW, St.Denis P, *supra* note 157, p.285.

tional level. Thus, the same principles as already mentioned in relation to the work of the FIU are also applicable in this area. These are the lifting of the bank secrecy rule and the principles of confidentiality and specialty.[168] Next, some issues on extradition need to be considered. These are the principle of *aut dedere aut judicare* (the duty to extradite or prosecute), the exceptions of political offence and fiscal offence. The principle of *aut dedere aut judicare* is in effect an alter ego of the principle of universality, and aims to prevent criminals from escaping criminal justice.[169] On the other hand, the political offence exception provides a country with a justification to refuse a request for extradition of political refugees.[170] With a similar mechanism, the fiscal offence exception allows a country to refuse the request for extradition of offenders in relation to fiscal offences such as tax evasion or the violation of customs regulations.[171] This is mainly to protect the economic interest of nationals of the requested country or to prevent the outflow of national wealth.[172]

In international criminal texts, the principle of *aut dedere aut judicare* is increasingly adopted as with Articles 4(2) and 6(9) of the Vienna Convention and most anti-terrorism conventions.[173] Likewise, the exceptions of the political offence and fiscal offence are disappearing gradually as illustrated by Article 3(10) of the Vienna Convention and recent anti-terrorism conventions.[174] All these phenomena serve to promote the development in mutual assistance in criminal matters.

---

[168] However, it should be noted that the principle of specialty finds its use also in respect of extradition. Namely, an extradited fugitive may not be detained, tried and punished for any offence other than the one for which extradition was granted (Stein T (1985) "Extradition", *Encyclopaedia of International Law*, vol.8, p.224).

[169] Clark RS, *supra* note 19, pp.49-50.

[170] Gilbert G (1998) *Transnational Fugitive Offenders in International Law*, p.204. For an overview of this concept, see Nadelmann EA (1993) *Cops across borders: the Internationalization of U.S. Criminal Law Enforcement*, pp.419-426.

[171] Stessens G, *supra* note 34, pp.299-300.

[172] It is criticised for an obsolete notion of sovereignty and protectionism and for immorality of, say conserving tax havens (*Ibid.*, pp.299-300).

[173] For instance, Article 6(4) of the 1997 convention on terrorist bombings contains the principle of *aut dedere aut judicare*.

[174] For instance, Article 11 of the 1997 convention on terrorist bombings excludes the political offence exception.

2.3.2 UN General Assembly and the 1999 Convention

2.3.2.1 Context

In 1996, the General Assembly once again established an *ad hoc* committee to deal with terrorism affairs with the adoption of Resolution 51/210.[175] This *ad hoc* committee has been involved in drafting several anti-terrorism conventions thus far.[176] The International Convention for the Suppression of the Financing of Terrorism (ICSFT) was one of the anti-terrorism convention series drafted by this committee. Originally in paragraph 3(f) of Resolution 51/210, the General Assembly called upon all states to take steps to prevent the financing of terrorists and terrorist organisations.[177] In May 1998, this attention of the General Assembly to the issue of terrorist financing was reinforced by a statement of the Foreign Ministers of the G-8 countries which identified the issue as a priority area for action. The President of France further called for the immediate negotiation of a convention against the financing of terrorism.[178] The idea of fighting terrorist financing then materialised with the adoption of Resolution 53/108 which required the *ad hoc* committee to elaborate a draft international convention for the suppression of terrorist financing, based on the French proposed draft text.[179] As a result, the ICSFT was adopted by the UN on 9 December 1999 and can be recorded as a significant

---

[175] UN, A/RES/51/210, 17 December 1996.

[176] The *ad hoc* committee first drafted the International Conventions for the Suppression of Terrorist Bombings, which was adopted by the UN in December 1997. Currently, this committee is involved in drafting a comprehensive convention on international terrorism as well as a convention for the suppression of acts of nuclear terrorism.

[177] The paragraph 3(f) of Resolution 51/210 is as follows: all states are called upon to "prevent and counteract, through appropriate domestic measures, the financing of terrorists and terrorist organizations, whether such financing is direct or indirect through organizations which also have or claim to have charitable, social or cultural goals or which are also engaged in unlawful activities such as illicit arms trafficking, drug dealing and racketeering, including the exploitation of persons for purposes of funding terrorist activities, and in particular to consider, where appropriate, adopting regulatory measures to prevent and counteract movements of funds suspected to be intended for terrorist purposes without impeding in any way the freedom of legitimate capital movements and to intensify the exchange of information concerning international movements of such funds".

[178] See also, Johnson CM (2000) "Introductory Note to the International Convention for the Suppression of the Financing of Terrorism", *International Legal Materials*, vol.39, p.268.

[179] UN, A/RES/53/108, 26 January 1998, para. 12.

breakthrough in the history of combating terrorism by directly targeting the financial infrastructure of terrorist movements.[180]

With the focus on the ICSFT, a comparative study will also be made in this section for the purpose of having an overview of the current development of the anti-money laundering framework, given that anti-money laundering provisions are increasingly included as an essential element in recent international criminal conventions such as the UN Convention against Transnational Organized Crime (the Palermo Convention),[181] and the UN Convention against Corruption.[182]

2.3.2.2 Nature and scope

Given its nature as a multilateral treaty, the ICSFT is legally binding on all state parties. However, it should also be admitted that there exist some limitations in enforcing the countermeasures of the ICSFT. For example, some of its articles are not drafted in mandatory terms and certain provisions are not detailed enough to expect any substantial change of attitude in state parties.[183] Nonetheless, with its binding nature the ICSFT for the first time promotes the harmonisation of national legislation and provides the minimum basis for police and judicial cooperation in the specific area of countering terrorist financing.

The scope of application of this instrument can be viewed from a couple of perspectives. Firstly, Article 3 of the ICSFT limits the scope of its application to terrorist financing involving elements from more than one country; i.e., it does not

---

[180] UN, A/RES/54/109, 9 December 1999.

[181] By resolution 53/111 of 9 December 1998, the General Assembly established an *ad hoc* committee open to all States to elaborate the international convention against transnational organised crime and three additional international legal protocols. The first session of the *ad hoc* committee took place in Vienna, Austria, from 19-29 January 1999 and the draft convention was later adopted by the General Assembly at its Millennium meeting in November 2000. It was opened for signature at a high-level conference in Palermo, Italy and thereby it is called "the Palermo Convention" (visited on 25 November 2003) <http://www.unodc.org/adhoc/palermo/theconvention.html>.

[182] In its resolution 55/61 of 4 December 2000, the General Assembly established an *ad hoc* committee which drafted the text of the United Nations Convention against Corruption through seven sessions, held between 21 January 2002 and 1 October 2003. The Convention was adopted by the General Assembly with resolution 58/4 of 31 October 2003. A high-level political conference was held by the government of Mexico in Merida for its signing in December 2003 (visited on 29 December 2004) <http://www.unodc.org /unodc/en/crime_convention_corruption.html>.

[183] For example, the lifting of the bank secrecy rule is not compulsory in Article 12(2). Moreover, the provisions on confiscation and mutual legal assistance lack a detailed content as illustrated by Articles 8 and 12.

apply to cases that lack an international aspect.[184] This limitation appears to reflect the influence of precedent anti-terrorism conventions including the International Convention for the Suppression of Terrorist Bombings (1997).[185] Secondly, Article 2 of the ICSFT excludes "legitimate military activities during an armed conflict" from the scope of its application. It results from the understanding that the activities of armed forces against lawful targets should be dealt with by international humanitarian law rather than in a counter-terrorism context.[186] This is also apparently following the position of the 1997 convention on terrorist bombings.[187] This issue will be revisited in more detail in the following section. Thirdly, the ICSFT cannot be applied beyond the limitation of public international law such as doctrines of sovereign equality and the territorial integrity of states, and that of non-intervention in the domestic affairs of others.[188] These are common safeguard provisions which can be found in most international criminal conventions.[189]

2.3.2.3 Public sector

Definition of terrorism

Logically, the international strategy to combat the financing of terrorism has to begin with the defining of terrorism. Without defining terrorism, it is clear that the financing of terrorism can neither be defined nor be criminalised. However, as explained above, the international community could not make progress on this issue until the late 1990s due to the divided positions among states. Instead it responded

---

[184] US Senate, *International Convention for Suppression of Financing Terrorism: Message from the President of the United States*, 106th Congress, 2nd Session, Treaty Doc.106049, Washington: US Government Printing Office, 2000, p.VIII.

[185] Article 3. See further the 1970 Convention Against the Taking of Hostages, Article 13; the 1971 Convention for the Suppression of Unlawful Acts Against the Safety of Civil Aviation, Article 4(4); the 1980 Convention on the Physical Protection of Nuclear Material, Article 2; the 1988 Convention for the Suppression of Unlawful Acts Against the Safety of Maritime Navigation, Article 4.

[186] Article 2(2); Aust A (2001) "Counter-Terrorism— A New Approach: The International Convention for the Suppression of the Financing of Terrorism", *Max Planck Institute UNYB*, vol.5, p.14; US Senate, *supra* note 184, p.VII.

[187] Article 19(2); Perera AR (2004) "Reviewing the UN Conventions on Terrorism: Towards a Comprehensive Terrorism Convention". In: Fijnaut C, Wouters J, Naert F (eds) *supra* note 21, pp.573-576.

[188] Articles 20 and 22.

[189] Similar provisions can be found in Article 2(3) of the Vienna Convention (see, Gilmore WC (1991) *Combating International Drugs Trafficking*, *supra* note 40, p.3) and in most anti-terrorism conventions including the 1997 convention on terrorist bombings (Articles 17 and 18).

to the increasing threats of terrorism by criminalising certain types of terrorist acts.[190]

Under these deadlock circumstances, the achievements of the ICSFT in drafting a definition of terrorism for the purpose of the Convention is highly commendable, although the definition is not entirely comprehensive in its formulation. To the surprise of the international community, it was a critical success made with unexpected ease.[191] In this regard, the text of Article 2(1) is of particular significance:

Article 2.
1. Any person commits an offence within the meaning of this Convention if that person by any means, directly or indirectly, unlawfully and wilfully, provides or collects funds with the intention that they should be used or in the knowledge that they are to be used, in full or in part, in order to carry out:
  (a) An act which constitutes an offence within the scope of and as defined in one of the treaties listed in the annex; or
  (b) Any other act intended to cause death or serious bodily injury to a civilian, or to any other person not taking an active part in the hostilities in a situation of armed conflict, when the purpose of such act, by its nature or context, is to intimidate a population, or to compel a government or an international organization to do or to abstain from doing any act.

The ICSFT thus adopts a two-fold approach: a *listing* of offences and a *mini*-definition.[192] The first approach is to list anti-terrorism conventions which deal with specific acts of terrorism such as hijacking and hostage-taking, allowing the acts prohibited by each convention to be considered as acts of terrorism.[193] On the other hand, the second approach to make a *mini*-definition initially did not seem to be a good option since it could "reopen the dormant debate" since the 1970s on what terrorism is.[194] However, to the astonishment of the participants in the negotiation process, this *mini*-definition for the purpose of this convention was approved and included in the main text without too much difficulty.[195] The *mini*-definition has several policy implications of significance. To facilitate understanding, two qualifiers are of note: "active" and "armed conflict". First, if a per-

---

[190] See, Section 2.2.1 of this chapter.
[191] Gilmore WC, *supra* note 34, p.72.
[192] Aust A, *supra* note 186, p.7.
[193] At present, nine conventions are listed in the annex, but new treaties could be added in accordance with Article 23, taking into account the development of treaty law in the field of counter-terrorism. This *listing* approach is quite similar to that adopted in the European Convention on the Suppression of Terrorism (1977) and its amending Protocol (2003) (Aust A, *supra* note 186, p.7).
[194] *Ibid.*, p.8.
[195] *Ibid.*, pp.7-15.

son is applicable to both qualifiers which means he takes an *active* part in *armed conflicts*, the attack on that person does not constitute an offence within the meaning of the ICSFT. In other words, the ICSFT excludes from the definition of terrorism "legitimate military activities during armed conflicts".[196] Importantly, it should be recalled that international humanitarian law is already in existence for this case. This law controls the conduct of hostilities during armed conflict and protects the victims of the war.[197] Second, let us consider the situation where a person is connected with only one qualifier. For the persons who do *not take any active* part in hostilities during armed conflicts, the assault on them constitutes terrorism. The attack on off-duty military personnel is a case in point.[198] In particular, the US government intended this phrase to encompass the attacks on off-duty military personnel, as in the cases of the 1996 Al Khobar Towers bombings in Dhahran, Saudi Arabia, and the 1983 Beirut barracks bombings.[199] Furthermore, it can be inferred from this reasoning that military personnel should be protected in peacetime, given that even during armed conflict, the persons who do not take an active part in the hostilities need to be protected. However, with regard to the situation where there is *no armed* conflict, further discussion is pointless since without an armed conflict, no part can be taken in it.

Another point of note is that the ICSFT evades the issue of national liberation movement, while retaining the *mini*-definition of terrorism as a whole. This aspect is of significance, given that the strong obstacle to the universal definition of terrorism mainly derives from the Third World's insistence to include an exceptional provision on the principle of self-determination and national liberation movements. For instance, the Convention of the Organisation of the Islamic Conference on Combating International Terrorism (1999) provides for a definition of terrorism[200] which is immediately followed by a provision on the exception of national

---

[196] This is a simpler form of the so-called "military carved-out" (*Ibid.*, p.14).

[197] See, Perera AR, *supra* note 187, p. 576. International humanitarian law has developed from two sources: the law of Geneva and the law of The Hague. The law of Geneva is to protect the victims of the war, while the law of The Hague is to control the conduct of hostilities during armed conflict (Bugnion, F., "Droit de Genèva et droit de la Haye", *International Review of the Red Cross*, no.844, p.901, abstract) (visited on 4 January 2005) <http://www.icrc.org/Web/Eng/siteeng0.nsf/html/57JRLQ?OpenDocument>.

[198] UN, "Measures to eliminate international terrorism", Report of the Working Group, A/C.6/54/L.2, 26 October 1999, pp.61-63.

[199] US Senate, *supra* note 184, p.VII.

[200] The OIC defines terrorism in a superficial way, for example making no specific reference to the type of affected persons. In Article 1(2), terrorism means:
"any act of violence or threat thereof notwithstanding its motives or intentions perpetrated to carry out an individual or collective criminal plan with the aim of terrorizing people or threatening to harm them or imperiling their lives, honour, freedoms, security or rights or exposing the environment or any facility or public or private property to haz-

liberation movements in the next article.[201] Given this attitude of the OIC convention whose drafting almost synchronised with the drafting period of the ICSFT, the absence of an exceptional provision of this kind apparently constitutes progress. Yet, given the controversial nature of "armed conflict" which might be interpreted to include national liberation movements, there still remains a possibility of legal dispute when the ICSFT is applied to a real case.[202]

Criminalisation of terrorist financing

In the negotiation process it was argued that the offence of terrorist financing could be punished with the provisions on accomplices in existing anti-terrorism conventions without making it an independent offence.[203] This skepticism is quite similar to that raised in relation to the criminalisation of money laundering. Yet, the criminalisation of terrorist financing is necessary for the following reasons.

Firstly, attention should be paid to the problems deriving from the likely absence of a principal offence; i.e., the terrorist act itself. This situation is similar to the background where the criminalisation of money laundering was required.[204] In other words, when the principal offence is hardly traceable, it is the offence of money laundering that helps law enforcement agencies to tackle the suspicious assets either in the hands of a frontman or the real owner. However, the need for "criminalisation" is far greater with terrorist financing since the principal offence of terrorist financing in most cases does not take place or is not yet attempted,

---

ards or occupying or seizing them, or endangering a national resource, or international facilities, or threatening the stability, territorial integrity, political unity or sovereignty of independent States."

[201] Article 2(a) of the OIC Convention on combating international terrorism stipulates that: "People's struggle including armed struggle against foreign occupation, aggression, colonialism, and hegemony, aimed at liberation and self-determination in accordance with the principles of international law shall not be considered a terrorist crime".

[202] UN, "Report of the Ad Hoc Committee established by General Assembly resolution 51/210 of 17 December 1996", A/54/37, 5 May 1999, p.64. Due to this ambiguity, for example, the US government included upon ratification an understanding that the term "armed conflict" does not include internal disturbances and tensions, such as riots, isolated and sporadic acts of violence and other acts of a similar nature. See, US Senate, *supra* note 184, p.VIII. Basically, "armed conflict" is classified into two categories: international armed conflict and non-international conflict. However, in practice, it is not so easy to make a clear-cut distinction. For the types of armed conflicts and relevant applicable rules of international humanitarian law, see, Wouters J, Naert F (2004) "Shockwaves through International Law after 11 September: Finding the Right Responses to the Challenges of International Terrorism". In: Fijnaut C, Wouters J, Naert F (eds), *supra* note 21, pp.476-477.

[203] Aust A, *supra* note 186, p.4.

[204] See, Section 2.3.1.2 of this chapter.

while money laundering cases are at least premised on the existence of a predicate offence.[205] In particular, it should be noted that in most jurisdictions, ancillary offences such as the acts of aiding and abetting only occur when the principal act is committed or at least attempted.[206] Under this constraint, without establishing the actual guilt for the principal terrorist offence, it would be nearly impossible to punish the act of financing of terrorism separately. Likewise, with regard to a conspiracy offence, it should be remembered that the financing of terrorism could be committed by one person acting alone, a situation that a theory of conspiracy cannot cover.[207]

Secondly, terrorist financing can be considered to constitute a separate primary harm rather than an ancillary harm. To this end, the concept of harm needs to be approached from a different perspective by way of two standards: endurance and size. The conventional harm of terrorism can be characterised as *sporadic* and *local*. However, reliable financing changes the nature of this conventional harm, making it *continuous* and *broader*. Reliable financing breathes everlasting life into the sporadic harm, and expands the scope of its influence across vast areas and diverse people. For instance, in Chapter One, it was indicated that reliable financing enabled the FARC to continuously recruit new members and supply itself with adequate weaponry. Similarly, Al-Qaida was capable of launching its operations anywhere in the world utilising its global network based on its solid financial infrastructure. In addition, although relatively minor, the logic for condemning money laundering can be similarly cited with regard to terrorism-related money laundering, for example such as the undermining of the integrity of the financial industry or the legitimate economy.[208]

In this context, the explicit criminalisation of the financing of terrorism in the ICSFT constitutes a major accomplishment.[209] Eventually the financing of terrorism can be dealt with as an independent offence rather than just an ancillary offence. As noted in Chapter One, the financing of terrorism is comprised of both money-making activities (criminal enterprises, legitimate businesses, donations) and distribution activities (terrorism-related money laundering), and the wording "provides or collects" in Article 2(1) of the ICSFT seems broad enough in scope

---

[205] Terrorist money is generally used for the preparation of terrorist acts at some future date(Aust A, *supra* note 186, p.13).

[206] IMF (2003) *Suppressing the Financing of Terrorism*, p.50.

[207] *Ibid.,* p.51.

[208] See, Section 2.3.1.2 of this chapter. For a case study of the BCCI in the context of terrorist financing, see, Ridley N (2003) "Law Enforcement". In: Clark A, Burrell P (eds) *A Practitioner's Guide to International Money Laundering Law and Regulation*, 1ˢᵗ edn, pp.46-47.

[209] Article 2(1).

to cover both aspects.[210] Interestingly, although the ICSFT does not make explicit reference to "money laundering", Article 18 provides for the detailed measures to prevent terrorism-related money laundering in the private sector.[211] Similarly, both the 2000 Palermo Convention and the 2003 Convention against Corruption provide for the employment of the AML framework in the private sector but their texts further includes express criminalisation of money laundering.[212]

Confiscation

The ICSFT provides for confiscation in Article 8, and it is worded as follows:

1. Each State Party shall take appropriate measures, in accordance with its domestic legal principles, for the identification, detection and freezing or seizure of any funds used or allocated for the purpose of committing the offence set forth in article 2 as well as the proceeds derived from such offence, for purposes of possible forfeiture.
2. Each State Party shall take appropriate measures, in accordance with its domestic legal principles, for the forfeiture of funds used or allocated for the purpose of committing the offences set forth in article 2 and the proceeds derived from such offences.

Firstly, it is of note that there is no specification of the types of confiscation in the ICSFT which individual states should or may adopt. Nonetheless, the ICSFT would definitely include criminal confiscation, given that its confiscation regime is tied to the offences as set forth in the convention. Yet, the decision of an appropriate model is still entirely at the discretion of each state as indicated by the phrase "in accordance with its domestic legal principles". The ICSFT is giving a general mandate, simply obliging each state to enact relevant legislation without further elaboration. However, by way of comparison, the 2000 Palermo Convention and the 2003 Convention against Corruption give a detailed treatment

---

[210] In the original French proposal, the word "financing" was used. The definition of "financing" included the concepts of both money-making activities and money distributing activities. However, during the negotiation process, the terminology was replaced by the current phrase "provides or collects". Nonetheless, considering the positions of national delegations, it seems clear that the basic concept of the French proposal has remained. See, UN, "Letter dated 3 November 1998 from the Permanent Representative of France to the United Nations addressed to the Secretary-General", A/C.6/53/9, 4 November 1998, Article 1 at p.3; UN Doc.A/54/37, *supra* note 202, p.26, 57; UN Doc., A/C.6/ 54/L.2, *supra* note 198, p.37,41, and pp. 57-58.

[211] However, in the past, attempts were already made to link the AML regime with terrorism by way of including terrorism in money laundering predicate offences. See, *supra* note 60.

[212] The Palermo Convention, Article 6; the Convention against Corruption, Articles 14 and 23.

to the issue which is quite similar in content to that of the Vienna Convention.[213] These conventions not only allow for five models of confiscation (object and value confiscation, confiscation of instrumentalities and proceeds, and criminal confiscation) but further introduce the concept of *the reversed burden of proof*.[214] In this regard, it leaves much to be desired in the approach of the ICSFT to this issue which is one of the most essential elments in fighting terrorist financing.

Secondly, other issues related to confiscation need to be considered. These are provisional measures, lifting of the bank secrecy rule, the protection of the rights of a third party, and compensation for victims of the offence. In respect of provisional measures, the ICSFT adopts a common provision such as "freezing and seizing" as with other conventions mentioned in comparison in this study. With regard to the lifting of the bank secrecy rule, however, the ICSFT takes a lukewarm position by referring to the lifting of the bank secrecy rule in a nonmandatory term and only in connection with international cooperation.[215] In contrast, to say nothing of the Vienna Convention, both the 2000 Palermo convention and the 2003 Convention against Corruption impose a binding obligation on all states to lift the bank secrecy rule for both domestic and international purposes.[216] In a broad and long-term context of fighting terrorist financing, this lack of binding force seems to be problematic, undermining the essential legal infrastructure. In relation to the rights of *bona fide* third parties, the ICSFT provides in Article 8(5) that "the provisions of this article shall be implemented without prejudice to the rights of third parties acting in good faith", which is a reflection of the Vienna Convention.[217] Considering the devastating effects of confiscation on *bona fide* third parties, each state needs to ensure that effective legal remedies are available in order for interested parties to preserve their rights as indicated by the 1990 Council of Europe Convention.[218] Lastly, the provision on the rights of victims which is absent in the Vienna Convention constitutes progress made by the ICSFT. Article 8(4) requires states to consider

---

[213] In fact, the more detailed an international instrument is, the more harmonised domestic legal systems are. For a discussion on this harmonisation effect of a detailed mandate, See, e.g., Keyser-Rignalda F (1992) "European Integration with regard to the Confiscation of the Proceeds of Crime", *European Law Review*, vol.17, pp.502-505.

[214] The Vienna Convention, Article 5; the Palermo Convention, Article 12; the Convention against Corruption, Article 31.

[215] Article 12, para. 2.

[216] The Vienna Convention mentions the bank secrecy rule two times in Article 5(3) (confiscation), and Article 7(5) (mutual legal assistance); the Palermo Convention also mentions this rule twice in Article 12(6) (confiscation), and Article 18(8) (mutual legal assistance); the Convention Against Corruption similarly deals with this rule twice in Article 31(7) (confiscation) and Article 46(8) (mutual legal assistance).

[217] The Vienna Convention, Article 5, para. 8.

[218] The 1990 Council of European Convention, Article 5.

the establishment of a mechanism to compensate victims of terrorist offences. However, no clarity is provided as to the manner in which this mechanism might operate. Similar provisions can also be found in the Palermo Convention[219] and the Convention against Corruption.[220]

General part of criminal law

Now let us review some issues relating to what might be termed the general part of criminal law. Of particular significance for present purposes is the approach taken to state of mind, inchoate offences and complicity, and corporate criminal liability.

Firstly, the issue of state of mind (*mens rea*) needs to be analysed in connection with the definition of terrorism and the financing of terrorism respectively. To begin with, for terrorism itself, the ICSFT adopts the standard of intent as a requirement to constitute terrorism as it is clear in the phrase "any other acts *intended* to cause death or serious bodily harm" of Article 2(b). Also in respect of terrorist financing, Article 1 requires the standard of intent (or alternatively knowledge) to make up terrorist financing offences by way of inserting of the phrase "with the *intention* that they should be used or in the *knowledge* that they are to be used".[221] Furthermore, another relevant issue of note is how to prove the intent or knowledge of perpetrators. With regard to this "test" of state of mind, the ICSFT indirectly follows the precedent of the Vienna Convention, which, as noted earlier, adopts the position that the subjective elements like intent, or knowledge may be inferred from objective factual circumstances.[222] In Article 2(b), the ICSFT implicitly adopts this position by inserting the phrase "by its nature and context" in the definition of terrorism. Considering that during the negotiation process the drafters adhered to the phrase "by its nature and context" with a view to including an "objective factual circumstance standard" within the text of the ICSFT, it can be understood that this standard is also applicable to terrorist financing offence in-

---

[219] The Palermo Convention, Article 14(2).

[220] Article 35. Interestingly, the Convention against Corruption further guarantees victims the right to initiate legal proceedings against those involved in corruption.

[221] In effect, the phrase "wilfully" is another indicator of this intent standard, however, it seems to be redundant, given the following phrase which explicitly includes both intent and knowledge (Aust A, *supra* note 186, p.11).

[222] This is a statement of the obvious simply because people cannot read other people's mind (Verbruggen F (2002) "On Containing Organised Crime Using "Container Offences": Some Reflections on Substantive Criminal Law Issues". In: Albrecht HJ, Fijnaut C (eds) *The Containment of Transnational Organised Crime: Comments on the UN Convention of December 2000*, p.124). Furthermore, the 1990 Recommendation 6 and 1996 Recommendation 5 contain a similar provision.

directly.[223] By comparison, both the 2000 Palermo Convention and the 2003 Convention against Corruption expressly include the "objective factual circumstance standard".[224]

Secondly, given that concepts of incomplete offences and complicity are highly controversial and subject to different interpretations under various legal systems, the ICSFT adopted a safer approach by copying a corresponding provision from the 1997 convention on terrorist bombings.[225] Article 2(4) provides for attempts; paragraph 5(a) deals with accomplices; paragraph 5(b) addresses organising and directing others to commit the offence; and, paragraph 5(c) concerns conspiracies. Indeed, the difficulty in drafting a universal formulation on these subjects did not seem to be met only by the drafters of the ICSFT. The drafters of the 1998 Rome Statute of the International Criminal Court already ran into this situation of considerable difficulty and likewise benefited greatly from a formulation of the 1997 convention against terrorist bombings.[226] In other words, the wording of paragraph 5(c) of the ICSFT which is concerned with conspiracy (a concept strongly advocated by common law countries but unknown in some civil law systems) already found its place in Article 25(3)(d) of the Rome Statute.[227]

Thirdly, the concept of corporate liability in Article 5 needs to be noted. In a similar context to money laundering, corporate criminal liability would be useful in dealing with, for example, the front charities for terrorist groups or securing the compliance of the private sector in terms of responsibilisation strategy. However, given the diverse national legal cultures in relation to this issue, it is provided that corporate liability may not necessarily be criminal but could also be civil or administrative in nature. This is a unique provision for an anti-terrorism conven-

---

[223] Initially a proposal was made during the negotiation that this phrase be deleted, however, opposition was raised in that it would suggest the offence require proof of the perpetrator's subjective state of mind (UN, A/C.6/54/L.2, *supra* note 198, p.62).

[224] The Palermo Convention, Article 6(2)(f); the Convention against Corruption, Article 28.

[225] UN, "Report of the Ad Hoc Committee established by General Assembly resolution 51/210 of 17 December 1996", A/52/37, 31 March 1997, p.51; Aust A, *supra* note 186, p.16. In fact, it is very difficult to find any consistent formulation on these subjects in the multilateral treaty practice so far. For further details, see, Clark RS, *supra* note 19, pp.78-81.

[226] Saland P (1999) "International Criminal Law Principles". In: Lee RS (ed) *The International Criminal Court: The Making of the Rome Statute: Issues, Negotiations, Results*, pp.198-200.

[227] In the common law system, a conspiracy is committed once two or more persons agree to commit a crime, whether or not the crime itself is committed. In contrast, under continental systems inspired from the Napoleonic tradition, conspiracy is generally viewed as a form of complicity or participation in an actual crime or attempt (Schabas WA (2001) *An Introduction to the International Criminal Court*, pp.82-83).

tion[228] but a similar approach can be frequently found in other recent international instruments containing anti-money laundering provisions such as the 2000 Palermo Convention,[229] the 2003 Convention against Corruption,[230] and the FATF Forty Recommendations.[231]

2.3.2.4 Private sector

This part of the ICSFT has been strongly influenced by the FATF Forty Recommendations, although this is not specifically acknowledged as with the 2000 Palermo Convention and the 2003 Convention against Corruption.[232] In Article 18, the ICSFT stipulates:

1. State Parties shall cooperate in the prevention of the offence.......by *taking* all practicable measures......including:
   (b) Measures requiring financial institutions and other professions involved in financial transactions to utilize the most efficient measures available for the identification of their usual or occasional customers, as well as customers in whose interest accounts are opened, and to pay special attention to unusual or suspicious transactions and report transactions suspected of stemming from a criminal activity. For this purpose, State Parties shall consider:
      (i) Adopting regulations prohibiting the opening of accounts the holders or beneficiaries of which are unidentified or unidentifiable, and measures to ensure that such institutions verify the identity of the real owners of such transactions;
         (iv) Requiring financial institutions to maintain, for at least five years, all necessary records on transactions, both domestic or international.
3. State Parties shall further cooperate in the prevention of offences......by considering:
   (a) Measures for the supervision, including, for example, the licensing, or all money-transmission agencies;
   (b) Feasible measures to detect or monitor the physical cross-border transportation of cash and bearer negotiable instruments, subject to strict safeguards to ensure proper use of information and without impeding in any way the freedom of capital movements.

---

[228] Aust A, *supra* note 186, p.17.

[229] Article 10.

[230] Article 26.

[231] The 1990 Recommendation 7; The 1996 FATF Recommedation 6. In some sense, the FATF is more aggressive since it only mentioned corporate criminal liability, unlike the ICSFT.

[232] Gilmore WC, *supra* note 34, p.73. See, the Palermo Convention, Article 7; the Convention against Corruption, Articles 23 and 52.

The scope of the affected industry

To begin with, the scope of affected industry by the responsibilisation strategy needs to be considered.[233] In paragraph 1(b), the ICSFT imposes the responsibility for proactive crime control on both financial institutions and "other professions" involved in financial transactions.[234] Thus, the ICSFT covers a far wider area than other anti-money laundering regimes envisaged in recent legal texts. Both the 2000 Palermo Convention and the 2003 Convention against Corruption confine the scope of affected industry only to bank and non-bank financial institutions, namely "financial institutions of any kind", and do not extend its anti-money laundering regime to non-financial institutions.

In addition, like the anti-money laundering framework as seen above, an individual is included in the responsibilisation regime by paragraph 3(b). This insertion was suggested by the German delegation based on their experience in the counter-terrorist financing area.[235] The 2000 Palermo Convention[236] and the 2003 Convention against Corruption[237] follow suit.

The content of responsibility

For the contents of responsibility, the ICSFT provides for the three basic measures: customer identification, record keeping, and reporting of suspicious transactions.

Firstly, the detailed treatment of the ICSFT to the measure of customer identification is worthy of note. The convention provides for the procedures and standards of customer identification over three sub-paragraphs, the text of which is very similar to that of the FATF Forty Recommendations.[238] In contrast, the 2000 Palermo Convention simply mentions customer identification as one of the requirements with no additional explanation.[239] This distinction in treatment becomes much clearer and more meaningful, considering that the Palermo Convention is more detailed than the ICSFT in most other aspects. Perhaps given that some terrorist money might be derived from legitimate sources and its amount might also be trivial unlike typical criminal proceeds, the improved identification

---

[233] For relevant discussions, see, Section 2.3.1.3 of this chapter.

[234] However, the approach of the ICSFT adopted leaves something to be desired in that these professions are not specified. The enumeration of "other professions" has eventually been made in the 2003 Forty Recommendations.

[235] UN, A/54/37, *supra* note 202, p.40.

[236] Article 7(2).

[237] Article 14(2).

[238] The 1996 FATF Recommendations 10 and 11.

[239] The Palermo Convention, Ariticle 7(1). The level of the touch of the 2003 Convention against Corruption in Article 52(1) falls between those of the ICSFT and the 2000 Palermo Convention.

of customers might be a major way of developing suspicion in most cases.[240] The added weight given to the customer identification issue within the ICSFT is in this regard beneficial to relevant authorities.

Secondly, with regard to the record keeping obligation, the ICSFT similarly borrowed the text of the FATF Recommendations.[241] However, in some sense it could be argued that the ICSFT follows the wording of the FATF too faithfully. It should be noted that under the initial French text, both financial institutions and other professions were obligated to keep records on necessary documents.[242] However, during the negotiation process, the text from the FATF Recommendations replaced the original phrase, thus resulting in the omission of *other professions* from the regime of record-keeping obligations.[243] In other words, the 1996 FATF text imposed a recording obligation only on financial institutions and the ICSFT borrowed the phrase of this 1996 text as it was, thus leaving out other professions from the reporting regime. This formulation of paragraph 1(b)(iv) seems be an error undermining consistency within the whole article, unless the drafters left out other professions on purpose.

Thirdly, in respect of the reporting obligation, the ICSFT adopts the suspicion-based reporting model. In fact, the choice of the ICSFT is not so different from the main international trend.[244] However, it should be noted that in some instruments such as FATF Forty Recommendations the choice of adding the threshold–based reporting model is open as well.[245] As argued earlier, the optimal mixture of both models might possibly create in practice more effective methods. Another point of note is that the ICSFT covers only a subjective test of suspicion by requiring financial institutions to report transactions "suspected of" stemming from criminal activities. In contrast, an objective test of suspicion means that financial institutions should report when they "have reasonable grounds to suspect".[246] Other conventions such as the 2000 Palermo Convention and the 2003 Convention against Corruption are not distinct from the approach of the ICSFT while the 2003 FATF Recommendations eventually adopts the objective test of suspicion as well.[247] Also, the two rules in connection with the reporting obligation should be re-

---

[240] See, the discussion in Section 1.3.2.2 of Chapter One of this book.

[241] See, the 1996 FATF Recommendation 12.

[242] UN, "Letter dated 3 November 1998 from the Permanent Representative of France to the United Nations addressed to the Secretary-General", A/C.6/53/9, 4 November 1998, Article 17.

[243] UN, A/54/37, *supra* note 202, p.44, p.63.

[244] See, e.g., the 1996 FATF Recommendations 14 and 15; the Palermo Convention, Article 7(1)(a); the 1991 European Communities Directive, Article 6.

[245] The 1996 FATF Recommendation 23.

[246] FATF, "Review of the FATF Forty Recommendations: Consultation Paper", 30 May 2002, p.43.

[247] The 2003 Recommendation 13.

viewed. These are the "safe harbour" provision to protect the private sector from the possible liability for breach of any restriction on disclosure of information, and the "no-tipping off" rule to secure the success of police investigation, should be reviewed. The ICSFT includes only the "safe harbour" provision but this partial treatment seems better than no treatment in that the 2000 Palermo Convention and the 2003 Convention against Corruption do not provide for any of these rules.

Last but not least, some flaws in the ICSFT mechanism for the responsibilisation strategy need to be indicated. The head text of paragraph 1 of Article 18 is worded in mandatory terms. Although at first glance there seems to be some neutralising words such as "cooperate", the whole sentence imposes a binding obligation if it is read together with the following phrase "by *taking* all practicable measures". Indeed, this binding effect is once again confirmed by way of comparison with the non-binding wording of paragraph 2 within the same article which drafts a provision in a similar way but employing a different and non-mandatory verb "consider".[248] In this regard, it should be pointed out that unlike the *binding* requirement of customer identification, record keeping is dealt with on an *optional* basis.[249] If this inconsistency in the degree of binding power is taken together with the *optional* requirement of the lifting of the bank secrecy rule, it might cause serious problems in the operational mechanism of the ICSFT as will be indicated below. For instance, given that the lifting of bank secrecy rule is not obligatory under the ICSFT regime,[250] domestic authorities might not get access to the data on the identity of suspicious customers if a bank refuses to cooperate on the ground of the bank secrecy rule. This logical flaw of the ICSFT is illustrated as follows:

> Data *should* be created through customer identification→ Data *may* be kept for a certain period within financial institutions → Authorities *may* be able to demand the data from the financial institutions

Indeed, it is apparent in the flow that the success of the next step is totally dependent upon the success of the former step. If data does not exist, it is not kept. Furthermore, although the data could be available, if relevant authorities could not get access to the data, the former two steps would be really meaningless. So to speak, there is no reason to make the first step obligatory, since the data on custo-

---

[248] The ICSFT, Article 18, para. 2 which provides:
"2. State Parties shall further cooperate in the prevention of offences... by *considering* measures...".

[249] It should be reminded, however, that an attempt was made during the negotiation process to render the provision mandatory by the delegation of the Netherlands but did not get public support. See, UN, A/54/37, *supra* note 202, p.62.

[250] For a relevant discussion, see, Section 2.3.1.3 of this chapter. Particularly, see, *supra* note 215 and its related text.

mer identification secured through the first step might be shredded anyway, or be inaccessible.

Monitoring and controlling the work of the private sector

In addition to these mentioned above, there are other necessary elements in building a successful strategy to combat money laundering and terrorist financing in the private sector. What is noteworthy among those are "internal control and training" and "supervision".[251] As said before, since the successful prevention of terrorist financing in the private sector is dependent on the proactive cooperation of the private sector, the need of the two elements is higher than ever before. However, the ICSFT is silent about them as are the 2000 Palermo Convention and the 2003 Convention against Corruption.

In respect of supervision, the ICSFT does not make a general statement but focuses on the "licensing aspect" of all money-transmission agencies.[252] The emphasis on the licensing efforts derived from the concern about *hawala*, an informal value transfer system, to which attention was increasingly given in the context of clarifying terrorist financing mechanism in the late 1990s. This is when the ICSFT was being drafted.[253] Interestingly and in contrast, the 2003 Convention against Corruption specifically focuses on the use of shell banks in the context of supervision.[254] The tendency to focus on a specific technique among such various typologies illustrates what is the drafters' major concern in their area of responsibility.

2.3.2.5 A bridging mechanism

As explained above, despite the significance of the FIU, most instruments were silent on this issue prior to 9/11.[255] For the ICSFT, its emphasis on the exchange of information is evident across several articles. Article 12(4) recommends countries to establish mechanisms to share information or evidence with other countries, and Article 18(3) requires countries to cooperate in exchanging information and to establish communication channels. Yet, this requirement is not detailed enough to conceive an FIU-style body in any respect. Alternatively, countries may exchange information through the Interpol.[256] In contrast to this, both the 2000 Palermo Convention and the 2003 Convention against Corruption make a quantum leap by explicitly urging countries to establish an FIU to serve as a national centre for the

---

[251] For a relevant discussion, see Section 2.3.1.3 of this chapter. Especially, see *supra* note 130, 131, 132 and their related text.

[252] Article 18(2)(a).

[253] UN, A/54/37, *supra* note 202, p.40.

[254] Article 52(4).

[255] This issue was directly dealt with only when the FATF issued a revised Forty Recommendations in 2003. See, the 2003 Recommendation 26.

[256] Article 18(4).

collection, analysis and dissemination of information regarding potential money laundering.[257]

In the context of a bridging function, additional points of note are with regard to the matters concerning the "smooth flow of information". These are the lifting of the bank secrecy rule and the principles of confidentiality and specialty. To begin with, as indicated in connection with the discussion of confiscation, the lifting of the bank secrecy rule is not obligatory in the ICSFT. To make matters worse, it is mentioned only regarding international cooperation.[258] Given that most recent global conventions such as the Vienna Convention, the 2000 Palermo Convention and the 2003 Convention against Corruption render the lifting of the bank secrecy rule obligatory in both local and international cooperation, the stance of the ICSFT appears somewhat retrogressive.[259] Furthermore, with regard to the two principles, the ICSFT mentions only the principle of specialty in Article 12 (mutual assistance) in binding terms. By comparison, the 2000 Palermo Convention and the 2003 Convention against Corruption provides for both principles with regard to mutual assistance.[260]

2.3.2.6 International cooperation

It should be pointed out that the main purpose of international cooperation in the field of the suppression of the financing of terrorism is to confiscate the terrorists' monies and their financial resources, thus undermining their capability of sustaining a terrorist campaign. With a specific emphasis on this aspect in mind, let us proceed to the following issues.

Firstly, with regard to the basis for jurisdiction, the ICSFT adopts the standard approach of other anti-terrorism conventions. This means that the ICSFT provides for the mandatory application of both the territorial principle and the active personality principle.[261] Given that the use of the active personality principle differs considerably between common law and civil law states,[262] and for this reason it is

---

[257] The Palermo Convention, Article 7(1)(b); the Convention against Corruption, 14(1)(b).

[258] Article 12(2).

[259] See, *supra* note 215.

[260] The Palermo Convention, Article 18(19) and (20); the Convention against Corruption, Article 46(19) and (20).

[261] The ICSFT, Article 7. For the examples of other conventions, see, e.g., IMO Convention for the Suppression of Unlawful Acts Against the Safety of Maritime Navigation (1988), Article 6; IAEA Convention on the Physical Protection of Nuclear Material (1980), Article 8; UN Convention Against the Taking of Hostage (1979), Article 5.

[262] The common law countries rely heavily on the territorial principle, while the civil law states insist on the inclusion of the active personality principle as well. This is for the reason that the civil law states are reluctant to extradite their own nationals. Irrespective of the original background, the establishment of active personal principle will contribute

mostly stipulated in a non-binding manner, the mandatory status of the active personality principle in the ICSFT could be regarded as progress.[263] In addition, several principles are inserted on an optional basis such as the passive personality principle, the protective principle, etc. However, given the unique financial nature of the offences set forth within the ICSFT regime, this conventional approach appears to be a bit trite. In this regard, the innovative formulation of the Palermo Convention is of particular note. To begin with, Article 15(1) designates the classic principle of territoriality as a minimum standard. Then, Article 15(2)(c)(ii) indicates the basis for jurisdiction in the context of money laundering offence on an optional basis. The requirements are (i) the offence has the characteristic of incomplete offence or complicity, and (ii) the offence is committed outside one's territory in order to commit the offence of converting or acquiring criminal proceeds within one's territory. In effect, it provides a jurisdictional basis for an extraterritorial reach. In relation to the issue concerning the conflict of jurisdictional claims, Article 6(5) of the ICSFT stipulates that state parties shall strive to coordinate their actions appropriately.[264]

Secondly, in respect of international cooperation, it should be recalled that this area is also the exact reflection of former anti-terrorism conventions. Namely, the ICSFT provides for a basic principle that countries should afford one another the greatest measure of mutual legal assistance without further elaboration.[265] The treatment of the ICSFT in this area is, however, dwarfed in its depth and variety when compared with other conventions mentioned in this study. For example, the Palermo Convention which was drafted during almost the same period as the ICSFT, goes several steps farther than the Vienna Convention whose provisions on international cooperation were already called "a treaty within a treaty".[266] In particular, given that the ultimate goal of international cooperation in this area is the confiscation of terrorists' financial resources, there should be some guideline on the cooperation concerning the enforcement of confiscation as with the Vienna

---

to the reduction of the possibility that criminals escape punishment (Gilbert G (1992) "Crimes Sans Frontiers: Jurisdictional Problems in English Law", *British Yearbook of International Law*, vol.63, p.416).

[263] The Vienna Convention, Article 4. Interestingly, the Palermo Convention adopted the Vienna Convention's approach, borrowing its text nearly word for word. See, Sproule DW, St.Denis P, *supra* note 157, p.275.

[264] For example, in practice, some solutions can be considered such as the harmonisation of legislation; arrangements for the settlement of disputes; and, international agreements concerning mutual assistance in criminal matters (The Council of Europe, *supra* note 150, pp.32-38).

[265] Article 12(1).

[266] Sproule DW, St. Denis P, *supra* note 157, p.285.

Convention, the 2000 Palermo Convention, and the 2003 Convention against Corruption.[267]

Thirdly, some principles related to international cooperation need to be reviewed. As explained above, the principles in relation to the flow of information are also applicable to international cooperation, and they have already been examined in the analysis of the bridging mechanism.[268] Next, the principle of *aut dedere aut judicare* and the exceptions of political offence and fiscal offence need to be considered. In a similar way to other anti-terrorism conventions, the ICSFT also stipulates the principle of "extradite or prosecute" in Article 10. Furthermore, the ICSFT contains provisions on non-recognition of the exceptions of both political offence and fiscal offence. This position stands in stark contrast with the existing anti-terrorism conventions which do not contain these exclusive provisions. Only the 1997 convention on terrorist bombings contains a relevant provision but it is only about the political offence exception.[269]

2.3.3 Security Council and the *Afghanistan* situation

While the General Assembly was striving to formulate a legal tool to tackle the financing of terrorism in the late 1990s, the Security Council had another opportunity to launch a major campaign against terrorism. It was on the occasion of the terrorist bombing of the US embassies in Kenya and Tanzania in 1998. However, this time the approach of the Security Council could be distinguished from the past since for the first time it engaged in financial warfare on terrorism in a real sense. The Security Council adopted Resolution 1267 (1999), demanding that the Taliban surrender Usama bin Laden to appropriate authorities in a country where he has been indicted, or to appropriate authorities in a country where he will be returned to such a country, or to appropriate authorities in a country where he will be arrested and effectively brought to justice.[270] In fact, this resolution was designed in a similar way to the *Lockerbie* case, imposing sanctions on the Taliban regime.

However, what makes the involvement of the Security Council at this time totally different from that of the *Lockerbie* incident is its subsequent Resolution 1333 (2000) that commenced to target Usama bin Laden (an individual) and his property. Indeed, the sanctions regime of the Security Council has for the first time begun to aim at undermining the financial infrastructure of terrorist groups; i.e., the financial property of Usama bin Laden and his organisation. Another thing of note is that an individual, who was a non-actor in international law with the ex-

---

[267] The Palermo Convention, Article 13.

[268] For a relevant discussion, see, Section 2.3.2.5 of this chapter. Particularly, *supra* notes 246, 247 and 248, and their related text.

[269] The ICSFT, Articles 13 and 14; the 1997 convention, Article 11.

[270] UN, S/RES/1267, 15 October 1999, para.2.

ception of the human rights area, has emerged as a subject of the international sanctioning regime. Following 9/11, the Security Council continues to maintain this sanctions regime with the adoption of subsequent resolutions.[271] Importantly, this approach has formed one of the two pillars that the Security Council has built to combat terrorist financing since 9/11. These two pillars will be dealt with in detail in the next chapter.

2.4 Conclusion

It was not until the 1990s that the international community started to pay serious attention to terrorist financing. The increased awareness of this issue then led to the adoption of the ICSFT by the General Assembly in 1999 and the utilisation of the Chapter VII powers of the Security Council in 2000.

Notwithstanding these precedents, the suppression of the financing of terrorism was quite a neglected area before the 9/11 attack, being marginalised both within the strategy to combat money laundering, as well as within the strategy to combat terrorism as a whole.

In these circumstances, it is the attack on the Twin Towers which has shaken the reticence of the international community, giving the financing of terrorism a status of the highest priority as an agenda item in the international community. Consequently, various international and regional organisations have since come to establish a broad coalition against the financing of terrorism. In the following chapters, this major change in the international community will be reviewed with a specific focus on the UN Security Council and other specialist bodies.

---

[271] UN, S/RES/1390, 28 January 2002.

3 The Role of the Security Council since 9/11

3.1 Introduction

In the past, the Security Council intermittently engaged in the suppression of the financing of terrorism on an operational basis, allowing a leading role to be taken by others such as the General Assembly. However, the September 11th attack marked a turning point in the role of the Security Council, placing the mighty UN organ into the vanguard of the international campaign against terrorism. Needless to say, this change also had a great impact in the field of the suppression of the financing of terrorism which is one of the crucial sub-areas of the counter-terrorism campaign.

In its efforts the Security Council has adopted two radically different strategies: a structural approach and an operational approach.[1] The structural approach comprises long-term measures to build up a counter-terrorism infrastructure at both the international and national level, and Security Council Resolution 1373 of 2001 might conceivably be said to be an unprecedented example for the international community in this category. By comparison, the operational approach refers to immediate measures taken in the context of an imminent or actual crisis or danger caused by some terrorists. In other words, this approach could be said to be a crackdown on particular terrorists, and Security Council Resolution 1390 of 2002 plays a pivotal role in this operational campaign.

Against this backdrop, this chapter aims at analysing the Security Council's role in suppressing the financing of terrorism since 9/11. For this purpose, Section 3.2 will examine the nature and function of Resolution 1373 and its monitoring mechanism. It will clarify how the Security Council constructs a counter-terrorism infrastructure in the international community. Then Section 3.3 will diagnose Resolution 1390 in a way similar to Section 3.2. After analysing these parallel efforts of the Security Council, Section 3.4 will draw some lessons to facilitate the Security Council's further involvement in this area.

---

[1] A similar categorisation was once employed by the UN Secretary-General in his report on the prevention of armed conflict, see, UN, "Report of the Secretary-General on Prevention of armed conflict", A/55/985-S/2001/574, 7 June 2001, p.7.

However, it should be emphasised that this chapter is focused only on the financial aspect among the contents of these two resolutions. Accordingly, although there are other important counter-terrorism measures contained in the resolutions, the discussion will be confined to the suppression of the financing of terrorism. For a similar reason, in-depth analysis will not be extended to Resolution 1540 of 2004 since it is mainly concerned with the weapons of mass destruction (WMD) issue and the weight given to the financial aspect is very light in comparison with Resolutions 1373 and 1390.[2]

3.2 Structural Approach: Resolution 1373

3.2.1 Background

With the terrorist attack on 11 September 2001, the international community was increasingly sensitised to the danger posed by international terrorism. There immediately arose a sense of urgency that the international community had to take action in the face of such an unprecedented and heinous attack. In Resolution 1368, which was adopted a day after the attack, the Security Council declared any act of international terrorism as a threat to international peace and security, thus laying the legal foundation for further action at Security Council level.[3] Once international terrorism was declared to be *a threat to international peace and security*, the Security Council was entitled to exert its powerful Chapter VII authority.[4] Subsequently, on 28 September 2001, the Security Council adopted Resolution 1373 which was the first manifestation in a concrete form of the international community's determination to combat international terrorism since 9/11. This time, the Security Council did not intend simply to take a one-off action but had it in mind to establish a permanent counter-terrorism legal and executive infrastructure within the international community. Considering that in the past, the international community lacked appropriate legal and administrative tools to cope with

---

[2]   Furthermore, Resolution 1540 adopts the same "structural approach" as Resolution 1373 and thus the working mechanism of its monitoring committee is almost identical to that of Resolution 1373. However, given that the financing issue mentioned in Resolution 1540 has still an overlapping aspect with that of Resolutions 1373 and 1390, Resolution 1540 will be briefly dealt with at the end of this chapter in the context of avoiding duplication among the relevant committees of the Security Council.

[3]   UN, S/RES/1368, 12 September 2001, para. 1.

[4]   See, e.g. Kirgis Jr FL (1995) "The Security Council's First Fifty Years", *The American Journal of International Law*,vol.89, p.512.

international terrorism and there was hardly any coordinated international response to it, Resolution 1373 seems to have great potential to counter this failing.[5]

3.2.2 The nature of Resolution 1373

The Security Council, acting under its Chapter VII powers, can make a simple recommendation or a *binding* decision to maintain international peace and security.[6] In the case of this *binding* decision, it could involve either non-forcible measures or military measures in accordance with Articles 41 and 42 respectively. Generally, the Security Council has exercised various functions under Article 41 such as quasi-judicial functions, quasi-legislative functions and territorial administration, especially since the end of the Cold War.[7] As pointed out in the *Prosecutor v. Tadic* case,[8] the measures set out in Article 41 are not exhaustive but merely illustrative. With a view to exercising these functions, the Security Council usually has had recourse to economic sanctions. This strategy appeared to be somewhat effective but also proved to entail negative side effects as well.[9] Accordingly, at-

---

[5] Ward CA (2003) "Legal Imperatives for Implementation of Resolution 1373 (2001)", Paper presented at the 2003 Caribbean Regional Conference of the International Law Association, Barbados, West Indies, 26-29 March 2003 (typescript), p.1.

[6] See, UN Charter, Article 39. The Security Council has the primary responsibility for the maintenance of international peace and security under Article 24(1) of the UN Charter. If the Security Council considers certain situations or acts as a threat to the peace, or breach of the peace, it can make recommendations or decide what measures should be taken, and these decisions are binding since UN member states agree to accept and carry out them under Articles 25 and 48 of the UN Charter. For the detailed explanation, see, e.g., Malanzuk P (ed) (1997) *Akerhurst's Modern Introduction to International Law*, pp.373-374 and pp.387-390.

[7] Simma B (ed) (2002) *The Charter of the United Nations: A Commentary*, pp.707-710. With regard to quasi-judicial functions, Resolution 662 (1990) is a case in point. In the resolution, the Security Council affirmed that the annexation of Kuwait by Iraq is null and void and that Iraq was liable for damages caused by the invasion of Kuwait. As regards quasi-legislative function, Resolution 1306 (2000) is an example. With the adoption of the resolution, the international diamond market has been forced to adopt an effective mechanism to verify the origin of diamonds. Indeed, these measures can lead to changes in state behaviour.

[8] See, *infra* note 136.

[9] It was the unintended side effects on the civilian population. For the general discussion on the remedies for victims of UN sanctions, see, e.g., Reinisch A (2001) "Developing Human Rights and Humanitarian Law Accountability of the Security Council for the Imposition of Economic Sanctions", *The American Journal of International Law*, vol.95, pp.863-869.

tempts were later made to develop targeted or smart sanctions.[10] While Resolution 1373 contains some elements of this smart sanctions policy, Resolution 1390 definitely falls into this category.[11]

Bearing this aspect in mind, let us look at the nature of Resolution 1373. Above all, since the resolution is also derived from Article 41, it could be said to be *binding*. Of course, there might be some criticism that not all contents of the resolution are binding since some of it takes the form of a recommendation. In relation to this criticism, however, it should be noted that although only paragraphs 1 and 2 of the resolution are explicitly mandatory, the remaining paragraphs also could be implicitly binding in practice. This reasoning is based on the fact that the Security Council has expressed its determination to ensure the *full* implementation of the resolution,[12] and at the same time, the Counter-Terrorism Committee (CTC) (examined in detail below) monitors the implementation of the resolution *as a whole* regardless of the degree of binding power of respective paragraphs.[13]

In addition to this binding nature, Resolution 1373 is distinct in two respects; *permanence* and *universality*, when compared with other Security Council resolutions prior to 9/11.[14] To begin with, the permanent nature of the resolution results from the exercise of a quasi-legislative function by the Security Council. Under the 1373 mandate, all states are required to construct the prescribed legal framework in their national laws and institutions, and furthermore to promote international cooperation.[15] By so doing, a *permanent* obligation seems to be placed on a national legal system to enforce the mandate. For example, whenever future ter-

---

[10] For relevant discussions, see, e.g., *infra* note 104.

[11] Smart sanctions is usually assumed to include: the freezing of financial assets of regime members or elites who support them; suspension of credits and grant aid; denial and limitation of access to overseas financial markets; trade embargoes on arms and luxury goods; flight ban; and, denial of overseas travel. See, UN, "Report of the Secretary-General to the Security Council on the Protection of Civilians in Armed Conflict", S/1997/957, 8 September 1997, p.16.

[12] Resolution 1373, para. 8.

[13] IMF (2003) *Suppressing the Financing of Terrorism: A Handbook for Legislative Drafting*, p.16; Ward CA, *supra* note 5, pp.3-4. For example, if we take a close look at the priorities of the CTC's review, no distinction is made based on the degree of the binding power between paragraphs of Resolution 1373, but only sequential priority has been given to the implementation of the resolution.

[14] The Working Group on the United Nation and Terrorism also noted that the character and scope of Resolution 1373 represents an important innovation and opens up new possibilities for inter-state cooperation. See, Policy Working Group Report, *infra* note 41, p.8.

[15] Ward CA, *supra* note 5, p.2. For the utility of UN resolutions in developing new law in national and international jurisprudence, see,e.g., Schachter O (1994) "United Nations Law", *The American Journal of International Law*, vol.88, pp.1-5.

rorists try to utilise the loopholes of existing legislation and regulations, there arises a need to improve the existing legislation and regulations. Perhaps, with continuous development of terrorists' skills and technology, the nature of a permanent mandate will be more highlighted in the future. In particular, the permanent nature is reinforced by the fact that the CTC, the monitoring body of the resolution, was virtually given a permanent mandate to do its job.

Interestingly, this aspect stands in sharp contrast to the operational aspect of other terrorism-related Security Council resolutions which have an end point to their mandate. For example, in Resolution 748 which was adopted in March 1992 following the aerial incident at Lockerbie, the Security Council demanded that Libya hand over the terrorist suspects to the US or UK and required UN member states to participate in a sanctions regime. This mandate eventually came to an end when Libya surrendered to the Security Council's demand.[16]

Now, let us proceed to the *universal* nature of this measure. First of all, this universality results from the fact that the mandate applies to all terrorist-related entities no matter whether they are state, organisation or individual, and no matter where they are.[17] This nature stands out against that of other Security Council resolutions which usually designated specific targets in a fixed region. Again the Lockerbie incident and the Taliban are cases in point. In both instances, the target was specified as the Libyan government and the Taliban regime respectively. Secondly, note should also be taken that Resolution 1373 is universal in terms of the *scope* of states that are under the *direct* mandate of the resolution.[18] This means that the 1373 mandate imposed active obligations on all states, while other binding Security Council resolutions usually imposed passive obligations thus affecting a limited number of states. Put simply, under active obligations, all states are obliged to take positive action by themselves as is the case with Resolution 1373 which obliges all states to actively build up counter-terrorism infrastructures in their legal and administrative system. In contrast, under passive obligations, states have only to refrain from some proscribed acts such as permitting the operation of the targeted state's airline within their territory and the supplying of specific industrial components.[19] Given that passive obligations might be considered as meaningless

---

[16] For the reference to the entire course of sanctioning, see, Gerson A, Adler J (2001) *The Price of Terror*, pp.104-108, pp.272-284.

[17] See, Policy Working Group Report, *infra* note 41, p.8.

[18] With regard to non-member states, the universal application of the UN resolution might be called into question. Indeed, the Security Council practice in this respect is not conclusive, although the Security Council recently addresses decision under Article 41 to 'all states', implying that non-member states are subject to enforcement actions. In any event, the problem become less important due to the decrease in number of non-member states. See, Simma B, *supra* note 7, p.715.

[19] UN, S/RES/748, 21 January 1992.

for most states which do not consider engaging in those activities with the targeted state, resolutions of this kind do not seem to enjoy universality in a real sense.

Symbolically, the uniqueness of Resolution 1373 in several respects is well illustrated by a UK comment in her state report to the UN Counter-Terrorism Committee that "the unanimous adoption of Security Council Resolution 1373 (2001) was a historic event. This was the first resolution to impose *obligations* on *all states* to respond to the *global threat of terrorism*".[20] Indeed, the resolution is binding because the Security Council, acting under its Chapter VII powers, sets the tone with an obligatory mandate; it is permanent because it is targeted at the endless threat of global terrorism; and, finally it is universal because it related to all states and to terrorism in general.

3.2.3 The general framework of the resolution

Resolution 1373 tries to cover every major aspect of counter-terrorism tactics and accordingly its content could be divided into four groups based on the area that the tactics focus on: suppression of financing of terrorism (para.1); general counter-terrorism measures at the national level (para.2); counter-terrorism measures at the international level (para.3); and, the expansion of the counter-terrorism campaign into a broader area (para.4).[21]

The common feature of these elements is that they impose legislative and administrative obligations on member states, and the implementation of these obligations could entail structural reform in legal and administrative systems at both national and international level. For example, in order to criminalise the provision of funds for terrorism, states need to create a criminal offence for this act of funding.[22] Furthermore, for the purpose of bringing terrorist-related persons to justice, states need to improve their legislation, and their judicial and administrative systems.[23]

Another aspect of note is that although Resolution 1373 attempts to deal with every possible tactic to combat terrorism, it is clear that this resolution adds more weight to the suppression of the financing of terrorism than to other areas. This is

---

[20] UN, "Report to the Counter-Terrorism Committee pursuant to paragraph 6 of Security Council resolution 1373 (2001) of 28 September 2001", enclosed in "Letter dated 19 December 2001 from the Chairman of the Security Council Committee established pursuant to resolution 1373 (2001) concerning counter-terrorism addressed to the President of the Security Council", S/2001/1232, 24 December 2001, p.3.

[21] In some sense, Resolution 1373 created a mini-treaty containing obligations that the majority of states had not been willing to accept in the recent past in treaty form (Bantekas I (2003) "Current Development: The International Law of Terrorist Financing", *The American Journal of International Law,* vol.97, p.326).

[22] Resolution 1373 (2001), para. 1(a).

[23] *Ibid.*, para. 2(e).

illustrated in opening paragraph 1(a) which requires that all states shall prevent and suppress the financing of terrorist acts.[24] However, this stance can also be implicitly found in other paragraphs. For example, the act of *financing* is inserted in the first place of proscribed offences in the original text of paragraph 2(c),(d),(e), and (f). Moreover, in paragraph 3(d), the International Convention for the Suppression of the Financing of Terrorism (ICSFT) (1999), which was examined in detail in the previous chapter, is alone mentioned as an example of the international legal conventions and protocols relating to terrorism.[25] Considering that Resolution 1373 was the first concrete and meaningful measure that the Security Council took following the unprecedented terrorists attack, this stance of the resolution alludes to the fact that the Security Council regards the suppression of financing as a top priority.

In this context, it seems noteworthy to make a comparative study between Resolution 1373 and the ICSFT which is the only multilateral convention of global reach regulating this area. In fact, there are distinct parts as well as similar provisions between these two instruments.

With regard to the similar provisions, paragraph 1(a) and (b) of Resolution 1373 are cases in point. Paragraph 1(a) which states that all states shall prevent and suppress the financing of terrorist acts can find a similar message in the preamble of the ICSFT. Also, paragraph 1(b) which requires the criminalisation of the provision or collection of funds for terrorist acts finds a very close counterpart in Articles 2 and 4 of the ICSFT.[26]

With regard to the distinctive parts, paragraph 1(c) and (d) are examples. Firstly, paragraph 1(c)[27] makes a step forward by way of requiring immediate action, while Article 8 of the ICSFT requires changes in domestic law to enable ac-

---

[24] This aspect is also well illustrated by the CTC's practice in carrying out the 1373 mandate. For example, the CTC set the priority of its review of states' reports in which it singled out counter-terrorist financing as a priority issue for developing executive machinery at stage A. This decision stands in marked contrast to the fact that as noted below the executive machinery for other areas was to be reviewed at stage B ("Focus Paper: Stage B", 22 November 2002, p.1).

[25] There are 19 global or regional treaties directly pertaining to the subject of international terrorism. For the full list of the conventions, see, Policy Working Group Report, *infra* note 41, pp.17-18.

[26] IMF, *supra* note 13, p.20.

[27] Paragraph 1(c) provides that "all states shall freeze without delay funds and other financial assets or economic resources of persons who commit, or attempt to commit, terrorist acts or participate in or facilitate the commission of terrorist acts, of entities owned or controlled directly or indirectly by persons; and of persons and entities acting on behalf of, or at the discretion of such persons and entities, including funds derived or generated from property owned or controlled directly or indirectly by such persons and associated persons and entities".

tion to be taken.[28] Namely, operative paragraph 1(c) stipulates that all states shall freeze without delay funds and other financial assets or economic resources of persons or entities associated with terrorist acts. In contrast, Article 8 provides that each state party shall take appropriate measures *in accordance with its domestic legal principles* for the identification, detection and freezing or seizure of any funds used or allocated for the purpose of committing the proscribed offences set forth in the ICSFT. On the other hand, paragraph 1(c) has some weak points in that it only contains a provision as to freezing whereas the ICSFT elaborates on freezing, seizing and forfeiture in Article 8. Secondly, in addition to dealing with the financing of "concrete terrorist acts" in paragraph 1(b), paragraph 1(d) touches upon the issue of the financing of "terrorists" aimed at supporting their infrastructure.[29] The practice of charities is a good example under this category. By comparison, the ICSFT does not deal with this aspect.[30]

Lastly, attention should be given to the fact that the Security Council tries to address the threat of terrorism more broadly and in a longer term. In paragraph 4, the Security Council pointed out the close link between international terrorism and transnational organised crime such as drug-trafficking, money-laundering, arms-trafficking, etc.[31] With the help of this paragraph 4, there is secured some room for dealing with terrorism and transnational organised crime together in the international arena in the future.[32]

---

[28] Gilmore WC (2003) "International Initiative". In: Graham T (ed) *Butterworths International Guide to Money Laundering Law and Practice*, pp.138-139.

[29] IMF, *Suppressing the Financing of Terrorism*, *supra* note 13, p.20. Paragraph 1(d) stipulates that "all states shall prohibit their nationals or any persons and entities from making any funds, financial assets or economic resources or financial or other related services available, directly or indirectly, *for the benefit of* persons who commit or attempt to commit or facilitate or participate in the commission of terrorist acts, of entities owned or controlled, directly or indirectly, by such persons and of persons and entities acting on behalf of or at the discretion of such persons" (emphasis added).

[30] Ward CA, *supra* note 5, pp.5-6.

[31] The link between terrorism and other transnational crimes was once again emphasised at the Security Council Meeting at the level of the Ministers for Foreign Affairs on 20 January 2003 (UN, S/RES/1456, 20 January 2003).

[32] With regard to this issue, Policy Working Group made a recommendation that the UN Office on Drugs and Crime, and the Department for Disarmament Affairs should study the links between terrorism and organised crime, including drug trafficking, money laundering, illicit trafficking of arms and corruption. See, Policy Working Group Report, *infra* note 41, p.15.

3.2.4 The monitoring mechanism

As the 1373 mandate is permanent in its nature, the will of the international community to continue to combat international terrorism might be assessed by whether it establishes a feedback mechanism or not. In this context, the mandate to establish the Counter-Terrorism Committee (CTC) could be said to be a milestone in the counter-terrorism campaign.[33] In fact, in the past, there did not exist such a *permanent* body to monitor and ensure compliance with the enforcement measures of Security Council resolutions but only some temporary mechanisms.[34] Furthermore, with a view to facilitating the monitoring process, the Security Council called upon all states to report to the CTC on the steps that they have taken to implement the resolution, no later than 90 days from the date of the adoption of the resolution.[35] This request might also set a real standard for the feedback on the implementation of a Security Council resolution in terms of its speed and scope. Since its birth, the CTC "has become the UN's leading body to promote collective action against international terrorism. Its mandate is to bring Member states to an acceptable level of compliance with Resolution 1373 and the terrorism-related conventions and protocols which were negotiated over four decades",[36] and indeed it "will remain at the centre of global efforts to build capacity to combat terrorism" in the future.[37]

3.2.4.1 The operating procedure of the CTC

The CTC consists of all members of the Security Council and meets in closed session, unless it decides otherwise. The Secretariat of the CTC is provided by the Secretariat of the UN. In addition to experts, the CTC may invite any member of the UN to participate in the discussion of any question brought before it, if the in-

---

[33] Resolution 1373, para. 6.

[34] Usually, the Security Council established a sanctions committee, the enforcement body, to ensure compliance with its measure under Article 41. Since the 1990s, two Sanctions Committees have been established in relation to combating terrorism. One is the Sanctions Committee established pursuant to Resolution 748 (1992) and in this case, the Sanctions Committee itself monitored the implementation of the resolution. The other is the Sanctions Committee established pursuant to Resolution 1267 (1999). To monitor the implementation of this resolution, a temporary monitoring group was established. For detailed information, see, section 3.3.4 of this chapter.

[35] UN, S/RES/1373, 28 September 2001, para. 6.

[36] UNODC, "The Global Programme Against Terrorism", in "Global Programmes", p.23 (updated May 2003 and visited on 28 July 2003) <http://www.unodc.org/pdf/crime/publications/cicp_global_programmes.pdf>.

[37] Ward CA (2003) "Building Capacity to Combat International Terrorism: The Role of the United Nations Security Council", *Journal of Conflict & Security*, vol.8, no.2, p.305.

terests of the invited member are specifically affected. When reaching a decision, the CTC generally acts by consensus of its members.[38] If consensus cannot be reached on a particular issue, the matter will be submitted to the Security Council. Lastly, the CTC will submit regular reports, including recommendations as necessary, to the Security Council on the implementation of Resolution 1373.[39]

3.2.4.2 The monitoring priorities of the CTC

Originally, given that Resolution 1373 is broad in scope, the CTC has divided its monitoring work into three phases, with plans to move from a lower to a higher stage as each stage is finished.[40]

Stage A
- Having in place legislation covering all aspects of 1373, and a process in hand for becoming a party as soon as possible to the 12 international conventions and protocols relating to terrorism;
- Having in place executive machinery for preventing and suppressing terrorist financing;

Stage B
- Having in place executive machinery covering all aspects of 1373;

Stage C
- Cooperation on bilateral, regional and international levels, including exchanges of information;
- Judicial cooperation between states and actions on bringing terrorists to justice;
- Increased attention to the links between terrorism and other transnational organised crime

From this division of the monitoring phases, it can be noticed that the CTC's first priority is to establish a national legislative infrastructure by placing it at stage A. Simultaneously, in line with Section 3.2.3 of this chapter, the CTC placed an emphasis on the area of the suppression of the financing of terrorism by mentioning only the executive machinery to cut off financing of terrorism at this stage. Then, the CTC moves to stage B at which point it touches upon the issue of building up the executive machinery covering all other aspects of Resolution

---

[38] Where the CTC agrees, decisions may be taken by a written procedure. In such cases, the chairman of the CTC will circulate the proposal to all members of the CTC, and if no objection is received within 48 hours, the decision will be deemed adopted.

[39] UN, "Guidelines of the Committee for the Conduct of Its Work", S/AC.40/2001/CRP.1, 16 October 2001.

[40] UN, "Focus Paper: Stage B", the CTC document, 22 November 2002.

1373. Finally at stage C, after vertically establishing a legislative and executive infrastructure to combat terrorism at national level, the CTC tries to horizontally weave a cooperative network within the international community. Moreover, in the long term, the CTC seems to pursue the broadening of its battle front to other areas such as drug-trafficking, money-laundering, arms trafficking, people-smuggling, etc.[41] It follows from the above that these stages are interrelated and could be classified into two categories: legislative and operational.[42]

In practice, however, a criticism has been raised that this categorisation has become increasingly artificial as the monitoring of the CTC proceeds and does not provide a clear picture of a state's real situation or development in its implementation of Resolution 1373.[43] In this regard, there arises a need for the revaluation of this categorisation.

3.2.4.3 The various activities of the CTC

The CTC renews its programme of work every 90 days. Since the first working programme covered the period from 28 September to 27 December 2001, as of 1 June 2005, the thirteenth working programme has been adopted. On analysing the development of the working programmes, it can easily be seen that it has been an evolving mechanism rather than a fixed one. The first working programme divided its area of interest into five fields: (a) establishment of contact points; (b) securing of advisers to the CTC; (c) reviewing of state reports; (d) provision of assistance to states; and, (e) promotion of the activities of the CTC.[44] This original format has been maintained throughout all programmes of work except an important change in the third programme in which there was added the issue of promoting dialogue with regional and subregional organisations.[45]

---

[41] See, e.g., UN, "Remarks of the Chairman at the Closing Session", S/AC.40/2003/SM.1/5, 26 March 2003, p.3. Furthermore, as the UN Conventions against Transnational Organized Crime entered into force, the UN Office at Vienna (where the secretariat of the Convention is located) seems to have an important role to play in further exploring the links and in promoting such coordination (UN, "Report of the Policy Working Group on the United Nations and Terrorism" (hereafter Policy Working Group Report), S/2002/875, 6 August 2002, p.7).

[42] UN, "Note by the President of the Security Council", S/2004/70, 26 January 2004, p.11.

[43] Ibid.

[44] UN, "CTC Programme of Work for the first 90-day period", attached to the Letter dated 19 October 2001 from the Chairman of the Counter-Terrorism Committee addressed to the President of the Security Council, S/2001/986, 19 October 2001.

[45] UN, "CTC Programme of Work for the third 90-day period", attached to the Letter dated 27 March 2002 from the Chairman of the Counter-Terrorism Committee addressed to the President of the Security Council, S/2002/318, 27 March 2002.

First of all, of note is that the CTC is trying to facilitate efficient dialogue with states and relevant international organisations, and among states themselves as to the matters covered by Resolution 1373. In this sense, the CTC collated a list of contact points, and published it in the period of the first programme of work. In principle, two contact points are to be designated: one in each state's Permanent Mission to the UN in New York and the other in each state's ministry or agency principally responsible for the implementation of the resolution. In the first instance, the CTC will approach the permanent mission contact points.[46] The CTC continues to update the directory of contact points at regular intervals.

Secondly, the CTC takes steps to furnish itself with the sources of appropriate expertise that it needs in order to do its work. To this end, the CTC invited states to submit lists of experts who would be available to be appointed to assist the CTC.[47] These experts, as independent advisers to the CTC, were first appointed during the period of the second programme,[48] and have since been assigned the task of reviewing state reports.[49]

Thirdly, the CTC takes as its primary task to review state reports.[50] The CTC established three sub-committees in the second programme, each made up of five of its members, to facilitate the reviewing process.[51] Initially, experts as mentioned above analyse each report, and the sub-committees provide a forum of discussion of the report with the presence of all concerned; i.e., members of the CTC, representatives of the state concerned, and experts. The sub-committee reports to the CTC on the conclusions reached and any proposed follow-up action. On receiving the report from its sub-committee, the CTC follows up with the state by way of informing the state of a time limit for the submission of further information or a further report. At the same time, the CTC sends a letter to the Chairman of the Se-

---

[46] The first programme of work, *supra* note 44, p.2. The contact points will be identified by (a) the name and address of the office and a general description of its function; (b) a telephone number; (c) a fax number; and, (d) an email address.

[47] The first programme of work, *supra* note 44, p.3.

[48] UN, "CTC Programme of Work for the second 90-day period", attached to the Letter dated 15 January 2002 from the Chairman of the Counter-Terrorism Committee addressed to the President of the Security Council, S/2002/67, 15 January 2002.

[49] Upon the request of the CTC, the UN Secretariat tries to maintain a list of a wider pool of experts who will be available to advise the CTC. The CTC itself also invited all states to consider whether they can put forward candidates (Note Verbal SCA 3/02(6)).

[50] In order to assist states in fulfilling their obligation in reporting, the CTC produced and circulated to all states guidelines for the preparation of their reports.

[51] For the example of these sub-committees' operation, see, "Tentative Timetable for Member States' Participation in the Process of Reviewing Reports" (visited in 28 July 2003) <http://www.un.org/Docs/sc/committees/1373/participation.html>.

curity Council for the purpose of recording the fact, and this letter would be circulated as a document of the Security Council.[52]

Fourthly, the CTC is trying to explore ways in which states could be assisted in their implementation of Resolution 1373.[53] For this purpose, the CTC has set up a database of available assistance which can be found on its web site.[54] This so-called CTC Assistance Database contains best practices, model legislation, available training programmes, etc.[55] The CTC encourages all states and international, regional, and sub-regional organisations to submit information to strengthen the database.[56] In addition, the CTC maintains a "Matrix of Assistance Requests" which summarises the assistance needs and requests in the areas covered by Resolution 1373. This matrix is intended to make it possible to comprehensively overview states' assistance needs, as well as information on any assistance being delivered.[57] However, the CTC mainly confines its role to that of a "switchboard" and does not directly provide assistance to states.[58]

Fifthly, the CTC promotes dialogue with international, regional and subregional organisations with a view to encouraging these organisations to play an active and coordinated role in combating terrorism within their areas of responsibility. A good example of its initial effort in this direction was a special meeting with some 60 international, regional, and subregional organisations on global action against

---

[52] UN, "Guidelines of the Committee for the Conduct of Its Work", S/AC.40/2001/CRP.1, 16 October 2001.

[53] In Resolution 1377 (2001), the Security Council asked the CTC to explore ways in which states can be assisted, and in particular to explore with international, regional and subregional organisations; the promotion of best practices; the availability of existing technical, financial, regulatory, legislative programmes; and, the promotion of possible synergies between these assistance programmes.

[54] (visited on 1 June 2005) <http://domino.un.org/ctc/CTCDirectory.nsf/frmSearch?Open Form>.

[55] The CTC divided the database into eight categories: legislation drafting; financial law & practice; customs law & practice; immigration law & practice; extradition law & practice; police & law enforcement; illegal arms trafficking; other areas. See, UN, "Information Note on Submissions to the CTC Directory", SCA /20/01(8), 27 November 2001.

[56] *Ibid.*

[57] However, this matrix is not available online, but accessible through the Technical Assistance Team <email: ctc@un.org>.

[58] Rosand E (2004) "Security Council Resolution 1373 and the Counter-Terrorism Committee: the Cornerstone of the United Nations Contribution to the Fight against Terrorism". In: Fijnaut C, Wouters J, Naert F (eds) *Legal Instruments in the Fight against International Terrorism: A Transnational Dialogue*, p.623.

terrorism, held on 6 March 2003.[59] This meeting was unprecedented in its scope of attendance, and might be regarded as a landmark in the history of combating terrorism. The CTC intends to encourage these organisations to develop guidance on best practices and codes, and to share information on monitoring. [60] The CTC meets periodically with these organisations and has called three follow-up Special Meetings as a result.[61]

Lastly, the CTC commits itself to maintaining transparency in its work. To this end, it remains in close contact with other UN organisations, and holds regular briefings of member states and of the media to promote the work of the CTC. This area seems to be very important in drawing the attention of the international community and maintaining the momentum of the work of the CTC.

3.2.4.4 The current progress and revitalisation of the CTC

Taking the monitoring priorities and working programmes of the CTC together, there automatically arises the question of which stage the CTC is now monitoring. Simply speaking, in order to finish stage A and to move to stage B, the CTC should not have any further comments at stage A. Thus, reviews of subsequent reports from many states will probably continue to focus on stage A until the CTC is satisfied that adequate legislation covering all aspects of Resolution 1373 is in place.[62]

Nonetheless, at this point, note should be taken that considering the ever-increasing complexity of terrorist tactics and technology in modern times,[63] it seems necessary that the CTC always keep an eye on the lower stages even after moving to a higher stage. As of 1 June 2005, all 191 UN member states had sub-

---

[59] For the wide range of participants, see, UN, "List of International, Regional and Subregional Organizations with which the Counter-Terrorism Committee Will Deepen Contact" attached to "Special Meeting of the Counter-Terrorism Committee with International, Regional and Subregional Orgnaizations", S/AC.40/2003/SM.1/6/Rev.1, 3 April 2003.

[60] UN, "Outcome Document of the Special Meeting of the Counter-Terrorism Committee with International, Regional and Subregional Organizations" (hereafter Special Meeting Document), S/AC.40/2003/SM.1/4, 31 March 2003, p.3.

[61] The first hosted by the OAS, was held in Washington on October 2003. The second, co-sponsored by the UNODC and the OSCE, took place in Vienna on March 2004. The third, co-hosted by the CIS and Kazakhstan, was held in Almaty on January 2005 <http://www.un.org/Docs/sc/committees/1373/ctc_meeting.html>.

[62] Rosand E, *supra* note 58, p.611.

[63] See, e.g., Monitoring Group Report II, *infra* note 93, p.5.

mitted their first report to the CTC, and most of them are now on the second or third round of their submissions.[64]

On the other hand, to cope with the increasing workload and sustain the momentum in implementing Resolution 1373, the Security Council adopted Resolution 1535 in March 2004 for the purpose of revitalising the CTC. This initiative included the establishment of the Counter-Terrorism Committee Executive Directorate (CTED) and provides for "on-site" visits by the CTC to member states. This CTED has replaced the group of experts with reinforced manpower and specialisation.[65] Furthermore, with an on-site visit available, it has become possible to assess the "ground truth" as well as the "paper truth" based on written reports.[66] The first on-site visit was made to Morocco in March 2005.[67]

3.2.5 The criticism

Perhaps the fundamental criticism is that the question of what is meant by terrorism is not answered by the resolution. In order to combat terrorism, there should be a clear definition of terrorism through which the international community could differentiate terrorists' activities from ordinary crime or a political campaign. However, Resolution 1373 does not address this matter, and up until now, there has been no such a definition available.[68] Accordingly, many problems arise in the course of the implementation of Resolution 1373 at both national and international level. For example, in order to create a criminal offence for the provision and collection of funds for terrorism, relevant legislation requires some definition of terrorism.[69] Without it, a terrorist or terrorist organisation in some state can be considered as patriotic or is a good cause in another state. For instance, in November 2001, Lebanon rejected a US demand to freeze the assets of Hezbollah

---

[64] The last report was received on 22 May 2003 from Sao Tome & Principe (Ward CA, *supra* note 37, p.299).

[65] The CTED was established for an initial period ending 31 December 2007. See, UN, "Letter dated 11 August 2004 from the President of the Security Council addressed to the Secretary-General, UN, S/2004/642, 12 August 2004, p.5.

[66] Rosand E, *supra* note 58, p.624. See also, CTC, "Procedures for CTC visits to member states", 15 September 2004.

[67] UN Information Service, "Country Visits Signal New Phase of Work for United Nations Counter-Terrorism Body", SC/8333, 15 March 2005.

[68] For the history of discussion on the definition of terrorism, see, e.g., Higgins R (1997) "The general international law of terrorism", pp.14-17 and Flory M (1997) "International Law: an instrument to combat terrorism". In: Higgins R, Flory M (eds) *Terrorism and International Law*, 1997, pp.31-33.

[69] Commonwealth Secretariat , "Report of Expert Working Group on Legislative and Administrative Measures to Combat Terrorism" (hereafter Commonwealth Secretariat Report), February 2002, pp.4-5.

since Lebanon noted the difference between resistance and terrorist organisations, considering Hezbollah as a political movement in opposition to Israel.[70]

Secondly, Resolution 1373 might be criticised for its lack of human rights protection provisions.[71] Most of the provisions in Resolution 1373 entail some restriction on civil liberties in a democratic society. In this case, there should be some exceptional clauses or paragraphs to buffer the shock of the aggressive mandate, striking a balance between protection of security and guarantees of basic human rights. However, Resolution 1373 contains no such a clause or paragraph anywhere within its mandate, and to make matters worse, it explicitly restricts the international human rights mechanism by demanding that all states ensure that the asylum-seeker who planned, facilitated or participated in the commission of terrorist acts is not granted refugee status, and that claims of political motivation are not recognised as grounds for refusing requests for the extradition of alleged terrorists.[72]

Thirdly, some of the provisions are not complete and therefore need further consideration. For example, given that Resolution 1373 adds more weight to the suppression of the financing of terrorism within its mandate, the measures for the freezing of financial resources play a pivotal role in this area. However, it is problematic that there are no further instructions concerning the situation following the freezing of assets. Indefinite freezing of assets, needless to say, might cause serious legal problems[73] as well as loss of opportunity. In other words, the

---

[70] See, e.g., Hardister AD (2003) "Can We Buy Peace On Earth?: The Price of Freezing Assets in a Post September 11 World", *North Carolina Journal of International Law & Commercial Regulation*, vol.28, at section V.

[71] The concerns for the lack of human rights protection have frequently been expressed in relation to the activities of the CTC. See, e.g., Policy Working Group Report, *supra* note 41, p.8; UN, Press Release, SG/SM/8583, 20 January 2003; UN, Press Release, SC/7667, 20 February 2003,p.7, 10; UN, "Letter dated 26 February 2003 from the Chairman of the Security Council Committee established pursuant to Resolution 1373(2001) Concerning Counter-Terrorism Addressed to the President of the Security Council", S/AC.40/2003/SM.1/2, 26 February 2003, p.129; UN, "Provisional Summary Record of the First Part of the 57th Meeting", S/AC.40/SR.57, 18 March 2003, pp.9-10; Special Meeting Document, *supra* note 60, p.2.
To make matters worse, there are some extreme cases in which some countries have used their counter-terrorism campaign as a tool for repressing citizen's freedoms. See, e.g., Hardister AD, *supra* note 70, at section VII.

[72] UN, S/RES/1373, para. 3(f) and (g). For the relevant national practices since 9/11, see, Sait S (2002) "International Refugee Law: Excluding the Palestinians". In: Strawson J (ed) *Law After Ground Zero*, p. 99. For more general criticism from human rights perspective, see, Talbot R (2002) "The Balancing Act: Counter-Terrorism and Civil Liberties in British Anti-Terrorism Law". In: Strawson J, *ibid.*, pp.123-135.

[73] See, e.g., Commonwealth Secretariat Report, *supra* note 69, p.9.

asset owner might seek to challenge the decision in a domestic court or before the international community. Moreover, there is the question of how to dispose of frozen assets that do not belong to any specific claimant.

Finally but most importantly, Resolution 1373 seems to have lost its initial momentum. Shortly after the September 11th attack, the international community was shocked into adopting Resolution 1373, consensus on which was reached out of sense of urgency. There was generated some sense of solidarity and sympathy in the international community seeing the collapse of the Twin Towers. Almost four years later, this sense of solidarity is being diluted, and the attention of the international community is shifting to other issues. In fact, considering that the 1373 mandate is permanent by its nature, it seems to be a great challenge to prevent the lessening of its momentum in practice.

3.3 Operational Approach: Resolution 1390

3.3.1 The context

The operational approach to the combat of terrorism at the Security Council level had already been adopted before the September 11th attack. Following the bombing of the US embassies in Kenya and Tanzania, the Security Council in its Resolution 1267 (1999) demanded that the Taliban surrender Usama bin Laden, and imposed sanctions on the Taliban regime such as the freezing of its overseas financial resources and applying aviation restrictions. It could be called *operational* in that this sanctions regime was aimed at bringing particular perpetrators and their organisation to justice and at preventing them from committing further attacks. The operational approach can be characterised in the main as an international administrative asset-freezing system.[74] This is of particular importance in that freezing orders can be issued even without criminal proceedings being instituted and they can (indeed must) be recognised immediately in each national legal system. In fact, this kind of international criminal cooperation was inconceivable under the conventional rules of mutual legal assistance which require strict standards to be met as a condition of assistance such as a formal decision of foreign or domestic courts, or dual criminality.

The sanctions regime which had been established by Resolution 1267, was reasserted in Resolution 1333 (2000),[75] and a monitoring mechanism was estab-

---

[74] The EU is also working on this issue. See, Council of the European Union, "The fight against terrorist financing", the note from the Secretary General/High Representative and the Commission to European Council, JAI 566, ECOFIN 424, EF 64, RELEX 655, COTER 91, 16089/04, Brussels, 14 December 2004, p.11.

[75] UN, S/RES/1333, 19 December 2000.

lished with the adoption of the subsequent Resolution 1363 (2001).[76] Resolution 1390 (2002), the first of an operational type since the September 11th attack, was on similar lines with previous resolutions aimed at the Taliban, Usama bin Laden, and entities associated with them.[77]

However, Resolution 1390 further strengthens this sanctions regime. For example, it provides momentum in monitoring process with the renewal of the mandate of the Monitoring Group that was established by Resolution 1363.[78] The resolution also requests all states to submit their state report, no later than 90 days from the date of the adoption of the resolution and thereafter according to a timetable to be proposed by the 1267 Sanctions Committee which will be explained below in detail. Thereby, a feedback mechanism of Resolution 1390 has been institutionalised. This aspect is in marked contrast with previous resolutions in which the Security Council simply urged states to submit their report without any time limit and any obligation to regularly report.[79]

3.3.2 The nature of Resolution 1390

As Resolution 1390 was adopted by the Security Council acting under Chapter VII, most of its content—in particular paragraph 2 relating to the suppression of the financing of Usama bin Laden and the Al-Qaida network—is as *binding* as Resolution 1373 is. However, whereas Resolution 1373 is universal and permanent in its nature, Resolution 1390 seems to be *particular* and *temporary* like other Security Council resolutions. Indeed, in Resolution 1390, the Security Council explicitly designated Usama bin Laden, members of the Al-Qaida organisation and the Taliban and other individuals, groups, undertakings and entities associated with them as targets of its sanctions regime. From this particularisation, a logical conclusion could be reached that once the designated individuals and entities are successfully dealt with, and their threat is substantially removed, the mandate of Resolution 1390 should expire thereafter. The practice of other Security Council's resolutions that have built their own sanctions regimes demonstrates this temporary nature of Resolution 1390. For example, since 1990, seventeen sanctions regimes have been set up by the Security Council, and seven of them were later terminated with the end to their mandate.[80] Yet, given that the war against Usama bin Laden and the Al-Qaida organisation is unlikely to come to an end in the near

---

[76] UN, S/RES/1363, 30 July 2001.

[77] UN, S/RES/1390, 16 January 2002.

[78] For the subsequent renewal of the mandate of the Monitoring Group, see, Section 3.3.4.3 of this chapter.

[79] Resolution 1267 has no fixed time limit, but it is questionable how many states followed the instruction. To make matters worse, Resolution 1363 has not even imposed an obligation to report.

[80] It is as of 1 June 2005 < http://www.un.org/Docs/sc/committees/INTRO.htm>.

future, this temporariness of Resolution 1390 mandate remains to be seen in practice.[81]

3.3.3 The general framework of the resolution

As noted above, the original framework of Resolution 1390 is derived from that of Resolution 1267 (1999). However, with the development of the situation in Afghanistan, substantial changes were made to the original framework.

First of all, the focus of the sanctions regime has shifted from the Taliban to Usama bin Laden and his Al-Qaida network. For example, in Resolution 1267, the Security Council decided that all states should freeze funds or other financial resources associated with the Taliban, whereas the freezing orders of Resolution 1390 have been extended to Usama bin Laden and his Al-Qaida network. As a matter of fact, it is not surprising, given that the Taliban regime almost collapsed at the time of the adoption of Resolution 1390, while Usama bin Laden and the cell network of the Al-Qaida organisation are still seen as posing a serious threat to international security.

Secondly and more precisely, considering that the target is not fixed in one place but very mobile and elusive around the world, Resolution 1390 focuses on the tackling of individual activities. Indeed, besides tackling the financing of terrorism, the Security Council also added travel bans and arms embargoes on these entities. At this point, note should be taken that a travel ban is different from the former aviation restrictions in that it is imposed on each individual rather than on the entire Afghanistan region. Likewise, arms embargoes aim at preventing arms supplies to the proscribed individuals and entities no matter where they are, rather than to Afghanistan as a whole. Obviously, this is the characteristic of the "smart sanction".[82]

Another important change in this line is that the Security Council gave a new mandate to the sanctions committee established by Resolution 1267 (1999) by requiring it to update the list of targeted entities based on relevant information provided by member states and regional organisations.[83]

---

[81] For the discussion on the future of the campaign against Usama Bin Laden and his Al-Qaida network, See, Gunaratna R (2002) *Inside Al Qaeda: Global Network of Terror*, pp.221-233.

[82] Wessel R (2004) "Debating the 'Smartness' of Anti-Terrorism Sanctions: The UN Security Council and the Individual Citizen". In: Fijnaut C, Wouters J, Naert F (eds), *supra* note 58, p.634.

[83] Resolution 1390, para. 5(a).

3.3.4 The enforcement body and the monitoring mechanism

While Resolution 1373 has only its monitoring mechanism, Resolution 1390 has its own enforcement body as well as a monitoring mechanism. Obviously, this aspect is due to the *operational* nature of Resolution 1390. Indeed since Resolution 1390 aims at dealing with individual terrorists, in some sense, the enforcement body might conceivably be compared to a police headquarter at the international level, directing each state to freeze this individual's asset or that organisation's property. This enforcement body is called the 1267 Sanctions Committee (hereafter Sanctions Committee) which was established by Resolution 1267 (1999) and whose mandate has been amended by Resolution 1390.

Furthermore, for the feedback on the outcome of its enforcement, as noted above resolution 1390 gave a new lease of life to the expiring Monitoring Group established by Resolution 1363 (2001) with the renewal of its mandate by one year.[84] With a new mandate which obligates all states to submit a state report within 90 days, this renewal of a monitoring mechanism provided critical momentum in the securing of states' compliance with the 1390 mandate as below.

3.3.4.1 The operating procedure of the Sanctions Committee

Basically, the operating procedure of the Sanctions Committee is quite similar to that of the CTC. The Sanctions Committee consists of all members of the Security Council and meets in closed session. It may invite any member of the UN to participate in the discussion of any question brought before it if the interests of the member are specifically affected, as well as the members of the Monitoring Group. When reaching a decision, the Sanctions Committee makes it by consensus of its members. If consensus cannot be reached on a particular issue, the matter is submitted to the Security Council. However, given the specific nature of the information, the Chairman may encourage bilateral negotiations between member states. Lastly, the Sanctions Committee submits regular reports, including recommendations as necessary, to the Security Council on the implementation of Resolution 1390.[85]

Added to this common aspect of the procedure, however, it should be noted that the Sanctions Committee has some additional operating procedures on listing and de-listing, which is obviously derived from its *operational* character. Firstly, so far as new listings are concerned, the Sanctions Committee follows the normal decision-making procedure but does so more quickly; i.e., within less than 48

---

[84] Originally, the 1363 mandate of the Monitoring Group was supposed to expire on 19 January 2002. For the history of the renewal of the mandate of this monitoring group, see, Section 3.3.4.3 of this chapter.

[85] UN, "Guidelines of the Committee for the Conduct of its Work", Sanctions Committee document adopted on 7 November 2002 and amended on 10 April 2003.

hours. When member states or regional organisations propose new additions of individuals or organisations to the list, the Sanctions Committee expeditiously considers the proposal and makes a decision by the consensus of its members.

Secondly, it is in relation to updating the existing data on the list that usually includes detailed information such as a name, acronyms, addresses, headquarters, subsidiaries, affiliates, fronts, the nature of business or activity, and the leadership of the entities.[86] If member states or regional organisations provide new information on the list, the Monitoring Group will review the information, and within four weeks, advise the Sanctions Committee on whether to update the existing data or not. In this case, the decision-making procedure does not seem to be as expeditious as that of the new listing.

Thirdly, there is a procedure for de-listing.[87] Under this procedure, (a) a petitioner (individuals, groups, or entities on the list) may petition the government of residence or citizenship to request a review of the case; (b) the government to which a petition is submitted should review all relevant information and approach bilaterally the designating government; (c) if the petitioned government wishes to pursue a de-listing request, it should seek to persuade the designating government to this end; (d) the petitioned government may submit a request for de-listing to the Sanctions Committee, either alone or jointly with the designating government; (e) the Sanctions Committee will reach decision by consensus, and if consensus cannot be reached, the Chairman of the Committee will undertake such further consultation as may facilitate agreement; and, (f) if, after consultation, consensus still cannot be reached, the matter may be submitted to the Security Council.

3.3.4.2 The activities of the Sanctions Committee

Since it was given a new mandate with the adoption of Resolution 1390, the two major tools of the Committee to implement its mandate have been the updating of the list and the reviewing of state reports.[88] As of 1 June 2005, there were 325 individuals and 117 entities on the list, while 5 individuals and 11 entities had been

---

[86] For individuals, name, date of birth, nationality, alias, and passport number.

[87] UN, "Statement of the Chairman of the 1267 Committee on De-listing Procedures", Press Release, SC/7487/AFG/203, 16 August 2002.

[88] For an overview of the Sanctions Committee activities, see,e.g., UN, "Report of the Security Council Committee established pursuant to resolution 1267 (1999) concerning Afghanistan" attached to "Letter dated 17 January 2002 from the Chairman of the Security Council Committee established pursuant to resolution 1267 (1999) concerning Afghanistan addressed to the President of the Security Council", S/2002/101, 5 February 2002; UN, "Report of the Security Council Committee established pursuant to resolution 1267 (1999) attached to "Letter dated 20 December 2002 from the Chairman of the Security Council Committee established pursuant to resolution 1267 (1999) addressed to the President of the Security Council", S/2002/1423, 26 December 2002.

removed from the list.[89] Progress has also been made in listing the names according to their actual cultural usage. As a result of this ongoing effort, approximately US$ 85 million in assets have been blocked worldwide mostly in the form of bank accounts since the September 11th attack.[90]

3.3.4.3 The Monitoring Group

As noted above, the monitoring mechanism was originally created by Resolution 1363 (2001) for a period of 12 months, and later its mandate was renewed twice through the adoption of Resolution 1390 (2002), and Resolution 1455 (2003) until 19 July 2004.[91] Shortly after the expiration of the mandate of the Resolution 1363 Monitoring Group, the Security Council again established for a period of 18 months a New-York based Analytical Support and Sanctions Monitoring Team (the Monitoring Team) by adopting Resolution 1526 (2004).[92] Once again, it could be pointed out that the temporary nature of the Monitoring Group also results from the *operational* aspect of Resolution 1390. By its mandate, the Monitoring Group is supposed to report to the Sanctions Committee regularly, and most of its reports submitted so far contained valuable assessments and recommendations.[93] This

---

[89] The 1267 Sanctions Committee web site <http://www.un.org/Docs/sc/committees/1267/1267ListEng.htm>.

[90] As of 30 July 2004. See, Monitoring Group Report VI, *infra* note 93, p.23.

[91] UN, S/RES/1455, 17 January 2003.

[92] UN, S/RES/1526, 30 January 2004.

[93] See, UN, "Report of the Monitoring Group established pursuant to Security Council resolution 1363 (2001) and extended by resolution 1390 (2002)" (hereafter Monitoring Group Report I) enclosed in "Letter dated 13 May 2002 from the Chairman of the Security Council Committee established pursuant to resolution 1267 (1999) concerning Afghanistan addressed to the President of the Security Council", S/2002/541, 15 May 2002; UN, "Second report of the Monitoring Group established pursuant to Security Council resolution 1363 and extended by resolution 1390 (2002)" (hereafter Monitoring Group Report II) enclosed in "Letter dated 19 September 2002 from the Chairman of the Security Council established pursuant to resolution 1267 (1999) addressed to the President of the Security Council", S/2002/1050 and Corr.1, 27 September 2002; UN, "Third report of the Monitoring Group established pursuant to Security Council resolution 1363 and extended by resolution 1390 (2002)" (hereafter Monitoring Group Report III) enclosed in "Letter dated 16 December 2002 from the Chairman of the Security Council Committee established pursuant to resolution 1267 (1999) addressed to the President of the Security Council", S/2002/1338, 17 December 2002; UN, "Fourth report of the Monitoring Group established pursuant to Security Council resolution 1363 and extended by resolution 1390 (2002)" (hereafter Monitoring Group Report IV) enclosed in "Letter dated 7 July 2003 from the Chairman of the Security Council Committee established pursuant to resolution 1267 (1999) addressed to the President of the Security

study deals with the viewpoint of the Monitoring Group and with other relevant criticisms of Resolution 1390 in the following sub-section.

3.3.5 The criticism

The strongest criticism against Resolution 1390 concerns its procedure for new listing and de-listing.[94] According to a UN report, individuals and entities have filed at least 13 lawsuits around the world directly related to the sanctions.[95] The most common grounds alleged were violation of basic human rights, particularly the right to a fair hearing and an effective counter remedy, right to property and freedom of association.[96] Understandably, in the case of a new listing, it is very difficult to maintain a degree of judicial control on the targeting process, and in the case of de-listing, it is a great challenge to make it happen.[97] The expeditious decision-making procedure which should be finished within less than 48 hours means that there is very little time for the involved states to check the listing process properly.[98] Particularly, the intelligence material provided to the Sanctions Committee may be of limited reliability.[99] In the case of de-listing, criticism becomes more serious. Once the suspected individuals or entities realise that their funds or assets are frozen, they might wish to complain about the decision. However, they have no choice but to make a petition to the state of residence or citi-

---

Council", S/2003/669, 8 July 2003; UN, "Letter dated 1 December 2003 from the Chairman of the Security Council Committee established pursuant to resolution 1267 (1999) addressed to the President of the Security Council containing the SECOND RE-PORT of the MONITORING GROUP pursuant to resolution 1455 (2003)" (hereafter Monitoring Group Report V), S/2003/1070, 2 December 2003; UN, "Letter dated 23 August 2004 from the Chairman of the Security Council Committee established pursuant to resolution 1267 (1999) concerning Al-Qaida and the Taliban and associated individuals and entities addressed to the President of the Security Council containing the FIRST REPORT of the MONITORING TEAM pursuant to resolution 1526 (2004)" (hereafter Monitoring Group Report VI), S/2004/679, 25 August 2004.

[94] See, e.g., Monitoring Group Report I, *supra* note 93, pp.5-6; Monitoring Group Report II, *supra* note 93, pp.7-9; De Wet E (2004) *The Chapter VII Powers of the United Nations Security Council*, p.354.

[95] UN, "Letter dated 14 February 2005 form the Chairman of the Security Council Committee established pursuant to resolution 1267 (1999) concerning Al-Qaida and the Taliban and associated individuals and entities addressed to the President of the Security Council", S/2005/83, 15 February 2005, p.16.

[96] *Ibid.*, p.16.

[97] Cameron I (October 2002), "Targeted Sanctions and Legal Safeguards", Report to the Swedish Foreign Office, pp.9-10.

[98] *Ibid.*, p.9.

[99] See, e.g., Monitoring Group Report II, *supra* note 93, p.10.

zenship for the purpose of getting the diplomatic protection of that state.[100] If that state is not sympathetic, the petition might not be presented to the Committee, regardless of its merits.[101] Indeed, on the international plane, the Security Council and the individuals are not on an equal legal footing. Whereas the Security Council sanctions have started to target individuals or non-government entities, they are totally denied the right to a fair trial. Based on common sense, when one's rights are undermined, there should be guaranteed the opportunity to protect one's legal interest on an equal legal basis.[102] To make matters worse, given that decisions in the Sanctions Committee are made by consensus of member states, just one negative vote could impede the de-listing process.[103]

Another criticism also has a human rights dimension. So long as individuals or entities remain on the list, there arises the issue of fundamental human rights of listed persons and their families.[104] For example, if the entire funds and assets of the listed person should be frozen, there arises a question of how the listed person and his or her family can sustain themselves without any economic resources. They need to buy food or go to hospital, etc. Fortunately, there has been some attempt to alleviate this negative effect as in the case with Resolution 1452 (2002).[105] This resolution constitutes the Security Council's major concession to the criticism against its rigid and inflexible attitude towards freezing orders. In the resolution, the Security Council admits some humanitarian exceptions to its sanctions regime such as basic expenses and legal service fees. However, the 1390 mechanism is still vulnerable to criticism since in reality, it is still difficult for the

---

[100] UN, S/2005/83, *supra* note 95, p.17.

[101] *Ibid.*, p.17.

[102] For the discussion on 'equality of arms' which means each party must be afforded a reasonable opportunity to present his case under on an equal basis in relations to his opponent, see, e.g., Reed R, Murdoch J (2001) *A Guide to Human Rights Law in Scotland,* pp.302-312.

[103] UN, S/2005/83, *supra* note 95, p.18.

[104] In more general terms, the negative side effect of the Security Council sanctions is already pointed out in much academic literature, and the 1390 sanctions regime could be described as sort of "smart sanction" in that it focuses on specific terrorists, in particular an elite class rather than a population in general. However, it does not entirely overcome the criticism in human rights context as illustrated here. For the discussion about smarter sanctions, see, e.g. "Security Council Sanctions Committee: An Overview" (visited on 28 July 2003) <http://www.un.org/Docs/sc/committees/INTRO.htm>; UN, "Report of the Secretary-General on the Humanitarian Implication of the Measures imposed by Security Council Resolution 1267 (1999) and 1333 (2000) on Afghanistan", S/2001/241, 20 March 2001; UN, "Report of the Secretary-General on the humanitarian implication of the Measures imposed by Security Council resolution 1267 (1999) and 1333 (2000) on Afghanistan", S/2001/695, 13 July 2001.

[105] UN, S/RES/1452, 20 December 2002.

listed person to obtain the "unfreezing" order. For instance, with regard to basic expenses, the unfreezing order can only be obtained after notification by the relevant state to the Sanctions Committee and in the absence of negative decision by the Committee within 48 hours of such notification.[106] In the case of extraordinary expenses, the unfreezing order can be obtained, provided that a request is made by the relevant state(s) to the Sanctions Committee and is approved by the Committee. However, in this case, there is no time limit to the decision-making process of the Sanctions Committee after the notification.[107]

Thirdly, there is a criticism that despite the effort of the Sanctions Committee, charities and the use of informal transfer mechanism such as *hawala,* continue to pose an important challenge in the war on terrorist financing.[108] The Monitoring Group noted that the funding of Al-Qaida and associated terrorist groups through charities and other organisations continued to be unregulated in many states.[109] Particularly, the current legal and administrative frameworks of most states is said to focus only on the formal financial sector while some informal sectors such as the diamond trade and the alternative remittance system are still left outside the regulation regime.[110] Considering some allegations that Al-Qaida diversified the movement of their finances such as acquiring gold and diamonds, and is resorting to long-established informal remittance system, this loophole looms large.[111]

Fourthly, some critics point out that the 1390 mechanism does not concentrate on the issue of the link between terrorism and other transnational crimes, in particular drug trafficking. Given that Afghanistan accounted for over 80 percent (4,200 metric tonnes, US$ 2.8 billion's worth) of the world's opium supply in 2004, the drug trade may remain a substantial source of Al-Qaida funding which is not directly dealt with under 1390 mandate.[112] Such concerns seem to hold water,

---

[106] Resolution 1452, para. 1(a).

[107] Resolution 1452, para. 1(b).

[108] For the related issues within the 1390 mechanism, see, e.g., Monitoring Group Report I, *supra* note 93 p.8; Monitoring Group Report IV, *supra* note 93, p.4. For a general overview of *hawala*, see, Gilmore WC (2004) *Dirty Money: The Evolution of Money Laundering Counter-Measures*, pp.37-38.

[109] Monitoring Group Report III, *supra* note 93, p.12. Surprisingly, Al-Qaida is presumed to receive US$ 16 million annually in donations. See, e.g., Monitoring Group Report IV, *supra* note 93 pp.13-14.

[110] An estimated US$ 80 billion moves yearly through such system. According to the estimation of the Pakistani bankers, *hawala* account for around US$ 3 billion entering Pakistan, while the formal banking system processed only US$ 1 billion (see, Monitoring Group Report IV, *supra* note 93, pp.17-18).

[111] Monitoring Group Report IV, *supra* note 93, p.16. For a further discussion, see, *supra* note 108.

[112] Monitoring Group Report IV, *supra* note 93, p.11; UNODC, *Afghanistan Opium Survey 2004*, p.4.

in particular considering some indications that Al-Qaida continued to profit from revenues connected with the Afghanistan illicit drug trade.[113]

Lastly, some of the criticisms of Resolution 1373 could also be true of the Resolution 1390 mechanism: *the issue of incomplete provision* and *maintaining of momentum.* For instance, Resolution 1390 also demanded that all states freeze financial resources of listed persons or entities, without further instruction. Moreover, the Sanctions Committee also has a difficulty in maintaining the original momentum. For example, the Security Council adopted Resolution 1455 (2003)[114] in which it demanded all states to submit their report on the measures to implement Resolutions 1267, 1333, and 1390, no later than 90 days from the date of the adoption of the resolution, but as of 1 June 2005, only some 130 states had responded to the call.[115]

3.4 Lessons for Future Campaign against Terrorist Financing

3.4.1 General

In order to successfully tackle the financing of terrorism, it is crucial to promote the synergy effect of the two distinctive approaches. For instance, the hands-on experience of the Sanctions Committee that has been accumulated in the course of pursuing these individuals and organisations could provide a valuable input to the work of the CTC. At the same time, the outcome from the structural approach could support the operation of the Sanctions Committee since the reinforced or newly established legal and administrative framework would create a more hostile environment in which Usama bin Laden and the Al-Qaida network operate.[116]

---

[113] Monitoring Group Report IV, *supra* note 93, p.14.

[114] UN, S/RES/1455, 17 January 2003.

[115] 1267 Sanctions Committee web site <http://www.un.org/Docs/sc/committees/1267/ 1455reportsEng.htm>.

[116] In fact this cooperative mechanism is already operating in the current system of the CTC and the Sanctions Committee. For instance, para. 5(f) of Resolution 1390 stipulates that the Sanctions Committee is required to cooperate with the CTC as well as other relevant Security Council Sanctions Committees. Furthermore, besides Resolution 1373, Resolution 1390 also imposes some obligations on all states to establish a legal and administrative framework on an operational basis that is necessary to pursue Usama bin Laden and the Al-Qaida network. Given that all states have to report to the Sanctions Committee on the measures to implement Resolution 1390, there is automatically established a sort of feedback mechanism between Resolution 1373 and 1390 on the effectiveness of the measures adopted under 1373 mandate in a real situation. See, e.g., UN, "Report of the Government of the United States called for under Security Council resolution 1455

Besides the promotion of a synergy effect, the Security Council needs to note some lessons to facilitate its further involvement in this area, which have already been teased out above. These lessons could be classified into two categories: *substantive* matters and *procedural* matters.

For instance, in substantive respects, the Security Council should introduce the definition of terrorism because the defining of terrorism is the logical step in taking any specific measure on a harmonised basis. Also, the Security Council needs to provide further instructions following its freezing orders, and to strengthen its regulation on charities and informal value transfer systems. Furthermore, the Security Council needs to clarify the link between terrorism and other transnational crimes for effective campaigns in both areas.[117]

In procedural respects, the Security Council should develop a fairer and more objective mechanism for listing and de-listing. Moreover, in the course of initiating the counter-terrorism campaign on a broader front than ever before, the Security Council should reduce the duplication of activities of relevant bodies as well as being an engine for maintaining international momentum.

Last but not the least, regardless of whether it is a substantive or procedural matter, note should be taken that "our response to terrorism, as well as our efforts to thwart it and prevent it should uphold human rights that terrorists would aim to destroy. Respect for human rights, fundamental freedoms and the rule of law are essential tools in the effort to combat terrorism—not privileges to be sacrificed at a time of tension."[118]

(2003)" attached to "Letter dated 17 April 2003 from the Permanent Representative of the United States of America to the United Nations addressed to the Chairman of the Committee", S/AC.37/2003/(1455)/26, 22 April 2003, p.3.

[117] To begin with, the link needs to be researched to prevent other crimes from being used as a means of terrorism. See, e.g., Monitoring Group Report IV, *supra* note 93, pp.18-31. In particular, the understanding of this link might be of value to fight other transnational crimes in the field of the suppression of financing of terrorism. This is because the countermeasure to tackle the link might end up with strengthening the crime-prevention infrastructure with regard to other transnational crime. However, the effort to elucidate the link has been quite limited so far. See, e.g., UN, "First Report of the Monitoring Group on Afghanistan Established Pursuant to Security Council Resolution 1363 (2001) attached to "Letter dated 14 January 2002 from the Chairman of the Security Council Committee established pursuant to resolution 1267 (1999) concerning Afghanistan addressed to the President of the Security Council", S/2002/65, 15 January 2002, p.5.

[118] Kofi Annan, the Secretary-General of the UN, at the "Special Meeting of Security Council's Counter-Terrorism Committee Hears Calls for Systematic International, Regional Cooperation" (UN, Press Release, SC/7679, 6 March 2003).

Fortunately, some progress has been made since in this respect. The Office of the UN High Commissioner for Human Rights (OHCHR) has exchanged views with the CTC and submitted a note with proposals for "Further Guidance" for the submission of a state

In fact, all of the above issues need to be dealt with in greater depth. However, given that the scope of study in this chapter is confined to the general role of the Security Council and that major substantive issues such as charities and an informal value transfer system are being undertaken in detail by the specialist bodies such as the FATF based on the soft law approach, this chapter will focus on four issues to which the Security Council needs to pay urgent attention: the definition of terrorism; the establishment of a fairer and more objective mechanism for listing and de-listing; the avoidance of duplication; and, the sustaining of momentum.

3.4.2 The definition of terrorism

So far, there has been no consensus on the definition of terrorism in international law, and relevant international instruments have bypassed the problem by usually dealing with specific types of terrorist acts.[119] Currently, the preponderant practice of the existing UN counter-terrorism conventions is to define terrorism in the form of a list of underlying acts with a requirement that these acts are committed to threaten the population or to force some change in government policy. Sometimes a requirement of a political or religious motivation is added.[120]

Of course, in the meantime, the General Assembly has been making efforts to draft a comprehensive convention against international terrorism and an international convention for the suppression of nuclear terrorism,[121] but it still remains to be seen if and when these initiatives will be finalised, signed, and brought into force.

---

report on the implementation of Resolution 1373 to the chairman of the CTC on 23 September 2002. This note and proposals included some guiding principles for protecting human rights in the course of combating terrorism such as the right to recognition everywhere as a person before the law, principle of due process, etc. (visited on 28 July 2003) <http://www.un.org./Docs/sc/committees/`1373/ohchr1.htm>.

Of course, the CTC could utilise the input from the monitoring by other international human rights protection bodies and NGOs as remarked by Ambassador Jeremy Greenstock, the then Chairman of the CTC, at the Symposium: "Combating International Terrorism: The Contribution of the United Nations", Vienna, 3-4 June 2002.

[119] This attitude was supported in the Special Meeting on March 2003. See, e.g. UN, "Provisional Summary Record of the First Part of the 57th Meeting", S/AC.40/SR.57, 18 March 2003, p.4.

[120] Commonwealth Secretariat Report, *supra* note 69, p.4.

[121] The drafting work is under way by the *ad hoc* committee established by General Assembly Resolution 51/210 of 17 December 1996, and it was given a mandate to harmonise legal structures for combating international terrorism. So far it has led to the adoption of two treaties: one on terrorist bombings and the other on suppression of financing of terrorist activities. For more information, see, UN, Press Release, L/2993, 1 February 2002.

Under these circumstances, given that the definition of terrorism directly affects the ongoing effort of the Security Council to construct an international counter-terrorism infrastructure, the Security Council cannot safely rely on the current imperfect practice. It needs to seek alternative ways. Indeed, it is important to provide states with some guidance and information as to the definition of terrorism, and some uniformity achieved by this effort will eventually enhance international cooperation to combat terrorism.[122] For this purpose, this study will suggest two methods. One is to borrow the definition of the ICSFT (1999), and the other is to consult some internationally recognised model law.[123]

Firstly, the Security Council might set an ICSFT-style standard. In the view of the writer, there exist solid grounds on which states can rely in adopting the ICSFT approach since the Security Council called upon all states to become parties to the ICSFT in Resolution 1373, thus establishing a bridge between the resolution and the ICSFT. Furthermore, the ICSFT has now secured substantial universality by itself, given that some 140 states have ratified it.

Secondly, the Security Council could recommend the definition of terrorism contained in an internationally recognised model law such as the "Model Legislative Provisions on Measures to Combat Terrorism" drafted by the Commonwealth Secretariat. On a broader look, the approach adopted in this model law does not deviate much from other international practice such as the ICSFT-style since it included both the *listing* approach and a supplementary definition. Of course, however, it should be noted that this model law has made some minor changes such as the direct enumeration of the acts which constitute offences, instead of indirectly referring to relevant conventions. Furthermore, it is broader in scope than the ICSFT because it touches upon new issues such as chemical and biological weapons, and the disruption of communication infrastructures, computer systems, and medical services.[124] In fact, this kind of advanced approach of the model law is already adopted in the EU Council Framework Decision on Combating Terrorism (2002) which also directly enumerates a list of offences and introduces new issues as well.[125] Generally, upon a closer look at the developing trend of these new instruments, the focus of the international community seems to shift from an attack on an individual object on a small scale to that on the social and financial infrastructure. Given that the CTC has referred to this "Model Legislative Provisions on Measures to Combat Terrorism" as an example of guidance, and it is quite

---

[122] Commonwealth Secretariat Report, *supra* note 69, p.4.

[123] See, e.g., Commonwealth Secretariat, "Model Legislative Provisions on Measures to Combat Terrorism", September 2002.

[124] See, e.g., Commonwealth Secretariat Report, *supra* note 69, p.4.

[125] Official Journal of the European Communities, L 164, 22.6.2002, p.3.

similar to the relevant international instrument, there also exists some room for the member states to safely benchmark it.[126]

3.4.3 The establishment of a fair and objective mechanism for listing and de-listing

As noted above, the most important lesson from the practice of the Sanctions Committee seems to relate to the listing and de-listing procedure. The list is indeed a key to the success of the sanctions regime. However, in order to remain as a useful tool in the future, it should focus on securing its international acceptance on as wide a basis as possible.[127] In this regard, some suggestions for improvement might be worthy of review. Firstly, it is conceivable to maintain the present system with some minor changes. For instance, a minimum standard by which the Sanctions Committee can make a decision of listing might be introduced with a view to making lists as accurate and consistent as possible, paying attention to the cultural usage of names.[128] Moreover, the Sanctions Committee might require a national indictment as a precondition to listing for the purpose of reinforced human rights protection.[129] In this case, national judges could scrutinise the relevant evidence and information, providing some legal safeguards at the national level.[130] Moreover, the Sanctions Committee could obligate all state to guarantee an effective appeal procedure in their domestic legal system.[131] This proposal has the merit of utilising existing infrastructures without dramatically introducing a new system.

However, it is vulnerable to criticism on the ground that it does not fundamentally address the issue of the right to a fair trial. Even if a national indictment or appeal procedure before national courts is introduced, these safeguards cannot guarantee the right to a fair trial in the full sense without a genuinely effective ju-

---

[126] Ambassador Jeremy Greenstock, the then chairman of the CTC, commented on this model legislative provision at the 4618th Meeting of the Security Council. See, e.g., UN, Press Release, SC/7522, 4 October 2002.

[127] Monitoring Group Report VI, *supra* note 93, p.10.

[128] This idea might substantially relieve the burden of financial institutions, given that with vague lists, computerised warning systems produce too many "false hits" entailing human double checks on the hits. See, Cameron I, *supra* note 97, p.11.

[129] *Ibid.*, p.42.

[130] *Ibid.*, pp.40-43. However, in order to maintain a minimum level of quality control on national legal systems, it might be conceivable that the authority to issue a national indictment is confined to the states that have joined the ICSFT (1999). Indeed, if a state ratified the ICSFT, the state may be presumed to in a degree have a will to participate in the international coalition to combat terrorism, compared with non-party states.

[131] *Ibid.*, p.43.

dicial review procedure operating in each national legal system.[132] Moreover, these changes could not guarantee the listed persons a fair opportunity of being allowed humanitarian exceptions at the international level.

Secondly and more fundamentally, the idea of establishing an international review mechanism can be considered. In this regard, the establishment of the Security Council's own sub-organ of a judicial nature is one of the options.[133] It definitely guarantees the individual's right to a fair trial, and the court's capacity for reviewing each case with relevant expertise and speed might be incomparable since it would be a specialised court for the sole purpose of dealing with terrorists. Furthermore, it is more likely to enjoy the support of the international community because it could be established by a decision of the Security Council. In fact, there are precedents to this scenario in the Security Council's recent practice as illustrated by the International Criminal Tribunal for the Former Yugoslavia (ICTY)[134] and the International Criminal Tribunal for Rwanda (ICTR).[135] Of course, there was a challenge against the authority of the Security Council to establish a subsidiary tribunal in the *Prosecutor v. Tadic* case but the court successfully justified it.[136]

---

[132] *Ibid.*, p.46.

[133] De Wet E (2004) *The Chapter VII Powers of the United Nations Security Council*, pp.354-357.

[134] The ICTY was established by the Security Council Resolutions 808 (22 February1993) and 827 (25 May 1993). This practice well illustrates the flexibility with which the Security Council interprets its Chapter VII powers. For the legal basis for the establishment of the international tribunal, see, UN, "Report of the Secretary-General under Security Council Resolution 808", S/2504(1993); Roman AK (1996) "An Ad Hoc International Tribunal for the Prosecution of Serious Violations of International Humanitarian Law in the Former Yugoslavia". In: Clark R, Sann M (eds) *The Prosecution of International Crimes*.

[135] UN, S/RES/955, 8 November 1994.

[136] *Prosecutor v. Tadic*, Case No.IT-94-1-AR72, 2 October 1995. In this case, Tadic challenged the authority of the Security Council in an interlocutory appeal before the Appeals Chamber of the ICTY on three grounds (a) the establishment of such a tribunal was never contemplated by the framers of the Charter as one of the measures to be taken under Chapter VII; (b) the Security Council is constitutionally or inherently incapable of creating a judicial organ, as it is conceived in the Charter as an executive organ, hence not possessed of judicial powers which can be exercised through a subsidiary organ; and, (c) the establishment of the International Tribunal has neither promoted, nor was capable of promoting, international peace, as demonstrated by the current situation in the former Yugoslavia.

In response to this argument, the Court said that (a) the measures set out in Article 41 are merely illustrative examples and the International Tribunal matches perfectly the description in Article 41 of 'measures not involving the use of force'; (b) the separation

However, this approach also is not free of criticism in that the establishment of a subsidiary body involves huge costs and manpower, especially at a time when the UN is trying to streamline its organisational structure.[137] With regard to this criticism, it should be pointed out that this new sub-organ might be designed to utilise temporary judges, which would enable the Security Council to launch a new mechanism with less cost and manpower. Furthermore, this body can meet the demand from all sanctions committees, thus considerably relieving the overall burden on the Security Council in terms of human rights criticism. As a matter of fact, the workload might not be so high in practice as is feared. For example, it is unlikely that most of the elusive terrorists, including Usama bin Laden himself, who have been put on the list by the Sanctions Committee, would officially challenge the decision as to listing.[138] Moreover, the body might restrict its role only to the reviewing of listing and de-listing procedures without extending its mandate to broader issues.[139]

Thirdly, the possibility of utilising the International Criminal Court (ICC) can be reviewed. Although earlier drafts of the statute for the ICC included jurisdiction over terrorist offence, drafters decided to include only crimes which are recognised under customary international law; i.e., the crime of genocide, crimes against humanity, war crimes, and the crime of aggression.[140] Treaty-based crimes were not considered.[141] The drafters feared that the investigation of the crime of terrorism requires long-term planning and infiltration into the organisations involved.[142] Furthermore, it became clear that there was no time to secure a generally acceptable definition of terrorism.[143] As a result, the ICC has no "explicit"

---

of powers has meaning only in a national system, and among the principal organs of the UN, the divisions between judicial, executive and legislative functions are not clear cut. However, more essentially, it is not the matter of delegation of its function but what is important is that the Security Council has chosen the option as an instrument for the exercise of its own principal function of maintenance of peace and security; and, (c) the legality of measures could not be tested by their success or failure to achieve their ends. Nonetheless, the effectiveness of the International Tribunal was repeatedly endorsed by the representative organ of the UN in various resolutions.

[137] Rosand E, *supra* note 58, p.621.

[138] See, e.g., Monitoring Group Report V, *supra* note 93, p.5.

[139] However, desirably, once the mechanism is established, the extension of its mandate to another area such as the trial of terrorist suspects could be reviewed, depending on the consensus of the international community and the situation at the time.

[140] Selbmann F, "Terrorism-A Case for the International Criminal Court", <http://voelker strafrecht.org/literatur/ICC_Terrorism.pdf>.

[141] Schabas WA (2001) *An Introduction to the International Criminal Court*, p.28.

[142] Arsanjani M (1999) "The Rome Statute of the International Criminal Court", *The American Journal of International Law*, vol. 93, p.29.

[143] *Ibid.*, p.29.

subject matter jurisdiction over the crime of terrorism. However, in a resolution annexed to the ICC statute, the participants of the Rome conference recognised terrorism as serious crimes of concern to the international community and stressed that the statute could be amended regarding terrorism in a review conference according to Article 123 of the ICC statute.[144] This conference should take place in 2009.[145]

Under these circumstances, it should also be noted that the category of crimes against humanity includes murder and extermination committed as part of a widespread or systematic attack on any civilian population. Thus, there is secured some room for the ICC to be involved in the fight against international terrorism. Perhaps, certain terrorist acts like the 9/11 attack might be tried under this category of crimes against humanity. In this regard, note should be made of Article 13(b) of the Rome statute which allows the ICC to exercise its jurisdiction with respect to such crimes if a situation in which one or more of these crimes appears to have been committed is referred to the Prosecutor of the ICC by the Security Council acting under Chapter VII powers. Accordingly, if there is a referral from the Security Council and certain terrorist acts could be interpreted to fall into the category of crimes against humanity, the ICC could exercise its jurisdiction over the case.[146] In this scenario, the individual right to a fair trial is perfectly guaranteed, and the ICC might operate efficiently to deal with each individual case since the ICC is a proper court for this purpose. This idea was also supported by the Policy Working Group on the United Nations and Terrorism.[147]

However, the ICC scenario is vulnerable to the criticism that the Rome statute is not accepted by all states in the international community. In particular, the US, a permanent member of the Security Council, did not sign the statute to establish the ICC. Furthermore, the possibility of its joining the statute in the near future seems

---

[144] Selbmann F, *supra* note 140; UN, "Final Act of the United Nations Diplomatic Conference of Plenipotentiaries on the Establishment of an International Criminal Court; Annex I", A/CONF.183/10*, 17 July 1998, pp.7-8.

[145] Selbmann F, *supra* note 140.

[146] Article 7(1) of the ICC statute. For an insight into the elements of crime against humanity, see, Robinson D (1999) "Defining "Crimes Against Humanity" at the Rome Conference", *American Journal of International Law*, vol.93, p.43. See also, Neff S (1998) "Past and Future Lessons from the Ad Hoc Tribunals for the Former Yugoslavia and Rwanda". In: Cullen PJ, Gilmore WC (eds) *Crime Sans Frontières: International and European Legal Approaches*, pp.63-65.

[147] See, Policy Working Group Report, *supra* note 41, p.8. For the cooperative relationship between the Security Council and the International Criminal Court, see, Yee L (1999) "The International Criminal Court and the Security Council: Article 13(b) and 16". In: Lee RS (ed) *The International Criminal Court: The Making of the Rome Statute-- Issues, Negotiations, Results*, pp.146-149.

extremely low.[148] Nonetheless, the Security Council recently made a breakthrough in its cooperative relationship with the ICC by adopting Resolution 1593 (2005).[149] This resolution was originally aimed at subduing armed conflicts in Sudan. However it provides significant policy implications in that for the first time the Security Council sought the assistance of the ICC in dealing with individuals suspected of committing international crimes during armed conflicts. It could act as a precedent for the future relationship between the Security Council and the ICC.[150] If accompanied by a consensus among the members of the Security Council, the current experiment with armed conflicts could be extended to other issues such as international terrorism.

Fourthly and theoretically, the establishment of other joint review mechanisms at the international level can be conceived such as involving the Human Rights Committee[151] and the International Court of Justice.[152] However, in terms of feasibility, these options are quite a remote possibility.

---

[148] The major concern of the US is that American servicemembers deployed overseas might be tried by the ICC. For details on the US objection, see, e.g., Everett R (2000) "American Servicemembers and the ICC". In: Sewall SB, Kaysen C (eds) *The United States and the International Criminal Court*, pp.137-148; Scheffer D (1999) "The United States and the International Criminal Court", *The American Journal of International Law*, vol.93, p.18.

[149] UN, S/RES/1593, 31 March 2005.

[150] However, Resolution 1593 excludes the nationals of states which are not a party to the Rome statute from the jurisdiction of the ICC. Furthermore, the resolution makes it clear that the expenses incurred with the activities of the ICC shall be borne by the parties to the Rome statute and those states that wish to contribute voluntarily.

[151] Given that the HRC could receive communications from individuals, it could allow individuals to initiate and make their own case. However, it is doubtful whether the HRC has adequate expertise to deal with intelligence material and make a proper decision. Furthermore, the HRC faces the problem of delay. Since the HRC meets three times a year while individual communications are increasing every year, it could not meet the requirement of efficiency and speed. In addition, the HRC does not enjoy universal membership. As at 8 June 2005, 154 states has became a party to the ICCPR, and 107 of them became a party to the Protocol <http://www.unhchr.ch/pdf/report.pdf>. Lastly, since the HRC is a treaty-based body and its decisions are not binding, there is an inherent limit to the HRC's involvement in the Security Council's primary area. For further information, see, e.g., Shaw M (1997) *International Law*, p.238.

[152] The ICJ option is also not desirable, because only a state could file a suit before the ICJ. Perhaps, in this case, a state might exercise its right of the diplomatic protection of its nationals, but this aspect fundamentally contradicts the idea of guaranteeing an individual the right to a fair trial. Moreover, the scenario might lead to a conflict between the Security Council and the ICJ, introducing the issue of a judicial review of the decision of the Security Council by the ICJ. In fact, several attempts were carefully made

3.4.4 The avoidance of duplication

As the counter-terrorism campaign involves numerous international organisations and regional bodies, the question of how to avoid duplication among these concerned parties in the implementation of their mandates becomes a crucial issue.[153]

First of all, within the Security Council, the duplication of the activities between the CTC and the Sanctions Committee should be avoided. Moreover, the new 1540 Committee has some overlapping areas with the CTC and the Sanctions Committee in general terms. For example, the CTC and the Sanctions Committee partly deal with the issue concerning the supply of weapons to terrorists, while the 1540 committee in the main aims at preventing the proliferation of the weapons of mass destruction as well as their means of delivery. Particularly in the context of terrorist financing, Resolution 1540 also makes a very brief remark on the need for the prevention of financing any non-State actor which involves the issue of WMD.[154] In this regard, although the weight given to the financial issue consider-

---

with regard to the issue of the judicial review, but the issue is still unsettled. See, e.g., Alvarez JE (1996) "Judging the Security Council", *The American Journal of International Law*, vol.90, pp.2-4; Vera GD (1994) "The Relationship between the International Court of Justice and the Security Council in the Light of the *Lockerbie* Case", *The American Journal of International Law*, vol.88, p.647, pp.661-675; Martenczuk B (1999) "The Security Council, the International Court and Judicial Review: What lessons from Lockerbie?", *European Journal of International Law*, vol.10, pp.525-546; Akande D (1997) "The International Court of Justice and the Security Council: Is there room for judicial control of decisions of the political organs of the United Nations", *International and Comparative Law Quarterly*, vol.46, pp. 325-342. From a different perspective, the ICJ might support the weak points of the Sanctions Committee by way of its advisory opinions. However, this option is also not attractive since this advisory opinion could be requested by an international organisation, and in this case, the Security Council itself. Moreover, there is no room for individuals to intervene on their behalf in this scenario. To make matters worse, the ICJ might be incapable of dealing with its heavy workloads expeditiously, considering its manpower and the current demands by states. With regard to the structure and activities of the ICJ, see, e.g., Oda S (1993) "The International Court of Justice viewed from the Bench (1976-1993)" *Recueil des Cours*, Tome 244, pp.110-111; Jennings RY (1995) "The United Nations At Fifty: The International Court of Justice After Fifty Years", *The American Journal of International Law*, vol.89, pp.496-497.

[153] See, e.g. UN, "Provisional Summary Record of the First Part of the 57th Meeting", S/AC.40/SR.57, 18 March 2003, p.4, 13; Special Meeting Document, *supra* note 60, p.2.

[154] UN, S/RES/1540, 28 April 2004, para.2.

ably varies, there is some room to coordinate the activities of these three Security Council committees.[155]

Furthermore, at the entire UN level, this duplication issue is also applicable to the relations between the Security Council and other relevant organs within the UN such as the Office on Drugs and Crime[156] and the Sixth Committee.

In a broad perspective, the issue of duplication could be further extended to the relations between the UN and other specialist bodies and regional organisations such as the FATF, IMF, World Bank, the Asia/Pacific Group on Money Laundering, etc. Given that the discussion on specialist bodies comes in the following chapters, the issue of duplication in a broad perspective will be revisited on that occasion in more detail.[157]

At this point, note should be taken that this aspect of duplication is a double-edged sword which could be turned into a benefit in disguise, depending on the management of the situation. In this context, the CTC could utilise the input from other UN organs and international and regional organisations in combating terrorism, as well as making use of their mechanisms in implementing the 1373 mandate. At the same time, these organisations also could enjoy the support of the Security Council in carrying out the mandate within their area of responsibility through the CTC's capability to communicate with the Security Council.[158]

Fortunately, the CTC have made a positive step in this direction as is shown by the special meeting held by the CTC on 6 March 2003, which brought together some 60 international, regional, and sub-regional organisations, all with their counter-terrorism programmes. Of course, there is also a contrary example that the CTC visits other relevant organisations to brief them on its work as illustrated by the regular attendance of the CTC's representatives at the FATF's plenary meetings.[159] Certainly, the effort to avoid duplication will contribute to the boosting of the synergy effect of cooperation in the future by way of giving a proper mandate to a suitable organisation, removing uncovered grey areas.

---

[155] UN, "Letter dated 14 February 2005 from the Chairman of the Security Council Committee established pursuant to resolution 1267 (1999) concerning Al-Qaeda and the Taliban and associated individuals and entities addressed to the President of the Security Council", S/2005/83, 15 February 2005, p.38.

[156] The United Nations Office on Drugs and Crime delivers technical assistance to strengthen a legal regime against terrorism. For details, see <http://www.unodc.org/unodc/en/terrorism.html>.

[157] Particularly, Chapter Six provides an overview of the duplication issue.

[158] Johnston RB, the representative of the IMF at the Special Meeting on 6 March 2003 (UN, "Provisional Summary Record of the First Part of the 57th Meeting", S/AC.40/SR.57, 18 March 2003, p.5).

[159] FATF, "Annual Report: 2002-2003", p.9.

3.4.5 The sustaining of momentum

Further success of all these counter-terrorism measures finally depends on the will of all parties concerned with the counter-terrorism campaign to follow up on these international efforts.[160] Indeed, every party has to take responsibility for maintaining the momentum in its own area. As far as the Security Council is concerned, it has made efforts in this context by way of adopting subsequent resolutions to urge all states, international, and regional organisations to implement the 1373 and the 1390 mandate as is illustrated by the Resolution 1455, 1456, 1535, 1566, etc.

Another point of note is to strengthen the CTC operation. If the Security Council could be said to be in the centre of the counter-terrorism campaign, the CTC could be said to be at the heart of that campaign. It is the CTC that helps and urges states to implement the instructions of the Security Council and other relevant organisations, and at the same time, coordinates and encourages other international and regional organisations to participate in combating terrorism. Thus, given the role of the CTC as an engine in the counter-terrorism campaign with a capacity to make a huge difference to the maintenance of momentum, it seems better to "become something more: a full-time, professional and global body of experts, working with the Security Council, but following up all avenues which resolution 1373 had opened".[161] In this vein, the revitalisation process of the CTC initiated by Resolution 1535 constitute a step forward. Particularly, the establishment of the CTED and "on-site" visits by the CTC would have substantial impacts on member states in terms of securing their continuous engagement in the counter-terrorism campaign.

3.5 Conclusion

This chapter has outlined the two parallel approaches to the suppression of financing of terrorism at the Security Council level since 9/11. One is the structural approach characterised by Resolution 1373 and its CTC. The other is the operational approach represented by Resolution 1390 and its Sanctions Committee. Both approaches are mutually complementary in that one is aimed at establishing a permanent counter-terrorism infrastructure in the international society and the

---

[160] The importance of sustaining momentum is frequently noted. See, e.g., Policy Working Group Report, *supra* note 41, p.11; UN, "Memorandum From the Russian Federation Submitted in accordance with Paragraph 12 of Security Council Resolution 1456 (2003) on the Issue of Combating International Terrorism" S/2003/191, 18 February 2003, p.4; UN, Press Release, SG/SM/8583, 20 January 2003.

[161] Jeremy Greenstock, the Chairman of the CTC, at the Security Council Meeting on Terrorism on 4 April 2000 (UN, Press Release, SC/7718, 4 April 2003).

other attempts to hunt down Usama bin Laden and his Al-Qaida network that are posing imminent threat to the international community.

However, these parallel efforts within the Security Council need some improvement to further its advancement. First of all, the Security Council needs to indicate some alternative ways to define terrorism. Then, the Security Council also needs to pay attention to procedural issues such as the establishment of a fair and objective procedure of listing and de-listing of terrorists, and the avoidance of duplication. However, needless to say, all these efforts should be made with continuous momentum to bear fruit in the field of the suppression of the financing of terrorism.

Lastly, considering that the Security Council noted the link between terrorism and other transnational crimes, and has indicated its will to deal with transnational crimes in the course of combating terrorism, the international community needs to be aware that the window of opportunity in this area is wide open, and consequently to make all efforts to ensure the best use of it.

4 Standards set by Specialist Bodies since 9/11

4.1 Introduction

The September 11th attack dramatically changed the legal regime in the field of the suppression of the financing of terrorism by inducing the full-scale involvement of the Security Council and the consequent introduction in this area of its *binding* Chapter VII powers.[1] Nevertheless, the work of the specialist bodies such as the FATF is of note since they have also played an important role in this area, especially in laying the groundwork long before 9/11.[2] Interestingly, their approach was quite distinct from that of the Security Council in the sense that importantly they rely upon what are technically *non-binding* standards supported by a soft enforcement mechanism. The approach of these specialist bodies deviates from the traditional law-making process of public international law such as custom and treaty. However, even though they employ non-binding methods, the approach of the specialist bodies does not appear to be less effective than that of the Security Council which can be characterised as a hard law approach.[3] Rather, the specialist bodies seem to be more effective and work more efficiently in some senses.[4] 9/11 has also brought about changes in the work of these specialist bodies through the

---

[1] See, e.g, the Security Council Resolutions 1267 (1999), 1333 (2000), 1363 (2001), 1373 (2001) and 1390 (2002).

[2] The FATF was established in 1989, and at first it dealt with the money laundering in the context of drug trafficking, but later in 1996 its mandate was extended to the proceeds of other crimes including indirectly financing of terrorism. See, e.g. FATF, *Annual Report: 1995-1996*, on 28 June 1996, p.7; the 1996 Recommendation 4 and its interpretative note.

[3] See, e.g., S/RES/1373, para. 1; UN, S/RES1390, para. 1. As mentioned below, there are three major standards to define hard law, and the resolutions of the Security Council seem to meet all these standards. For discussions on the effectiveness of soft law, see, Section 4.4 of this chapter.

[4] For example, the soft law approach of specialist bodies can avoid difficulties involved in the law-making process by relieving a state's concern about their sovereignty or may supplement the interpretation of already-existing hard law by fleshing out its simple structure. For details, see, the utility of soft law in Section 4.1.2 of this chapter.

attraction of more participants and strengthening of their commitment in the campaign.[5]

Bearing this perspective in mind, this chapter will analyse developing international standards in the field of the suppression of the financing of terrorism. Then, the next chapter (Chapter Five) will examine the way in which these standards are monitored and enforced. At the end of these two chapters, note will also be made of the soft law implication of these activities. Given the weight of soft law in the main discussions of these two chapters, it firstly would be of value to review what soft law means.

4.1.1 The definition of soft law

In general, there is no clear-cut definition of soft law,[6] but several elements have been identified as relevant in making a distinction between soft law and hard law. Among these, the absence of three prevalent elements can be noted as follows: (a) a binding force; (b) precision; and, (c) compulsory binding dispute settlement.[7]

Firstly, in terms of a binding force, if an international agreement has a legal binding force it might be hard law, whereas if not, it has definitely a soft law element. By this standard, the legal form is decisive in differentiating soft law from hard law.[8] If the form is a treaty, it cannot be soft law under this category.[9] Gener-

---

[5]   As mentioned below, since 9/11, actors not related to the banking sector have actively involved in the AML/CFT areas, and, furthermore, the regulatory regime goes deeply into the heart of supervisory bodies and the supervised businesses as illustrated by the 2003 FATF Forty Recommendations and the Nine Special Recommendations.

[6]   Indeed, the difficulty of defining soft law is expressed by many scholars. See, e.g., Schachter O (1997) "The Twilight Existence of Nonbinding International Agreement", *The American Journal of International Law*, vol.71, pp.297-298; Chinkin CM (1989) "The Challenge of Soft Law: Development and Change in International Law", *International and Comparative Law Quarterly*, vol.38, p.852; Tadeusz GW (1984) "A Framework for Understanding "Soft Law"", *McGill Law Journal*, vol.30, p.44; Guzman AT (2002) "A Compliance-Based Theory of International Law", *California Law Review*, vol.90, pp.1879-1880.

[7]   See, Boyle AE (1999) "Some Reflection on the Relationship of Treaties and Soft Law", *International and Comparative Law Quarterly*, vol. 48, pp.901-902; Chinkin CM, *supra* note 6, p.852; Abbott KW, Snidal D (2000) "Hard and Soft Law in International Governance", *International Organization*, vol.54, pp.422-424; Elias O, Lim C (1997) " 'General Principle of Law', 'Soft' Law and the Identification of International Law", *Netherlands Yearbook of International Law*, vol.28, pp.44-45; Cullet P (1999) "Differential Treatment In International Law: Towards A New Paradigm of Inter-State Relations", *European Journal of International Law*, vol.10, p.575.

[8]   Boyle AE, *supra* note 7, p.902.

[9]   *Ibid.*

ally, resolutions of the UN General Assembly, guidelines and declarations of international conferences are cases in point.[10] In a counter-terrorist financing context, the FATF's 2003 Forty Recommendations and the Nine Special Recommendations on Terrorist Financing can be pointed out.

Secondly, depending on the precision of the contents of law, a distinction can be made between soft law and hard law.[11] From this perspective, hard law involves clear and specific commitments whereas soft law is more open-textured or general in its content.[12] Soft law under this category may be found even in a binding treaty. Particularly, some provisions are considered to be soft in that they impose no real obligations on the parties.[13] For example, Article 12 of the International Convention for the Suppression of the Financing of Terrorism (ICSFT) imposes a binding obligation on all state parties to afford one another the greatest measure of assistance in criminal matters, but it is merely hortatory and not precise enough to identify a concrete violation of the obligation of the convention in a real situation.

Thirdly, in respect of methods of dispute settlement, a contrast can be made between soft law and hard law. In a case of non-compliance, hard law can resort to compulsory binding settlement of disputes, while soft law makes use of non-binding compliance procedures.[14] The obvious cases of hard law in this category are what involves the Chapter VII powers of the Security Council. As was seen in Chapter Three of this study, the operative paragraphs of Resolution 1373 and 1390 are good examples.[15] Put simply, the financing of terrorism as well as terrorism itself are prohibited under international law and those who violate this mandate, whether states or individuals, are subject to international sanctions imposed by the Security Council. Moreover, the 1982 UN Convention on the Law of the Sea is another case in point, equipped as it is with a sophisticated scheme for compulsory dispute settlement involving various international courts.[16] By way of contrast, some soft law instruments have recourse to soft enforcement which consists of a

---

[10] *Ibid.*

[11] Dupuy PM (1991) "Soft law and the International Law of the Environment", *Michigan Journal of International Law*, vol.12, pp.429-430; Baxter RR (1980) "International Law in "Her Infinite Variety"", *International and Comparative Law Quarterly*, vol.29, pp.561-562; Chinkin CM, *supra* note 6, p.851; Elias O, Lim C, *supra* note 7, p.45.

[12] Boyle AE, *supra* note 7, p.902.

[13] *Ibid.*, p.906.

[14] *Ibid.,* p.909; Abbott KW, Snidal D, *supra* note 7, p. 421; Tadeusz GW, *supra* note 6, p.49.

[15] Resolution 1373, para.1 and 2; Resolution 1390, para.1 and 2.

[16] Boyle AE, *supra* note 7, p.909. For details of the scheme, see, Boyle AE (1997) "Dispute Settlement and the Law of the Sea Convention: Problems of Fragmentation and Jurisdiction", *International and Comparative Law Quarterly,* vol.46, p.37.

wide variety of methods of "inducements" and "value deprivations".[17] The combination of non-confrontational inducement and value deprivation is best exemplified by the non-compliance procedure adopted by the parties to the 1987 Montreal Protocol to the 1985 Ozone Convention.[18] When a non-compliant state is identified by an Implementation Committee of the convention, the state may be given financial and/or technical assistance as an incentive to secure compliance. If these measures are inadequate, a caution can be issued or as a last resort, rights and privileges under the treaty can be suspended in the full Meeting of the Parties in accordance with the law of treaties.[19]

Lastly it should be pointed out that, in reality, all these standards do not exist separately but work in close connection with each other. In other words, when all these standards are satisfied, an international instrument can be called *hard law* in its true sense, but "the realm of soft law begins" once one of these standards is not met and "this softening can occur in varying degrees".[20] Thus, every international agreement can be placed somewhere on the broad spectrum between hard law and soft law that exist at either end in their strictest sense.

4.1.2 The utility of soft law

The contribution that soft law makes to the development of international law cannot be ignored for the following reasons. Firstly, soft law can avoid difficulties involved in the law-making process in a specific area by relieving a state's concern about its sovereignty.[21] By adopting a non-binding form or vague provisions or a soft enforcement mechanism, soft law may make it possible for states to reach an agreement faster or sometimes with a more detailed content.[22] Furthermore, soft law makes it easier for states to avoid the domestic parliamentary ratification process, or to amend or replace its text in the future.[23] Soft law may also provide more immediate evidence of international support and consensus than a treaty, given

---

[17] Chinkin CM, *supra* note 6, p.862; Bothe M (1980) "Legal and Non-Legal Norms— A Meaningful Distinction in International Relations?", *Netherlands Yearbook of International Law*, vol.11, p.88; Tadeusz GW, *supra* note 6, p.48; Contini P, Sand PH (1972) "Methods to Expedite Environment Protection: International Ecostandards", *The American Journal of International Law*, vol.66, p.54.

[18] *Ibid.*, p.910. For the text of the non-compliance procedure revised in 1992, see, UN Doc., UNEP/OzL.Pro/WG.3/3/3, 9 November 1991 <http://www.unep.org/ozone/Meeting_Documents/adhoc/adhoc-nc-3-3-3.91-04-08.pdf>.

[19] *Ibid.*

[20] Abbott KW, Snidal D, *supra* note 7, p.422.

[21] Bothe M, *supra* note 17, p.90, 92; Elias O, Lim C, *supra* note 7, p.45.

[22] Bothe M, *supra* note 17, pp.90-92; Lipson C (1991) "Why are some international agreements informal?", *International Organization*, vol.45, pp.514-518.

[23] Boyle AE, *supra* note7, p.903; Bothe M, *supra* note 17, p.90.

that the legal effect of a treaty is often heavily qualified by reservations and it takes time to ratify a multilateral treaty and secure its entry into force.[24] Perhaps, this role of soft law to facilitate a law-making process is best illustrated by the success of the OECD in its dealing with the issue of corruption. The OECD first adopted a soft law approach in the law-making process and it eventually brought about the conclusion of a binding treaty.[25]

Secondly, soft law may supplement the interpretation or implementation of already-existing hard law by fleshing out its simple structure.[26] For instance, UN General Assembly Resolution 1514 (1960) provided authoritative guidance to the interpretation of the UN Charter as indicated in *Western Sahara Advisory Opinion* (1975).[27] So to speak, the principle of self-determination enshrined in Articles 1 and 55 of the UN Charter can be interpreted by way of Resolution 1514 to support the process of decolonisation based on a free and genuine expression of the will of the peoples concerned.[28] Furthermore, as an example of complementing implementation, the 2003 FATF Forty Recommendations and Nine Special Recommendations on Terrorist Financing can be quoted. The recommendations and their interpretative notes provide detailed guidelines on many issues related to the implementation of Resolution 1373, 1390 and the ICSFT, such as how to criminalise terrorist financing in a national legal system or how to deal with non-profit charity organisations.

Thirdly, soft law may contribute to the formation of hard law in a specific area. Soft law instruments may lead to the conclusion of a new treaty as exemplified by the relationship between UN General Assembly Resolution XVIII on Outer Space of 1963 and the Treaty on Outer Space of 1967.[29] Furthermore, soft law may generate widespread and consistent state practice and/or provide evidence of *opinio juris* in support of customary law. To begin with, non-binding soft law may generate state practice by way of creating the expectations that have an impact on state behaviour in a specific area.[30] This is true especially where there are no rules or standards for states to benchmark. It would be far better for states to have some kind of guidance rather than an *all or nothing* situation when faced with uncer-

---

[24] Boyle AE, *supra* note 7, p.903; Bothe M, *supra* note 17, p.92.

[25] For the detailed process how soft law approach enmeshed negotiating governments over time, see, Abbott KW (2001) "Rule-Making in the WTO: Lessons From the Case of Bribery and Corruption", *Journal of International Economic Law,* vol.4, p.275.

[26] Hillgenberg H (1999) "A Fresh Look at Soft Law", *European Journal of International Law*, vol.10, p.506.

[27] Boyle AE, *supra* note 7, p.905.

[28] UNGA Resolution 1514(1960) titled "Declaration on the Granting of Independence to Colonial Countries and People". See also, *Western Sahara Advisory Opinion*(1975), I.C.J. Report, para. 55, 57 and 58.

[29] Baxter RR, *supra* note 11, p.564.

[30] See, e.g, Tadeusz GW, *supra* note 6, pp.46-47; Chinkin CM, *supra* note 6, p.862.

tainty in a certain area.[31] The legal vacuum created by the rapid development of space technology in the 1960s, and the use of UN General Assembly Resolution XVIII as mentioned above is once again a good example.[32] Also, soft law instruments may provide evidence of *opinio juris* as shown in the *Nicaragua Case* (1986) with regard to the legal effects of several UN General Assembly resolutions.[33]

In sum, from these useful aspects of soft law, it can hardly be denied that soft law constitutes "another tool in the professional lawyer's armoury".[34]

4.2 The Major International Standard Setter: the FATF

4.2.1 Context

Following the 9/11 attack the FATF met in extraordinary session on 29-30 October 2001 in Washington DC to consider necessary measures to combat terrorist financing activities. Consequently, the FATF expanded its mandate to formally include terrorist financing, and adopted Eight Special Recommendations to this end.[35]

In addition, action was taken to amend the 1996 version of the Forty Recommendations on money laundering. It was a natural response from the FATF given that the Forty Recommendations should be subject to periodic review to reflect the ever-developing techniques and methods used by criminals as recognised in the 1990 annual report.[36] The experience gained through the Non-Cooperative Countries and Territories (NCCT) process also provided a catalyst for the FATF decision to review and revise the 1996 version of the Forty Recommendations.[37] To this end, the FATF issued a public consultation document, entitled "Review of the FATF Forty Recommendations: Consultation Paper" on 30 May 2002, which examined many issues of concern and proposed options for dealing with them. All

---

[31] Contini P, Sand PH, *supra* note 17, p.49; Gold J (1983) "Strengthening the Soft International Law of Exchange Arrangements", *The American Journal of International Law*, vol.77, p.443.

[32] For example, para. 3 declares the prohibition of sovereignty claims to outer space and celestial bodies, and para. 8 provides for the liability of a state for the harm done by its object launched in outer space.

[33] *Military and Paramilitary Activities in and against Nicaragua*(1986), I.C.J. Report, para. 188.

[34] Boyle AE, *supra* note 7, p.913.

[35] FATF, "Annual Report: 2001-2002", 21 June 2002, p.4.

[36] FATF, "Annual Report: 1989-1990", 7 February 1990, p.16.

[37] FATF, "Annual Report: 2002-2003", 20 June 2003, p.4.

states, international organisations, and interested parties were invited to provide their comments to the FATF on these issues.[38] As a result, new Forty Recommendations were formally agreed at the June 2003 Plenary Meeting in Berlin.[39] More recently, cash smuggling has been repeatedly highlighted as one of the major tools for terrorist financing,[40] and the FATF consequently issued Special Recommendation IX (cash couriers) on 22 October 2004, thus making a total of Nine Special Recommendations. At this point, however, it should be noted that the revised Forty Recommendations are not separated from the Nine Special Recommendations, but should be read together, thus providing a combined set of enhanced measures to combat terrorist financing.[41]

Since its inception in 1989, the FATF which has been operating under a temporary life-span, has made considerable progress in the fight against money laundering and the financing of terrorism. However, it is clear that the FATF still has a major task to perform in continuing to set standards, considering the increasingly sophisticated international financial system.[42] In this context, the mandate of the FATF was extended for a further eight years (i.e., expiration of the mandate in December 2012) to promote better the AML/CFT strategy worldwide.[43]

---

[38] FATF, "Review of the FATF Forty Recommendations: Consultation Paper", 30 May 2002, pp.3-4.

[39] FATF, "Annual Report: 2002-2003", 20 June 2003, p.4.

[40] See its use for Bali bombing (2002) as illustrated in APG, "APG Typologies Report 2003-04", June 2004, p.38.

[41] FATF, "Annual Report: 2002-2003", 20 June 2003, p.5.

[42] *Ibid.*, p.1.

[43] FATF, "Annual Report: 2003-2004", 2 July 2004, p.1; FATF, "Mandate For the Future of the FATF", 14 May 2004, p.4.
The FATF was established by the G-7 Economic Summit in Paris in July 1989 as an independent international body whose Secretariat is housed at the OECD. It is a temporary body and its mandate has been renewed four times (1989-1994,1994-1999,1999-2004, 2004-2012). The thirty-one member jurisdiction of the FATF are: Argentina; Australia; Belgium; Brazil; Canada; Denmark; Finland; France; Germany; Greece; Hong Kong, China; Iceland; Italy; Japan; Luxembourg; Mexico; the Kingdom of the Netherlands; New Zealand; Norway; Portugal; the Russian Federation; Singapore; South Africa; Spain; Sweden; Switzerland; Turkey; the United Kingdom; and, the United States. The European Commission and the Gulf-Cooperation Council are also FATF members. In addition, the People's Republic of China is an observer.

4.2.2 The general framework of the Nine Special Recommendations on Terrorist Financing and the 2003 Forty Recommendations

4.2.2.1 Major changes

First of all, the FATF began to make direct reference to the financing of terrorism in its standards. Indeed, it goes without saying that the Special Recommendations have been adopted for the sole purpose of dealing with terrorist financing. Nevertheless, the issue of terrorist financing has been once again highlighted and has also been given a significant status in the 2003 Forty Recommendations as illustrated by the subtitles that afford equal footing to money laundering and terrorist financing.[44]

Secondly, under the new regime, the scope of application *ratione personae* has been substantially extended to include non-financial institutions with explicit enumeration,[45] such as casinos, real estate agents, dealers in precious metals and stones, lawyers, notaries, other independent legal professionals and accountants, and trust and company service providers.[46]

Thirdly, the standards themselves have also become more sophisticated as illustrated by the detailed provisions on customer due diligence (CDD) measures in general and specifications on the CDD procedures in relation to individual categories of subjects and activities such as politically exposed persons, intermediaries and cross-border correspondent banking.[47]

Fourthly, in line with the above, attempts have also been made to alleviate the consequent burden in terms of implementation and in supervision,[48] such as the introduction of a risk-based approach[49]; the exemption of non-financial institutions

---

[44] See the subtitles of the 2003 Forty Recommendations in the following;
"B. Measures to be taken by financial institutions and non-financial businesses and
Professions to prevent *money laundering* and *terrorist financing*;
C. Institutional and other measures necessary in systems for combating *money
laundering* and *terrorist financing*"

[45] Recommendations 12, 16, and 24.

[46] For the examples of these professions' involvement in money laundering, See, e.g., Egmont Group, "FIU's in action: 100 cases from the Egmont Group", 2000, pp.50-69; Bell RE (2002) "The Prosecution of Lawyers for Money Laundering Offences", *Journal of Money Laundering Control,* vol.1, no.1, pp. 17-22.

[47] Recommendations 5-9.

[48] IMF (2004) *Financial Intelligence Unit: An Overview*, pp.39-42.

[49] Of course, in 1990 and 1996 versions, the elements of risk based approach existed such as the reporting obligation based on the suspicion which stood in contrast with the objective threshold model. However, in 2003, this trend becomes stronger as illustrated by Recommendations 5, 23, and 24. Risk based approach allows the discretion of individual states and makes the application of AML/CFT framework flexible according to each

from the strict application of "no professional secrecy privilege" in respect of sus-picious transaction reports[50]; lenient standards of "no-tipping off" for non-financial institutions; and, the narrowing down of the scope of activities of non-financial institutions that are subject to the reporting of suspicious transactions.[51] Indeed, these measures seems to be an effort to guarantee the successful operation of the Anti-Money Laundering and Combating the Financing of Terrorism (AML/CFT) regime, while at the same time minimising the accompanying cost such as duplication of resources and the resistance from related sectors.

Fifthly, the concept of the FIU has been explicitly dealt with for the first time in the main text of the Forty Recommendations. Given the significance of the role of the FIU in the public, private and international sectors, it seems clear that this change will make a great contribution to the successful worldwide operation of the AML/CFT framework.

Lastly but interestingly, specific reference is increasingly made to the standards set by other organisations in the text of the 2003 Forty Recommendations.[52] For example, in the 1990 Forty Recommendations, only the 1988 Vienna Convention and the then draft Convention of the Council of Europe on Confiscation of the Proceeds from Offences were referred to.[53] In the 1996 Forty Recommendations, nothing changed except the title of the Council of Europe Convention (1990) since that convention had been finally agreed. However, in the Special Recommenda-tions and the 2003 version of the Forty Recommendations,[54] in addition to the above, specific reference has been made to numerous other standards such as the International Convention for the Suppression of the Financing of Terrorism (ICSFT) (1999), the Security Council Resolution 1373 (2001),[55] the 2000 Palermo Convention, "Core Principles",[56] and the 2002 Inter-American Convention against

---

state's own assessment of the vulnerability of a certain domestic sector. See, FATF, "Annual Report: 2002-2003", 20 June 2003, p.7; Interpretative Note to Recommenda-tion 5, para. 9-13. For further discussions on the application of this concept in the con-text of the Forty Recommendations, see, FATF, "Review of the FATF Forty Recom-mendations: Consultation Paper", pp.22-35.

[50] Recommendation 16; Interpretative Note to Recommendation 16.

[51] Recommendation 16. For the detailed discussion on the qualifications imposed on the reporting of suspicious transaction in relation to non-financial institutions, see, FATF, "Review of the FATF Forty Recommendations: Consultation Paper", 30 May 2002, p.86, 90, 94, 98, 101, 106, and 109.

[52] I am indebted to Professor Gilmore WC for sparking this point.

[53] The 1990 Recommendations 1, 4, 6, 8, and 35.

[54] The 2003 Recommendations 1,2,3, 23, and 35.

[55] The Special Recommendation 1 in respect of Resolution 1373.

[56] The Glossary of the 2003 Forty Recommendations defines the Core Principles as fol-lows:

Terrorism. In some sense this is understandable because the FATF alone is not in a position to cover every aspect of the counter-measures, given the fast-developing techniques of money laundering and terrorist financing and the interdisciplinary nature of such measures. Accordingly, the standards set by other organisations are believed to significantly complement the gap in applying the FATF Forty Recommendations to a specific area of their responsibility. In the following, the changes will be analysed in more detail under the specific categories of the AML/CFT framework.[57]

4.2.2.2 The criminal justice measures in the public sector

The criminalisation of the financing of terrorism and money laundering[58]

Special Recommendation II provides that each country should criminalise the financing of terrorism, terrorist acts and terrorist organisations, and should also ensure such offences are designated as money laundering predicate offences.[59] In addition, the revised 2003 Recommendation 1 stipulates that countries should apply the crime of money laundering to all serious offences, with a view to including the widest range of predicate offences. To this end, the recommendation suggests

---

"The Core Principles refers to the Core Principles for Effective Banking Supervision issued by the Basel Committee on Banking Supervision, the Objective and Principles for Securities Regulation issued by the International Organisation of Securities Commissions, and the Insurance Supervisory Principles issued by the International Association of Insurance Supervisors."

[57] The AML/CFT framework can be divided into four categories: (a) public sector; (b) private sector; (c) a bridging mechanism; and, (d) international cooperation. For backgrounds of this categorisation, see, Gilmore WC (2004) *Dirty Money: The evolution of international measures to counter money laundering and the financing of terrorism*, 3rd edn, pp.19-23 and pp.93-94; Mitsilegas V (2003) *Money Laundering Counter-Measures in the European Union: A New Paradigm of Security Governance versus Fundamental Legal Principles*, pp.8-14; UN (1998) "Commentary on the United Nations Convention Against Illicit Traffic in Narcotic Drugs and Psychotropic Substances 1988", pp.65-70. For further details, see also, Section 2.3.1.1 of Chapter Two.

[58] For the justification for criminalisation of the financing of terrorism, see Section 2.3.2.3 of Chapter Two.

[59] Generally, money laundering predicate offence means the original offence that precedes money laundering offence. However, there is some controversy on the nature of financing of terrorism as money laundering predicate offences because in some case, it is difficult to prove the unlawfulness of the money related to terrorism when terrorist activity has not taken place yet. For a detailed discussion, see, e.g., Kersten A (2002) "Financing of Terrorism—A Predicate Offence to Money Laundering?". In: Pieth M (ed) *Financing of Terrorism*, See also, FATF, "Interpretative Note to Special Recommendation II", 2 July 2004.

three approaches to describe predicate offences: an all-inclusive approach, a threshold approach and a list approach. The all-inclusive approach means that all serious offences could be predicate offences. The threshold approach describes a predicate offence by reference to a threshold linked either to a category of serious offences or to the penalty of imprisonment. Lastly, the list approach simply enumerates a list of predicate offences. Of course, countries could use a combination of all three approaches. However, whichever approach is adopted, Recommendation 1 makes it mandatory that predicate offences should comprise at a minimum the designated categories of offences in the Glossary of the 2003 text.[60] This specifically includes terrorist financing.

Moreover, Recommendation 1 attempts to remove jurisdictional obstacles based on the territoriality of the offence by stipulating that predicate offences should be extended to conduct that occurred in another country, which constitutes an offence in that country, and which would have constituted a predicate offence had it occurred domestically.[61] However, Recommendation 1 does not make it obligatory to apply the offence of money laundering to persons who committed the predicate offence.[62] These measures constitute considerable progress in relation to the criminalisation aspect of terrorist financing and associated money laundering,

---

[60] The designated categories of offences by the FATF are as follows:
  - Participation in an organised criminal group and racketeering;
  - Terrorism, including terrorist financing;
  - Trafficking in human beings and migrant smuggling;
  - Sexual exploitation, including sexual exploitation of children;
  - Illicit trafficking in narcotic drugs and psychotropic substances;
  - Illicit arms trafficking;
  - Illicit trafficking in stolen and other goods;
  - Corruption and bribery;
  - Fraud;
  - Counterfeiting currency;
  - Counterfeiting and piracy of products;
  - Environmental crime;
  - Murder, grievous bodily injury;
  - Kidnapping, illegal restraint and hostage-taking;
  - Robbery or theft;
  - Smuggling;
  - Extortion;
  - Forgery;
  - Piracy; and,
  - Insider trading and market manipulation.
[61] Recommendation 1, para. 5.
[62] Recommendation 1, para. 6. For a relevant discussion, see, Schott PA (2003) *Reference Guide to Anti-Money Laundering and Combating the Financing of Terrorism*, p.V-10.

particularly given that the 1996 Forty Recommendations placed the decision of predicate offences at the discretion of individual countries without giving any detailed guidance, let alone mentioning terrorism itself.[63]

Confiscation

Special Recommendation III provides that each country should implement measures to freeze terrorist-related funds or assets in accordance with relevant UN resolutions, and should have measures in place that would enable the competent authorities to seize and confiscate them. Moreover, its interpretative note and best practices paper provide additional guidance to strengthen the freezing regime as well as facilitating cooperation with foreign governments and the private sector, and subsequent confiscation.[64]

Furthermore, a major breakthrough was made in the revised 2003 Recommendation 3 for the purpose of strengthening confiscation measures.[65] To begin with, the revised recommendation cautiously introduces the controversial concept of civil confiscation by stipulating that countries may consider adopting measures that allow such proceeds or instrumentalities to be confiscated without requiring a criminal conviction.[66] What is more, the recommendation also prudently touches upon a concept of the reversed burden of proof, a powerful legal tool, by saying that "countries may require an offender to demonstrate the lawful origin of the property alleged to be liable to confiscation".[67]

---

[63] The 1996 Recommendation 4.

[64] FATF, "Interpretative Note to Special Recommendation III", 3 October 2003; FATF, "Freezing of Terrorist Assets: International Best Practice", 3 October 2003.

[65] Basically, it should be recalled that the provisional measures such as freezing and seizing that were included in the 1990 version, remain in the 2003 revised text.

[66] While criminal confiscation is operating *in personam* (against a specific person) and needs a criminal confiscation, the civil confiscation is an *in rem* (against a thing) procedure by nature and is not conditional upon a criminal confiscation. For an overview of the civil confiscation, see, Palm CW (1991) "RICO Forfeiture and the Eighth Amendment: When is Everything too much?", *The University of Pittsburgh Law Review*, vol.53, at section II; Jankowski MA (1990) "Tempering the Relation-Back Doctrine: A More Reasonable Approach to Civil Forfeiture in Drug Cases", *Virginia Law Review*, vol.76, p.165; Tonry M (1997) "Forfeiture Laws, Practices and Controversies in the US", *European Journal of Crime, Criminal Law and Criminal Justice*, vol.5, pp.294-307; Gallant MM (2005) *Money Laundering and the Proceeds of Crime: Economic Crime and Civil Remedies*. For details of civil confiscation, see also, Section 2.3.1.2 of Chapter Two, and its footnote 68.

[67] For justification of the reversed burden of proof, see, Stessens G (2000) *Money Laundering*, p.67; Bell RE (2003) "The Confiscation, Forfeiture and Disruption of Terrorist Finances", *Journal of Money Laundering Control*, vol.7, no.2, p.113; Gallant MM (2005) *Money Laundering and the Proceeds of Crime: Economic Crime and Civil*

Indeed, besides the system of value confiscation which had already found its place in the 1990 and 1996 Forty Recommendations, these new legal tools that appear in the main text of the revised recommendations would, without doubt, give added impetus to the development of confiscation law in the international arena.

4.2.2.3 The prevention of money laundering in the private sector[68]

Customer due diligence

The customer due diligence (CDD) regime in the Special Recommendations and the 2003 Forty Recommendations can be characterised by reference to three modifications: (a) the incorporation of the basic principles on the CDD process in more detail; (b) specification of the CDD procedures dependent upon the type of activity and subject; and, (c) the introduction of flexibility.[69]

First of all, as suggested in the review process,[70] the 2003 Forty Recommendations explicitly set out guidelines on the basic principles of the CDD process in the context of answering the following three questions:

- What does the customer due diligence process consist of ?;
- When does customer identification and verification need to be carried out ?;

Remedies, pp.30-32; Smellie A (2004) "Prosecutorial Challenges in Freezing and Forfeiting Proceeds of Transnational Crime and the Use of International Asset Sharing to Promote International Cooperation", *Journal of Money Laundering Control*, vol. 8, no.2, p.107. Particularly, Smellie notes that someone who acquires property lawfully should be able to establish that fact with relative ease as the standard is only a balance of probabilities. See also, Section 2.3.1.2 of Chapter Two and its footnote 68.

[68] This section should be understood in the context of the *responsibilisation* strategy. As explained in Chapter Two, since there is a limit to the capacity of a state in preventing crime in every corner of society in the modern era, contemporary governments have developed a strategy by which a government delegates its responsibility for crime control to relevant actors in the private sector. It regards the private sector as a valuable counterpart to share the burden of policing society and at the same time, attempts to utilise the expertise and resources of the private sector to the maximum. See, Garland D (1996) "The Limits of the Sovereign State: Strategies of Crime Control in Contemporary Society", *The British Journal of Criminology*, vol.36, p.448; Mitsilegas V, *supra* note 57, p.12.

[69] Basically, the CDD regime of the Special Recommendations and the 2003 Forty Recommendations is heavily influenced by the Basel Committee's "Customers due diligence for banks"(2001). For relevant discussions, see, Gilmore WC, *supra* note 57, p.108; Zagaris B (2003) "Basel Group Supports FATF's Revised Recommendations", *International Law Enforcement Reporter*, vol.19, issue 9, pp.333-334.

[70] FATF, "Review of the FATF Forty Recommendations: Consultation Paper", 30 May 2002, pp.9-10.

and,
- What should the obligations be if customer identification and verification cannot be carried out ?

With regard to the question "what", the revised Recommendation 5 enumerates four measures which are,

- Identifying the customer and verifying the customer's identity;
- Identifying the beneficial owner and verifying the identity of the beneficial owner;
- Obtaining information on the purpose and intended nature of the business relationship; and,
- Conducting ongoing due diligence on the business relationship and scrutiny of transactions.

Moreover, in respect of the question "when", the revised recommendation indicates four situations which are:

- Establishing business relations;
- Carrying out occasional transactions; (i) above the applicable threshold,[71] or ii) that are *wire transfers* in the circumstances covered by the Interpretative Note to Special Recommendation VII;
- There is a suspicion of money laundering or terrorist financing; or
- The financial institution has doubts about the veracity or adequacy of previously obtained customer identification data.

Lastly, in relation to the question of "what to do if the identification is not possible", the revised Recommendation 5 suggests that the financial institution:

- Should not open the account, commence business relations or perform transactions; or
- Should terminate the business relationship; and,
- Should consider making a suspicious transactions report in relation to the customer.[72]

---

[71] Interpretative Notes indicates the designated thresholds for transactions (under Recommendation 5 and 12) as follows:
- Financial Institutions (for occasional customers under Recommendation 5): USD/€15,000;
- Casinos, including internet casinos (under Recomendation12): USD/€3,000; and,
- For dealers in precious metals and dealers in precious stones when engaged in any cash transaction (under Recommendation 12 and 16): USD/€15,000.

[72] For the issue of simply attempted and not completed transactions, see, FATF, "Review of the FATF Forty Recommendations: Consultation Paper", 30 May 2002, p. 43.

Given that the 1996 version included some guidelines to the question of "what" and "when", the answer to the third question of "what to do if the identification is not possible" is of particular note in the context of change in the revised new text.

Secondly, the Special Recommendations and the 2003 Forty Recommendations afford distinctive treatment to some categories of *subject* and *activity*, by way of providing individual specifications on the CDD procedures in each case. To begin with, in respect of the *subject*, the 2003 Forty Recommendations allocate a single recommendation to the issue of a "politically exposed person", the content of which is a reflection of the guidelines set by the Basel Committee.[73] Also another independent recommendation is provided for the sole purpose of dealing with the matter of "intermediary or the third parties" which is also heavily influenced by the Basel Committee's guidance.[74] Moreover, in a very detailed independent recommendation, the 2003 version fully engages with the issue of "non-financial institutions". Without doubt, this special treatment of the non-financial institutions, so-called "gate keepers", has benefited greatly from the groundwork laid by the 2nd EU Money Laundering Directive (2001).[75] In the 2003 text, non-financial institutions are enumerated with limited situations which trigger CDD process.[76] The 2003 version also leaves the possibility of the expansion of the list open, by providing that "countries should consider applying the FATF Recommendations to businesses and professions, other than designated non-financial businesses and professions, that pose a money laundering or terrorist financing risk".[77] Furthermore, it should be remembered that cash smuggling was mentioned as a unique case of the responsibilisation strategy which is imposed, mainly, on an individual

---

[73] Recommendation 6. For the details of the guideline of the Basel Committee, see, BCBS, "Customer due diligence for banks", October 2001, pp.10-11. This document suggests several measures such as: banks should gather sufficient information from a new customer, and check quickly available information, in order to establish whether or not the customer is a PEP; banks should investigate the source of funds before accepting a PEP; and, the decision to open an account for a PEP should be taken at a senior management level.

[74] Recommendation 9. For the details of the guidelines of the Basel Committee, see, *ibid.*, pp.9-10. The document suggests that all beneficial owners of the accounts held by the intermediary should be identified. However, at the same time, the document show some flexibility by providing that banks may not need to look beyond the intermediary, for example, when the intermediary applies the same CDD standards to client as the bank does.

[75] See, the 2001 EU Directive Amending Council Directive 91/308/EEC on Prevention of the Use of the Financial System For the Purpose of Money Laundering, Article 2.a. For further details, see, Gilmore WC, *supra* note 57, p.109, pp.202-206.

[76] Recommendation 12. For a further discussion on the qualification, see, FATF, "Review of the FATF Forty Recommendations: Consultation Paper", 30 May 2002, pp.79-110.

[77] Recommendation 20.

rather than an institution.[78] Special Recommendation IX provides detailed guidelines on this issue such as the establishment of a declaration and disclosure system.[79]

Similarly, in respect to the *activity,* Special Recommendation VII throws the issue of "wire transfer" into sharp relief, by stipulating that countries should require financial institutions to include accurate and meaningful originator information on funds transfers and requiring that the information remain with the transfer through the payment chain. This special recommendation also requires the enhanced scrutiny of the transaction process.[80] Indeed, given the role of "wire transfers" in the events leading up to the 9/11 attack, this issue was deserving of special treatment by the FATF.[81] It is also dealt with in the 2003 Forty Recommendations in the context of customer due diligence.[82] Furthermore, the important issue of "correspondent banking" is highlighted in the 2003 Recommendation 7, again reflecting the influence of the Basel Committee's guidance.[83] The issue was once again emphasised in a subsequent recommendation on "shell banks".[84]

In sum, the sophistication of the CDD principles and the separate treatment of individual categories of problematic areas which are attempted under the new regime constitute a step forward, in comparison with the 1996 Forty Recommendations which simply contains a general description of the CDD principles with no specific treatment of individual issues in this area.

Thirdly, the 2003 Forty Recommendations introduce several elements of flexibility as a buffer, given that with the hardening of the AML/CFT regime relevant sectors would be overburdened, possibly incurring their resistance.[85] First of all, the concept of the "risk-based approach" comes to the fore in the 2003 Forty

---

[78] See, Section 2.3.1.3 of Chapter Two of this study, and its footnote 111.

[79] FATF, "Interpretative Note to Special Recommendation IX", 22 October 2004.

[80] FATF, "Interpretative Note to Special Recommendation VII", 10 June 2003.

[81] Wire transfer was the main tool of financing the 9/11 terrorists. See, Gunaratna R (2002) *Inside Al Qaeda: Global Network of Terror*, pp.64-65.

[82] Recommendation 5. For the text, see the italicised part of the text in relation to the question "when" as above.

[83] See, BCBS, "Customer due diligence for banks", October 2001, p.12. The Basel Committee suggests that banks should gather sufficient information about their respondent banks, and if they have strong suspicion on the nature of the respondent banks, they should refuse to enter into or continue a correspondent banking relationship with the respondent banks.

[84] The 2003 Recommendation 18.

[85] See, e.g., IMF (2004) *Financial Intelligence Unit: An Overview*, pp.39-42; Zagaris B (2005) "Lawyers Challenge to Money Laundering Delays Gatekeepers Law in Zimbabwe", *International Enforcement Law Reporter*, vol.21, issue 5, p.177.

Recommendations.[86] Through the adoption of this approach, the 2003 Forty Recommendations afford great discretion to individual countries in the implementation of relevant measures.[87] Namely, individual countries assess the risk of money laundering and terrorist financing in a specific domestic business sector, and based on the assessment, they may tailor the right level of measures to types of customers, transactions or products. This risk-based approach can be found across the main text of the 2003 Forty Recommendations. For instance, simplified and reduced CDD procedures are applied where the risk of terrorist financing and money laundering is lower, say because information on the identity of the customer and the beneficial owner is publicly available, or adequate checks and controls exists elsewhere in the national system or in any other jurisdiction.[88] Also financial institutions do not have to repeatedly identify and verify the identity of each customer whenever a customer conducts a transaction, unless they have doubts about the veracity of the relevant information.[89] Furthermore, in exceptional situations, the Interpretative Notes allow verification of customer identity to be completed

---

[86] See, e.g., Recommendations 5, 23 and 24. For the benefit of the "risk-based approach", see, Bazley S, Foster C (2004) *Money laundering: business compliance*, pp.118-119. Bazley and Foster emphasise that businesses which have limited financial resources must apply these resources in a responsible manner by concentrating on those areas that are more likely than others to face regulatory risk, and that regulators who also do not have limitless resources should have a process by which they can focus its attention on those things which matters most in the market place.

[87] For a comparison between simplified CDD procedures and reinforced CDD procedures resulting from the risk-based approach, see, Gilmore WC, *supra* note 57, pp.108-109.

[88] The Interpretative Notes for Recommendation 5 set out examples of customer where simplified or reduced CDD measures could apply are:
- Financial institution- where they are subject to requirement to combat money laundering and terrorist financing consistent with the FATF Recommendations and are supervised for compliance with those controls;
- Public companies that are subject to regulatory disclosure requirements;
- Government administrations or enterprises;
- Life insurance policies where the annual premium is no more than USD/ €1,000 or a single premium of no more than USD/ €2,500;
- Insurance policies for pension schemes if there is no surrender clause and the policy cannot be used as collateral; and,
- A pension, superannuation or similar scheme that provides retirement benefits to employees, where contributions are made by way of deduction from wages and the scheme rules do not permit the assignment of a member's interest under the scheme.

For the justification for the simplified CDD measures, see, FATF, "Review of the FATF Forty Recommendations: Consultation Paper", 30 May 2002, p.25.

[89] Interpretative Note to Recommendation 5, para.5.

after the establishment of the business relationship because it would be essential not to interrupt the normal conduct of business.[90]

Another element of flexibility at this stage can be found in connection with non-financial institutions. Being conscious of the rapid extension of regulations to non-financial institutions, the 2003 Forty Recommendations provide a kind of buffer zone. In the context of the CDD procedures, Recommendation 12 sets out some qualifications with regard to the scope of activities of non-financial institutions that are subject to the reporting of suspicious transaction.[91] For instance, dealers in precious metals and stones are required to apply CDD measures only when they engage in *any cash transactions* with customers equal to or above an applicable designated threshold.[92] Similar qualifications can be found in relation to other non-financial institutions and professions such as casinos, real estate agents, lawyers, and, trust and company service providers.[93]

---

[90] Interpretative Note to Recommendation 5, para.6. The examples include:
- Non face-to-face business;
- Security transactions; and,
- Life insurance business.

[91] Recommendation 16. For the detailed discussion on the qualifications imposed on the reporting of suspicious transaction in relation to non-financial institutions, see, FATF, "Review of the FATF Forty Recommendations: Consultation Paper", p.86, 90, 94, 98, 101, 106, and 109.

[92] Originally, there were three options as follows:
- Option 1: An agreed minimum list of dealers in high value items e.g., dealers in precious stones or metals, or in works of art or auctioneers;
- Option 2: Such other dealers in high value items as are perceived by each jurisdiction to be vulnerable to money laundering.
- Option3: Option 1or 2, but only if it involves cash transaction (including multiple linked transactions) exceeding a certain threshold e.g., USD/€15,000.

For the revised 2003 Forty Recommendations, the Option 3 was chosen. See, FATF, "Review of the FATF Forty Recommendations: Consultation Paper", p.89.

[93] For example, with regard to lawyers, notaries, other independent legal professionals and accountants, they do not have to exercise due diligence for all their activities but only for the following activities:
- Buying and selling of real estates;
- Managing of client money, securities or other assets;
- Management of bank, savings, or securities accounts;
- Organisation of contributions for the creation, operation or management of companies; and,
- Creation, operation or management of legal persons or arrangements, and buying and selling of business entities.

These provisions are heavily influenced by the 2nd EU money laundering directive (2001) and the limited Swiss approach. For relevant discussions, see, Gilmore WC, *su-*

Reporting obligation

Special Recommendation IV provides that if financial institutions or other businesses or entities suspect, or have reasonable grounds to suspect that funds are related in some way to terrorism, they should be required to report promptly their suspicions to the competent authorities. In the revised 2003 Recommendation 13, if a financial institution suspects or has reasonable grounds to suspect, that funds are the proceeds of a criminal activity, or are related to terrorist financing, it should be required, directly by law or regulation, to report promptly its suspicions to the financial intelligence unit (FIU).[94] By way of comparison with the 1996 Forty Recommendations, three changes are of note. Firstly, the requirement applies to both proceeds of a criminal activity and funds related to terrorist financing.[95] Secondly, the new regime now provides for a negligence standard as well, by adding "have reasonable grounds to suspect". Thus, it is clear that the obligation imposed on financial institutions becomes far stricter than before.[96] Thirdly, according to the Interpretative Notes, attempted suspicious transactions must also be reported regardless of the amount of the transaction. If a financial institution chooses not to enter into a suspicious transaction without reporting it, the suspected customer might go "on the loose", thus finding a loophole somewhere else.[97]

Interestingly, another element of flexibility can be found at this stage. The 2003 Recommendation 16 provides that non-financial businesses and professions such as lawyers, notaries, and accountants are not required to report their suspicions if

---

pra note 57, p.109; Zagaris B (2003) "FATF Gatekeepers Likely to Settle on a Modified Swiss Version of the Law", *International Enforcement Law Reporter*, vol.19, issue 7, pp.249-250.

[94] This is a suspicion-based reporting model. For an overview of this model, see, Stessens G (2000) *Money Laundering: A New International Law Enforcement Model*, p.161. For the comparison of a suspicion-based model and a threshold-based model, see, Noble PK, Golumbic CE (1998) "A New Anti-Crime Framework For the World: Merging The Objective and Subjective Models for Fighting Money Laundering", *New York University Journal of International Law and Politics*, vol. 30, p. 79; Grant TD (1995) "Toward a Swiss Solution for an American Problem: An Alternative Approach for Banks in the War on Drugs", *Annual Review of Banking Law*, vol.14, p.225. See also, Section 2.3.1.3 of Chapter Two of this book and its footnote 121.

[95] FATF, "Annual Report: 2002-2003", 20 June 2003, p.5.

[96] Indeed, by the negligence standard, it is not necessary to prove that a responsible officer actually suspected illegality, but just that a reasonable person should and would have suspected illegality based on the circumstances surrounding the transaction. Thus, the negligence standards test is generally regarded as a wider reporting requirement than the standard of intent. See, FATF, "Review of the FATF Forty Recommendations: Consultation Paper", p.43; FATF, "Guidance notes for the Special Recommendations on Terrorist Financing and the Self-Assessment Questionnaire", 27 March 2002, p.4.

[97] FATF, "Review of the FATF Forty Recommendations: Consultation Paper", p.43.

the relevant information was obtained in circumstances where they are subject to professional secrecy or legal professional privilege.[98] In addition, while the 1996 Forty Recommendations provided for a "no-tipping off" obligation in relation to financial institutions and the main text of the 2003 Recommendation 14(b) also adheres to this position, exceptions can be found only with regard to "non-financial businesses and professions". The Interpretative Note to Recommendation 14(b) says that "where lawyers, notaries......seek to dissuade a client from engaging in illegal activity, this does not amount to tipping off".[99] Indeed, these elements of flexibility once again prove the intention of the drafters of the 2003 Revised Forty Recommendations to alleviate the overburdening and to reduce the resistance in implementation of the international standards in specific sectors that come under the influence of AML/CFT regime.

Internal controls

The 2003 Recommendation 15 provides for internal controls by financial institutions and non-financial institutions themselves such as the development of internal policies and procedures, an ongoing training programme, and auditing procedures to test the entire system. This position is nearly identical to that of the 1996 position. However, interestingly, this provision is also permeated by an element of the "risk-based approach". For instance, the Interpretative Note to Recommendation 15 explains that the type and extent of measures to be taken for each of the requirements set out in the recommendation should be appropriate having regard to the risk of money laundering and terrorist financing and the size of the business.[100]

---

[98] A similar position can be found in the preamble of the 2nd EU Money Laundering Directive (2001) which stipulates that:

"Where independent members of professions providing legal advice which are legally recognised and controlled, such as lawyers, are ascertaining the legal position of a client or representing a client in legal proceedings, it would not be appropriate under the Directive to put these legal professionals in respect of these activities under an obligation to report suspicion of money laundering."

These difficulties in reconciling a reporting obligation with the professional secrecy rules have been frequently indicated in literature. For relevant discussions, see, e.g, Gilmore WC, *supra* note 57, pp.202-206; Mitsilegas V, *supra* note 57, pp.146-151; IMF (2004) *Financial Intelligence Unit*, pp.39-41. For an overview of professional confidentiality, see also, Auburn J (2000) *Legal Professional Privilege: Law and Theory*, pp.57-78.

[99] A similar attitude can be found in the recital 17 of the 2001 EU directive.

[100] To this end, first of all, it would be necessary to conduct a thorough risk assessment identifying the areas which are more likely than others to face a regulatory risk. For a relevant discussion, see, Bazley S, Foster C (2004) *Money laundering: business compliance*, p.118.

Supervision

The 2003 Forty Recommendations provide for supervision in a manner which is remarkably different from the treatment of the 1996 version.[101] It covers a wider area in scope and gives detailed guidelines to each type of institutions or businesses to be supervised.

Firstly, in relation to financial institutions, the 2003 Recommendation 23 divides them into two categories: one is of the sectors that are subject to the Core Principles, namely, banking, securities, and insurance industries, and the second is simply all other institutions. With regard to the first category, an element of flexibility can be identified again. Given that these three sectors already have supervisory mechanisms in place which are also relevant to money laundering and terrorist financing, they do not have to develop a new review system but deal with AML/CFT issues within their existing mechanisms, thus avoiding duplication of resources.[102] In respect of the second category (all other institutions), the approach of the 2003 Recommendation 23 is aimed at pulling these institutions into a formal supervisory regime, by providing that they should be licensed or registered, and then be subject to an effective system for monitoring. In fact, given that informal value transfer systems such as *hawala* are causing a serous problem in terms of the AML/CFT efforts, this approach had already been adopted in Special Recommendation VI.[103]

Secondly, for designated non-financial businesses and professions, the 2003 Recommendation 24 provides for a two-track treatment which is similar to the prior Recommendation 23 in terms of structure. Namely, one is to focus solely on

---

[101] Of course, the text of the 1996 Recommendations has an impact on the 2003 Recommendations in the sense that the 1996 Recommendations 26-29 have been integrated into the 2003 Recommendation 23 which describes the general principles of supervision.

[102] This attitude can be well illustrated by the Interpretative Note to the 2003 Recommendation 23 which says:

"Recommendation 23 should not be read so as to require the introduction of a system of regular review of licensing of controlling interests in financial institutions merely for anti-money laundering purposes, but as to stress the desirability of suitability review for controlling shareholders in financial institutions (banks and non-banks in particular) from a FATF point of view. Hence, where shareholder suitability (or "fit and proper") tests exist, the attention of supervisors should be drawn to their relevance for anti-money laundering purposes."

[103] For example, in order to prevent the abuse of alternative remittance systems, the paper "International best practices" points out five areas of focus: (a) Licensing/registration; (b) Identification and awareness raising; (c) Anti-money laundering regulations; (d) Compliance monitoring; and, (v) Sanctions. In each area, very detailed procedures are illustrated. For details, see, FATF, "Interpretative Note to Special Recommendation VI", 14 February 2003; FATF, "Combating the Abuse of Alternative Remittance System: International Best Practices", 20 June 2003.

casinos, and the other is to simply deal with all other businesses and professions in very general terms.[104] With regard to the former, the 2003 Recommendation 24 sets out several measures for effective supervision such as the licensing of casinos, the prevention of criminals from owning a casino in any form, etc. In respect of the second category (all other businesses or professions), the 2003 Recommendation 24(b) adopts an element of flexibility by stipulating that countries should ensure the effective supervision of all other designated non-financial businesses and professions "on a risk-sensitive basis". Indeed, the new 2003 regime affords discretion to individual countries in relation to supervision of non-financial businesses and professions.[105]

Thirdly, non-profit organisations which are highly likely to be misused by terrorists need to be supervised in a broader perspective. The structure and activities of non-profit organisations could be made in reality much more complicated and clandestine if they so intended. Thus, the ordinary AML/CFT measures employed by the private sector may not suffice to prevent the misuse of these organisations. In this regard, competent government authorities may need to supervise the overall activities of the entities rather than simply focusing on the financial aspects of their activities. With this perception, Special Recommendation VIII extends its supervisory regime to cover the entire management of non-profit organisations.[106] Of course, to this end, supervisory roles may be shared among relevant government authorities or law enforcement bodies if necessary.

Fourthly, minor changes can be seen in relation to a general requirement for supervision in the 2003 text. To begin with, while the 1996 version provided for only criminal corporate liability, the 2003 text mentions civil and administrative

---

[104] Recommendation 23:
- Financial institutions subject to the Core principles;
- All other institutions.

Recommendation 24:
- Casino;
- The other categories of designated non-financial businesses and professions.

[105] Also interestingly, and in a similar context of flexibility, the 2003 text sets out two options with regard to the question of who is going to supervise concerning the second category. Namely, the supervision may be performed either by a government authority or by an appropriate self-regulatory organisation. See, Recommendation 24, b).

[106] For detailed strategies, see, FATF, "Combating the Abuse of Non-Profit Organisations: International Best Practices", 11 October 2002. For example, the monitoring regime of governments could be extended to the following areas: the securing of the transparency of the financial accounting of non-profit organisations; the overseeing of the implementation of projects of non-profit organisations, including field inspection; the examination of the administrative and managerial documents, etc.

corporate liability as well.[107] Furthermore, the 2003 text stipulates that supervisors should have adequate powers to monitor and ensure compliance, including the authority to conduct inspections.[108] Last but not least, the 2003 text requires that the competent authorities should establish guidelines, and "provide feedback" for the purpose of assisting financial institutions and designated non-financial businesses and professions in applying the AML/CFT measures.[109]

4.2.2.4 The FIU: a bridging body between relevant sectors

The 2003 Forty Recommendations not only for the first time introduce the concept of the FIU but also provide added weight to the role of the FIU in the overall text.[110] With a summary definition of the FIU, the 2003 text provides for a state's obligation to establish its own FIU. Furthermore, it is also made obligatory for the private sector to submit a suspicious transaction report to the FIU.[111] The 2003 text also requires that states should provide their competent authorities with adequate powers, such as authority to get access to records held by financial institutions as well as adequate financial, human, and technical resources.[112] Moreover, the 2003 text indicates the importance of coordinating mechanism between all relevant par-

---

[107] The 1996 Recommendation 6 vs. the 2003 Recommendation 17. For discussions on the corporate liability between different legal systems, see also, Schott PA (2003) *Reference Guide to Anti-Money Laundering and Combating the Financing of Terrorism*, p.V-9; Council of Europe, "Liability of enterprises for offences: Recommendation No.R(88) adopted by the Committee of Ministers of the Council of Europe on 20 October 1988 and explanatory memorandum", 1990, pp.10-11; Savla S (2001) *Money Laundering and Financial Intermediaries*, pp.186-188.

[108] Recommendation 29.

[109] Recommendation 25. The provision of feedback is of significance to promote a climate of mutual trust between the public sector and the private sector. Thus it could elicit more proactive cooperation from the private sector. For detailed guidelines, see, FATF, "Annual Report 1997-1998: Annex E-Providing Feedback to Reporting Financial Institutions and Other Persons: Best Practice Guidelines", June 1998.

[110] With the introduction of the responsibilisation strategy into the private sector, there could be generated a flow of substantial financial data from the private sector to the public sector, for example by way of record-keeping and reporting requirements. The FIU acts as an intermediary between the two sectors in effect providing a service of information-filtering, and encouraging a climate of mutual trust (Stessens G (2000) *Money Laundering*, p.185). For detailed functions and categorisations of the FIU, see, IMF (2004) *Financial Intelligence Units: An Overview*, pp.33-82; Mitsilegas V, *supra* note 57, 2003, pp.155-170.

[111] Recommendations 13 and 26. For the revised definition of the FIU, see "Statement of Purpose of the Egmont Group of Financial Intelligence Units", 23 June 2004.

[112] Recommendations 28 and 30.

ties such as the FIU, law enforcement authorities, supervisors, and policy makers.[113]

4.2.2.5 International cooperation

Like the 1996 text, the 2003 Forty Recommendations provide for general principles on mutual legal assistance and extradition.[114] However, the revised text is
more developed and refined,[115] and in this regard, some changes are of particular
note. Firstly, the 2003 Recommendation 36 explicitly eliminates the fiscal offence
exception[116] and lifts financial institutions' secrecy rules in the context of international cooperation. Furthermore, given that the 2003 Recommendation 35 and
Special Recommendation I requires states to become party to and implement fully
the ICSFT (1999), it could be interpreted that the political offence exception is also implicitly eliminated in the counter-terrorist financing context.[117]

Secondly, the 2003 Recommendation 40 makes a most important addition for
the sole purpose of dealing with international cooperation other than mutual legal
assistance and extradition, namely cooperation between administrative and law enforcement authorities, including the FIUs.[118] This addition touches upon the matter
of a clear and effective gateway for cooperation.[119] It also supports the elimination

---

[113] Recommendation 31.

[114] For an overview of international cooperation in criminal matters, see, McClean D (2002)
International Co-operation in Civil and Criminal Matters.

[115] See, e.g., FATF, "Annual Report: 2002-2003", 20 June 2003, p.7.

[116] The specific removal of the fiscal offence exception was in the main due to the treatment
that this issue is afforded in NCCT criteria 18 and 22 (Gilmore WC, *supra* note 57,
p.107).

[117] Article 14 of the ICSFT stipulates:
"None of the offences set forth in article 2 shall be regarded for the purposes of extradition or mutual legal assistance as a political offence or as an offence connected with a
political offence or as an offence inspired by political motives."
For an overview of the relationship between terrorism and the political offence exemption, see, e.g., Gilbert G (1998) *Transnational Fugitive Offenders in International Law*,
pp.203-246, and pp.251-261.

[118] FATF, "Annual Report: 2002-2003", 20 June 2003, p.7.

[119] For example, Recommendation 40 indicates the manner in which to establish a gateway
as follows:
"Where the ability to obtain information sought by a foreign competent authority is not
within the mandate of its counterpart, countries are also encouraged to permit a prompt
and constructive exchange of information with non-counterparts. Co-operation with foreign authorities other than counterparts could occur directly or indirectly. When uncertain about the appropriate avenue to follow, competent authorities should first contact
their foreign counterparts for assistance."

of restrictive conditions such as the bank secrecy rule and fiscal offence exemption once again following the position of Recommendation 36.

4.3 Other Standard Setters

4.3.1 Context

Generally, the FATF has played a leading role in setting the relevant international standards. Yet, as the development of the techniques used by terrorists and criminals to finance their activities and launder their money involves not only financial institutions but also other businesses and professions, it has become clear that the FATF alone cannot cover every aspect of problems effectively. In this regard, there arises a need for setting standards in more detail which are tailored to specific businesses or professions, thus complementing the FATF framework. For example, the securities sector and insurance sectors were recently subsumed under the AML/CFT framework.[120] Furthermore, in order to facilitate cooperation between the government sector and the private sector, an association of the FIUs to set up their own standards and to promote best practices has also been established; namely, the Egmont Group.

In sum, the standards set by these specialist bodies are playing a significant role in supplementing the FATF Forty Recommendations. These complementary standards will be introduced briefly in what follows, but note should also be taken that the scope of these complementary international standards might be extended further, depending on the development in techniques of money laundering and terrorist financing, as pointed out in the 2003 Recommendation 20.

4.3.2 Basel Committee on Banking Supervision

The Basel Committee on Banking Supervision (BCBS) is a committee of banking supervisory authorities that was established by the central bank governors of the Group of 10 countries in 1974, and meets four times a year.[121] The BCBS has no

---

[120] See, e.g., FATF, "Methodology for Assessing Compliance with Anti-Money Laundering and Combating the Financing of Terrorism Standards", 11 October 2002; FATF, "Methodology for Assessing Compliance with the FATF 40 Recommendations and the FATF 8 Special Recommendations", 27 February 2004.

[121] Lee LLC (1999) "The Basle Accords as Soft law: Strengthening International Banking Supervision", *Virginia Journal of International Law*, vol.39, pp.16-17. See also (visited on 1 March 2004) <http://www.bis.org/bcbs>. As of 1 June 2005, its membership consists of 13 countries: Belgium, Canada, France, Germany, Italy, Japan, Luxembourg, the Netherlands, Spain, Sweden, Switzerland, United Kingdom and United States.

formal international supervisory authority, and its conclusions have no legally binding force.[122] Rather, "it formulates broad supervisory standards and guidelines and recommends statements of best practice in the expectation that individual authorities will take steps to implement them through detailed arrangements - statutory or otherwise - which are best suited to their own national systems".[123] The BCBS aims at closing gaps in international supervisory coverage, with a specific reference to two basic principles: that no foreign banking establishment should escape supervision; and, that supervision should be adequate.[124] To this end, the BCBS has issued a series of documents since 1975, and the following are of relevance in terms of the global AML/CFT framework. Already from the 1990s, the BCBS has expressed its will to support the work of the FATF, and recently, also engaged in the revision of the Forty Recommendations.[125]

4.3.2.1 Prevention of Criminal Use of the Banking System for the Purpose of Money-Laundering (1988)

This historic paper "Prevention of criminal use of the banking system for the purpose of money-laundering" is aimed at the outlining of basic principles and procedures that banks' managements should ensure are in place within their institutions with a view to assist in suppressing money laundering through the banking system, national and international.[126] This document is of value since it heavily influenced the initial composition of the 1990 Forty Recommendations with its four major principles: (a) know your customer; (b) conduct business in compliance with high ethical standards and laws; (c) cooperate fully with law enforcement authorities; and, (d) have in place policies and procedures to carry out the above three principles.[127]

4.3.2.2 Core Principles for Effective Banking Supervision (1997)

In September 1997, through the adoption of the document entitled "Core Principles for Effective Banking Supervision", the BCBS established twenty-five principles that need to be in place for a supervisory system to operate effectively. Besides the principles themselves, this document also includes explanations of the various methods which supervisors can employ to implement them. Indeed, these

---

[122] Schott PA, *supra* note 62, p.III-12.

[123] *Ibid.*, p.III-12.

[124] (visited on 1 June 2005) <http://www.bis.org/bcbs/aboutbcbs.htm>.

[125] FATF, "Methodology for Assessing Compliance with Anti-Money Laundering and Combating the Financing of Terrorism Standards", 11 October 2002, p.4; FATF, "Annual Report: 2002-2003", 20 June 2003, p.4.

[126] Schott PA, *supra* note 62, p.III-13.

[127] For a further analysis, see, Drage J (1993) "Countering Money Laundering: The Response of the Financial Sector". In: Macqueen HL (ed) *Money Laundering*, p.65.

principles cover a wide range of topics, and one of these principles deals directly with money laundering. It is Core Principle 15 which stipulates:[128]

> "Banking supervisors must determine that banks have adequate policies, practices and procedures in place, including strict "know your customer" rules, that promote high ethical and professional standards in the financial sector and prevent the bank being used, intentionally or unintentionally, by criminal elements."

However, as is pointed out in the document, the key objective of supervision is to maintain stability and confidence in the financial system, thereby reducing the risk of loss to depositors and other creditors.[129] In this sense, although not in a direct way, the application of all other twenty-four principles is essential to support the AML/CFT framework as a whole package.[130]

4.3.2.3 Core Principles Methodology (1999)[131]

The Core Principles (1997) as above were originally designed to provide general guidance. However, in terms of implementation, the BCBS realised that national supervisory authorities might misinterpret them.[132] At the same time, also with regard to the assessment of compliance with the Core Principles, it was important that concerned parties, such as the IMF, the World Bank, and regional development banks, should be provided with a common basis of interpretation. Otherwise it was possible that they might misunderstand the principles and have varied interpretations possibly resulting in the provision of inconsistent advice.[133] In this context, the BCBS developed a methodology for use in compliance assessment in 1999 which is entitled the "Core Principles Methodology". This document discusses each Core Principle in detail. Namely, for each Core Principle, various criteria are enumerated, which are then divided into two categories: "essential criteria" and "additional criteria".[134] Consequently, the application of the Core Principle 15 (1997) is considerably strengthened with the provision of eleven essential criteria and five additional criteria by the 1999 methodology.[135]

---

[128] <http://www.bis.org/publ/bcbs30a.pdf>.

[129] BCBS, "Core Principles for Effective Banking Supervision", p.8.

[130] See, e.g., IMF/World Bank, "Enhancing Contributions To Combating Money Laundering: Policy Paper; Annex II", 26 April 2001, pp.29-32.

[131] (visited on 31 March 2004) < http://www.bis.org/publ/bcbs61.htm>.

[132] BCBS, "Core Principles Methodology", p.5

[133] *Ibid.*, p.5.

[134] *Ibid.,* p.2. This division facilitates the discerning of the priority among the criteria.

[135] For the details of the criteria, see *ibid.*, pp.33-34.

4.3.2.4 Customer due diligence for banks (2001)[136]

Without due diligence, banks can become subject to reputational, operational, legal and concentrational risks, which can result in significant financial cost.[137] Accordingly, the BCBS issued another crucial paper on the know-your-customer (KYC) issue in October 2001, which is entitled "Customer due diligence for banks". This paper builds upon the three documents as explained above, thus dealing with the KYC issue in more detail.[138] For instance, in addition to the general elements of KYC standards, the paper provides for an in-depth analysis of specific identification issues such as trust, corporate vehicles, introduced business, politically exposed persons, and correspondent banking. In February 2003, the "General Guide to Account Opening and Customer Identification" was issued as an addition to this KYC paper. These guidelines are also of value beyond the money laundering context in that they aim to protect the safety and soundness of banks.[139] More recently, in October 2004, the BCBS issued another supporting document for the 2001 KYC paper, the "Consolidated KYC Risk Management". This document emphasises the importance of a centralised approach in promulgating KYC standards. In other words, international banking groups should establish a centralised process for coordinating and promoting KYC policies and procedures as well as sharing information across the head office and all branches and subsidiaries worldwide.

---

[136] <http://www.bis.org/publ/bcbs85.htm>.

[137] Reputational risks take place where a bad reputation may result in the loss of confidence by depositors, creditors and the general market place. Operational risk is with regard to a situation where failed internal processes, or systems may bring about direct or indirect loss to banks. Legal risks exist where banks may be subject to lawsuits resulting from the failure to observe mandatory KYC procedures. Concentration risks are concerned with a situation where banks are exposed to single borrowers or groups of related borrowers without knowing precisely who the customers are (BCBS, "Customer due diligence for banks", pp.4-5). For a further discussion, see, Codd E (2003) "Reputational Risk". In: Clark A, Burrell P (eds) *A Practitioner's Guide to International Money Laundering Law and Regulation*, 1st edn, pp.69-76.

[138] For a relevant discussion, see, Clark A, Russell M (2003) "Know Your Customer". In: Clark A, Burrell P (eds) *A Practitioner's Guide to International Money Laundering Law and Regulation*, 1st edn., pp.88-89.

[139] See, Schott PA, *supra* note 62, p.III-15.

4.3.3 Wolfsberg Group of Banks

The Wolfsberg Group of Banks, which was established in 2000 and named after a town in Switzerland, is an association of twelve international private banks.[140] Interestingly, while the BCBS is an association of *supervisory* bodies in the banking industry, the Wolfsberg Group is an association of the *supervised* banks themselves. In fact, the Wolfsberg Group of Banks is the only international AML/CFT initiative which is taken by the private sector. Indeed this aspect stands in stark contrast with the "public" nature of practices of other international standard setters such as the BCBS and IOSCO. Outwith this comparison, there naturally arose a question of why the private sector should become active in this area. As a matter of fact, this change in position of the private banks was brought about by virtue of the existence of a non-level playing field in the banking industry. Namely, although banking supervisors struggled to implement international AML/CFT standards in the 1990s, the outcome was the "creation of a patchwork of rather diverse rules which enabled money launderers to profit from the discrepancies between various financial centres".[141] Under these circumstances, it is indeed intolerable for internationally active banks which had to apply all these diverse standards while at the same time they constantly risked losing clients to competitors operating under a more flexible regulatory framework elsewhere.[142] It was apparently necessary for these major banks to be guaranteed the "level playing field" but for some time, they waited for the regulators to make the next move.[143] However, at the end of the 1990s, the FATF developed other priorities such as non-cooperative countries and territories (NCCT) rather than refining the existing standards and its own performance.[144] Furthermore, another pressure was placed on the banking industry by a series of banking scandals in connection with highly placed political officials in the 1990s, seriously damaging the reputation of the involved banks.[145] Thus, this time "the affected banks themselves" made the next move by adopting their own guidelines as explained below. This movement influenced not only the

---

[140] The members of the Wolfsberg Group are as follows: BN AMRO NV, Banco Santander Central Hispanco, S.A., Bank of Tokyo-Mitsubishi, Ltd., Barclays Bank plc, Citigroup, Credit Suisse Group, Deutsche Bank AG, HSBC Holdings plc, J.P.Morgan Chase, Société Générale, UBS AG.

[141] Pieth M, Aiofi G, "The Private Sector becomes active: The Wolfsberg Process", p.3.

[142] *Ibid.*, p.3.

[143] *Ibid.*, p.3.

[144] *Ibid.*, p.3.

[145] For examples of the banking scandals, see, e.g., US Senate, "Minority Staff Report for Permanent Subcommittee on Investigation; Hearing on Private Banking and Money Laundering: A Case Study of Opportunities and Vulnerabilities", 9 November 1999; Hinterseer K (2002) *Criminal Finance: The Political Economy of Money Laundering in a Comparative Legal Context*, pp.262-264.

banking industry itself but also the regulators in the public sector.[146] With this momentum, the Wolfsberg Group also participated as a key partner in the drafting process of the 2003 Forty Recommendations.[147] Thus, the reciprocal process between the private sector and public sector has been put into full effect. By so doing, both sectors will, without doubt, benefit from narrowing the gap of the understanding of diverse issues concerning the AML/CFT campaign.[148] In fact, the real strength of the Wolfsberg Group lies in the fact that its members allegedly make up more than 60% of the world market in private banking.[149]

4.3.3.1 Anti-Money Laundering Principles for Private Banking (2000)

The first relevant initiative of the Wolfsberg Group was to adopt "Anti-Money Laundering Principles for Private Banking" in October 2000 which were subsequently revised in 2002. These principles cover the full set of preventive anti-money laundering measures, ranging from customer due diligence to supervision and internal control.[150] The eleven principles are related to the following issues:

- Client acceptance: general guidelines;
- Client acceptance: situations requiring additional diligence/attention;
- Updating client files;
- Practices when identifying unusual or suspicious activities;
- Monitoring;
- Control responsibilities;
- Reporting;
- Education, training and information;
- Record retention requirements;
- Exceptions and deviations based on risk assessment; and,
- Adequately staffed independent department responsible for the prevention of money laundering.[151]

---

[146] Pieth M, Aiofi G, "The Private Sector becomes active: The Wolfsberg Process", p.5.

[147] *Ibid.*, p.5.

[148] It could be said that one of the main achievements of the banking industry in the early 21st century has been to win the regulators over to follow a "risk-based approach" when developing norms rather than a "rule-based approach"(*Ibid.*, pp.5-6).

[149] *Ibid.*, p.5.

[150] See, Wolfsberg Group, "Wolfsberg Press Releases", 30 October 2000.

[151] <http:///www.wolfsberg-principles.com/privat-banking.html>.

4.3.3.2 Statement on the Suppression of the Financing of Terrorism (2002)

Following 9/11, the Wolfsberg Group adopted the "Statement on the Suppression of the Financing of Terrorism" in May 2002.[152] This document first points out that funds used in the financing of terrorism do not necessarily derive from criminal activity. Then it emphsises the role of financial institutions in the fight against terrorism such as proper identification of customers and enhanced due diligence.[153] Interestingly, this document includes human rights aspects of the counter-terrorism campaign, by mentioning that the Wolfsberg Group is committed to participate in the counter-terrorism campaign in a manner which is non-discriminatory and is respectful of the rights of individuals.[154]

4.3.3.3 Anti-Money Laundering Principles for Correspondent Banking (2002)

Shortly after 9/11, global correspondent banking was highlighted as playing an important role in the financing of terrorism and money laundering.[155] However, at the time, no initiative existed to focus on this issue, thus making it difficult to tackle it as a means to frustrate the financing of terrorism and criminal activity.[156] In this regard, the Wolfsberg Group adopted the "Wolfsberg Anti-Money Laundering Principles for Correspondent Banking" in November 2002. It affords an in-depth treatment to the issue concerning correspondent banking as illustrated by the due diligence standards with regard to client banks,[157] and the elements requiring enhanced due diligence.[158] In addition, what is peculiar in this document is its use

---

[152] (visited on 20 March 2004) <http://www.wolfsberg-principles.com/financing-terrorism.html>.

[153] Principles 2, 4, 5, and 6.

[154] Principle 3.

[155] See, Wolfsberg Group, Press Release, 5 November 2002.

[156] *Ibid.*

[157] Principle 5 provides that a bank shall consider the client bank's:
- Client domicile and organisation;
- Client ownership and executive management;
- Correspondent banking client's business;
- Products or services offered;
- Regulatory status and history;
- Anti-money laundering controls;
- No business arrangements with shell banks; and,
- Client visit

[158] Principle 6 provides for the elements that require enhanced due diligence as follows:
- Ownership and management;
- PEP involvement;

of the risk-based approach.[159] It encourages each institution to give appropriate weight to each risk factor as it deems necessary and stipulates that it may adjust the level of due diligence subsequently.[160]

4.3.3.4 Monitoring Screening and Searching Wolfsberg Statement (2003)[161]

Since its inception, the Wolfsberg Group has issued three documents for the purpose of combating terrorist financing and money laundering in the banking industry. However, these documents lacked a detailed standard operating procedure as to monitoring and reporting matter based on the assessment of risk that each type of transaction poses.[162] In this context, the Wolfsberg Group issued the "Monitoring Screening and Searching Wolfsberg Statement" in September 2003 for the purpose of filling the gap by introducing three important concepts: real-time screening; retroactive search; and, risk-based transaction monitoring.[163] Indeed, this refinement of the risked-based CDD process provides more clear-cut guidance in the implementation of the AML/CFT standards for supervisory authorities as well as for the banking industry itself.

4.3.4 International Association of Insurance Supervisors

The International Association of Insurance Supervisors (IAIS), established in 1994, is an organisation which represents the insurance supervisory authorities from some 130 jurisdictions.[164] The functions of the IAIS are to:

- Promote cooperation among insurance regulators;
- Set international standards for insurance supervision;
- Provide training to members; and,

- Correspondent banking client's anti-money laundering controls; and,
- Downstream correspondent banking.

[159] Schott PA, *supra* note 62, p. IV-5.

[160] See, e.g., Principles 4,5,6, and 8.

[161] <http://www.wolfsberg-principles.com/monitoring.html>.

[162] See, *ibid.*, preamble.

[163] See, *ibid.*, article 2 (definitions). Real-time screening means the screening or filtering of payment instructions prior to their execution in order to prevent making funds available in breach of sanctions, embargoes and other measures. Retroactive searches are defined as the identification of specific past transactions, as well as existing and closed accounts. Transaction monitoring means the process of monitoring transaction after their execution in order to identify unusual transactions, including monitoring single transactions, as well as transaction flows.

[164] (visited on 1 June 2005) <http://www.iaisweb.org>.

- Coordinate work with regulators in the other financial sectors and
  international financial institutions.[165]

4.3.4.1 Anti-Money Laundering Guidance Notes for Insurance Supervisors and Insurance Entities (2002)

In relation to the AML/CFT issues, the IAIS issued the "Anti-Money Laundering Guidance Notes for Insurance Supervisors and Insurance Entities" in January 2002.[166] Like other documents issued by specialist bodies, the notes are just guidance in a literal sense, and implementation is entirely at the discretion of individual countries. For the insurance entities, these guidance notes indicate the following basic principles:

- Comply with anti-money laundering laws;
- Know your customer;
- Cooperate with law enforcement authorities, insurance supervisors, and
  other investigative and supervisory authorities; and,
- Have in place anti-money laundering policies, procedures and a training
  programme.

Indeed, these four principles are very similar to the four principles in the BCBS's "Statement of Principle on Money Laundering" (1988).[167] The notes provide an insight into how to apply the AML/CFT framework, such as customer identification and suspicious transactions, within the insurance industry. Later, in order to reflect the revised 2003 text of the FATF Forty Recommendations, another guidance note of a similar nature entitled "Guidance Paper on Anti-Money Laundering and Combating the Financing of Terrorism", was issued in October 2004.[168] This document is in effect the revised version of the 2002 guidance notes, and is seeking more harmonisation with the FATF text.

4.3.4.2 Insurance Core Principles and Methodology (2003)

In October 2003, the IAIS adopted the "Insurance Core Principles and Methodology" for the purpose of clarifying essential principles that need to be in place for a supervisory system to be effective. The IAIS sets out twenty-eight Core Principles the last of which provides for the AML/CFT strategy:

---

[165] *Ibid.*
[166] For an overview of these notes, see, Butterworth S (2003) "Regulators: IAIS Anti-Money Laundering Guidelines". In: Clark A, Burrell P (eds) *A Practitioner's Guide to International Money Laundering Law and Regulation*, 1st edn, pp.231-242.
[167] Schott PA, *supra* note 62, p.III-16.
[168] <http://www.iaisweb.org/041013_GP5_Guidance_paper_on_anti_money_laundering _and_combating_the_financing_of_terrorism_approved_040107.pdf>.

"The supervisory authority requires insurers and intermediaries, at a minimum those insurers and intermediaries offering life insurance products or other investment related insurance, to take effective measures to deter, detect and report money laundering and the financing of terrorism consistent with the Recommendations of the Financial Action Task Force on Money Laundering (FATF)."[169]

Furthermore, the five essential criteria attached to this principle provides detailed guidelines concerning its application in practice in relation to such as powers and resources of supervision, authority to cooperate with the domestic FIU, and consistency with the FATF Recommendations.

4.3.5 International Organization of Securities Commissions

The International Organization of Securities Commissions (IOSCO) was established in 1983 as an association of securities regulatory agencies.[170] Currently the IOSCO consists of regulatory bodies from some 110 jurisdictions.[171] In fact, there are three kinds of membership categories which are ordinary, associate, and affiliate. Usually, a governmental regulatory body becomes an ordinary member, and an associate member means any other eligible public body with an appropriate responsibility for securities regulation beyond the ordinary member in a country. Lastly, the affiliate members are self-regulatory organisations. Among these three categories of membership, only the ordinary membership can exercise voting powers.[172] Exceptionally, however, if there is no governmental regulatory body in a country, a self-regulatory organisation, such as a stock exchange, from that country is eligible for ordinary membership of the Organisation.[173] The IOSCO have three core principles in place with regard to securities regulation:

- The protection of investors;
- Ensuring that markets are fair, efficient and transparent; and,
- The reduction of systemic risk.[174]

4.3.5.1 Resolution on Money Laundering (1992)

The IOSCO became involved in dealing with money laundering in the early 1990s. An important step was taken with the adoption of the "Resolution on Mon-

---

[169] Core Principle 28.

[170] (visited on 23 March 2004) <http://www.iosco.org/about/>.

[171] (visited on 1 June 2005) <http://www.iosco.org/lists/>.

[172] (visited on 23 March 2004) < http://www.iosco.org/about/about.cfm?whereami=page5>.

[173] Schott PA, *supra* note 62, p. III-17.

[174] IOSOC, "Objectives and Principles of Securities Regulation", May 2003, pp.5-6.

ey Laundering" in 1992 which briefly touched upon the basic rules for combating money laundering such as customer identification, and record keeping requirements.[175]

4.3.5.2 Principles on Client Identification and Beneficial Ownership for the Securities Industry (2004)

In May 2003, the IOSCO adopted a document on the basic principles of securities regulations entitled "Objectives and Principles of Securities Regulations". This document allocated one principle to the money laundering issue but it was drafted in such a general way that no detailed guidelines could be drawn.[176] Indeed, the progress of the AML/CFT strategy in the securities sector seems to have been slower than in other sectors despite its earlier initiative in 1992.[177] However, a major breakthrough was made with the adoption of "Principles on Client Identification and Beneficial Ownership for the Securities Industry" in May 2004. These principles are heavily influenced by the 2003 FATF Forty Recommendations and are very detailed providing specific advice to the staff in the industry. These include requirements that compel authorised securities service providers (ASSP) to: identify their clients; obtain adequate information about their clients' circumstances and investment objectives; as well as maintaining records of this data.[178]

4.3.6 Egmont Group of Financial Intelligence Units

The Egmont Group which is named for the location of its first meeting in the Egmont-Arenberg Palace in Brussels in 1995, is an informal organisation of FIUs.[179] The Egmont Group aims at providing a forum for FIUs to improve support for

---

[175] For the detailed text, see (visited on 23 March 2003) < http://www.iosco.org/ resolutions/pdf/IOSCORES5.pdf>.

[176] Principle 8.5 provides for the basic position of the IOSCO with regard to money laundering as follows:
"Securities regulators should consider the sufficiency of domestic legislation to address the risks of money laundering. The regulator should also require that market intermediaries have in place policies and procedures designed to minimize the risk of the use of an intermediaries business as a vehicle for money laundering."

[177] For the explanation on the delayed progress in securities sector, see, "The Initiatives by the BCBS, IAIS and IOSCO to combat money laundering and the financing of terrorism", June 2003, pp.8-9.

[178] IOSCO, "Principles on Client Identification and Beneficial Ownership for the Securities Industry", p.2.

[179] Egmont Group "Information Paper on Financial Intelligence Units and the Egmont Group", p.3. Thus, the Egmont Group has no permanent Secretariat and administration functions are shared on a rotating basis.

each of their national AML/CFT programmes and to coordinate AML/CFT initiatives.[180] For the purpose of membership, an operational AML/CFT agency should
meet the definition of the FIU established by the Egmont Group, which is:

> "A central, national agency responsible for receiving (and, as permitted, re-
> questing), analysing and disseminating to the competent authorities, disclosures
> of financial information (i) concerning suspected proceeds of crime and potential
> financing of terrorism, or (ii) required by national legislation, in order to counter
> money laundering and terrorism financing."[181]

Membership of the Egmont Group is in the region of 100 states and territories.[182] With a view to promote the cooperation of the FIUs, it has set out international standards called "Principles for Information Exchange between Financial
Intelligence Units for Money Laundering Cases" on 13 June 2001. This document
provides for cooperation based on mutual trust and reciprocity, and conditions for
the exchange of information such as the rules of specialty and confidentiality.[183] It
was subsequently reinforced with the adoption of "Best Practices for the Exchange
of Information Between Financial Intelligence Units" on 15 November 2004.[184]
The Egmont Group became an observer to the FATF in February 2002,[185] and the
interpretative notes to the revised 2003 FATF Forty Recommendations make direct reference to the Egmont Group as a standard-setter concerning the role and
functions of FIUs.[186]

4.4 Soft law phenomena: non-binding but detailed provisions

To begin with, it needs to be clarified whether all these standards could be classified as soft law. In fact, what all these standards of specialist bodies as mentioned
above have in common is that firstly, they are legally non-binding in nature. Thus,
as it is symbolically indicated by the BCBS, these standards "will become the
benchmark for supervisors to establish national practices and for *the supervised* to
design their own programmes."[187] Secondly, all these standards are very detailed

---

[180] Schott PA, *supra* note 62, p.III-19.
[181] Egmont Group, "Statement of the Purpose", p.2. Terrorist financing has been inserted
through the revision in June 2004 Plenary meeting.
[182] <http://www.egmontgroup.org>.
[183] *Ibid.*
[184] <http://www.egmontgroup.org/bestpractices.pdf>.
[185] FATF, "Annual Report: 2003-2004", 2 July 2004, p.18.
[186] Interpretative Note to the 2003 Recommendation 26.
[187] BCBS, "Customer due diligence for banks", October 2001, p.2. The italicised phrased is
replaced by the author.

and tailored to particular institutions and risks in a specific industry, thus complementing the generality of the hard law with regard to implementation in practice. Namely, in the field of terrorist financing, the hard law in the strictest sense has been developed by the Security Council through the adoption of Resolution 1267, Resolution 1373, and its subsequent resolutions.[188] One of the major obligations imposed by these resolutions is to suppress the financing of terrorism, for example, by way of criminalising terrorist financing or freezing terrorism-related assets.[189] However, the resolutions do not provide additional guidance for their implementation in a real situation. In these circumstances, the standards set up by specialist bodies are very useful in filling the gap between the general hard law and various problematic circumstances which require tailored countermeasures. For instance, the FATF Special Recommendation III along with its supporting documents[190] and the revised 2003 Recommendation 3, provide valuable guidance and legal weapons to deal with frozen terrorist assets. To be more particular,[191] the International Best Practice of Special Recommendation III encourages countries to develop a system for mutual, early, and rapid pre-notification of pending designations of terrorists, through diplomatic and other appropriate channels. Moreover, it also calls upon countries to prepare a packet of information for each potential designation that include as much information as is available to identify the designated person, and to submit it with the request of designation. This practice would apparently render assistance to the government which intends to file a judicial proceeding in relation to the assets which are frozen following the designation of a owner as a terrorist suspect. If these measures could be coupled with the legal tools such as civil confiscation or the reversed burden of proof as mentioned in the 2003 Recommendation 3, they would definitely help the prosecution office to win the case. Similarly, with regard to alternative remittance systems on which the Security Council's resolutions are silent, the FATF Special Recommendation VI accompanied by its supporting documents, gives detailed instructions and promotes best practices to tackle the issue.[192] Likewise, in respect of non-profit organisa-

---

[188] See, e.g., Resolution 1333 (2000), para.8; Resolution 1373 (2001), para.1; Resolution 1390 (2001), para.2. First of all, these resolutions impose binding obligations on all states. Moreover, the contents of the obligations are clear enough to point out their violation in a real situation. Furthermore, the Security Council itself can act as an independent dispute settlement mechanism which can make a compulsory binding decision.

[189] For further details, see, Section 3.2.3 and Section 3.3.3 of Chapter Three of this book.

[190] See, FATF, "Interpretative Note to Special Recommendation III: Freezing and Confiscating Terrorist Assets", 3 October 2003; FATF, "Freezing of Terrorist Assets: International Best Practices", 3 October 2003.

[191] FATF, "Freezing of Terrorist Assets: International Best Practices", 3 October 2003.

[192] For details, see, *supra* note 103.

tions, the FATF Special Recommendation VIII provides for detailed guidelines and "food for thought" in order to crack down on their clandestine operations.[193]

Another point of note in relation to the development of international standards is the contribution made by the private sector. As was seen above, the Wolfsberg Group of Banks, in the absence of coercion by the public sector, has taken the initiative in establishing a set of principles concerning money laundering and the financing of terrorism.[194] Although some may dismiss this kind of movement as a mere public relation exercise,[195] in practice these voluntary codes of conduct can be of considerable value in underpinning regulatory guidance, by giving practical advice to banks on operational matters.[196] Of course, it should be noted that such codes cannot be regarded as a substitute for formal regulatory guidance,[197] but they indeed have the potential to make a meaningful contribution to the development of AML/CFT standards based on the consensus of both the private and public sectors.[198] In terms of the development of soft law, the voluntary participation of the private sector can promote great synergy effects since they are the ones who actually implement the "non-binding" standards.[199]

All in all, the Security Council is supported by the FATF in general terms, and the FATF is assisted by other specialist bodies in a specific sub-areas, such as the BCBS, Wolfsberg Group, IAIS, IOSCO, and the Egmont Group.[200] In sum, all these are excellent cases of the usage of soft law as non-binding law with detailed contents. The standards set by specialist bodies are indeed supplementing the authoritative approach of the Security Council in fighting terrorist financing by way of fleshing out the simple structure of its resolutions with their own "specialty".[201]

---

[193] For details, see, *supra* note 106.

[194] I owe much to Professor Gilmore WC for sparking this point.

[195] Hinterseer K (2002) *Criminal Finance: The Political Economy of Money Laundering in a Comparative Legal Context,* p.264.

[196] BCBS, "Customer due diligence for banks", October 2001, p.5.

[197] *Ibid.*, p.5.

[198] Hinterseer K, *supra* note 195, p.282.

[199] For relevant discussions on soft law, see also, Section 4.1 of this chapter.

[200] Indeed, the FATF aids the Security Council in a practical sense. However, other specialist bodies openly express their will to assist the FATF. See, e.g., BCBS, "Customer due diligence for banks", October 2001, p.2; Pieth M, Aiofi G, "The Private Sector becomes active: The Wolfsberg Process", p.7; IAIS, "Insurance Core Principles and Methodology", October 2003, p.45; The Joint Forum, "The Initiatives by the BCBS, IAIS and IOSCO to combat money laundering and the financing of terrorism", June 2003, pp.9-10.

For details on the monitoring and enforcement mechanisms of specialist bodies, see, Chapter Five of this study.

[201] Hillgenberg H, *supra* note 26, pp.506-507.

5 Monitoring and Enforcing Standards by Specialist Bodies

5.1 Introduction

Following the discussion in the last chapter (Chapter Four) on the establishment of international standards in the suppression of the financing of terrorism by specialist bodies, this chapter will examine the manner in which these standards are being monitored and enforced by them. After reviewing this monitoring and enforcement work, some soft law implications will also be highlighted as well as the prospects of the transformation from soft law into hard law of certain of the standards in question. Lastly, considering the fast development of terrorist financing and money laundering techniques, attention is paid to the importance of establishing level playing fields in relation to the setting up of international standards, and their monitoring and enforcement.

5.2 FATF

5.2.1 The monitoring of standards

5.2.1.1 Context

For the purpose of monitoring countries' implementation of its Forty Recommendations, the FATF has developed four methods: self-assessment, mutual evaluation, cross-country review, and, the non-cooperative countries and territories (NCCT) initiative. The self-assessment and mutual evaluation processes were adopted during the FATF II period (1990-1991)[1] and continued to be used as the main tools for monitoring. The cross-country review was first tried during the FATF VI period (1994-1995)[2] but was not a frequently-used method, being last

---

[1]   FATF, "Annual Report: 1990-1991", 13 May 1991, p.3.
[2]   FATF, "Annual Report: 1994-1995", 8 June 1995, p.15.

used during the FATF VIII period (1996-1997).[3] Finally, the NCCT initiative was launched to in effect deal with non-FATF member countries during the FATF X period (1998-1999).[4] Based on their current status of usage, the three main devices for monitoring except the cross-country review will be analysed as follows.

5.2.1.2 Self-assessment

A self-assessment exercise was invented out of the need to check the FATF member countries' progress in the implementation of the specialist body's standards. Given that it usually took more than three years to finish one round of mutual evaluations of the all FATF member countries, the annual self-assessment exercise provided a yearly inventory record of member countries' counter-measures in the related area.[5] Self-assessment also played a complementary role by way of providing the necessary preliminary information for a coming round of mutual evaluations.[6]

In this exercise, each member country was required to provide information on their implementation of the Forty Recommendations by way of filling in a questionnaire.[7] This information was then compiled and analysed, and provided the basis for an in-depth assessment at the final Plenary meeting for each yearly cycle of the level of the implementation of the Forty Recommendations by both individual countries and the group as a whole.[8]

---

[3] FATF, "Annual Report: 1996-1997", 19 June 1997, p.20. The cross-country evaluation was conducted on the basis of questionnaires which sought information on the nature and results so far achieved of measures taken by FATF members to implement specific Recommendations. Namely, it was an intensified theme-specific approach. The subject chosen for this evaluation was "suspicious transaction report" during the FATF VI period (1994-1995): "identifying, freezing, seizing and confiscating the proceeds of crime" from the FATF VII (1995-1996) to the FATF VIII period (1996-1997). Since then no cross-country evaluation has been taken thus far.

[4] FATF, "Annual Report: 1998-1999", 2 July 1999, p.35.

[5] FATF, "Annual Report: 2002-2003", 20 June 2003, p.28.

[6] FATF, "Review of FATF Anti-Money Laundering Systems and Mutual Evaluation Procedures 1992-1999", 16 February 2001, p.1.

[7] The questionnaire was subject to constant review and change dependent upon the development of situations. In 1999, two important changes were made to the questionnaire. Firstly, in the past there had been two sets of questionnaires on legal and financial matters respectively but these two questionnaires were combined into a single document and considerably reduced in size. Secondly, compliance analysis focused only on specific recommendations which require a mandatory action or specific measures. See, FATF, "Annual Report 1999-2000", 22 June 2000, p.20.

[8] FATF, "Annual Report: 1997-1998", 25 June 1998, p.10.

Following the adoption of the Special Recommendations on Terrorist Financing, the FATF also started to assess the status of the implementation of the special recommendations through a self-assessment exercise.[9] The questionnaire used in the exercise took into account and was cross-referenced to the requirements of the Security Council Resolutions 1373 (2001) and 1390 (2002).[10] Importantly, the scope of the self-assessment exercises on this occasion was not confined to the FATF member countries but was extended to non-FATF member countries. The FATF invited all countries around the world to join the exercise. As a result, some 130 countries responded to the call.[11]

However, given that the new standards and monitoring methods developed following 9/11 are significantly broader in scope and detail than the 1996 Recommendations, in 2004, the FATF decided not to conduct self-assessment exercises modelled on previous exercises any longer.[12] Instead, the FATF decided to initiate a process of following-up reports to mutual evaluations.[13] These follow-up reports directly build up on the results from the mutual evaluation reports by providing an annual update of progress made on specific issues highlighted in the mutual evaluation.[14]

5.2.1.3 Mutual evaluation

Within the FATF, mutual evaluation was created as "the primary measurement of the FATF member countries' progress" in implementing the AML/CFT standards.[15] It also serves as a principal means of evaluating the overall effectiveness of the national AML/CFT framework.[16]

The mutual evaluation process begins with the preparation for an on-site visit.[17] Generally, experts are selected from lists which the FATF Secretariat has received from each member country.[18] Then a questionnaire is sent to the country concerned and later collected by the FATF Secretariat at least 30 days prior to the on-site

---

[9] FATF, "Annual Report: 2002-2003", 20 June 2003, p.8.

[10] FATF, " Annual Report: 2001-2002", 21 June 2002, p.5.

[11] For the list of the responding countries as of 24 February 2004, see (visited on 19 April 2004) <http://www1.oecd.org/fatf/SAQTF_en.htm>.

[12] FATF, "Annual Report: 2003-2004", 2 July 2004, p.10.

[13] *Ibid.*, p.10.

[14] *Ibid.*, p.10.

[15] FATF, "Annual Report: 2001-2002 ", 21 June 2002, p.13.

[16] *Ibid.,* p.19.

[17] FATF, "Review of FATF Anti-Money Laundering Systems and Mutual Evaluation Procedures 1992-1999", 16 February 2001, p.37.

[18] Each examination team consists of a legal, a financial, and a law enforcement expert, with the examiners being drawn from different jurisdictions (*Ibid.*, p.37).

visit.[19] Usually, the on-site visit lasts for three working days, and meetings are arranged with individual agencies.[20] When the on-site visit is finished, the FATF Secretariat prepares the draft report through communication with the examiners and the examined country.[21] Upon the completion of the draft report, the FATF Secretariat sends it to all delegations, and it is discussed in the FATF Plenary meeting.[22] The report is then revised as necessary and formally adopted at the following Plenary meeting.[23]

The first round of mutual evaluations lasted from 1992 to 1995, focusing on the description of the laws and other anti-money laundering measures in place.[24] The second round then focused on the effectiveness of the implementation of the 1990 Forty Recommendations, ending in 1999 with regard to the then 26 member countries.[25] The third round of mutual evaluations was due to start in 2002, but was delayed during the review period of the 1996 FATF Forty Recommendations.[26] In the meantime, the FATF, the International Monetary Fund (IMF), the World Bank, and other related organisations jointly developed a common methodology to monitor countries' compliance with the AML/CFT standards in October 2002.[27] However, with the revision of the Forty Recommendations in 2003, this common methodology was also revised in February 2004.[28] This 2004 methodology is broader in scope and detail than the 2002 methodology. In particular, it

---

[19] *Ibid.*, p.37.

[20] *Ibid.*, pp.38-39.

[21] *Ibid.*, pp.39-41.

[22] *Ibid.*, p.42.

[23] The procedure for the discussion of the draft report at the Plenary meeting is as follows: The examiner briefly present their report; the examined country makes its opening statement; and, the discussion is launched by two intervenor countries, selected by the President on a proposal by the Secretariat. The draft report is then open for general discussion by the Plenary. See, *ibid.*, p.42.

[24] *Ibid.*, p.35.

[25] *Ibid.*, p.35. Given that it took several years to finish one round of mutual evaluations, only the 1990 version of Forty Recommendations was used as a standard of reference during this period of mutual evaluation. Argentina, Brazil, and Mexico became FATF members in June 2000 and their mutual evaluation was finished during 2003-2004 period. Furthermore, the mutual evaluation of Saudi Arabia was also made during this period, completing the evaluation process of all six Gulf Co-operation Council (GCC) countries. See, FATF, "Annual Report: 2003-2004", 2 July 2004, p.8.

[26] FATF, "Annual Report: 2002-2003", 20 June 2003, p.29.

[27] FATF, "Methodology for Assessing Compliance with Anti-Money Laundering and Combating the Financing of Terrorism Standards", 11 October 2002.

[28] FATF, "Methodology for Assessing Compliance with the FATF 40 Recommendations and the FATF 8 Special Recommendations", 27 February 2004.
For a relevant discussion, see also, Section 5.3.2 of this chapter.

provides useful guidance on new concepts or topics introduced by the 2003 Forty Recommendations, including the concept of the risk-based approach and the issue of non-financial institutions (e.g. lawyers and notaries).[29] The FATF commenced a third round of mutual evaluation at the end of 2004, using the 2004 AML/CFT Methodology as well as evaluation documentation as agreed between the FATF, the IMF, the World Bank, FATF-style regional bodies (FSRBs) and the Offshore Group of Banking Supervisors (OGBS).[30] This will allow for increased consistency at a global level.[31]

5.2.1.4 NCCT

Unlike other monitoring mechanisms, the NCCT initiative has been developed, in fact if not in form, for the purpose of dealing with non-FATF member countries. It is based on the concerns that as the FATF member countries have strengthened their AML/CFT framework, terrorists and criminals have had recourse to loopholes that can be found in non-FATF member countries. It was felt that this situation could considerably undermine the overall effectiveness of the FATF system.[32]

To this end, in February 2000, the FATF set out twenty-five criteria which are consistent with the 1996 version of the Forty Recommendations with a view to identifying non–cooperative jurisdictions outside the FATF circle.[33] At the same time, the FATF also set up four *ad hoc* regional groups (Americas; Asia/Pacific; Europe; and Africa and the Middle East) to analyse the AML/CFT regime of a number of jurisdictions against these criteria.[34]

Then the jurisdictions to be reviewed were informed of this monitoring work to be conducted by the FATF.[35] The review process involved the gathering of such

---

[29] FATF, "Annual Report: 2003-2004", 2 July 2004, p. 9.

[30] *Ibid.*, p.9.

[31] *Ibid.*, p.9.

[32] FATF, "Review to Identify Non-Cooperative Countries or Territories: Increasing The Worldwide Effectiveness of Anti-Money Laundering Measures", 22 June 2000, p.1.

[33] FATF, "Report on Non-Cooperative Countries and Territories", 14 February 2000, pp.10-12.

[34] *Ibid.*, pp.1-2. For the details of the NCCT criteria, see the appendix. However, there was criticism that the twenty-five criteria were much stricter than the 1996 Forty Recommendations, thus placing a heavier burden on the non-FATF member countries. For example, NCCT criterion 25 provides for the concept of the FIU upon which the 1996 version of the Forty Recommendations did not touch. For further discussions, see, Levi M, Gilmore WC (2002) "Terrorist Finance, Money Laundering and the Rise and Rise of Mutual Evaluation: A New Paradigm for Crime Control?". In: Pieth M (ed) *Financing Terrorism*, p.104.

[35] FATF, "Review to Identify Non-Cooperative Countries or Territories: Increasing The Worldwide Effectiveness of Anti-Money Laundering Measures", 22 June 2001, p.6.

information as laws and regulations, any mutual evaluation reports, related progress reports, and self-assessment surveys.[36] Following this work, draft reports were prepared and sent to the reviewed jurisdictions for comment.[37] These comments and the draft reports were then discussed between the FATF and the reviewed jurisdictions during a series of face-to-face meetings.[38] The assessment of whether a jurisdiction was non-cooperative was first made by the *ad hoc* group, and then discussed and endorsed in the FATF Plenary meetings.[39]

The last round of the NCCT review was carried out in 2001, and since then, the FATF suspended the third round of the NCCT review of any new jurisdiction, for the purpose of promoting cooperation with the IMF and the World Bank.[40] Nonetheless, the FATF continues to monitor the jurisdictions on the current list and those once on the list but later removed.[41]

5.2.2 The enforcement of standards

5.2.2.1 FATF member countries

Although the FATF does not have a formal binding enforcement mechanism, it has developed a non-compliance policy to ensure that all FATF member countries reach a satisfactory level of compliance with the Forty Recommendations. For the purpose of applying the policy, it has relied on a combination of the findings of both mutual evaluations and self-assessment exercises.[42] The measures contemplated by this policy represent a graduated approach aimed at enhancing peer pressure.[43] The formal policy which had been developed by 1994 is as follows:

1. Requiring the members to provide regular reports on their progress in implementing the Recommendations within a fixed timeframe;

---

[36] FATF, "Report on Non-Cooperative Countries and Territories", 14 February 2000, p.7.
[37] FATF, "Review to Identify Non-Cooperative Countries or Territories: Increasing The Worldwide Effectiveness of Anti-Money Laundering Measures", 22 June 2001, p.6.
[38] *Ibid.*, p.6.
[39] FATF, "Report on Non-Cooperative Countries and Territories", 14 February 2000, p.7.
[40] The tension between the FATF and the IMF/World Bank over the NCCT initiative will be dealt with in more detail in Section 5.3.2.2 of this chapter and Section 6.2.3 of Chapter Six.
[41] IMF, "Report on the Outcome of the FATF Plenary Meeting and Proposal for the Endorsement of the Methodology for Assessing Compliance with Anti-Money Laundering and Combating the Financing of Terrorism (AML/CFT) Standard", 8 November 2002, p.4.
[42] FATF, "Review of FATF Anti-Money Laundering Systems and Mutual Evaluation Procedures 1992-1999", 16 February 2001, p.43.
[43] FATF, "Annual Report: 1996-1997", 19 June 1997, p.10.

2. Sending a letter from the FATF President to the relevant minister(s) in the member jurisdiction drawing their attention to non-compliance with the FATF Recommendations;

3. Arranging a high-level mission to the member jurisdiction in question to reinforce this message;

4. In the context of the application of Recommendation 21[44] by its members, issuing a formal FATF statement to the effect that a member jurisdiction is insufficiently in compliance with the FATF Recommendations; and,

5. Suspending the jurisdiction's membership of the FATF until the Recommendations have been implemented.[45]

Since the adoption of this non-compliance policy, it has been employed in a couple of cases. For instance, Turkey and Austria are cases in point. Both were subject to measures above the second step of the procedure. In 1995 during the first round of mutual evaluations, Turkey was found to lack the necessary laws to cope with money laundering. Accordingly, the measures contained in Recommendation 21 were imposed in 1996, and it responded to this sanction by enacting the necessary laws and regulations, thus resulting in the lifting of Recommendation 21 in 1997.[46] Similarly, in 1997 during the second round of mutual evaluations, Austria was designated to be a non-compliant member. However, this time despite continuous attempts at persuasion by the FATF, Austria persistently adhered to its position with regard to anonymous passbooks for Austrian residents, thus incur-

---

[44] The 2003 FATF Recommendation 21 is as follows:

"Financial institutions should give special attention to business relationships and transactions with persons, including companies and financial institutions, from countries which do not or insufficiently apply the FATF Recommendations, Whenever these transactions have no apparent economic or visible lawful purpose, their background and purposes should, as far as possible, be examined, the findings established in writing, and be available to help competent authorities. Where such a country continues not to apply or insufficiently applies the FATF Recommendations, countries should be able to apply appropriate countermeasures".

Thus, when this Recommendation 21 is put into effect, there should be corresponding measures of the FATF member countries to support it. For example, in the UK, the 2003 Money Laundering Regulation 28 provides that "the treasury may direct any person or institution carrying out relevant business not to enter into a business relationship or carry out any one-off transaction, or not to proceed any further with a customer relationship or transaction, if the customer is based or incorporated in a country to which the FATF has decided to apply countermeasures....." (See, Joint Money Laundering Steering Group (2003) "Prevention of Money Laundering: Guidance Notes for the UK Financial Sector", p.29).

[45] FATF, "Review of FATF Anti-Money Laundering Systems and Mutual Evaluation Procedures 1992-1999", 16 February 2001, p.43.

[46] FATF, "Annual Report: 1996-1997", 19 June 1997, pp.10-11.

ring the imposition of a further step according to the above procedure.[47] Finally, since no major breakthrough seemed to be plausible in the near future, the FATF issued a public statement on 3 February 2000 which stipulated that Austria would be suspended as a member of the FATF unless by 20 May 2000 the Austrian government took corrective actions. Interestingly, following this statement, the Austrian government responded immediately. Consequently the suspension of membership did not take place.[48]

5.2.2.2 Non-FATF member countries

With regard to non-member countries, first of all, the FATF can apply the measures of Recommendation 21 as it does with member countries.[49] However, sometimes the FATF can recommend broader countermeasures which should be "gradual, proportionate and flexible regarding their means and taken in concerted action towards a common objective".[50] For instance, in the NCCT context, stronger measures are in place as follows:[51]

1. Actions to put an end to the detrimental rules and practices
    (i) Actions designed to encourage non-cooperative jurisdictions to adopt laws in compliance with FATF recommendations;[52] and,
    (ii) Application of Recommendation 21
2. Counter-measures designed to protect economies against money of unlawful origin
    (i) Customer identification obligations for financial institutions in FATF members with respect to financial transactions carried out with or by individuals or legal entities whose account is in a "non-cooperative

---

[47]   FATF, "Annual Report: 1997-1998", 25 June 1998, p.24.

[48]   For the details on the FATF's dealing with the Austrian government, see, FATF, "Annual Report: 1999-2000", 22 June 2000, pp.20-22.

[49]   For example, Seychelles, as a non-member, was subject to the measures of Recommendation 21 in 1996 due to its investment law. For further details, see, FATF, "Financial Action Task Force on Money Laundering Condemns New Investment Law in Seychelles", SG/COM/NEWS (96) 9.

[50]   FATF, "Review to Identify Non-Cooperative Countries or Territories: Increasing The World-Wide Effectiveness of Anti-Money Laundering Measures", 21 June 2002, p.6.

[51]   FATF, "Report on Non-Cooperative Countries and Territories", 14 February 2000, pp.7-9.

[52]   At this stage, the FATF seeks a dialogue, in conjunction with relevant FATF-style regional bodies or appropriate international organisations/bodies, with the identified jurisdictions in order to prompt them to amend their laws and change their practices. Specific actions could also be taken by other multilateral fora (e.g., the G-7, the OECD, the BCBS, IOSCO, IAIS) to seek the issuance of public statements or other appropriate action (*Ibid.*, p.7).

jurisdiction";

(ii) Specific requirements for financial institutions in FATF members to pay special attention to or to report financial transactions conducted with individuals or legal entities having their account at a financial institutions established in a "non-cooperative jurisdiction"; and,

(iii) Conditioning, restricting, targeting or even prohibiting financial transactions with non-cooperative jurisdictions.

As a result of the two rounds of the NCCT initiative which were carried out in 2000 and 2001, a total of 47 jurisdictions were reviewed and 23 of them were identified as NCCTs.[53] The NCCT practices have been "extremely productive" in that many jurisdictions enacted significant reforms and are well on their way towards a comprehensive AML regime.[54] Consequently, as of 1 June 2005, only 3 jurisdictions (Myanmar, Nauru, and Nigeria) remain on the list.[55]

However, it should be admitted that the NCCT initiative is quite unique and controversial in the sense that a *non-universal* body seeks to enforce *non-binding* standards on *non-member* countries.[56] Thus, the countries assessed may view this unilateral stigmatisation as a form of "normative imperialism" on their fragile economies.[57] In relation to this criticism, however, the current development of treaty and customary law in this area would be worthy of note. So to speak, in the past the unilateral nature of the NCCT certainly met with great difficulties in terms of legal justification. Yet, as will be seen in the last section of this chapter, multilateral instruments concerning criminal matters increasingly include the AML measure as an essential tool in their strategy to combat crime, and they are being widely ratified.[58] Furthermore, a majority of countries in the international community are nowadays participating voluntarily in AML assessment exercises

---

[53] See, FATF website (visited on 8 May 2005) <http://www.fatf-gafi.org/document/ 51/0,2340,en_32250379_32236992_33916403_1_1_1_1,00.html>.

[54] FATF, "Review to Identify Non-Cooperative Countries or Territories: Increasing The World-Wide Effectiveness of Anti-Money Laundering Measures", 21 June 2002, p.19.

[55] See, the FATF website (visited on 1 June 2005) < http://www.fatf-gafi.org/document/4/ 0,2340,en _32250379_32236992_33916420_1_1_1_1,00.html>.

[56] Professor Gilmore WC at an LL.M seminar on international criminal law, Edinburgh, 5 December 2003. As of 1 June 2005, the FATF membership consists of 31 countries and two regional organisations.

[57] Mitsilegas V (2003) "Countering the chameleon threat of dirty money: 'Hard' and 'soft' law in the emergence of a global regime against money laundering and terrorist finance". In: Edwards A, Gill P (eds) *Transnational organised crime: perspectives on global security*, p.205. Furthermore, the NCCT review was critisised for its nature of a "double standard". For a relevant discussion, see, Gilmore WC (2003) "Changes to the Global Regime". In: Clark A, Burrell P (eds) *A Practitioner's Guide to International Money Laundering Law and Regulation*, 1st edn, pp.286-287.

[58] For a relevant discussion, see, Section 5.5.2 of this chapter.

of some kind by way of their relationship to the FATF, FSRBs, IMF/World Bank, and other specialist bodies. In this sense, the ground for justification seems to be gradually being built up.[59] In the end, if the legal basis for the AML strategy can be firmly established in the international community by way of either treaty or custom, the NCCT initiative might take on the nature of soft enforcement, say in the context of "reprisals" by the affected peer countries.[60]

Moreover, although the current NCCT criteria do not contain CFT elements, if they included these elements in the future, there could be secured a link to the binding resolutions of the Security Council. In other words, Security Council Resolution 1373 imposes binding obligations on all states to suppress the financing of terrorism and in this sense, there could be further justification for the NCCT initiative under the authority of the Security Council.[61]

---

[59] Johnson J (2003) "Repairing Legitimacy after Blacklisting by the Financial Action Task Force", *Journal of Money Laundering Control*, vol.7, no.1, p.40. Johnson argues that the legitimacy of the FATF is "growing" by an ever increasing number of countries and organisations that want to become aligned with its goal and objectives, and that the FATF's authority continues to increase as more and more countries enact AML legislation as a result of the 9/11 and the following war against the funding of terrorist and its associated terrorist groups. For a relevant discussion, see also, Section 5.5.2 of this chapter.

[60] If it does not involve use of force, it can be understood that reprisal is still permitted under public international law (Seidl-Hohenveldern I (1979) "International economic "soft law"", *Recueil des Cours*, tome 163, p.205).

The important elements of "reprisals" are (i) that the acting state and the addressee be states; (ii) that the act be a retort to a previous act of the addressee which the act can reasonably consider to be a violation of international law of any kind; and, (iii) that its purpose be to coerce the addressee to change its policy and to bring it into line with the requirements of international law, thus being a measure to implement the observance of the law (Partsch KJ (2000) "Reprisals", *Encyclopedia of Public International Law*, vol.4, London: Elsevier, p.201).

In this regard, it is interesting to note the title of the countermeasures of the NCCT as stipulated in the cited paragraph above which says "Counter-measures designed to protect economies against money of unlawful origin". Thus, it can be inferred from the wording that the FATF member countries consider the domestic policies and legal systems of identified NCCTs to be undermining their legitimate national interest.

[61] Furthermore, if the Security Council made explicit reference to the FATF guidelines as international standards in the context of combating terrorist financing, it could lay a solid groundwork for the FATF in all aspects.

5.2.3 Other supporting activities

For the purpose of promoting the effectiveness of its AML/CFT framework as a whole, the FATF is involved in a number of supporting activities. Firstly, the FATF has conducted research activities of terrorist financing and money laundering typologies since its establishment in 1989.[62] These research activities provide the groundwork for diagnosing the deficiencies in practice, thus facilitating the amendment of relevant standards, and the development of enforcement methods. Secondly, the FATF attempts to spread the AML/CFT framework all around the world. It expands its membership to strategically important countries,[63] and resorts to regional mobilisation through cooperation with other international organisations, such as FSRBs and United Nations Office on Drugs and Crime, and through the arrangement of regional seminars and conferences. However, given the mandate of the FATF as a "policy-making body"[64] and the inadequate manpower and resources of its Secretariat,[65] the FATF itself does not actively engage in the rendering of technical assistance.

---

[62] Originally, the analysis of money laundering typologies had been included in the Annual Report but since the FATF VIII period (1996-1997), the FATF has published a separate document "Report on Money Laundering Typologies" on an annual basis.

[63] Originally the FATF is not active in expanding its membership for the reason that it might undermine the effective and efficient operation of the FATF itself. However, in the review of the FATF future which was carried out in 1998, the FATF decided to expand its membership to include a limited number of strategically important countries which could play a major role in their regions. In this sense, the requirements of new membership is quite demanding which is as follows:
-   To implement the 1996 Recommendations within a reasonable timeframe (three years), and (ii) to undergo annual self-assessment exercises and two rounds of mutual evaluations;
-   To be a full and active member of the relevant FATF-style regional body (where one exists), or be prepared to work with the FATF or even to take the lead, to establish such a body (where none exists);
-   To be a strategically important country;
-   To have already made the laundering of the proceeds of drug trafficking and other serious crimes a criminal offence; and,
-   To have already made it mandatory for financial institutions to identify their customers and to report unusual or suspicious transactions (FATF, "Annual Report: 1998-1999", 2 July 1999, p.34).

[64] (visited on 1 June 2005> <http://www.fatf-gafi.org/pages/0,2987,en_32250379_3223 5720_1_1_1_1_1,00.html>.

[65] There are around 10 people who work at the FATF Secretariat which is financed by the individual contributions from the 31 member countries and 2 member organisations (Vandergrift K, "Re: Inquiry", E-mail to Jae-myong Koh, 8 March 2004).

5.3 IMF / World Bank

5.3.1 Context

The IMF is an international organisation of 184 member countries, and it was established to promote international monetary cooperation, exchange stability, and economic growth.[66] To this end, the IMF is involved in three essential operations which are surveillance, financial assistance, and technical assistance.[67] Namely, the IMF monitors the development of international financial situations, and assists member countries in maintaining orderly exchange arrangements among themselves. Particularly, if the IMF identifies a crisis of foreign exchange in member countries, it provides temporary financial assistance to the countries with a view to helping them to adjust their balance of payments without resorting to measures destructive of national or international prosperity.[68] Thus, symbolically, the IMF can be said to play the role of the "fire brigade" in the international financial system.[69]

By comparison, the World Bank is an organisation which operates with a long-term perspective and its membership is also comprised of 184 countries. In principle, this membership of the World Bank overlaps with that of the IMF since countries first join the IMF to become members of the World Bank.[70] The mission of the World Bank is to fight poverty and improve the living standards of people in the developing world. For these purposes, the World Bank provides loans, analysis and policy advice, as well as technical assistance to low and middle income countries.

Despite the fundamental difference between these two organisations in their goals, one common area is that they both focus on the protection and improvement in the financial sector in the course of pursuing their objectives.[71] Accordingly, both organisations have sought cooperation in dealing with the financial sector by way of jointly launching assessment programmes or rendering technical assis-

---

[66] See, the purposes in the "Articles of Agreement of the IMF", the IMF website (visited on 20 March 2004) < http://www.imf.org/external/pubs/ft/aa/aa01.htm>.

[67] See, "About the IMF", the IMF website (visited on 20 March 2004) <http://www.imf.org/external/about.htm>.

[68] Schott PA (2003) *Reference Guide to Anti-Money Laundering and Combating the Financing of Terrorism*, p.X-2.

[69] Forget L, Interview at the headquarters of the IMF, Washington DC, 19 February 2004.

[70] See the World Bank website (visited on 3 March 2004)<http://web.worldbank.org/WBSITE/EXTERNAL/EXTABOUTUS/0,,pagePK:43912~piPK:36602~theSitePK:29708,00.html>.

[71] IMF/World Bank, "Strengthening IMF-World Bank Collaboration on Country Programs and Conditionality-Progress Report", 19 August 2002, p.7.

tance, thus attempting to avoid duplication and promoting a synergy effect.[72] Under these circumstances, as money laundering increasingly becomes seen as a threat to the financial sector, the IMF and World Bank began to consider their engagement in this area to protect the global financial system since early 2001.[73] However, it was 9/11 which provided critical momentum to both organisations' involvement in the AML/CFT area.[74] In the view of the IMF, money laundering and terrorist financing have a full range of macroeconomic consequences, such as unpredictable changes in money demand and risks to the soundness of the financial systems.[75] Also in terms of the World Bank, money laundering and terrorist financing have potentially devastating economic, political and social consequences for developing countries.[76]

---

[72] In this context, the division of labour between the IMF and the World Bank has been continuously reviewed. Originally, in 2001, both organisations endorsed a joint paper with a view to promoting the cooperation between themselves (IMF/World Bank, "Strengthening IMF-World Bank Collaboration on Country Programs and Conditionality", 23 August 2001).

The IMF/World Bank also issued a staff guidance note on "Operationalizing Bank-Fund Collaboration in Country Programs and Conditionality" in April 2002 which stresses division of labour based on the concept of a "lead agency", "discussions and coordination at an early stage", "adequate information sharing", and "transparency in presenting information to the Boards". More recently, the IMF/World Bank published progress reports such as: (i) "Strengthening IMF-World Bank Collaboration on Country Programs and Conditionality-Progress Report", 19 August 2002; (ii)"Strengthening IMF-World Bank Collaboration on Country Programs and Conditionality-Progress Report", 24 February 2004. For the text of the 2002 guidance note, see, the first progress report published in August 2002, pp.21-24.

[73] The IMF/World Bank issued a joint policy paper which proposed both organisations strengthen their role in the global fight against money laundering. See, "Enhancing Contributions to Combating Money Laundering: Policy Paper", 26 April 2001.

[74] IMF, "Intensified Fund Involvement in Anti-Money Laundering Work and Combating the Financing of Terrorism", 5 November 2001.

[75] Schott PA, *supra* note 68, p.X-2.

[76] *Ibid.*, X-2. Although it would not be an objective analysis of the adverse effects of terrorist financing, it is interesting to note the remarks of Usama bin Laden of the impact of 9/11 on the global economy, which reads as follows:

"I say the events that happened on Tuesday 11 September in New York and Washington, that is truly a great event in all measures, and its claims until this moment are not over and are still continuing.... According to their own admissions, the share of the losses on the Wall Street market reached 16%. They said that this number is a record, which has never happened since the opening of the market more than 230 years ago. This large collapse has never happened. The gross amount that is traded in that market reaches $ 4 trillion. So if we multiply 16% by $ 4 trillion to find out the loss that affect-

Accordingly, the IMF and the World Bank developed action plans with regard to the AML/CFT issue in November 2001 and January 2002, respectively.[77] The action plans call for joint action in the following areas:

1. Expanding Fund/Bank involvement in AML work to include CFT;
2. Expanding Fund/Bank AML work to cover legal and institutional framework issues in addition to financial sector supervisory issues;
3. Agreeing with the FATF on a converged global AML/CFT standard and associated Reports on Observance of Standards and Codes(ROSC) process;[78]
4. Increasing Fund/Bank technical assistance in response to members' requests to strengthen AML/CFT regimes; and,
5. Conducting a joint Fund/Bank study of informal funds transfer systems.

In addition, under its Action Plan, the IMF is:

1. Circulating over time a voluntary questionnaire on AML/CFT in the context of Fund Article IV missions[79]; and,
2. Accelerating the Fund's OFC assessment program.

Under its Action Plan, the World Bank is also:

1. Integrating AML/CFT issues in Country Assistance Strategies (CASs).[80]

5.3.2 The monitoring of standards

As mentioned above, in broader terms, the work of the IMF and the World Bank falls into three major categories: *assessment of a country's situation, lending* and *technical assistance.* Thus, the monitoring of the AML/CFT standards can be un-

---

ed the stocks, it reaches $ 640 billion of losses from stocks, by Allah's grace. So this amount, for example, is the budget of Sudan for 640 years. They have lost this, due to an attack that happened with the success of Allah lasting one hour only." (reproduced from Gunaratna R (2002) *Inside Al Qaeda: Global Network of Terror*, pp.225-226). For relevant discussions, see, Johnston RB, Nelelescu OM, "The Impact of Terrorism on Financial Markets", *IMF Working Paper*, WP/05/60.

[77] For the IMF Action Plan, see, "Intensified Fund Involvement in Anti-Money Laundering Work and Combating the Financing of Terrorism", 5 November 2001, pp.14-17. For the World Bank Action Plan, see, "Proposed Action Plan for Enhancing the Bank's Ability to Respond to Clients in Combating Money Laundering and the Financing of Terrorism", 22 January 2002.

[78] For details on ROSCs, see *infra* note 89.

[79] For details on Article IV missions, see *infra* note 101 and its related text.

[80] IMF/World Bank, "Intensified Work on Anti-Money Laundering and Combating Financing of Terrorism (AML/CFT)", 17 April 2002, p.3. For details on the CASs, see, *infra* note 112 and its related text.

derstood in the context of the *assessment* activities. However, given that the IMF/World Bank are not standard-setting bodies, these organisations simply borrowed internationally recognised standards for their purposes. In other words, the IMF/World Bank agreed to adopt the FATF 8+40 Recommendations as relevant standards in the AML/CFT area in July 2002, with some conditions that should be met by the FATF.[81] Of particular note among the conditions are the development of a common assessment tool and the suspension of a further NCCT round.[82] Consequently, both sides (the IMF/World Bank and the FATF) jointly developed and adopted a common assessment tool, namely, the "Comprehensive Methodology for Assessing Compliance with AML/CFT Standards" in October 2002. It was mainly based on the 8+40 Recommendations. Then, both sides jointly launched a 12-month pilot programme of AML/CFT assessment on 15 November 2002, using this common methodology.[83] The FATF kept the promise not to take the third

---

[81] "Anti-Money Laundering and Combating the Financing of Terrorism (AML/CFT): Proposals To assess A Global Standard And To Prepare ROSCs", 17 July 2002, pp.6-7. The conditions were as follows:
- The FATF Secretariat, in consultation with Fund/Bank staff, satisfactorily completes the draft of the comprehensive and integrated assessment methodology by the Annual Meetings for consideration at the October Plenary;
- In its October Plenary, the FATF endorses the comprehensive methodology and its use in undertaking FATF/FSRB mutual evaluations and Fund/Bank staff-led assessments;
- In its October Plenary, the FATF agrees to undertake its mutual evaluations consistent with the ROSC process; and,
- The FATF does not undertake a further round of the NCCT process, at least during the period of a 12-month pilot project.

For the response of the FATF, see, IMF, "Report on the Outcome of the FATF Plenary Meeting and Proposal for the Endorsement of the Methodology for Assessing Compliance with Anti-Money Laundering and Combating the Financing of Terrorism (AML/CFT) Standard", 8 November 2002, p.3.

[82] The reason for the demand for the suspension of the NCCT initiative is that usually, the assessment of the IMF and World Bank is conducted on a voluntary basis at the request of the assessed country, while the NCCT initiative is a unilateral measure of assessment toward unwilling countries. For a good comparison between the NCCT process and the work of the IMF/World Bank, see, IMF/World Bank, "Anti-Money Laundering and Combating the Financing of Terrorism (AML/CFT): Materials Concerning Staff Progress Towards the Development of a Comprehensive AML/CFT Methodology and Assessment Process", 11 June 2002, p.10.

[83] For the progress and the results of the 12-month pilot programme, see, IMF/World Bank, "Twelve-Month Pilot Program of Anti-Money Laundering and Combating the Financing of Terrorism (AML/CFT) Assessments and Delivery of AML/CFT Technical Assistance", 31 March 2003; IMF/World Bank, "Status Report of the Work of the IMF

round of the NCCT initiative at least during the period of the pilot programme.[84] With the success of this programme, the IMF/World Bank decided in March 2004 to make the assessment practice a regular part of their work, and endorsed the revised 2003 Forty Recommendations and its revised 2004 AML/CFT methodology as well.[85] This 2004 methodology became effective for IMF/World Bank from September 2004.[86] Correspondingly, the FATF reciprocated the cooperation from the IMF/World Bank by declaring that it "has no plans at present to conduct a third round of the NCCT reviews".[87]

The cooperative mechanism which has been developed through the 12-month pilot programme is as follows. For their part, the IMF/World Bank decided to participate in the pilot programme in the main in the context of their normal operation of the Financial Sector Assessment Program (FSAP)[88] and the Offshore Financial Center (OFC) programme.

---

and the World Bank on the Twelve-Month Pilot Program of AML/CFT assessments and Delivery of AML/CFT Technical Assistance", 5 September 2003; IMF/World Bank, "Twelve Month Pilot Program of AML/CFT Assessments: Joint Report on the Review of the Pilot Program", 10 March 2004.

[84] IMF, "Report on the Outcome of the FATF Plenary Meeting and Proposal for the Endorsement of the Methodology for Assessing Compliance with Anti-Money Laundering and Combating the Financing of Terrorism (AML/CFT) Standard", 8 November 2002, p.3.

[85] IMF, "IMF Executive Board Reviews and Enhances Efforts for Anti-Money Laundering and Combating the Financing of Terrorism", Public Information Notice (PIN) No.04/33, 2 April 2004; FATF, "Annual Report: 2003-2004", 2 July 2004, p.9.

[86] <http://www1.worldbank.org/finance/html/amlcft/methodology.htm>.

[87] "Letter from the FATF President to Mr.Kohler", in IMF/World Bank, "Twelve-Month Pilot Program of AML/CFT Assessments", 10 March 2004, p.63.

[88] In fact, the FSAP, a joint IMF/World Bank effort introduced in May 1999, aims to identify the strengths and vulnerabilities of a country's financial system; to determine how key sources of risk are being managed; to ascertain the sector's developmental and technical assistance needs; and, to help prioritise policy responses. See, IMF/World Bank, "Financial Sector Assessment Program-Review, Lessons, and Issues Going Forward", 24 February 2003, p.8. Initially, there was a criticism that it was not desirable for the IMF and World Bank to assess legal/criminal enforcement measures since these areas are beyond the mandate of both organisations. However, it should be noted that the FATF Forty Recommendations were designed to be assessed as a unified whole rather than separately (IMF/World Bank, "Strengthening IMF-World Bank Collaboration on Country Programs and Conditionality", 23 August 2001.p.16). Thus, subsequently, the work of the IMF/the World Bank has been expanded to cover legal and institutional framework issues (IMF/World Bank, "Intensified Work on Anti-Money Laundering and Combating Financing of Terrorism (AML/CFT)", 17 April 2002, p.3). However, for the pilot programme, the IMF/World Bank staff assess compliance with all criteria except

Firstly, for the purpose of implementing the FSAP, the IMF/World Bank have set the standards and codes in 12 areas under which the AML/CFT issue is subsumed.[89] By the FSAP, the IMF/World Bank prepare country reports. These reports analyse each country's status on the implementation of the 12 standards and codes, thus being called "Reports on Observance of Standards and Codes (ROSCs). Then, these ROSC modules constitute the basis for the publication of the documents called the "Financial System Stability Assessments (FSSAs)" in the IMF context, and the "Financial Sector Assessment (FSA)" in the World Bank context, respectively.[90] Namely the same ROSCs are incorporated into the texts of each organisation's document. Given the voluntary nature of the ROSC procedure, the assessment process of the IMF/World Bank can be triggered only at the request of the assessed country.[91]

---

those relating to the implementation of criminal justice measures and to sectors that are not macroeconomically relevant. One or more independent AML/CFT experts (IAEs) assessed the remaining criteria (IMF/World Bank, "Twelve-Month Pilot Program of AML/CFT Assessments", 10 March 2004, p.8). Later, the IMF decided to expand its AML/CFT assessment and technical assistance work to cover the full scope of the 2004 FATF Forty Recommendations including the criminal justice area, and non-financial institutions such as lawyers and notaries (IMF, "IMF Executive Board Reviews and Enhances Efforts for Anti-Money Laundering and Combating the Financing of Terrorism", Public Information Notice (PIN) No.04/33, 2 April 2004).

[89] The list of the 12 areas are: transparency standards; fiscal transparency; financial sector standards; banking supervision; securities; insurance; payments systems; anti-money laundering and combating the financing of terrorism; standards concerned with market integrity; corporate governance; accounting; auditing; insolvency and creditor rights. See, the IMF website (visited on 25 January 2005) <http://www.imf.org>.

[90] IMF/World Bank, "Financial Sector Assessment Program-Review, Lessons, and Issues Going Forward", 24 February 2003, p. 7.

[91] The four guiding principles for the ROSC process:
- The staff's involvement in assessing non-prudently-regulated financial sector activities should be confined to those that are macro-economically relevant and pose a significant risk of money laundering/terrorism financing;
- All assessment procedures should be transparent and consistent with the mandate and core expertise of the different institutions involved, and compatible with the uniform, voluntary, and cooperative nature of the ROSC exercise;
- The assessments should be followed up with appropriate technical assistance at the request of the countries assessed in order to build their institutional capacity and develop their financial sectors; and,
- The assessments would be conducted in accordance with the comprehensive and integrated methodology (IMF, "Report on the Outcome of the FATF Plenary Meeting and Proposal for the Endorsement of the Methodology for Assessing

Secondly, the OFC programme was initiated by the Executive Board in July 2000 to address potential vulnerabilities in the global financial system.[92] It assesses financial regulation and supervision in jurisdictions with significant financial activity and few previous assessments of standards, following a request from the jurisdiction.[93] On this occasion, jurisdictions' AML/CFT regime is also assessed using the version of the common methodology available at the time of assessment.[94]

In contrast, the FATF and FATF-Style Regional Bodies (FSRBs) joined the 12-month pilot programme in the context of conducting their own mutual evaluation. The results of these mutual evaluations were subsequently transformed into the ROSC format for IMF/World Bank purposes.[95] A total of 8 assessments were completed by the FATF or FSRBs during this test period.[96] To this end, the FATF and FSRBs used the 2002 methodology shared by the IMF/World Bank.[97] In terms of reciprocity, it is interesting to note that the IMF/World Bank agreed to incorporate the results of the mutual evaluation exercises by the FATF into the ROSCs when available, urging a reciprocal approach by the FATF and FSRBs to use a Fund/Bank-led assessment in lieu of a mutual evaluation.[98] Fortunately, some FSRBs such as the Asia/Pacific Group on Money Laundering (APG) and the Caribbean Financial Action Task Force (CFATF) decided that they would use an IMF/World Bank-led assessment when available in lieu of mutual evaluation in the future.[99]

In addition to the major assessment exercises as mentioned above, the IMF alone conducts assessment exercises in the context of Article IV consultations.[100] The

---

Compliance with Anti-Money Laundering and Combating the Financing of Terrorism(AML/CFT) Standard", 8 November 2002, p.2).

[92] IMF, "Offshore Financial Center Reform: A Progress Report", 14 March 2003, p.4.

[93] IMF, "Offshore Financial Centers: The Assessment Program: An Information Note", 29 August 2002.

[94] IMF, "Offshore Financial Center Reform: A Progress Report", 14 March 2003, p.12.

[95] FATF, "Annual Report: 2002-2003", p.22; IMF/World Bank, "Twelve-Month Pilot Program of AML/CFT Assessments", 10 March 2004, p.9, p.13.

[96] IMF/World Bank, "Twelve-Month Pilot Program of AML/CFT Assessments", 10 March 2004, p.4.

[97] FATF conducted assessment on South Africa, Russia, and Germany as part of the pilot programme. See, IMF/World Bank, "Twelve Month Pilot Program of AML/CFT Assessments", 10 March 2004, p.13.

[98] For a relevant discussion, see, *ibid.*,p.9. The IMF/World Bank-led missions conducted assessments of some FATF member countries such as the UK and Austria but these reports were not adopted as formal mutual evaluation reports by the FATF.

[99] IMF/World Bank, "Twelve Month Pilot Program of AML/CFT Assessments", 10 March 2004, p.9.

[100] *Ibid.*,p.17.

IMF shall oversee the international monetary system to ensure its effective operation and for this reason, member countries are required to undertake consultation with the IMF on their exchange rate policies usually on a yearly basis.[101] However, it should be pointed out that the scope of consultation topics is not narrowly confined to exchange rate policies but covers all aspects of an economic situation because exchange rate policies are one of the variables which operate linked with each other in a national economy.[102] Thus, the IMF included the AML/CFT issue in the topics for consultation and consequently, it developed an AML/CFT questionnaire and has distributed it to member countries to be visited by Article IV consultation missions since early 2002. However, it should be seen as a complement to and not as a substitute for FSAPs and OFC assessments.[103]

5.3.3 Other supporting activities

The IMF and the World Bank are actively involved in supportive activities for the purpose of spreading the AML/CFT message worldwide. Interestingly, it should be noted that although they do not have a formal enforcement policy,[104] some of these supportive activities can be characterised as a kind of soft enforcement (examined in detail below).

Firstly, the IMF and the World Bank render technical assistance based on the findings from the FSAPs and separate AML/CFT assessments.[105] The World Bank includes technical assistance in respect of the AML/CFT issue in its Country Assistance Strategy (CAS) for developing countries.[106] Moreover, for the purpose of improving systematic and coordinated technical assistance follow-up procedures, the Financial Sector Reform and Strengthening (FIRST) initiative was developed.[107] The FIRST initiative seeks to support countries' implementation of re-

---

[101] Articles of Agreement of the International Monetary Fund, Article IV, section 3(b).

[102] Gold J (1983) "Strengthening the Soft International Law of Exchange Arrangements", *The American Journal of International Law*, vol.77, p.474 (This article provides an excellent overview of the relationship between the Article IV and its soft law nature).

[103] IMF, "Intensified Work on Anti-Money Laundering and Combating the Financing of Terrorism (AML/CFT)", 10 September 2002, section II, para. 3-6.

[104] See, e.g., IMF/World Bank, "Anti-Money Laundering and Combating the Financing of Terrorism (AML/CFT): Materials Concerning Staff Progress Towards the Development of a Comprehensive AML/CFT Methodology and Assessment Process", 11 June 2002, p.28.

[105] Schott PA, *supra* note 68, p.X-7.

[106] IMF/Word Bank, "Intensified Work on Anti-Money Laundering and Combating the Financing of Terrorism (AML/CFT): Joint Progress Report on the Work of the IMF and World Bank", 25 September 2002, para. 38.

[107] IMF/World Bank, "Implementation of the Basel Core Principles for Effective Banking Supervision, Experiences, Influences, and Perspectives", 23 September 2002, p.39.

commendations made from the assessment reports.[108] Also the IMF/World Bank publish reference guides on AML/CFT issues to facilitate the establishment of countries' legislative and institutional frameworks.[109] Furthermore, the World Bank is operating a database on its website for the purpose of matchmaking the requests and the donation of technical assistance.[110] As a result, by way of illustration, during the period January 2002-December 2003, the IMF/World Bank delivered 116 TA projects, including 85 direct TA to 63 countries, and 32 regional projects reaching more than 130 countries.[111]

Secondly, as indicated above, the IMF/World Bank provide *lending assistance.* For instance, the World Bank includes the AML/CFT components in its lending projects. It integrates the findings of the FSAP in respect of the AML/CFT issues into the broader Country Assistance Strategy (CAS),[112] and incorporates the AML/CFT component into country programmes or individual lending operations. In this context, several loans by the World Bank already have the AML/CFT components in place in relation to the reform in the financial sector.[113]

---

[108] The FIRST Initiative is a multi-donor trust fund aimed at promoting robust and diverse financial sectors in developing and transition countries, utilising the resources pledged by initial donors (UK, Canada, Sweden, Switzerland, the World Bank, and the IMF). The initial commitment was approximately US$ 10-12 million over four years (IMF/World Bank, "Intensified Work on Anti-Money Laundering and Combating Financing of Terrorism (AML/CFT)", 17 April 2002, p.13).

[109] Schott PA, *supra* note 68, p.X-9.

[110] IMF/World Bank, "Twelve-Month Pilot Program of Anti-Money Laundering and Combating the Financing of Terrorism (AML/CFT) Assessments and Delivery of AML/CFT Technical Assistance", 31 March 2003, p.16.

[111] IMF/World Bank, "Twelve Month Pilot Program of AML/CFT Assessments: Joint Report on the Review of the Pilot Program", 11 March 2004, p.14.

[112] For the purpose of achieving the goal of "development", the World Bank employs several strategies as a means. The CAS is one of these strategies. It is a development framework for the World Bank's assistance in a client country, in the sense that it sets out the priorities for the World Bank's programme on a three-year basis in consultation with the concerned government. Its objective is to identify the key areas where the World Bank's assistance can have the largest impact on poverty reduction. In producing its CAS, the World Bank conducts extensive analysis of the country's economic and social situation in consultation with the government (visited on 19 April 2004) <http://www.worldbank.org/html/extdr/casconsult.htm>.

[113] For example, the AML/CFT Technical Assistance totaling US$ 2.2 million has been included in lending programs for 4 countries-Bangladesh, Guatemala, Honduras, and Pakistan. In addition, for Serbia/Montenegro, the AML/CFT is an area to be covered in the adjustment loan (IMF/World Bank, "Twelve Month Pilot Program of AML/CFT Assessments: Joint Report on the Review of the Pilot Program", 11 March 2004, p.17); Halligan J, Interview, Washington, DC, 19 February 2004.

Thirdly, the IMF/World Bank conduct research into the AML/CFT typologies, a case in point being the recent analysis of the *hawala* System.[114] These studies examine the operational characteristics of the informal value transfer system, and discuss the implications for regulatory and supervisory responses to the system.[115]

Lastly, the IMF/World Bank also focus on the awareness raising campaign in the AML/CFT area, as illustrated by the recent Global Dialogue Series which is a live video conference for the purpose of establishing a communication network on AML/CFT issues with leading experts and high level country officials.[116]

5.4 FATF-Style Regional Bodies (FSRBs)

5.4.1 The development of FSRBs

As one of the regional mobilisation strategies to combat money laundering, the FATF has supported or fostered the development of FATF-style regional bodies all over the world. This cooperative relationship between the FATF and FSRBs is of considerable importance for several reasons. For instance, the FSRBs could engage "non-FATF" member countries in the AML/CFT campaign in the "FATF" manner. Furthermore, given the small size of the FATF Secretariat in Paris, FSRBs could play an essential role in ensuring the appropriate provision of technical assistance and other follow-up activities in non-FATF member countries.[117] These aspects are well illustrated by the agreement of FATF Plenary meeting in 1998 :

> ".... the ideal model for an FATF-style regional body would be: a local group exerting peer pressure among its members and whose mutual evaluation procedures had been endorsed by the FATF; one or several FATF members present in it and a secretariat which would liaise regularly with the FATF. Moreover, the presidents/secretariats of each FATF-style regional body should become full members of the FATF. The FATF-style regional bodies should also be commit-

---

[114] The IMF and the World Bank recently published their work on the *hawala* system, respectively. See, Qorchi ME, Maimbo SM, Wilson JF, "Informal Funds Transfer Systems: An Analysis of the Informal Hawala System", *Occasional Paper 222*, 18 August 2003; Maimbo SM (2003) "The Money Exchange Dealers of Kabul: A Study of the Hawala System in Afghanistan".

[115] Schott PA, *supra* note 68, p.X-9.

[116] The first of the series started in January 2002 (IMF/World Bank, "Intensified Work on Anti-Money Laundering and Combating the Financing of Terrorism (AML/CFT)", 25 September 2002).

[117] Gilmore WC (2004) *Dirty Money: The evolution of international measures to counter money laundering and the financing of terrorism*, pp.144-145.

ted to the Forty Recommendations and to any other anti-money laundering principles they wish to endorse to reflect local problems. The main task of these bodies should include conducting mutual evaluations of their members and carrying out self-assessment surveys and regional typologies exercises".[118]

In this context, there have been established seven FSRBs thus far: the Caribbean Financial Action Task Force (CFATF)[119]; the Asia/Pacific Group on Money Laundering (APG);[120] the Council of Europe Select Committee of Experts on the Evaluation of Anti-Money Laundering Measures (MONEYVAL) (formerly PC-R-EV)[121]; the Eastern and Southern Africa Anti-Money Laundering Group (ESAAMLG)[122]; the Financial Action Task Force on Money Laundering in South America (GAFISUD)[123]; the Eurasian Group on Money Laundering and Terrorism Funding (EAG)[124]; and, the Middle East & North African Financial Action Task Force on Money Laundering (MENAFATF).[125]

Given that the operating mechanism of all these FSRBs is not so different from each other and utilising the writer's familiarity with the Asia/ Pacific region, this chapter will make a case study of the APG to examine the role of the FSRBs in the global AML/CFT campaign.

5.4.2 The nature and scope of the FSRBs work

5.4.2.1 The background to the APG

Like other regions, the Asia/Pacific region has also suffered from transnational criminal activities. This is, for example, the case with the trade in heroin based on the Golden Triangle and Golden Crescent area and trafficking in people and small arms in South Asia.[126] Moreover, the region includes the home countries of major

---

[118] FATF, "Review of the Future of FATF: Strategic Issues", FATF-IX, PLEN/12.BIS.REV 1, reproduced from Gilmore WC, *supra* note 117, pp.145-146.

[119] For details, see its website <http://www.cfatf.org/>.

[120] For details, see its website < http://www.apgml.org/>.

[121] For details, see its website <http://www.coe.int/T/E/Legal_affairs/Legal_co-operation/ Combating_economic_crime/Money_laundering/>.

[122] For details, see its website <http://www.esaamlg.org/>.

[123] For details, see its website <http://www.gafisud.org/>.

[124] The EAG was founded in Moscow in October 2004. The founding members are Belarus, Kazakhstan, People's Republic of China, the Russian Federation and Tajikstan.

[125] The MENAFATF was created in November 2004 in Bahrain. For details, see its website <http://www.mofne.gov.bh/menafatf/ArticleDetail.asp?rid=548>.

[126] McFarlane J (2001) "Transnational Crime and Asia-Pacific Security". In: Simon SW (ed) *The Many Faces of Asian Security*, Boston: Rowman & Littlefield Publishers, Inc., pp.202-208.

world criminal organisations such as *the Japanese Yakuza, the Chinese Triads, and the Russian Mafia*.[127] Furthermore, in the money laundering context, the extensive and efficient underground banking systems have been operating either as a substitute for or as a complement to the orthodox financial sector in the region.[128] Under these circumstances, the vast geographical area and loose governmental control, and corruption have contributed to the aggravation of the problems.[129] Consequently, Asia/Pacific was one of the regions to which the FATF gave priority consideration. In conjunction with the Commonwealth Secretariat, the FATF began an "awareness raising" campaign in the region.[130] A number of symposia were held. The first was held in Singapore in April 1993. The second took place in Kuala Lumpur, Malaysia in November/December 1994, at which the 16 attending governments endorsed and agreed to implement the FATF Forty Recommendations.[131] In order to achieve more concrete results, Australia agreed in 1995 to set up a Secretariat in Australia.[132] The Secretariat, in cooperation with the Commonwealth Secretartiat and other international bodies, worked to garner support for anti-money laundering measures.[133] As a result, Typologies Workshops were held in Hong Kong in October 1995 and November 1996, and the Third Asia Money Laundering Symposium was held in Tokyo in December 1995.[134] Eventually, the APG was officially established as a regional anti-money laundering body in February 1997 at the Fourth (and last) Asia Money Laundering Symposium in Bangkok.[135]

5.4.2.2 The structure and functions of the APG

The purpose of the APG is to facilitate the adoption, implementation and enforcement of internationally accepted anti-money laundering and counter-terrorist financing standards, such as the FATF Forty Recommendations and Special Rec-

---

[127] For an overview of these organisations, see, Williams P, Savona EU (1996) *The United Nations and Transnational Organised Crime*, pp.14-18.

[128] Gilmore WC, *supra* note 117, pp.228-229.

[129] Koh JM (2002) "Transnational Organised Crime and International Countering Efforts". In: Ministry of Foreign Affairs and Trade (ROK) *Theory and Practice of Multilateral Security Policy*, p.245.

[130] APG, "First Annual Report: 1999-2000", April 2001, p.6.

[131] *Ibid.*, p.6.

[132] *Ibid.*, p.6.

[133] *Ibid.*, p.6.

[134] *Ibid.*, p.6.

[135] See, "Relationship to the FATF", the APG website (visited on 3 March 2004)<http://www.apgml.org/content/relationship_to_the_fatf.jsp>; APG, "Annual Report 1 July 2001-30 June 2002", December 2002, p.1.

ommendations, while taking into account regional factors.[136] The APG was established by agreement among its members rather than being based on an international treaty. In the 2004 Annual Meeting, it was agreed that the APG continue in existence until December 2012, corresponding to the recent extension of the mandate of the FATF until December 2012.

The requirements for the APG membership are as follows:

- Recognises the need for action to be taken to combat money laundering and terrorist financing;
- Recognises the benefits to be obtained by sharing knowledge and experience;
- Has taken or is actively taking steps to develop, pass and implement anti-money laundering and anti-terrorist financing legislation and other measures based on accepted international standards;
- Subject to its domestic laws, commits itself to implementing the decisions made by the APG;
- Commits itself to participate in the mutual evaluation programme;
- Contributes to the APG budget in accordance with arrangements agreed by the APG.[137]

It is interesting to note that these requirements are not as strict as those of the FATF. Indeed, it is not necessary that candidates jurisdictions be considered as strategically important or that they have AML laws already in place.[138] In this sense, the APG seems to be quite open to nearly all regional jurisdictions. At present, it comprises 28 member jurisdictions,[139] 11 observer jurisdictions,[140] and 15 observer international and regional organisations.[141]

---

[136] APG, "Terms of Reference" in "Annual Report: 1 July 2001-30 June 2002", December 2002, pp.34-35.

[137] APG, "Terms of Reference" in "Annual Report: 1 October 2003-30 June 2004", November 2004, p.35.

[138] For the FATF criteria for admission, see, *supra* note 63.

[139] Australia; Bangladesh; Brunei Darussalam; Cambodia; Chinese Taipei; Cook Islands; Fiji Islands; Hong Kong, China; India; Indonesia; Japan; Korea, Republic of; Macau, China; Malaysia; Marshall Islands; Mongolia; Nepal; New Zealand; Niue; Pakistan; Palau; Philippines; Samoa; Singapore; Sri Lanka; Thailand; United States of America; Vanuatu. See, the APG's website (visited on 1 June 2005) <http://www.apgml.org/content/member_jurisdiction.jsp>.

[140] Canada; France; Kiribati; Lao People's Democratic Republic; The Maldives; Nauru; Papua New Guinea; Tonga; Myanmar; United Kingdom; Vietnam. See, *ibid.*

[141] ADB; APEC; ASEAN; CFATF; Commonwealth Secretariat; Egmont Group; FATF; IMF; INTERPOL; OGBS; Pacific Financial Technical Assistance Centre (PFTAC); Pacific Islands Forum Secretariat (PIFS); UNODC; World Bank; World Customs Organisation (WCO). See *ibid.*

The APG meets at least once a year, and decisions are made by consensus.[142] The Secretariat is located in Sydney, Australia. With regard to the leadership of the APG, there are two co-chairs, and originally it was agreed that during the formative stage, one co-chair position would be held by Australia which should host the annual meeting on alternative years,[143] and the other co-chair would be rotated every two years amongst member jurisdictions.[144] At the 2004 Annual Meeting, however, it was decided that while the "formative stage" should be considered completed, the status quo be maintained and that no change to APG's Co-Chairing arrangements should be made for some time.[145] This is mainly due to the fact that the current system is operating well and Australia has been providing an essential support to the APG by hosting the secretariat or other financial means.

Generally, the APG develops a Strategic Plan every three years, and makes an annual Business Plan of a detailed nature.[146] At present, the 2nd Strategic Plan has been adopted for the period of 2003-06 which reads as follows.[147]

1. Provide an autonomous regional body for APG members and observers to work together against money laundering and the financing of terrorism (ML/FT);
2. Conduct outreach activities to promote membership of the APG and encourage non-member to cooperate in the global fight against ML/FT;
3. Participate in and cooperate with the global AML network primarily the FATF and other regional anti-money laundering groups;
4. Carry out education, research and analysis activities to enhance the understanding of the ML/FT environment and the global fights against it;
5. Assist APG members to implement the global standards against ML/FT; and,
6. Assess APG members' compliance with the global standards against ML/FT.

With regard to the implementation of these strategic and action plans of the APG, of particular note is the role of the APG Steering Group which was established at the Annual Meeting in September 2003.[148] The major functions of the Steering Group are:[149] (a) to consider governance and other issues of strategic importance referred to it; (b) to engage and consult with APG members to obtain their input on key issues; (c) to provide advice to the APG Co-chairs and APG members through the Secretariat; (d) to assist with engaging and influencing all

---

[142] APG, "Terms of Reference" in "Annual Report: 1 October 2003-30 June 2004", November 2004, p.36.

[143] *Ibid.*, p.37.

[144] *Ibid.*, p.37.

[145] *Ibid.*, p.14.

[146] *Ibid.*, p.36.

[147] APG, "Annual Report: 1 July 2002-30 September 2003", September 2004, p.4.

[148] APG, "Annual Report: 1 October 2003-30 June 2004", November 2004, p.13.

[149] *Ibid.*, pp.12-13.

APG members to effectively participate in its activities, including leading or sponsoring specific APG projects; and, (e) to encourage non-members in their geographic area to join the APG. The membership of the Steering Group includes a representative from each of five broad geographical areas within the Asia/Pacific region, namely North Asia, Pacific Islands, South Asia, South East Asia, and 'Other'.[150] Each representative will be selected by consensus within each geographical area on an annual basis.[151] In addition, the current Co-Chairs and immediate past and nominated future Co-Chair are also subsumed under the membership.[152] Without doubt, these functions considerably reinforce the activities of the APG, especially in securing political momentum and solid financing. This *implementation-oriented* administrative structure stands in contrast with the simple organisational structure of the FATF which mainly focuses on standard-setting activities.[153] This is one of aspects which characterise the relationship between the FATF and FSRBs.

5.4.2.3 The monitoring of standards by the APG

Having its origins in the initial awareness-raising efforts of the FATF, the APG naturally adopted the FATF Forty Recommendations as the AML/CFT standard.[154] Moreover, as it is stipulated in its terms of reference, the APG can also review the best way to apply the standards within the region considering regional factors.[155] The CFATF already tried this approach by adopting the Nineteen Recommendations.[156] However, at the 2002 Annual Meeting, APG agreed not to develop its own standards at this time but rather to feed into the review of the global standards set up by the FATF.[157] In this context, the APG endorsed the revised 2003 FATF Forty Recommendations in September 2003 and its revised 2004 AML/CFT methodology in June 2004.[158]

Being influenced by the FATF, the APG similarly employed self-assessment and mutual evaluation with a view to the monitoring of the regional implementa-

---

[150] Under the category of "others", Australia, New Zealand, and US are subsumed.

[151] *Ibid.,* p.13.

[152] *Ibid.,* p.13.

[153] Basically, the administrative structure of the FATF simply consists of a Chair and Secretariat, but it does not have a Steering Group of an APG type. For details on the structure of the FATF, see, Gilmore WC, *supra* note 117, pp.91-92.

[154] APG, "First Annual Report: 1999-2000", April 2001, p.1.

[155] APG, "Terms of Reference", in APG, "Annual Report: 1999-2000", April 2001, p.35.

[156] For the 1999 revised Nineteen Recommendation, see (visited on 1 June 2005) <http://www.cfatf.org/documentation/getfile.asp?fileid=12&option=1>.

[157] APG, "Annual Report: 1 July 2001-30 June 2002", December 2002, p.17.

[158] APG, "Annual Report: 1 July 2002-30 September 2003", September 2004. p.17; APG, "Annual Report: 1 October 2003-30 June 2004", November 2004, p.26.

tion of international standards. For the self-assessment exercise, the APG used the FATF's self-assessment questionnaire, and the procedures of analysis and discussion in the annual meetings are quite similar to those of the FATF.[159] In fact, the APG conducted its own self-assessment exercises as well as participating in the FATF self-assessment exercise on terrorist financing.[160] The self-assessment exercise was first conducted in 1997 and continued to be a valuable information source on the status of the AML/CFT measures in much of the region. It also served to enable the participating jurisdictions to assess their situation against the world's best practice.[161] However, at the 2003 Annual Meeting, members postponed a decision on whether and when to conduct further self-assessment exercises until the next APG Annual Meeting.[162] More recently, at the 2004 Meeting, it was agreed to postpone any self-assessment exercise for a further year until the release of a revised self-assessment methodology by the FATF.[163] However, given that in 2004, the FATF decided not to conduct self-assessment exercises any more,[164] it remains to be seen how the APG will proceed in this area in the future.[165]

Likewise, the APG's mutual evaluation process is not so different from that of the FATF.[166] Interestingly, however, all evaluated APG members are required to provide a follow-up report at each APG Annual Meeting on the progress they have made.[167] The APG intends to assess a minimum of five APG members each year, either through an APG mutual evaluation or an IMF/World Bank-led assessment.[168] APG members who are also members of the FATF, are evaluated by the FATF or jointly by the FATF and the APG.[169]

---

[159] For the details of the procedure, see, "Self-Assessment Exercises" on the APG website <http://www.apgml.org/content/self_assessment_exercises.jsp>.

[160] APG, "Annual Report: 1 October 2003-30 June 2004", November 2004, p.24.

[161] APG, "First Annual Report: 1999-2000", April 2001, p.13.

[162] APG, "Annual Report: 1 July 2002-30 September 2003", September 2004, p.23.

[163] APG, "Annual Report: 1 October 2003-30 June 2004", November 2004, p.25.

[164] For a relevant discussion, see, Section 5.2.1.2 of this chapter.

[165] It is expected that future planning will be outlined following the 2005 APG Annual meeting.

[166] For the details of the procedure, see, APG, "Procedures for APG mutual evaluations: As adopted at the Sixth APG Annual Meeting, Macau, China", September 2003.

[167] *Ibid.*, p.6. Moreover, this obligation is stricter than that of the MONEYVAL which requires all countries to present written progress reports to the plenary one year after their report has been adopted. For the details of the MONEYVAL practices, see, Gilmore WC, *supra* note 124, pp.173-176.

[168] APG, "Annual Report: 1 October 2003-30 June 2004", November 2004, p.24.

[169] The six APG/FATF member jurisdictions are Australia; Hong Kong, China; Japan; New Zealand; Singapore; and, the U.S. (APG, "Annual Report: 1 July 2001-30 June 2002", December 2002, p.26). For the first round of mutual evaluations, the APG accepted the

The first round of mutual evaluations began with Vanuatu in March 2000, and as of 30 June 2004, 16 had been completed.[170] The APG's six FATF members have also undergone an FATF evaluation, and the APG shares reports with the FATF on a reciprocal basis.[171] For instance, New Zealand was assessed by a joint APG/FATF mission in October 2003. The APG also shares reports with the IMF/World Bank.[172] As explained above, the APG agreed to use a Fund/Bank-led assessment when available in lieu of a mutual evaluation.[173] The seven remaining APG members (Brunei Darussalam; India; Marshall Islands; Nepal; Niue; Pakistan; and, Sri Lanka) are to be evaluated by mid 2005.[174] Interestingly, the APG has used the 2004 revised AML/CFT methodology for the first round of mutual evaluations of the remaining jurisdictions conducted since January 2005.[175] Although this approach is vulnerable to a criticism in terms of the equality of treatment of this remaining jurisdictions which are to be evaluated by the higher standards of the revised 2003 version,[176] the APG appears to put a more emphasis on consistency with most recent international standards and the increased reciprocity with other specialist bodies such as the IMF/World Bank.[177] The second round of mutual evaluations will commence following the APG's 2005 Annual Meeting.[178]

5.4.2.4 The enforcement of standards by the APG

The APG's non-compliance policy is also influenced by that of the FATF. In its "Explanatory Note on Membership" (2002), the APG provides for the following measures to be taken which include:

1. Requiring the member to provide regular reports on their progress in meeting the membership requirements within a fixed timeframe;
2. Sending a letter from the APG Co-Chairs to the relevant minister(s) in the

---

FATF's mutual evaluation reports for APG purposes of the six members who are also FATF members.

[170] APG, "Annual Report: 1 October 2003-30 June 2004", November 2004, p.24.

[171] *Ibid.*, p.24.

[172] *Ibid.,* p.24.

[173] For a relevant discussion, see, *supra* note 105 and its related text.

[174] APG, "Annual Report: 1 October 2003-30 June 2004", November 2004, p.25.

[175] *Ibid.,* p.26. Brunei Darussalam became one of the first countries in the world to be assessed by this 2004 methodology (APG, *The Asia/Pacific Group on Money Laundering Information Quarterly*, February 2005, p. 2).

[176] This is due to the fact that most of jurisdictions were assessed against the 1996 FATF Forty Recommendations during this first round (APG, "Annual Report: 1 October 2003-30 June 2004", November 2004, p.24).

[177] The IMF/World Bank have already started to use the 2004 methodology since the last quarter of 2005.

[178] APG, "Annual Report: 1 October 2003-30 June 2004", November 2004, p.25.

member jurisdiction drawing their attention to non-compliance with the APG membership requirements;

3. Arranging a high-level mission to the member jurisdiction in question to reinforce this message;

4. Suspending the jurisdiction from some of the APG's activities, for example its technical assistance and training program until all membership requirements have been met; and,

5. Suspending the jurisdiction's APG membership entirely until all membership requirements have been met.

The steps proposed are divided into two parts. Steps 1, 2 and 3 essentially involve enhanced peer pressure to assist non-complying members in expediting implementation of the Recommendations,[179] while Steps 4 and 5 entail more serious action.[180] Indeed, this non-compliance policy is nearly identical to that of the FATF. However, it is of note that there is a lack of countermeasures which correspond to FATF Recommendation 21. In this sense, the APG's non-compliance policy is not as powerful as that of the FATF. It does not directly interfere with the flow of international financial transactions. Nevertheless, the application of the non-compliance policy itself could serve as a strong incentive for the applied jurisdiction to correct its behaviour by way of damaging its reputation in the regional society.

In practice, concerns about non-compliance have been raised with regard to the failure in financial contributions which are necessary for membership.[181] Thus, in the 2004 Annual Meeting, it was agreed that the APG Secretariat should make a formal contact at a high level with any members who have failed to pay their contributions or who have been late with payments in order to encourage their future compliance and explain the possible consequences of non-payment.[182]

5.4.2.5 Other supporting activities

Besides the monitoring and enforcing activities of relevant international standards, the APG is involved in other important activities to support the spread of the AML/CFT message in the region. First of all, technical assistance is of particular note. In fact, the role of the FSRBs in coordinating technical assistance was endorsed at a meeting of AML bodies and various donor organisations held in Washington in April 2002.[183] In this meeting which was co-hosted by the IMF/World Bank, the participants agreed that the needs of technical assistance

---

[179] APG, "Explanatory Note on Membership", August 2002, para.4.3.

[180] *Ibid.*, para.4.3.

[181] APG, "Annual Report: 1 October 2003-30 June 2004", November 2004, p.14.

[182] *Ibid.*, p.14.

[183] IMF/World Bank, "Intensified Work on Anti-Money Laundering and Combating the Financing of Terrorism (AML/CFT)", 25 September 2002.

should be identified and the delivery of technical assistance should also be coordinated, on a regional basis through the FSRBs. In this context, the APG plays an active role in coordinating technical assistance in the region. For example, the Annual Forum on Technical Assistance and Training was held on 14 June 2004 just prior to the Annual Meeting in Seoul, with the attendance of all APG jurisdictions and the APG's Donors and Providers Group. Subsequently throughout the Annual Meeting period (15-18 June 2004), a series of individual meetings were held between priority jurisdictions and interested donors and providers, including a combined meeting involving Myanmar, Lao PDR, Vietnam and Cambodia.[184] Interestingly, this position of the APG on technical assistance stands in contrast with the practice of the FATF that does not actively engage in the area.[185] This is due to the *implementation-oriented* nature of the APG and also one of aspects that characterise the relationship between the FATF and FSRBs.

Secondly, the APG operates several Working Groups of a temporary nature to cope with various tasks. For instance, the Typologies Working Group was established at the 2003 Annual Meeting for the purpose of the better understanding of the nature, extent and impact of money laundering in the region.[186] Moreover, the APG Implementation Issues Working Group was set up at the 2003 Annual Meeting to undertake a series of coordinated and intensive examinations of particular AML/CFT implementation issues; to support and develop a network of APG experts on key implementation issues; and, to act as an informal consultation group to provide practical advice to APG members on AML/CFT issues.[187] This aspect once again illustrates the *implementation-oriented* nature of the APG.

Thirdly, the APG actively participates in the activities of the global AML/CFT network. For example, it participated in all activities undertaken by the FATF, including attendance at Plenary Meetings as an observer and participation in reviews of AML/CFT standards.[188] In June 2005, the FATF even held a joint Plenary with the APG in Singapore-the first FATF Plenary with an FSRB in attendance.[189] More recently, in the FATF Plenary meeting held in Paris on 12-14 October, it was also decided that the APG and the FATF launch an ambitious project to explore the symbiotic relationship among corruption, money laundering and terrorist financing and how the AML/CFT experiences following 9/11 can best be used to

---

[184] APG, "Annual Report: 1 October 2003-30 June 2004", November 2004, p.22.

[185] For relevant discussions, see, Section 5.2.3 of this chapter and Section 6.2.3.2 of Chapter Six.

[186] APG, "Annual Report: 2000-2001", November 2001, p.10; APG, "Annual Report: 1 July 2002-30 September 2003", September 2004, p.10.

[187] APG, "Annual Report: 1 July 2002-30 September 2003", September 2004, p.12.

[188] *Ibid.*, p.16.

[189] FATF, "Annual Report: 2004-2005", 10 June 2005, p.10.

combat these combined threats.[190] Furthermore, the APG Secretariat attends the FATF NCCT Review Group meetings as an observer and, where appropriate, seeks to provide a bridge for communication and information to APG members and observers on the NCCT list.[191]

5.4.3 The FSRBs strategy : developments and prospects

Currently, efforts to create similar regional bodies in western and central Africa are under way. Following the December 1999 Summit of the Heads of State and Government of the Economic Community of West African States (ECOWAS) in Lomé, Togo, it was decided to establish an Inter-Governmental Action Group against Money Laundering (GIABA).[192] A permanent secretariat is in the process of being established.[193] Similarly, an Action Group against Money Laundering in Africa (GABAC) was created in December 2000, in N'Djamena, Chad, by the Conference of the Heads of State of the Economic and Monetary Community (CEMAC).[194] If these initiatives are consolidated, nearly all countries in the world will be placed under the AML/CFT regime through their commitment to their regional FSRBs and thus establishing a close link with the FATF.

In sum, as a case study of the APG suggests, the strategy to spread FSRBs all over the world proved very useful, inducing "non-FATF" member countries to engage in the AML/CFT campaign in the "FATF" manner. Furthermore, it is clear that FSRBs play an essential role in ensuring the appropriate provision of technical assistance and other follow-up activities in non-FATF member countries.

What is more, note should also be given to a pivotal policy implication in relation to the FSRBs strategy particularly in the post 9/11 context. Namely, as seen above, there is some tension in the ongoing cooperation between the FATF and IMF/Word Bank since the IMF/World Bank conditioned their collaboration with the FATF on the agreement that the FATF does not undertake a further round of the NCCT exercise.[195] Accordingly, it is possible that the IMF/World Bank might withdraw from the AML/CFT campaign if the NCCT exercise should be resumed

---

[190] FATF, "FATF will explore the symbiotic relationship among corruption, money laundering and terrorist financing", 13 October 2005.

[191] *Ibid.*, p.17. Among the APG member jurisdictions, Cook Islands, Indonesia, Marshall Islands, Niue, Philippines were once designated as an NCCT. As of 1 June 2005, however, all these jurisdictions were removed from the NCCT list. However, Myanmar which is an observer jurisdiction of the APG is still on the NCCT list.

[192] FATF, "Annual Report: 2003-2004", 2 July 2004, p.15.

[193] *Ibid.*, p.15.

[194] *Ibid.*, p.15.

[195] For a relevant discussion, see, Section 5.3.2 of this chapter, and particularly *supra* note 89.

at some time in the future.[196] Then, it is apparent that the global AML/CFT campaign could not avoid suffering a serious setback since the IMF/World Bank are particularly noteworthy contributors in this area.[197] In these circumstances, the FSRBs strategy can be used as a backup plan for the global reach of the AML/CFT regime.[198] In other words, the FSRBs can play a buffer role between the FATF and non-FATF member countries. In the case of the withdrawal of the IMF/World Bank from the AML/CFT campaign, the FSRBs could be a reliable mediator to link non-compliant non-FATF member countries to an institutionalised circle in the international arena. Furthermore, when there can hardly be found any major technical assistance provider comparable to the IMF/World Bank,[199] it is the FSRBs that can play a crucial role in delivering technical assistance to the non-FATF member countries. All in all, they would hold the "alienated" countries within the institutionalised world in the AML/CFT context encouraging them to listen to the message of the international community.

5.5 The soft law phenomena

5.5.1 The soft enforcement and the blurring boundary between monitoring and enforcement

In Section 4.1 of Chapter Four, the requirement for hard enforcement is defined as compulsory binding settlement of disputes. If not, the realm of soft enforcement begins. In this context, various cases of soft enforcement can be identified. For example, the technical assistance provided by the IMF/World Bank or the FSRBs can be subsumed under the category of soft enforcement through "inducement".[200]

Moreover, soft enforcement can be sought by way of various methods of "value deprivation".[201] The conditionality of the IMF/World Bank linked to their lending assistance is a case in point. When these organisations provide financial loans to needy countries, they generally attach some conditionality to the loans, and if the

---

[196] The FATF still seems to regard the NCCT initiative as an important policy tool. See, FATF, "Annual Report: 2004-2005", p.12.

[197] These organisations have played a significant complementary role in relation to the FATF, given their capability of mobilising a good level of manpower and resources as well as their near universal membership which lends both organisations legitimacy and acceptance. For a relevant discussion, see also, Section 6.2.3 of Chapter Six.

[198] I am grateful to Professor Gilmore WC for an insightful seed comment in this respect.

[199] For a relevant discussion, see also, Section 5.2.3 of this chapter.

[200] For a relevant discussion, see, Section 4.1.1 of Chapter Four, and particularly footnote 17 and its related text.

[201] See, footnote 17 of Chapter Four and its related text.

needy countries are not willing to agree on the conditionality, the IMF/World Bank might not render financial assistance.[202] Also even when the contract is already established and the loans are being provided, further loans might be stopped if the assisted countries are not complying with the conditionality. Moreover, if both organisations could closely collaborate on conditionality, it would further strengthen this *de facto* enforcement powers.[203]

What is more, the non-compliance policies of the FATF and FSRBs provide further insight into the current analysis of the soft enforcement phenomena. When the result of a mutual evaluation exercise which indicate a country's serious deficiencies is submitted to an FATF plenary meeting, it would work as a form of stigmatisation of the country concerned.[204] This is in effect a soft sanction, "naming and shaming measure", designed to inflict damage to a country's reputation. If counter-measures go further such as the application of Recommendation 21, the economy of the country can be seriously affected because all other countries pay special attention to business relationships and transactions with the country in question. For example, the major banks of other FATF member jurisdictions may reject the letters of credit drawn by the banks of non-compliant FATF member jurisdictions or by NCCT banks.[205] They may also impose tight scrutiny and premium charges on any transactions conducted by the banks of non-compliant jurisdictions, and thus create a high-cost economy.[206]

---

[202] The possibility that the IMF/World Bank might use its lending power as a *de facto* enforcement tool has often been pointed out. See, e.g., Bothe M (1980) "Legal and Non-Legal Norms-A Meaningful Distinction in International Relations?", *Netherlands Yearbook of International Law*, vol.11, pp.82-83; Hillgenberg H (1999) "A Fresh Look at Soft Law", *European Journal of International Law*, vol.10, p. 511; Tadeusz GW (1984) "A Framework for Understanding "Soft Law"", *McGill Law Journal*, vol.30, p.77, p.85. Conditionality is central to policy-based lending. It elaborates the basis of a commitment between the country and the IMF or the World Bank throughout the period of a policy reform program. It also provides the basis for financing assurances for the country and for ensuring that funds are used in support of the objectives of the program (IMF/World Bank, "Strengthening IMF-World Bank Collaboration on Country Programs and Conditionality-Progress Report", 19 August 2002, p.7, at para. 6).

[203] This aspect was once pointed out by a joint paper. See, IMF/World Bank, "Strengthening IMF-World Bank Collaboration on Country Programs and Conditionality", 23 August 2001, p.iv. For the history of the cooperation between the IMF and World Bank on conditionality, see, the annex of this joint paper.

[204] For details of the procedure, see, FATF, "Review of FATF Anti-Money Laundering Systems and Mutual Evaluation Procedures 1992-1999", 16 February 2001, pp.35-42.

[205] Witular RA, "Govt upbeat RI to be dropped from money laundering list", *The Jakarta Post*, 8 February 2005.

[206] *Ibid.,* With regard to the tight scrutiny on the transactions between the FATF member jurisdictions and NCCTs, for example, concerns were raised in the Philippines that it

Sometimes, correspondent banking relations between the banks of non-compliant jurisdictions and their counterparts in FATF countries may be halted.[207] All these countermeasures may also trigger capital flight.[208] Indeed, these can be understood as a kind of political pressure under the category of soft enforcement rather than formal legal sanctioning, given the non-binding nature of the original instrument.

All in all, the potential damage which a non-compliant jurisdiction might suffer is not to be ignored, and it is apparent that the jurisdictions in question could hardly resist the request of the FATF as illustrated by the responses of jurisdictions to the two rounds of mutual evaluations.[209] Interestingly, for most jurisdictions, the indication of their deficiencies was enough to secure their compliance and further measures beyond it, in reality, were seldom necessary.[210] In short, this kind of "naming and shaming" measures exerts a huge influence on the behaviour of individual jurisdictions, and at the core of this enforcing power lies the manipulation of jurisdictions' concerns about their "reputation", which can be regarded as a typical type of soft enforcement.[211]

---

could lead to delays in the transmittal of overseas Filipino work remittances, which are an important source of foreign exchange (Tenorio AS, "RP excluded in FATF Feb. meet, remains blacklisted", *The Manila Times*, 8 March 2004).

[207] For example, the non-compliance policy of the FATF with regard to NCCTs allows member jurisdictions to condition, restrict, target or even prohibit financial transactions with non-cooperative jurisdictions (FATF, "Report on Non-Cooperative Countries and Territories", 14 February 2000, pp.7-9).

[208] For instance, the blacklisting was a severe threat to the Panamanian international banking system, which accounts for 80 percent of the country's gross domestic product. Bank Superintendent Delia Cárdenas of Panama said a number of banks left Panama because the blacklist made it difficult for them to make international transactions ("Money laundering list", *Latinamerica Press*, 9 July 2001). See also, Council for Security Cooperation in Asia Pacific (CSCAP), "Report on the 11th Meeting of the CSCAP Working Group on Transnational Crime", 13-14 May 2002, Shanghai, China, p. 7.

[209] FATF, "Review of FATF Anti-Money Laundering Systems and Mutual Evaluation Procedures 1992-1999", 16 February 2001, pp.43-44.

[210] *Ibid.*, pp.43-44. During two rounds of mutual evaluations, 12 countries took part in follow-up measures. As a result, except Turkey and Austria, all other countries enacted the necessary anti-money laundering measures in a speedy fashion, without being subject to any substantial sanctions such as the application of Recommendation 21 or the suspension of the FATF membership. In fact, reporting itself results in considerable political pressure.

[211] For further discussions on reputation, see, e.g., Guzman A (2002) "A Compliance-Based Theory of International Law", *California Law Review*, vol.90, pp.1861-1864; Tadeusz GW (1984) "A Framework for Understanding "Soft Law"", *McGill Law Journal*, vol. 30, p.86.

In this sense, the relationship of soft law with the market economy is also worthy of note. The system of the market economy can significantly strengthen the enforcement power of soft law. In a global market economy which is characterised as an unlimited competitive environment, reputation is a crucial factor to be taken into account for success.[212] The confidential nature of mutual evaluation reports by the FATF and FSRBs should also be understood in this context.[213] This is particularly true for the financial industry whose success is based on the trust of clients and the cooperative network with foreign counterparts.[214] The remarkable speed with which the assessed countries under the second round of the FATF mutual evaluations responded to the criticism of peer countries is already providing hard evidence of this trend.[215]

Furthermore, in this context of soft enforcement, another interesting phenomenon can be found with regard to the two separate concepts: monitoring and enforcement. In other words, the pressure on the "reputation" already starts with the monitoring process, and consequently, monitoring itself might well fit into the concept of "enforcement" by soft law standards.[216] For instance, the results of the FATF self-assessment exercises are collected and analysed by the Secretariat, and later they are put on the table for discussion at the FATF Plenary meeting with the attendance of all member countries and observers. During this process, it is needless to say that the self-assessing countries are placed under considerable peer pressure. In the case of mutual evaluations, peer pressure would work earlier than in self-assessment exercises and the degree of psychological pressure would be much higher, given the objective and demanding nature of this assessment mecha-

---

[212] For the important relationship between reputation and market economy, see, e.g., Wai R (2003) "Countering, Branding, Dealing: Using Economic And Social Rights In and Around The International Trade Regime", *European Journal of International Law*, vol.14, issue 1, at section 6; Simmons BA (2000) "Legalization of International Monetary Affairs", *International Organization*, vol.54, pp.586-587, and p.595; Simmons BA (2000) "Money and the Law: Why Comply with the Public International Law of Money?", *The Yale Journal of International Law*, vol.25, pp.361-362.

[213] Mostly, only summaries of the mutual evaluation reports are publicly available.

[214] For examples of firms' concern about their reputation in a market economy system, see, Bazley S, Foster C (2004) *Money laundering: business compliance*, pp.266-267. Bazley and Foster emphasise that firms have to appreciate that bad news travels fast and, with modern technology, is prominent, no matter how skillful the work of a PR company.

[215] See, e.g., FATF, "Review of FATF Anti-Money Laundering Systems and Mutual Evaluation Procedures 1992-1999", 16 February 2001, pp.43-45.

[216] FATF, "Annual Report: 1998-1999", 2 July 1999, p.7. This phenomenon was correctly pointed out by Chinkin. See, Chinkin CM (1989) "The Challenge of Soft Law: Development and Change in International Law", *International and Comparative Law Review*, vol.54, p.862.

nism.[217] It is an international system of periodic peer review under which each member is subject to a form of on-site examination.[218] Thus, even before the results of the evaluation are produced in the plenary meeting, the peer pressure is already working, i.e., from the beginning of the monitoring process. In short, even "before" or "in the absence of" the official employment of non-compliance policy, a substantial degree of peer pressure is operating in the monitoring work of the specialist bodies. This can then be regarded as another kind of soft enforcement situation. The FATF's success in enforcing its standards with mutual evaluation exercises was so impressive that the OECD and the Council of Europe 'GRECO'[219] followed suit by introducing similar mutual evaluation procedures in dealing with corruption issues.[220] In addition, the similar effect of a soft enforcement can be found in the monitoring process of the IMF and the World Bank.[221] However, in that case, the implication of monitoring would be much more far-reaching, given the two organisations' universal membership.[222]

In sum, it is apparent that even without invoking a strong non-compliance measure, the reputation formed through this monitoring process would already have a tremendous impact on changing the practices of individual countries in the international financial system and other concerned areas.[223] Indeed, this phenomenon of the blurring boundary between the monitoring stage and the enforcement stage seems to derive from the unique nature of soft enforcement.

---

[217] See, Section 5.2.2.3 of this chapter.

[218] Levi M, Gilmore WC (2002) "Terrorist Finance, Money Laundering and the Rise and Rise of Mutual Evaluation: A New Paradigm for Crime Control?". In: Pieth M (ed) *Financing Terrorism*, p.97.

[219] The GRECO is the "Group of States against Corruption" established by the Council of Europe in 1998 < http://www.greco.coe.int/Default.htm>.

[220] Article 12 of the OECD 1997 bribery convention provides for monitoring and follow-up to be undertaken by the OECD Working Group on Bribery (WGB) and the terms of reference of the WGB adopts self- and mutual evaluations for these purposes. Furthermore, the 1998 Council of Europe agreement establishing GRECO contains detailed procedures (Levi M, Gilmore WC, *supra* note 218, p.107).

[221] For details of the monitoring activities of the IMF/World Bank, see, Section 5.3.2 of this chapter.

[222] For details of the work and membership of the IMF/World Bank, see, Section 5.3.1 of this chapter.

[223] For the role of reputation in securing a country's compliance, see, e.g., Guzman AT, *supra* note 211, pp.1860-1865.

5.5.2 Future developments: transformation from soft law into hard law

In general, there seem to exist two positions on the issue of the transformation of soft law into hard law. The first insists that transformation is not desirable and soft law should exist as it is, while the second argues that the final goal of soft law is to reach the status of hard law. In fact, it is not right to say that one side is correct while the other is wrong. Rather, it should be reviewed in the context of the nature of specific issue areas. In other words, (a) when an issue area is always full of uncertainty and thus, it is very difficult to establish any concrete norms; (b) the legal norms play the role of coordinating conflicting interests, it is soft law that fits the needs of that area rather than inflexible hard law.[224] For example, in the field of arms control where it is very difficult to predict the development of technologies, states may prefer to leave agreements imprecise rather than to face the possibility of being caught with unfavorable commitments in the form of hard law or to face an *all or nothing* situation.[225] Let us consider the case of the anti-ballistic missile (ABM) treaty between the U.S. and the then Soviet Union. In this case, it is the U.S. that was caught with unfavorable and strict commitments.[226] Although the U.S. had widened its lead in the relevant new technologies with its more advanced economy, its detailed earlier commitment in the ABM treaty undermined its legal basis to develop the Strategic Defense Initiative (SDI) project and the testing of new weaponry.[227] Learning from this experience, states might be tempted not to conclude an agreement of a similar nature with potential rivals in the future.[228] Nonetheless, it would be better for states to have some kind of regulatory regime in the form of soft law, thus minimising uncertainty in a specific issue area rather than facing an *all or nothing* situation.

---

[224] Abbott KW, Snidal D (2000) "Hard and Soft Law in International Governance", *International Organization*, vol.54, p. 442.

[225] *Ibid.*, p.442.

[226] For example, see, Article V of the ABM treaty (1972) which stipulates:
"1. Each Party undertakes not to develop, test, or deploy ABM systems or components which are sea-based, air-based, space-based, or mobile land-based.
2. Each Party undertakes not to develop, test or deploy ABM launchers for launching more than one ABM interceptor missile at a time from each launcher, not to modify deployed launchers to provide them with such a capacity, not to develop, test, or deploy automatic or semi-automatic or other similar systems for rapid reload of ABM launchers."

[227] Lipson C (1991) "Why are some international agreements informal?", *International Organization*, vol.45, pp.522-523.

[228] The US eventually withdrew from the ABM treaty in June 2002. For details, see, Rivas MP, "US quits ABM treaty", 14 December 2001, CNN.com <http://archives.cnn.com/2001/ALLPOLITICS/12/13/rec.bush.abm/>.

However, (a) when uncertainty in an issue area is of a lesser degree; (b) legal norms play the role of promoting common good, it seems desirable to have hard law in the concerned area, considering the stability that established hard law accords. Of course, due to the difficulty in the course of establishing hard law in a specific area, the soft law form might be provisionally preferred as an alternative, but in this case, it should be understood as a means to achieve the status of hard law, rather than as the goal itself.[229] In the view of the writer, the AML/CFT area falls into this second category and thus, it is desirable that soft law ultimately develops into hard law.

Generally, soft law develops into binding hard law such as treaty or custom. In the course of this, soft law operates alone, or sometimes in conjunction with the hard law.[230]

With regard to the transformation into treaty form, the process is already triggered, and currently there can be identified three types of transformation.[231] The first type is that the content of a soft law is incorporated into the text of a treaty without any specific reference to the original sources, as illustrated by the International Convention for the Suppression of the Financing of Terrorism (1999).[232] The second type is that the content of a soft law is integrated into the text of a treaty with implicit reference to the original sources, as with the case of the Palermo Convention (2000).[233] The third type is that the content of soft law is reflected in the text of a treaty with explicit reference to the original sources like the Inter-American Convention Against Terrorism (2002),[234] and the Council of Eu-

---

[229] For a successful case study of the utility of soft law as a means to achieve the status of hard law, see, e.g., Abbott KW (2001) "Rule-Making in the WTO: Lessons From The Case Of Bribery and Corruption", *Journal of International Economic Law,* vol.4(2), pp.275-296.

[230] To this end, one of the methods that the soft law approach employs is the reiteration of principles through the proliferation of instruments and standards in order to reinforce the dynamics as illustrated by the practices of the specialist bodies such as the FATF, the BCBS, the Wolfsberg Group, etc. See, Thomas C (2002) "Trade-Related Labour and Environment Agreements?", *Journal of International Economic Law*, vol. 5(4), at section I.A.

[231] I am grateful to Professor Gilmore WC for this classification of three types of transformation.

[232] Article 18.

[233] Article 7(3) stipulates that:

"In establishing a domestic regulatory and supervisory regime under the terms of this article, ...State Parties are called upon to use as a guideline the relevant initiatives of regional, interregional and multilateral organizations against money-laundering."

[234] Article 4(2) provides that:

"When implementing paragraph 1 of this article, state parties shall use as guidelines the recommendations developed by specialized international and regional entities, in par-

rope Convention on Laundering, Search, Seizure and Confiscation of the Proceeds from Crime and on the Financing of Terrorism (2005).[235] Particularly, this 2005 Council of Europe Convention can be considered to be a very advanced instrument in that by providing for a simplified amendment procedure, it can even deal with a situation when the standards of the FATF have evolved considerably with time.[236]

On the other hand, with regard to the transformation into customary law, it is a bit difficult to produce clear-cut evidence, but it is basically because customary law requires *opinio juris* which is a psychological element as well as general and consistent state practice.[237] Of course, it is argued that sometimes only one requirement can in effect establish customary law.[238] However, this does not seem to be the case in the AML/CFT area since recent evidence suggests that customary law-making processes are already under way in terms of both requirements. For example, some 150 states are now members of either the FATF or FSRBs, or both, and they are regularly participating in self-assessment and mutual evaluation exercises. What is more, the existence of the multilateral treaty is also a significant factor to be taken into account. 137 states have already ratified the ICSFT, binding themselves to the CFT regime.[239] This commitment to FATF standards and multi-

---

ticular the Financial Action Task Force and, as appropriate, the Inter-American Drug Abuse Control Commission, the Caribbean Financial Action Task Force, and the South American Financial Action Task Force."

[235] Article 13(1) stipulates that:

"Each Party shall adopt such legislative and other measures as may be necessary to institute a comprehensive domestic regulatory and supervisory or monitoring regime to prevent money laundering and shall take due account of applicable international standards, including in particular the recommendations adopted by the Financial Action Task Force on Money Laundering (FATF)".

[236] See, Article 54; the explanatory report, p.54. Indeed, there arises a question of how to re-draw consensus among state parties when the standards of the FATF are considerably revised after the initial adoption of the convention.

[237] Brownlie I (2003) *Principles of Public International Law*, pp.4-11; Dixon M (2002) *Textbook on International Law*, pp.32-33; Akehurst M (1974/1975) "Custom as a Source of International Law", *The British Yearbook of International Law*, vol.47, pp.1-53.

[238] Brownlie I, *supra* note 237, p.8; D'Amato AA (1971) *The Concept of Custom in International Law*, pp.51-56; Roberts AE (2001) "Traditional and Modern Approaches to Customary International Law: A Reconciliation", *The American Journal of International al Law*, vol.95, pp.757-758; Cheng B (1982) "United Nations Resolutions on Outer Space: "Instant" International Customary Law". In: Cheng B (ed) *International Law: Teaching and Practice*, pp.249-252.

[239] It is as of 1 June 2005. If the focus is extended further to the Palermo Convention (2000), some 110 countries are placed overlappingly under the AML/CFT framework (It entered into force on 29 September 2003. As of 1 June 2005, there are 106 parties).

lateral treaties can provide valuable evidence of *opinio juris* as well as state practices.[240] Also other specialist bodies are repeatedly adopting and promoting the
FATF-drafted AML/CFT standards as their rules of reference as exemplified by
the practices of the IMF, World Bank, BCBS, IOSCO, and IAIS.[241] In particular,
the IMF/World Bank which has 184 jurisdictions as members, actively promote
the AML/CFT standards on various occasions. Last but not least, the role of the
Security Council should be remembered. As mentioned before, the resolutions of
the Security Council regard terrorism as a threat to international peace and impose
binding obligations on all countries to suppress terrorist financing.[242] In particular,
with the adoption of Security Council Resolution 1617, an explicit link has been
established between the mandate of the FATF and that of the Security Council.[243]
Accordingly, there is building up a strong basis for the transformation of the
FATF-inspired AML/CFT soft law into customary law under the umbrella of the
Security Council's direct mandate.[244]

In sum, there are developing customary law as well as treaty law in the
AML/CFT area, and both soft law and hard law interact with each other or within
themselves thus creating synergy in the transformation processes. However, given
that international standards in this area develop fast and become increasingly detailed to cover various typologies and situations, it should be remembered that the
transformation process cannot be completed simply as a one-off operation. Thus,

---

[240] Baxter RR (1965/1966) "Multilateral Treaties as Evidence of Customary International
Law", *The British Yearbook of International Law*, vol. 41, pp.277-278; Byers M (1999)
Customs, Power and the Power of Rules, pp.166-170; D'Amato AA, *supra* note 238,
pp.70-71; Boyle AE (1999) "Some Reflection on the Relationship of Treaties and Soft
Law", *International and Comparative Law Quarterly*, vol. 48, p.906. In particular, Akehurst emphasised that a treaty is not a physical act; it is a statement and a promise. For
further details, see, Akehurst M, *supra* note 237, pp.3-4.

[241] For the effect of "repetition", see, e.g, Dupuy PM (1991) "Soft law and the International
Law of the Environment", *Michigan Journal of International Law*, vol.12, pp.424-428;
Thomas C (2002) "Trade-Related Labour and Environment Agreements?", *Journal of
International Economic Law*, vol.5(4), at section I (A).

[242] See, e.g., UN SC Resolution 1373 and 1390.

[243] UN SC Resolution 1617, para.7.

[244] In our fast-changing times, the requirements to be customary law such as *opinio juris* as
well as general, uniform and consistent country practices, may prove to be obstacles in
the timely application of new rules which are necessary due to new developments. Thus,
the role of the Security Council is once again highlighted in the sense that it could have
a strong influence on the requirements through the adoption of relevant binding resolutions as an opinion leader. For the relevant discussion, see, Seidl-Hohenveldern I (1980)
"International Economic Soft Law", *Recueil des Cours*, tome 163, pp.188-191.

continuous attention should be given to sustaining this transformation process engaging relevant and necessary actors.[245]

5.6 Conclusion

Not to mention reviewing international standards, whening analysing the monitoring and enforcement work, it is interesting to make note of a common threshold underlying all initiatives; namely the establishment of a "level playing field". There seems to be three areas to which this concept is of relevance. Firstly, a level playing field is to be secured within an industry itself. Then, a level playing field should be extended between industries. Lastly and more broadly, there should be a level playing field between countries.

This concept of the level playing field has significant policy implications since it is aimed at: (i) reducing loopholes within the AML/CFT framework; (ii) encouraging fair competition between concerned parties; and, (iii) promoting efficiency. For example, if one bank has a well-organised AML/CFT framework in place while another is not equipped with adequate AML/CFT measures, criminals or terrorists will be motivated to deal with the latter bank in order to exploit the loophole. Moreover, ordinary customers might prefer to establish business relationships with the latter bank since it is simpler and less troublesome.[246] It would undermine the rule of fair competition between banks. Furthermore, under these circumstances, it would be difficult for the former bank to apply simplified AML/CFT measures with regard to customers introduced by the latter bank, for example, based on a correspondent banking contract since it could not trust the customer due diligence (CDD)-related data provided by the latter bank. This would cause the duplication of a surveillance regime, eventually undermining the efficiency of the AML/CFT measures.[247]

In a broader context, if the banking industry has strong AML/CFT measures in place whereas other industries such as securities or insurance sectors have not adequate AML/CFT measures in place, dirty money could be expected to flow into these sectors. This would compromise the rule of fair competition between sectors since other sectors would benefit from the capital inflow from the banking industry. Moreover, the banking industry could not trust the results of the surveillance measures of other sectors, thus generating duplication of AML/CFT efforts.

---

[245] This will be revisited in Section 6.2.3 of Chapter Six.

[246] Pieth M, Aiofi G, "The Private Sector becomes active: The Wolfsberg Process", p.4.

[247] See, e.g., the simplified CDD regime which is intended in the 2003 FATF Forty Recommendations.

If these monitoring systems by other sectors were not reliable, the concerned sector would have to re-apply its own CDD measures from scratch.[248]

A similar logic can be applied between states. Terrorists or criminals will be tempted to approach a state with a weak AML/CFT infrastructure in order to find a loophole. Furthermore, a state with a strong AML/CFT framework will be placed at a disadvantage in comparison with states with a weak one. What is more, states cannot rely on the inadequate CDD measures already taken by other states, causing the duplication of AML/CFT resources in the international arena.

In sum, considering the diversification of the terrorist financing and money laundering phenomena *ratione personae*[249] and *ratione materiae*,[250] it is essential to pay continuous attention to the establishment of a level playing field throughout the campaign in various dimensions.

---

[248] On the contrary, as noted in the revised 2003 FATF Forty Recommendations, when adequate checks and controls exist elsewhere in the national systems, simplified CDD measures can be applied See, Interpretative Note to Recommendation 5, para.9.

[249] The vehicle for money laundering and the financing of terrorism may sprawl across various professions such as lawyers and accountants.

[250] Money laundering and the financing of terrorism may be carried out involving various things such as securities, insurance policies, or diamonds.

6 The Financing of Terrorism: a Trojan Horse

6.1 Context

Through the analysis of the evolution and implementation of international standards on the financing of terrorism, two major findings should be noted. Firstly, the strategy to combat the financing of terrorism (CFT) has considerably contributed to the development of the anti-money laundering (AML) strategy which was originally created in the context of targeting criminal finances — these criminal finances are in the main from transnational organised crime such as drug trafficking and people smuggling. Secondly, the CFT strategy provided a prototype of a new law enforcement weapon to wage a financial war on criminal groups; i.e. the international administrative asset-freezing system as illustrated by the practices of the 1267 Sanctions Committee.[1]

In this context, strategies will be explored that make best use of these new CFT mechanisms as a Trojan horse in order to further facilitate the anti-money laundering campaign and to target criminal finances in general.

6.2 Further Support for the AML Campaign

6.2.1 The impact of 9/11 on the AML campaign

In Chapter One, the relationship between the financing of terrorism and money laundering was examined. As a matter of fact, these two concepts are essentially different.[2] Money laundering begins with brushing out the audit trail of dirty money and ends by achieving legitimisation. In contrast, the financing of terrorism which is used to promote a political cause by terrorist organisations begins with money-making activities and ends by distributing the money to final users. Despite the difference in their final goals, what money laundering and terrorist financing share are the concerns about how to erase money trails. Out of this simi-

---

[1] For details, see, Section 3.3 of Chapter Three.
[2] For in depth discussions, see, Section 1.3.2 of Chapter One.

larity, it should be noted that the skills of the money launderer have already become an indispensable tool for terrorists to hide the flow of their money as well as to keep sustainable financing sources intact.[3] Correspondingly, the anti-money laundering tools have been employed by policy makers in order to combat the distribution process of terrorist financing.

When this partnership was established between the CFT and AML areas, it seemed that the CFT side was getting a "free ride", utilising the already-established AML infrastructure. However, it has gradually become clear that in reality this was not the case. It was the AML area that benefited most from the partnership.

Chapter Three indicated that the Security Council became involved in the CFT area with its binding Chapter VII powers. Under these circumstances, it was in the main an AML framework that the Counter-Terrorism Committee (CTC) has requested each state to establish in its legal and executive system in the name of the CFT campaign. For instance, the checklist of on-site visits to member states includes anti-money laundering legislation; structures for the oversight of the financial system; supervision of the non-financial sector; mechanisms for the seizure and confiscation of the proceeds of crime, etc.[4] Similarly, it should be noted that the 1267 Sanctions Committee has indirectly supported the global AML campaign through its operational approach. For example, its monitoring group has urged states, in the context of targeting the finances of currently active terrorists, to take some (in effect) AML measures such as the establishment of FIUs; regulation of cash couriers, alternative remittance systems, and trade in precious commodities; and, cooperation with FATF, FSRBs, and IMF/World Bank.[5]

Furthermore, Chapters Four and Five showed that specialist bodies gained more importance and justification with regard to their work in the international community by inserting the word "CFT" behind their original slogan "AML". The 9/11 also engaged new, but previously reluctant, international organisations such as the IMF and World Bank in the AML/CFT area.[6] The participation of these organisations is important because they have the resources and manpower to mobilise as well as near universal membership. What is more, the 9/11 reinforced regional

---

[3]   Thachuk KL (May 2002) "Terrorism's Financial Lifeline: Can It be Severed?", *Strategic Forum*, Institute for National Strategic Studies, National Defense University, no.191, p.3.

[4]   See, UN CTC, "Framework document for CTC visits to states in order to enhance the monitoring of the implementation of resolution 1373 (2001)", 9 March 2005.

[5]   For details, see, UN, "Letter dated 14 February 2005 from the Chairman of the Security Council Committee established pursuant to resolution 1267 (1999) concerning Al-Qaeda and the Taliban and associated individuals and entities addressed to the President of the Security Council", UN Doc., S/2005/83, 15 February 2005.

[6]   Gilmore WC (2004) *Dirty Money: The evolution of international measures to counter money laundering and the financing of terrorism*, p.150.

AML movements as exemplified by the increase in the membership of the APG and other FSRBs. Similarly, the number of national FIUs, which are key players in the AML/CFT campaign, almost doubled following 9/11.[7]

In short, the CFT has been a very useful engine in promoting the AML strategy on a global scale following 9/11, making the AML/CFT a universal cause which no one dared challenge.[8] While this window of opportunity is open, however, there are still many tasks of significance to be carried out to make as much progress as possible in this area. To this end, several suggestions will be made in what follows.

6.2.2 Issues concerning duplication

Since a number of international organisations engage in diverse activities in the AML/CFT area, there arise issues concerning duplication. For the purposes of this study, they are classified into four categories: assessment, technical assistance, research, and sanctions.

6.2.2.1 Assessment

Given that various organisations have become involved in the AML/CFT campaign since 9/11, and that their first step usually begins with the assessment of current development, there arises a concern about the duplication of assessment efforts and resources in three dimensions: (a) within the Security Council between the works of the CTC, the 1267 Sanctions Committee, and the 1540 Committee; (b) within the circle of specialist bodies such as the FATF and the IMF/World Bank; and, (c) in broad terms, between the Security Council and the specialist bodies.

To begin with, in relation to the duplication of assessment in the first two dimensions, points have already been made in Chapter Three and Five. There have been repeated calls for greater coordination between the CTC, the Sanctions Committee, and the 1540 Committee particularly with regard to reporting requirements and the potential to share information.[9] Furthermore, considerable pro-

---

[7] As of July 2005, some 100 jurisdictions established their FIU.

[8] Johnson J (2002) "11th September, 2001: Will It Make a Difference to the Global Anti-Money Laundering Movement?", *Journal of Money Laundering Control*, vol.6, no.1, p.9.

[9] Although the weight to given to the financial aspect is considerably different from each other, these three committees have some room to coordinate their activities in the context of terrorist financing. For relevant discussions, see, Section 3.4.4 of Chapter Three of this study.
    See also, UN SC, "Letter dated 23 August 2004 from the Chairman of the Security Council Committee established pursuant to resolution 1267 (1999) concerning Al-Qaida

gress is already being made with respect to the duplication within the circle of specialist bodies. The FATF and the IMF/World Bank have sought to cooperate in assessing the implementation of the AML/CFT standards, illustrated by the 12-month pilot programme.[10] Given that this 12-month programme proved to be a success, the IMF/World Bank decided further to make AML/CFT assessments a regular part of their work.[11] They also endorsed the revised 2003 FATF Forty Recommendations as the standard for which AML/CFT ROSCs will be prepared, as well as the revised 2004 methodology to assess compliance with that standard.[12]

Accordingly, priority attention needs to be given to the duplication between the Security Council and the specialist bodies, since the least systematic approach is found in this dimension. It should be noted that the CTC is now conducting on-site visits to member states.[13] This mission is, however, not so different from the mutual evaluation exercise by the FATF/FSRBs or assessments by the IMF/World Bank.[14] Thus, although the visiting team led by the CTC includes experts from the FATF,[15] both sides need to develop further a mechanism to coordinate the assessment activity and to share the results of assessment exercises as is the case with the relationship between FATF/FSRBs and the IMF/World Bank. Perhaps, in the course of this, given that the Security Council covers wider issue areas thus addressing the CFT issue in a relatively general sense, added weight might be given

---

and the Taliban and associated individuals and entities addressed to the President of the Security Council", S/2004/679, 25 August 2004, pp.20-21; UN SC, 5059th Meeting, S/PV.5059, 19 October 2004, p.4.

[10] See, Section 5.3.2 of Chapter Five.

[11] However, considering the FATF's perception of the NCCT practice as a very effective policy tool, the future of the relationship between the FATF and IMF/World Bank is still uncertain as the following remarks of the FATF president suggests:

"While the FATF has no plans at present to conduct a third round of the NCCT reviews, it will retain the possibility of applying countermeasures to protect the international financial system from abuse including in situations where the FATF's recommendation are not applied or are insufficiently applied" (IMF/World Bank, "Twelve-Month Pilot Program of AML/CFT Assessments", 10 March 2004, p.63).

[12] IMF, "The IMF and the Fight against Money Laundering and the Financing of Terrorism", *A Factsheet*, September 2004.

[13] The CTC conducted its first visit to one of member states in March 2005.

[14] This is to develop a direct dialogue with the authorities of the visited states and to identify more precisely the technical assistance needs of the visited states for the purpose of effective implementation of the Security Council Resolution 1373 (2001). See, UN CTC, "General guidelines for conducting CTC visits to member states", 4 August 2004.

[15] UN Information Service, "Country Visits Signal New Phase of Work for United Nations Counter-Terrorism Body", SC/8333, 15 March 2005.

to the role of the specialist bodies which focus on the AML/CFT issue with greater manpower and more resources.[16]

However, in this last dimension, there remain some factors to be considered further. Firstly, whereas the relevant committees of the Security Council generally make all state reports public, specialist bodies usually keep them confidential, publishing only brief summaries. Thus, in order to share information and reports, it seems necessary for concerned parties to develop some rules of reference, especially with regard to the level of confidentiality.[17] Perhaps, the practices of the OECD Working Group on Corruption and the Council of Europe "GRECO" are of use in this regard since they maintain quite open attitudes, making their mutual evaluation reports fully public.[18] Fortunately, the FATF also decided, as a general rule, in 2005 to publish all future mutual evaluation reports.[19] Secondly, the composition of the Security Council permanent membership also needs to be taken into account. Given that China is not a member of the FATF, the initiative of the Security Council to establish a solid cooperative relationship with the FATF might meet with difficulties in gathering universal support.[20] In this regard, the current effort to expand the FATF membership to China needs to be promoted further.[21]

6.2.2.2 Technical assistance

Once the status of the national and international AML/CFT framework is assessed, there automatically arises a need to render technical assistance for the purpose of complementing the gap found in the assessment process. In these circumstances, in order to achieve the best efficiency and effectiveness, technical assistance should be gathered from the most suitable providers and distributed to the most needed receivers.

---

[16] For a relevant discussion, see, UN, "Letter dated 14 February 2005 from the Chairman of the Security Council Committee established pursuant to resolution 1267 (1999) concerning Al-Qaeda and the Taliban and associated individuals and entities addressed to the President of the Security Council", UN Doc., S/2005/83, 15 February 2005, p.9.

[17] In the case of the CTC, it has developed some rules of confidentiality in relation to its on-site visit reports. See, UN CTC, "Framework document for CTC visits to states in order to enhance the monitoring of implementation of resolution 1373 (2001)", 9 March 2005.

[18] Levi M, Gilmore WC (2002) "Terrorist Finance, Money Laundering and the Rise and Rise of Mutual Evaluation: A New Paradigm for Crime Control?". In: Pieth M (ed) *Financing Terrorism*, p.105.

[19] FATF, "Annual Report: 2004-2005", 10 June 2005, p.11.

[20] FATF, "Annual Report: 2003-2004", 2 July 2004, p.12.

[21] China was given an observer status of the FATF in February 2005, and currently is a member of the Eurasian Group on Money Laundering and Terrorism Funding (EAG) which was founded in October 2004.

In this regard, although the current system seems to be in some degree satisfactory, several points are to be noted for further improvement. Generally, there are two ways of delivering technical assistance: through multilateral channels or bilateral channels. With regard to the multilateral channels, the practices of the CTC and IMF/World Bank are good examples. If the CTC finds a need for technical assistance, it directs the need either to other international organisations or to donor states via its match-making database.[22] If the IMF/World Bank finds a need for technical assistance, they either deliver technical assistance directly to states or pass the request to FSRBs to solve the matter on a regional basis. The World Bank is also operating a database to provide match-making services.[23] On the other hand, in respect of the bilateral channel, it is simply that one state approaches another state for technical assistance.

Under this system, the major problem is the lack of a *centralised* coordination mechanism. For example, as a command post to coordinate technical assistance, at least nine entities might be identified currently: the CTC database, the World Bank database, and the Secretariats of the seven FSRBs. In these circumstances, it is difficult to consolidate all relevant information and make a central database. Inevitably, it would entail some kind of inefficiency in coordinating all those needs and the delivery of technical assistance.

Consequently, it is desirable to establish or designate a central coordination centre. With this mechanism, all technical assistance donors and receivers may be required to provide relevant information to it. Perhaps, upon designation, either the CTC or the World Bank may play the role of this central coordinating body. Then, it would facilitate the flow of information between relevant parties, and assume a feedback function as well, ensuring the assistance provided by a donor is fully satisfactory.[24]

Furthermore, the duplication of the CTC database and the World Bank database should also be pointed out. Given the similar function of these two databases and the close relations between the two organisations, some streamlining may be possible without too much trouble, thus preventing duplication of resources.[25]

---

[22] See <http://www.un.org/sc/ctc>.

[23] IMF/World Bank, "Intensified Work on Anti-Money Laundering and Combating the Financing of Terrorism (AML/CFT)", 25 September 2002, para. 45-48. It was agreed in a meeting of key technical assistance providers, organised by the IMF/World Bank in 2002 that the coordination of technical assistance should be organised on a regional basis through the FSRBs.

[24] UN SC, 5059th Meeting, S/PV.5069, 19 October 2004, p.11.

[25] IMF/World, "Twelve-Month Pilot Program of Anti-Money Laundering and Combating the Financing of Terrorism (AML/CFT) Assessments and Delivery of AML/CFT Technical Assistance", 31 March 2003, p.16.

6.2.2.3 Research

Another important field of the AML/CFT strategy is research on the typologies of money laundering and terrorist financing. At present, various organisations such as the Security Council, the FATF, the UNODC, the IMF/World Bank, and many of the FSRBs are involved in these research activities, and a high level of duplication can be identified among the efforts of these organisations.[26] Of course, if more resources are invested in research, the quality of output might be better. However, given the inadequacy of the resources and manpower in this area, it seems reasonable to establish a coordinating mechanism for research purposes. Considering that experts of various organisations attend seminars or workshops hosted by others to discuss the results of their research, the international community could use those occasions to pick up necessary research issues, and to distribute appropriate topics to proper organisations, thus preventing a double investment of resources. Fortunately, the recent initiative made by the FATF to conduct joint typology exercises with FSRBs is the right step forward in this direction.[27]

6.2.2.4 Sanctions

When a country is found to be non-compliant with the international AML/CFT standards, the international community might impose sanctions on that country. Ironically, however, in order to promote the effectiveness of "sanctions", it might be better to encourage duplication among relevant organisations rather than preventing it. This is indeed contrary to the treatment of other issues (assessment, technical assistance, and research) as mentioned above.

Theoretically, the Security Council could impose a hard enforcement with its Chapter VII powers while specialist bodies apply only soft enforcement. However, in practice, the Security Council, more precisely, the CTC has not applied its Chapter VII powers to impose sanctions on states which are non-compliant with the requirements of Resolution 1373. Furthermore, the committee does not seem to intend to do so in the near future, considering its cautious approach in dealing with individual states.[28] In this vein, the idea of how to engage the Security Coun-

---

[26] For example, the typologies of terrorist financing have been researched by all these organisations. See, the reports of the monitoring group of the 1267 Sanctions Committee, the typologies exercises of the FAFT, the research on the *hawala* system by the IMF and the World Bank, etc.

[27] The FATF held a joint Typologies meeting with MONEYVAL in December 2004, and will hold another joint meeting with GAFISUD in November 2005. See, FATF, "Annual Report: 2004-2005", 10 June 2005, p.11.

[28] Rosand E (2004) "Security Council Resolution 1373 and the Counter-Terrorism Committee: the Cornerstone of the United Nations Contribution to the Fight against Terrorism". In: Fijnaut C, Wouters J, Naert F (eds) *Legal Instruments in the Fight against International Terrorism: A Transnational Dialogue*, pp.610-611.

cil in a sanctions regime deserves attention as a promotion strategy of the AML/CFT campaign worldwide.

To this end, it should be remembered that although the CTC is not willing to act as a Sanctions Committee at present, it continues to report a list of states who are late in submitting state reports in accordance with Resolution 1373.[29] Thus, at the current stage of development, what seems realistically possible is to engage the Security Council in the regime of soft enforcement, say by way of a naming and shaming approach. For example, when the FATF is determined to apply its Recommendation 21 measure to states for not observing its AML/CFT recommendations, it can also inform the CTC of this fact. In this case, the CTC could report this to the Security Council based on its mandate.[30] In other words, this is to announce the listing of a state twice.[31] This kind of initiative would provide increased justification for the efforts of the specialist bodies to promote the AML/CFT strategy worldwide.[32]

6.2.3 Securing further involvement of influential actors

In order to provide further support to the AML/CFT campaign, it is important to secure further involvement of influential actors. First of all, it should be noted that currently the CTC is not only monitoring national progress by requiring all 191 UN member states to submit their state reports on the implementation of Resolution 1373 but also consequently turning them into an unprecedented database of national legislative and executive practices. In these circumstances, if the CTC stops operating for reasons such as that terrorist activities are decreasing or political momentum has been lost, the international community would lose valuable opportunities to harmonise national AML/CFT law and executive practices, not to

---

[29] *Ibid.*, p.612. For example, on 16 October 2003, the Security Council issued a warning that 48 states were late in submitting their reports to the CTC and that the CTC Chairman would send to the Council the list of states which might be late in submitting their reports by 31 October 2003 (UN SC, "Statement by the President of the Security Council", S/PRST/2003/17, 16 October 2003).

[30] See, UN SC, "Guidelines of the Committee for the Conduct of Its Work", S/AC.40/2001/CRP.1, 16 October 2001.

[31] However, given that China is not yet an FATF member state, a prudent approach would be necessary when consensus is sought within the Security Council in relation to the establishment of cooperative relationship with the FATF. See, *supra* note 20.

[32] However, with a longer perspective, it is desirable that the international community take more active measures, coordinating all possible sanctions, irrespective of whether it is a hard enforcement or a soft enforcement, for the greater good (Tanzi V (1998) "Macroeconomic aspects of offshore centres and the importance of money-laundering in offshore financial flows". In: *UNODC, Attacking the Profits of Crime: Drugs, Money and Laundering*, p13).

mention the already accumulated database and know-how in this area. What is more, although the work of the CTC is of direct relevance to the financing of terrorism, it should also be remembered that it is connected with various issues concerning transnational organised crime in general such as border control, extradition, illegal arms trafficking, etc. Thus, given this significant role of the CTC in the fight against the financing of terrorism and acquisitive crime in general, it is important that its current momentum be sustained, for example, through further revitalisation and awareness-raising campaigns.

Secondly, the IMF/World Bank are noteworthy participants in the AML/CFT area. It should be noted that although not directly allocated for AML/CFT purposes, the IMF/World Bank have relatively strong budgetary powers and well-trained experts in various fields.[33] Moreover, with near universal membership which lends both organisations legitimacy and acceptance, the IMF/World Bank could be a natural global forum for sharing information and developing common approaches to the AML/CFT issues.[34] Also, the assessed countries may find it not a bad option to have recourse to the IMF/World Bank, since the overall assessment of these two organisations —including the AML/CFT area—might work as a free "consulting service" to diagnose the soundness of the assessed countries' economy. Sometimes this "consulting service" may also trigger subsequent lending and technical assistance.[35]   However, there still remains a possibility that the IMF/World Bank may withdraw from the AML/CFT campaign should the NCCT exercise be resumed.[36] In this case, the international community may suffer a serious setback in the fight against terrorism and criminal finances.[37] Accordingly, it is of significance for policy makers to make continuous efforts to engage the IMF and the World Bank in the AML/CFT campaign as long as the effectiveness of

---

[33] For example, the IMF has historically provided a large amount of TA to member countries. In terms of person-years, TA activities in the field account for about 18% of the total resources of area and specialised functional departments. See, IMF, "Issues paper for an evaluation of technical assistance provided by the IMF", 5 November 2003, p.1.

[34] IMF, "Intensified Fund Involvement in Anti-Money Laundering Work and Combating the Financing of Terrorism", 5 November 2001, p.10. Furthermore, in terms of public relations the IMF could secure the solid dialogue channel with national legislators. See, e.g., "Report of the Working Group of IMF Executive Directors on Enhancing Communication with National Legislators", 15 January 2004.

[35] IMF/World Bank "Financial Sector Assessment Program-Review, Lessons, and Issues Going Forward", 24 February 2003, p.4.

[36] The IMF/World Bank conditioned their collaboration with the FATF on the agreement that the FATF does not undertake a further round of the NCCT exercise. See, *supra* note 11.

[37] For the potential of the IMF in complementing the work of the FATF, see also, LEE, LLC (1999) "The Basle Accords as Soft law: Strengthening International Banking Supervision", *Virginia Journal of International Law*, vol.39, pp.36-39.

"inducement" measures is not called into serious question. Lastly, even if the time comes for a change in "tactics"; namely from "inducement" to "value deprivation", the decision on this timing should be made in close coordination with and the understanding between the concerned parties.

6.2.4 Introducing intrusive legal tools

The AML/CFT strategy is basically aimed at the "financial devastation" of terrorist groups and criminal organisations. However, if the AML/CFT strategy is not effective in undermining the financial infrastructure of terrorist groups and criminal organisations, there arises a skeptical question of what all these measures are for. In this sense, some legal tools should be promoted with a view to enhancing the effectiveness of the financial warfare on these organisations, especially utilising the current political momentum of the CFT campaign. To begin with, attention should be given to the introduction of civil confiscation. In most of countries, local confiscation regimes depending on criminal confiscation systems do not seem to be so effective in incapacitating criminal organisations.[38] However, civil confiscation has proved to be quite effective in launching financial warfare on criminal organisations, exemplified by the experiences of the US, given that annually its law enforcement authorities confiscate as much as one billion dollars.[39] Moreover, the introduction of the reversal of burden of proof should also be considered in that it is often be very difficult for the prosecution to prove, beyond reasonable doubt, the criminal origin of proceeds, for example when they have been generated in violation of foreign criminal law,[40] or when suspicious assets are owned by legal persons that are domiciled in offshore finance centres.[41] In particular, it should be taken into account that many predicate offences are without a victim to give evidence on the nature of the offences and the extent of the proceeds.[42]

---

[38] Levi M (1997) "Taking the Profit Out of Crime: The UK Experience", *European Journal of Crime, Criminal Law and Criminal Justice*, vol. 5, p.239; Daams CA (2003) *Criminal Asset Forfeiture*, p.145, p.158.

[39] FATF, "Review of FATF Anti-Money Laundering System and Mutual Evaluation Procedures 1992-1999", 16 February 2001, Annex I; Tonry M (1997) "Forfeiture Laws, Practices and Controversies in the US", *European Journal of Crime, Criminal Law and Criminal Justice*, vol. 5, p.294; Smellie A (2004) "Prosecutorial Challenges in Freezing and Forfeiting Proceeds of Transnational Crime and the Use of International Asset Sharing to Promote International Cooperation", *Journal of Money Laundering Control*, vol.8, no.2, p.108.

[40] Stessens G (2000) *Money Laundering: A New International Law Enforcement Model*, p.67.

[41] Council of Europe (August 2004) *Combating organised crime*, p.44.

[42] Stessens G, *supra* note 40, p.67. Especially, with regard to the difficulties of conviction for terrorist finance offences, Bell explains as follows:

Accordingly, the FATF explicitly included these legal tools in the text of the 2003 Recommendation 3. In fact, however, they are introduced in non-mandatory terms since it is difficult to require every state to introduce these concepts at the current stage of development of international law and national legal systems. Nonetheless, if policy makers truly intend to make a real difference in their work on crime control by targeting terrorists' financial sources and other criminal finances, consideration should be given to the introduction of these intrusive legal tools into their domestic legal system.

6.3 Extending the Operational Approach to Criminal Finances

As seen in Chapter Three, the *operational* approach of the Security Council is of importance in that the international community established for the first time an administrative asset-freezing system with the participation of all 191 UN member states.[43] The policy implication from this approach is that freezing orders can be issued even without criminal proceedings and they can (indeed must) be recognised immediately in each national legal system. In fact, this kind of international criminal cooperation was inconceivable under the conventional rules of mutual legal assistance which require strict standards to be met as a condition of assistance such as a formal decision of foreign or domestic courts, or dual criminality.[44]

With such an innovative mechanism in place as a result of the CFT campaign, policy makers cannot help being tempted to apply this mechanism to fight other criminal finances. In fact, many of the measures taken in the wake of 9/11 are aimed at combating terrorism but also they tend to have a long-term effect on the fight against organised crime.[45] This is, for example, the case with the introduction

---

"The primary difficulty for the prosecution in terrorist finance cases is to prove beyond a reasonable doubt that the property is terrorist property. The difficulty is exacerbated when the funds are raised in support of terrorism overseas. It is noteworthy that there have been no successful prosecutions for terrorist funding offences in Northern Ireland over the last 30 years" (Bell RE (2003) "The Confiscation, Forfeiture and Disruption of Terrorist Finances", *Journal of Money Laundering Control*, vol.7, no.2, p.113).

[43] The EU is also running its own listing mechanism. See, Council of the European Union, "The fight against terrorist financing", the note from the Secretary General/High Representative and the Commission to European Council, JAI 566, ECOFIN 424, EF 64, RELEX 655, COTER 91, 16089/04, Brussels, 14 December 2004, p.11.

[44] *Ibid.*, p.11.

[45] Wouters J, Naert F (2004) "Police and Judicial Cooperation in the European Union and Counterterrorism: an Overview", p.110 and Bruggeman W (2004) "Countering the Threat of Terrorism in the EU in a Broader Organised Crime Perspective". In: Fijnaut C, Wouters J, Naert F (eds) *Legal Instruments in the Fight against International Terrorism: A Transnational Dialogue*, p.166.

of the "European Arrest Warrant"[46] and the setting up of the Eurojust within the European Union.[47] It is due to the fact that the infrastructures to fight terrorism and organised crime share much in common. Accordingly, it can be said that one area benefits from the progress made by the other. In this context, given that in the 21st century, transnational organised crime and its massive finances pose a serious challenge to the international community,[48] the extension of the *operational* approach to this area merits further research and consideration. Under the UN Charter, it is not impossible since as pointed out in the *Prosecutor v. Tadic* case (1995), the Security Council has the discretion to adopt appropriate measures to maintain international peace and security.[49] If this initiative materialises, the Security Council might freeze the financial resources of the so-called drug barons and the senior command of transnational criminal organisations.[50]

To this end, first of all, "a threat to international peace and security" needs to be determined in relation to transnational organised crime as the involvement of the Security Council with its Chapter VII powers is premised on the existence of this "threat". Given that this notion of "a threat to international peace and security" has undergone considerable evolution over the last decade,[51] this scenario is not a remote possibility. For example, the threat has already been determined in various

---

[46] By the European Arrest Warrant system, EU member states automatically recognise each other's judicial decisions that order the arrest of a suspect (Wouters J, Naert F, *supra* note 45, p.114). For its contribution to the judicial cooperation, see, Gilmore WC, "The Twin Towers and the Third Pillar: Some Security Agenda Developments", *European University Institute Working Papers*, Law no.2003/7, pp.5-9.

[47] The Eurojust which consists of prosecutors and judges coming from all EU member states, aims to promote European judicial cooperation. For further details, see, Coninsx M (2004) "Europjust and EU Judicial Cooperation in the Fight against Terrorism". In Fijnaut C, Wouters J, Naert F (eds) *Legal Instruments in the Fight against International Terrorism: A Transnational Dialogue*, pp.181-182.

[48] Williams P, Savona EU (1996) *The United Nations and Transnational Organised Crime*, p.32.

[49] Case No.IT-94-1-AR72, 2 October 1995. For details, see, footnote 136 of Chapter Three of this study.

[50] Recently, a precedent of the extension of this *operational* approach beyond the CFT context was already set with the adoption of Resolution 1591 (2005). This resolution aims at securing a cease-fire agreement between the government and rebel groups in Sudan. In light of the failure of all concerned parties including the Sudanese Government, the Sudan Liberation Movement/Army and the Justice and Equality Movement, to implement a cease-fire agreement, the resolution requires all those who impede the peace process to be designated as such and be subject to sanctions. Under these sanctioning measures, the freezing of listed individuals' assets is subsumed.

[51] Simma B (2002) *The Charter of the United Nations: A Commentary*, 2nd edn, vol.1, p.726.

contexts[52] in relation to such as internal armed conflict,[53] violations of human rights and humanitarian law,[54] violation of democratic principles,[55] terrorism,[56] and WMD control.[57] In 2000, even the possibility of defining HIV/AIDS as a threat to peace and security was reviewed.[58]

At the same time, however, there is also a growing concern about the "over"-extension of the chapter VII powers. In other words, if the Security Council were increasingly given the status of world government, it could undermine the overall efficiency and effectiveness of the organ.[59] Neither the Security Council nor the Charter system is structured to accommodate such a role.[60] Thus, the strategy to utilise the operational approach in the fight against transnational organised crime should be dealt with prudently, firstly building up the consensus of the international community that the issue of transnational organised crime is indeed a matter of a priority consideration.

Additionally, as already indicated in Chapter Three,[61] some questions relating to due process and legal safeguards, and delisting procedures should be studied further.[62] To this end, consideration should be given to options such as the establishment of the Security Council's own sub-organ of a judicial nature and utilisation of the International Criminal Court. In any case, it should be remembered that while most of the terrorists who have been put on the list by the 1267 Sanctions Committee are elusive and seldom challenge the decision on the listing,[63] potential candidates to be listed in relation to transnational organised crime might act more actively, utilising enormous financial resources and legitimatised institutional powers.

---

[52] *Ibid.,* p.722-726.

[53] See, e.g., Resolution 733 (1992) concerning Somalia.

[54] See, e.g., Resolution 929 (1994) concerning Rwanda.

[55] See, e.g., Resolution 841 (1993) concerning Haiti.

[56] See, e.g., Resolution 1373 (2001) following 9/11.

[57] See, e.g., Resolution 1540 (2004) concerning the weapons of mass destruction.

[58] De Wet E (2004) *The Chapter VII Powers of the United Nations Security Council,* pp.172-174.

[59] De Wet E, *supra* note 58, pp.176-177.

[60] *Ibid.,* p.177.

[61] See, Section 3.4.3 of Chapter Three.

[62] Council of the European Union, *supra* note 43, p.11.

[63] UN, "Letter dated 1 December 2003 from the Chairman of the Security Council Committee established pursuant to resolution 1267 (1999) addressed to the President of the Security Council containing the SECOND REPORT of the MONITORING GROUP pursuant to resolution 1455 (2003)", S/2003/1070, 2 December 2003, p.5.

6.4 Food for Further Research

Throughout this study, the writer has attempted to clarify the evolution and implementation of international standards on the countering of the financing of terrorism and money laundering. However, during these efforts, there are some issues of significance which could not be dealt with in a comprehensive manner due to the restraint of space as well as the thematic focus of the study. However, further research is definitely merited.

Firstly, it would be a worthwhile effort in academic terms to re-examine the changing relationship between international and national law following 9/11.[64] For instance, Resolution 1373 (2001) and the CTC are establishing international standards in connection with terrorism, and importantly, these are binding on all states. The 1267 Sanctions Committee also provides indirect support to the work of the CTC with its compulsory enforcement mechanism. A similar phenomenon can be found in relation to Resolution 1540 (2004) and its monitoring committee, which deals with the non-proliferation issue of WMD. Thus, it might be said that the "Security Council-made text law" with its monitoring and/or enforcement mechanisms is emerging as a new source of international law, fundamentally "destabilising" the balance between international and national law.

Secondly, new mechanisms for the protection of human rights tailored to AML/CFT context should be researched and reviewed. It is the flip side of the campaign against terrorism and TOC. Without a reliable human rights protection device, the ongoing AML/CFT campaign cannot be justified and cannot be successful in the long term. However, initially, the Security Council and the specialist bodies seemed to surrender to the urgent need to combat terrorism and other criminal finances, in effect delegating this task to other human rights watch organisations.[65] The legal dispute concerning the listing operation of the 1390 committee and the inadequate discussions on human rights in the Security Council Resolution 1373 and the FATF recommendations confirm this tendency. Furthermore, the introduction of intrusive legal tools as suggested above also inevitably entails legal controversies over the poor protection of civil rights.[66] In this regard,

---

[64] Rider BAK, Nakajima C (eds) (2003) "The Funding of Terror: The Legal Implications of the Financial War on Terror", *Journal of Money Laundering Control*, vol.6, no.3, p.211.

[65] See, e.g., the presentation by Ambassador Greenstock, the then Chairman of the CTC at the Symposium: "Combating International Terrorism: The Contribution of the United Nations", held in Vienna on 3-4 June 2002; UN, "Provisional Summary Record of the First Part of the 57th Meeting", S/AC.40/SR.57, 18 March 2003, pp.9-10.

[66] For civil confiscation, even within the U.S there are many criticisms, and some regional courts such as the ECtHR also seems to be still very cautious in introducing these intrusive concepts. See, e.g., Der Walt V (2000) "Civil Forfeiture of Instrumentalities and Proceeds of Crime and the Constitutional Property Clause", *South African Journal on*

a golden combination of the poison and the antidote needs to be sought through an in-depth study in the near future.

Human Rights, vol. 16, pp. 24-31. Similarly, in relation to the controversial nature of the reversed burden of proof, see, e.g., Tadros V, Tierney S (2004) "The Presumption of Innocence and the Human Rights Act", *Modern Law Review*, vol.67, pp.416-422.

References

Books and Articles

Abbot KW, Snidal D (2000) "Hard and Soft Law in International Governance", *International Organisation*, vol. 54.

Abbott KW (2001) "Rule-Making in the WTO: Lessons From the Case of Bribery and Corruption", *Journal of International Economic Law*, vol.4(2).

Adams J (1998) *The Financing of Terror*, UK: New English Library.

Adams W (1993) "Effective Strategies for Banks in Avoiding Criminal, Civil, and Forfeiture Liability in Money Laundering Cases", *Alabama Law Review*, vol. 44.

Ahmed R (2002) *Jihad: The Rise of Militant Islam in Central Asia*, New Haven and London: Yale University Press.

Akande D (1997) "The International Court of Justice and the Security Council: Is there room for judicial control of decisions of the political organs of the United Nations", *International and Comparative Law Quarterly*, vol.46.

Akehurst M (1974/1975) "Custom as a Source of International Law", *The British Yearbook of International Law*, vol.47.

Albrecht HJ (1997) "The Money Trail, Developments in Criminal Law, and Research Needs: An Introduction", *European Journal of Crime, Criminal Law and Criminal Justice*, vol.5.

Alldridge P (2003) *Money Laundering Law: Forfeiture, Confiscation, Civil Recovery, Criminal Laundering and Taxation of the Proceeds of Crime*, Oxford: Hart Publishing.

Alvarez JE (1996) "Judging the Security Council", The American Journal of International Law, vol.90.

Anonymous (2003) *Through Our Enemy's Eyes: Osama bin Laden, Radical Islam, and the Future of America*, Washington, DC: Brassey's Inc.

Arquilla J, Ronfeldt D, Zanini M (2002) "Networks, Netwar, and Information-Age Terrorism". In: Howard RD, Sawyer RL (eds) *Terrorism and Counterterrorism: Understanding the New Security Environment, Connecticut*, US: McGraw-Hill.

Auburn J (2000) *Legal Professional Privilege: Law and Theory*, Oxford: Hart Publishing.

Aust A (2000) "Lockerbie Case", *International and Comparative Law Quarterly*, vol. 49.

Aust A (2001) "Counter-Terrorism—A New Approach: The International Convention for the Suppression of the Financing of Terrorism", *Max Planck UNYB*, vol. 5.

Bartlett BL (May 2002) "The Negative Effects of Money Laundering on Economic Development", For the Asian Development Bank Countering Money Laundering in The Asian and Pacific Region Regional Technical Assistance Project No.5967.

Baxter RR (1965/1966) "Multilateral Treaties as Evidence of Customary International Law", *The British Yearbook of International Law*, vol.41.

Baxter RR (1980) "International Law in "Her Infinite Variety"", *International and Comparative Law Quarterly*, vol.29.

Bazley S, Foster C (2004) *Money laundering: business compliance*, UK(Croydon): Lexisnexis UK.

Bell RE (2002) "The Prosecution of Lawyers for Money Laundering Offences", *Journal of Money Laundering Control*, vol.6, no.1.

Bell RE (2003) "The Confiscation, Forfeiture and Disruption of Terrorist Finances", *Journal of Money Laundering Control*, vol.7, no.2.

Berry LV, Curtis GE, Hudson RA, Kollars NA (May 2002) "A Global Overview of Narcotics-Funded Terrorist and Other Extremist Groups", Library of Congress.

Bittle LF (1987) "Punitive Damages and the Eighth Amendment: An Analytical Framework for Determining Excessiveness", *California Law Review*, vol. 75.

Bodansky Y (1999) *Bin Laden: The Man Who Declared War on America*, Roseville, CA: Prima Publishing.

Bosworth-Davies R (1997) *The Impact of International Money Laundering Legislation*, London: Financial Times Financial Publishing.

Bothe M (1980) "Legal and Non-Legal Norms—A Meaningful Distinction in International Relations?", *Netherlands Yearbook of International Law*, vol. 11.

Boyle AE (1997) "Dispute Settlement and the Law of the Sea Convention: Problems of Fragmentation and Jurisdiction", *International and Comparative Law Quarterly*, vol. 46.

Boyle AE (1999) "Some Reflection on the Relationship of Treaties and Soft Law", *International and Comparative Law Quarterly*, vol. 48.

Brownlie I (2003) *Principles of Public International Law*, 6th edn, Oxford: Oxford University Press.

Buckmaster D (ed) (1996) *Islamic Banking: an overview*, London: Institute of Islamic Banking and Insurance.

Byers M (1999) *Custom, Power and the Power of Rules: International Relations and Customary International Law*, Cambridge: Cambridge University Press.

Cameron I (1994) *The Protective Principle of International Criminal Jurisdiction*, England: Dartmouth Pub. co.

Cameron I (October 2002) "Targeted Sanctions and Legal Safeguards", Report to the Swedish Foreign Office, October 2002 <http://www-hotel.uu.se/juri/sii>.

Campbell D (1992) (ed) *International Bank Secrecy*, London: Sweet & Maxwell.

Candler LJ (1997) "Tracing and Recovering Proceeds of Crime in Fraud Cases: A Comparison of U.S. and U.K. Legislation", *The International Lawyer*, vol. 31.

Capitanchik D (1986) "Terrorism and Islam". In: O'Sullivan N (ed) *Terrorism, Ideology, and Revolution*, Sussex: Wheatsheaf Books Ltd.

Cassese A (1989) *Terrorism, Politics and Law: The Achille Lauro Affair*, Cambridge: Polity Press.

Cheng B (1982) "United Nations Resolutions on Outer Space: "Instant" International Customary Law". In: Cheng B (ed) *International Law: Teaching and Practice*, London: Stevens & Sons.

Chinkin CM (1989) "The Challenge of Soft Law: Development and Change in International Law", *International and Comparative Law Quarterly*, vol. 38.

Clark A, Burrell P (2003) "The Money Laundering Threat". In: Clark A, Burrell P (eds) *A Practitioner's Guide to International Money Laundering Law and Regulation*, 1st edn, UK(Surrey): City & Financial Publishing.

Clark A, Russell M (2003) "Know Your Customer". In: Clark A, Burrell P (eds) *A Practitioner's Guide to International Money Laundering Law and Regulation*, 1st edn, UK(Surrey): City & Financial Publishing.

Clark A, Russell M (2003) "Reporting Regimes". In: Clark A, Burrell P (eds) *A Practitioner's Guide to International Money Laundering Law and Regulation*, 1st edn, UK(Surrey): City & Financial Publishing.

Clark N (1996) "The Impact of Recent Money Laundering Legislation on Financial Intermediaries". In: Rider B, Ashe M (eds) *Money Laundering Control*, Dublin: Sweet & Maxwell.

Clark RS (1998) "Offenses of International Concern: Multilateral State Treaty Practice in the Forty Years Since Nuremberg", *Nordic Journal of International Law*, vol. 57.

Codd E (2003) "Reputational Risk". In: Clark A, Burrell P (eds) *A Practitioner's Guide to International Money Laundering Law and Regulation*, 1st edn, UK(Surrey): City & Financial Publishing.

Comb C (2003) *Terrorism in the Twenty-First Century*, 3rd edn, New Jersey: Prentice Hall.

Contini P, Sand PH (1972) "Methods to Expedite Environment Protection: International Ecostandards", *American Journal of International Law*, vol. 66.

Council of Europe (August 2004) *Combating organised crime: Best practice surveys of the Council of Europe*, August 2004.

Cullen PJ (1993) "Money Laundering: The European Community Directive". In: Macqueen HL (ed) *Money Laundering*, Edinburgh: Edinburgh University Press.

Daams CA (2003) *Criminal Asset Forfeiture: One of the most effective weapons against (organised) crime?*, The Netherlands: Wolf Legal Publishers.

D'Amato AA (1971) *The Concept of Custom in International Law*, London: Cornell University Press.

De Wet E (2004) *The Chapter VII Powers of the United Nations Security Council*, Oxford: Hart Publishing.

Der Walt V (2000) "Civil Forfeiture of Instrumentalities and Proceeds of Crime and the Constitutional Property Clause", *South African Journal on Human Rights*, vol. 16.

Dinse J, Johnson S (1993) "Ideologies of Revolutionary Terrorism: Some Enduring and Emerging Themes". In: Han HH (ed) *Terrorism & Political Violence: Limits & Possibilities of Legal Control*, London: Oceana Publications, Inc.

Dixon M (2002) *Textbook on International Law*, 4th edn, London: Blackstone.

Drage J (1993) "Countering Money Laundering: The Response of the Financial Sector". In: Macqueen HL (ed) *Money Laundering*, Edinburgh: Edinburgh University Press.

Dupuy PM (1991) "Soft law and the International Law of the Environment", *Michigan Journal of International Law*, vol.12.

Ehrenfeld R (2003) *Funding Evil: How Terrorism Is Financed-and How to Stop It*, Chicago and Los Angeles: Bonus Books.

Elias O, Lim C (1997) " 'General Principle of Law', 'Soft' Law and the Identification of International Law", *Netherlands Yearbook of International Law*, vol. 28.

Esposito JL (2002) *Unholy War: Terror in the name of Islam*, Oxford: Oxford University Press.

Everett R (2000) "American Servicemembers and the ICC". In: Sewall SB, Kaysen C (eds) *The United States and the International Criminal Court*, US: Rowmand & Littlefield Publishers, Inc.

Fleur KR (1992) "European Integration with regard to the Confiscation of the Proceeds of Crime", *European Law Review*, vol. 17.

Floy M (1997) "International Law: an instrument to combat terrorism". In: Higgins R, Floy M (ed) *Terrorism and International Law*, London: Routledge.

Fried DJ (1988) "Rationalizing Criminal Forfeiture", *The Journal of Criminal Law & Criminology*, vol. 79.

Fukuyama F (2002) "History and September 11". In: Booth K, Dunne T, *World in Collision: Terror and the Future of Global Order*, New York: Palgrave MacMillan.

Gallant MM (2005) *Money Laundering and the Proceeds of Crime: Economic Crime and Civil Remedies*, UK(Glos): Edward Elgar Publishing Ltd.

Garland D (1996) "The Limits of the Sovereign State: Strategies of Crime Control in Contemporary Society", *The British Journal of Criminology*, vol. 36.

Gerson A, Adler J (2001) *The Price of Terror*, US: Harper Collins Publishers.

Gearson J (2002) "The Nature of Modern Terrorism". In: Freedman L (ed) *Superterrorism: Policy Responses*, Oxford: Blackwell Publishing.

Gilbert G (1992) "Crimes Sans Frontiers: Jurisdictional Problems in English Law", *British Yearbook of International Law*, vol. 63.

Gilbert G (1998) *Transnational Fugitive Offenders in International Law*, The Hague: Martinus Nijhoff Publishers.

Gilmore WC (1991) *Combating International Drugs Trafficking: The 1988 United Nations Convention Against Illicit Traffic in Narcotic Drugs and Psychotropic Substances*, London: Commonwealth Secretariat.

Gilmore WC (1993) "Money Laundering: The International Aspect". In: Macqueen HL (ed) *Money Laundering*, Edinburgh: Edinburgh University Press.

Gilmore WC (2003) "International Initiative". In: Graham T (ed) *Butterworths International Guide to Money Laundering Law and Practice*, 2nd edn, London: LexisNexis Butterworths Tolley.

Gilmore WC (2003) "Changes to the Global Regime". In: Clark A, Burrell P (eds) *A Practitioner's Guide to International Money Laundering Law and Regulation*, 1st edn, UK(Surrey): City & Financial Publishing.

Gilmore WC (2003) "The Twin Towers and the Third Pillar: Some Security Agenda Developments", *European University Institute Working Papers*, Law no.2003/7.

Gilmore WC (2004) *Dirty Money: The evolution of international measures to counter money laundering and the financing of terrorism*, 3rd edn, Strasbourg: Council of Europe Publishing.

Gilmore WC (2004) "International Financial Counterterrorism Initiatives". In: Fijnaut C, Wouters J, Naert F (eds) *Legal Instruments in the Fight against International Terrorism: A Transnational Dialogue*, Leiden and Boston: Martinus Nijhoff Publishers.

Giovanoli M (1993) "Switzerland. Some Recent Developments in Banking". In: Cranston R (ed) *European Banking Law: The Banker-Customer Relationship*, London: LLP.

Gold J (1983) "Strengthening the Soft International Law of Exchange Arrangements", *The American Journal of International Law*, vol. 77.

Gordon GH (2000) *Criminal Law*, 3rd edn, vol. 1, Edinburgh: W. Green.

Grant TD (1995) "Toward a Swiss Solution for an American Problem: An Alternative Approach for Banks in the War on Drugs", *Annual Review of Banking Law*, vol. 14.

Gunaratna R (2002) *Inside Al Qaeda: Global Network of Terror*, London: Hurst & Company.

Guzman AT (2002) "A Compliance-Based Theory of International Law", *California Law Review*, vol. 90.

Halberstam M (2003) "The Evolution of the United Nations Position on Terrorism: From Exempting National Liberation Movements to Criminalizing Terrorism Wherever and by Whomever Committed", *Columbia Journal of Transnational Law*, vol. 41.

Han HH (1993) "Autocracy of the Shah of Iran: Views of the Media Reporters". In: Han HH (ed) *Terrorism & Political Violence: Limits & Possibilities of Legal Control*, London: Oceana Publications, Inc.

Hardister AD (2003) "Can We Buy Peace On Earth? : The Price of Freezing Assets in a Post September 11 World", *North Carolina Journal of International Law & Commercial Regulation*, vol. 28.

Higgins R (1997) "The general international law of terrorism". In: Higgins R, Flory M (eds) *Terrorism and International Law*, London: Routledge.

Hillgenberg H (1999) "A Fresh Look at Soft Law", *European Journal of International Law*, vol. 10.

Hinterseer K (2002) *Criminal Finance: The Political Economy of Money Laundering in a Comparative Legal Context*, London: Kluwer Law International.

Hoffman B (1999) *Inside Terrorism*, London: Indigo.

Hyland M (2003) "Corporate Culture". In: Clark A, Burrell P (eds) *A Practitioner's Guide to International Money Laundering Law and Regulation*, 1st edn, UK(Surrey): City & Financial Publishing.

International Institute for Strategic Studies (2004) *Strategic Survey 2003/2004*.

IMF (2003) *Suppressing the Financing of Terrorism: A Handbook for Legislative Drafting*, Washington, D.C.: IMF Publication Services.

IMF (2004) *Financial Intelligence Units: An Overview*, Washington, D.C.: IMF Publication Services.

Jacquard R (2002) *In the name of Osama Bin Laden*, Durham, NC: Duke University Press.

Jankowski MA (1990) "Tempering the Relation-Back Doctrine: A More Reasonable Approach to Civil Forfeiture in Drug Cases", *Virginia Law Review*, vol. 76.

Jenkins BM (1975) "International Terrorism: A New Mode of Conflict". In: Carlton D, Schaerf C (eds) *International Terrorism and World Security*, London: Croom Helm.

Johnson CM (2000) "Introductory Note to the International Convention for the Suppression of the Financing of Terrorism", *International Law Material*, vol. 39.

Johnson J (2002) "11th September, 2001: Will It Make a Difference to the Global Anti-Money Laundering Movement?", *Journal of Money Laundering Control*, vol.6, no.1.

Johnson J (2003) "Repairing Legitimacy after Blacklisting by the Financial Action Task Force", *Journal of Money Laundering Control*, vol.7, no.1.

Johnston RB, Nelelescu OM (2005) "The Impact of Terrorism on Financial Markets", *IMF Working Paper*, WP/05/60.

Kersten A (2002) "Financing of Terrorism—A Predicate Offence to Money Laundering?". In: Pieth M (ed) *Financing Terrorism*, Dordrecht: Kluwer Academic Publishers.

Kirgis Jr FL (1995) "The Security Council's First Fifty Years", *The American Journal of International Law*, vol. 89.

Kittichaisaree K (2001) *International Criminal Law*, New York: Oxford University Press.

Koh JM (November 2002) "Transnational Organised Crime and International Countering Efforts". In: Ministry of Foreign Affairs and Trade (ROK), *Theory and Practice of Multilateral Security Policy*, Seoul.

Kolodkin RA (1996) "An Ad Hoc International Tribunal for the Prosecution of Serious Violations of International Humanitarian Law in the Former Yugoslavia". In: Clark R, Sann, M (eds) *The Prosecution of International Crimes*, London: Transaction Publishers.

Kressel NJ (2002) *Mass Hate: The Global Rise of Genocide and Terror*, Cambridge MA: Westview Press.

Levi M (1997) "Taking the Profit Out of Crime: The UK experience", *European Journal of Crime, Criminal Law and Criminal Justice*, vol. 5.

Levi M, Gilmore WC (2002) "Terrorist Finance, Money Laundering and the Rise and Rise of Mutual Evaluation: A New Paradigm for Crime Control?". In: Pieth M (ed) *Financing Terrorism*, Dordrecht: Kluwer Academic Publishers.

Lewis MK, Algaud LM (2001) *Islamic Banking*, UK(Cheltenham): Edward Elgar.

Lilley P (2003) *Dirty Dealing: The Untold Truth about Global Money Laundering, International Crime and Terrorism*, London: Kogan Page Ltd.

Lipson C (1991) "Why are some international agreements informal?", *International Organization*, vol. 45.

Maimbo SM (2003) "The Money Exchange Dealers of Kabul: A Study of the Hawala System in Afghanistan", World Bank.

Malanzuk P (ed) (1997) *Akerhurst's Modern Introduction to International Law*, 7th edn, London: Routledge.

Martenczuk B (1999) "The Security Council, the International Court and Judicial Review: What lessons from Lockerbie?", *European Journal of International Law*, vol. 10.

McClean D (2002) *International Co-operation in Civil and Criminal Matters*, New York: Oxford University Press.

McKay F (2004) "U.S. Unilateralism and International Crimes: The International Criminal Court and Terrorism", *Cornell International Law Journal*, vol. 36.

Mitsilegas V (2003) *Money Laundering Counter-Measures in the European Union: A New Paradigm of Security Governance versus Fundamental Legal Principles,* London: Kluwer Law International.

Mitsilegas V (2003) "Countering the chameleon threat of dirty money: 'Hard' and 'soft' law in the emergence of a global regime against money laundering and terrorist finance". In: Edwards A, Gill P (eds) *Transnational organised crime : perspectives on global security,* London: Routledge.

Morris M (2004) "Terrorism and Unilateralism: Criminal Jurisdiction and International Relations", *Cornell International Law Journal*, vol. 36.

Murphy SD (2003) "Contemporary practice of the United States relating to international law: the U.S. Adoption of New Doctrine on Use of Force", *The American Journal of International Law*, vol. 97.

Nadelmann EA (1993) *Cops across borders: the Internationalization of U.S. Criminal Law Enforcement,* US: Pennsylvania University Press.

Napoleoni L (2003) *Modern Jihad: Tracing the Dollars Behind the Terror Networks,* London: Pluto Press.

Navias MS (2002) "Financial Warfare as a Response to International Terrorism". In: Freedman L (ed) *Superterrorism: Policy Responses,* Oxford: Blackwell Publishing.

Neff S (1998) "Past and Future Lessons from the Ad Hoc Tribunals for the Former Yugoslavia and Rwanda". In: Cullen PJ, Gilmore WC (eds) *Crime Sans Frontières: International and European Legal Approaches,* Edinburgh: Edinburgh University Press.

Nilsson HG (1991) "The Council of Europe Laundering Convention: A Recent Example of a Developing International Criminal Law", *Criminal Law Forum*, vol. 2.

Noble PK, Golumbic CE (1998) "A New Anti-Crime Framework For the World: Merging The Objective and Subjective Models for Fighting Money Laundering", *New York University Journal of International Law and Politics*, vol. 30.

Qorchi ME, Maimbo SM, Wilson JF (August 2003) "Informal Funds Transfer systems: An Analysis of the Informal Hawala System", *Occasional Paper 222*, IMF.

Oxman B (1997) "Jurisdiction of States", *Encyclopaedia of Public International Law*, vol.3, Oxford: Elsevier.

Palm CW (1991) "RICO Forfeiture and the Eighth Amendment: When is Everything too much?", *The University of Pittsburgh Law Review*, vol. 53.

Partsch KJ (2000) "Reprisals", *Encyclopedia of Public International Law*, vol.4, London: Elsevier.

Perera AR (2004) "Reviewing the UN Conventions on Terrorism: Towards a Comprehensive Terrorism Convention". In: Fijnaut C, Wouters J, Naert F (eds) *Legal Instruments in the Fight against International Terrorism: A Transnational Dialogue,* Leiden and Boston: Martinus Nijhoff Publishers.

Ranstorp M (2002) "Terrorism in the Name of Religion". In: Howard RD, Sawyer RL (eds) *Terrorism and Counterterrorism: Understanding the New Security Environment,* Connecticut, US: McGraw-Hill.

Reeve S (1999) *The New Jackals: Ramzi Yousef, Osama bin Laden and the future of Terrorism*, London: André Deutsch Limited.

Reinisch A (2001) "Developing Human Rights and Humanitarian Law Accountability of the Security Council for the Imposition of Economic Sanctions", *The American Journal of International Law*, vol. 95.

Richardson L (2002) "Global Rebels: Terrorist Organisations as Trans-National Actors". In: Howard RD, Sawyer RL (eds) *Terrorism and Counterterrorism: Understanding the New Security Environment*, Connecticut, U.S.: McGraw-Hill.

Rider BAK, Nakajima C (eds) (2003) "The Funding of Terror: The Legal Implications of the Financial War on Terror", *Journal of Money Laundering Control*, vol.6, no.3.

Robbins JS (2002) "Bin Laden's War". In: Howard RD, Sawyer RL (eds) *Terrorism and Counterterrorism: Understanding the New Security Environment*, Connecticut, U.S.: McGraw-Hill.

Roberts AE (2001) "Traditional and Modern Approaches to Customary International Law: A Reconciliation", *The American Journal of International Law*, vol. 95.

Roman AK (1996) "An Ad Hoc International Tribunal for the Prosecution of Serious Violations of International Humanitarian Law in the Former Yugoslavia". In: Clark R, Sann M (eds) *The Prosecution of International Crimes*, News Brunswick: Transaction Publishers.

Rosand E (2004) "Security Council Resolution 1373 and the Counter-Terrorism Committee: the Cornerstone of the United Nations Contribution to the Fight against Terrorism". In: Fijnaut C, Wouters J, Naert F (eds) *Legal Instruments in the Fight against International Terrorism: A Transnational Dialogue*, Leiden and Boston; Martinus Nijhoff Publishers.

Rosie G (1987) *The Directory of International Terrorism*, New York: Paragon House.

Russell CA, Banker Jr LJ, Miller BH (1979) "Out-Inventing the Terrorist". In: Alexander Y, Carlton D, Wilkinson P (eds) *Terrorism: Theory and Practice*, Colorado, US: Westview Press, Inc.

Sait S (2002) "International Refugee Law: Excluding the Palestinians". In: Strawson J (ed) *Law After Ground Zero*, London: The Glass House Press.

Saland P (1999) "International Criminal Law Principles". In: Lee RS (ed) *The International Criminal Court: The Making of the Rome Statute: Issues, Negotiations, Results*, The Hague: Kluwer Law International.

Savla S (2001) *Money Laundering and Financial Intermediaries*, London: Kluwer Law International.

Schabas WA (2001) *An Introduction to the International Criminal Court*, Cambridge: Cambridge University Press.

Schachter O (1977) "The Twilight Existence of Nonbinding International Agreement", *The American Journal of International Law*, vol. 71.

Schachter O (1994) "United Nations Law", *The American Journal of International Law*, vol. 88.

Scheffer D (1999) "The United States and the International Criminal Court", *The American Journal of International Law*, vol. 93.

Schmid AP, De Graaf J (1982) *Violence as Communication: Insurgent Terrorism and the Western News Media*, London: Sage.

Schneider F (2004) "Macroeconomics: The Financial Flows of Islamic Terrorism". In: Maschiandaro D (ed) *Global Financial Crime: Terrorism, Money Laundering and Off-shore Centres*, England: Ashgate Publishing Limited.

Schott PA (2003) *Reference Guide to Anti-Money Laundering and Combating the Financing of Terrorism*, Washington, D.C.: World Bank.

Sederberg PC (1989) *Terrorist Myths: illusion, rhetoric, and reality*, New Jersey: Prentice-Hall, Inc.

Seidl-Hohenveldern I (1979) "International Economic Soft Law", *Recueil des Cours*, tome 163.

Shaw M (1997) *International Law*, 4th edn, Cambridge : Cambridge University Press.

Sherman T (1993) "International Efforts to Combat Money Laundering: The Role of the Financial Action Task Force". In: Macqueen HL (ed) *Money Laundering*, Edinburgh: Edinburgh University Press.

Shutte JJE (1991) "Extradition for Drug Offences: New Developments Under the 1988 U.N. Convention Against Illicit Traffic In Narcotic Drugs and Psychotropic Substances", *International Review of Penal Law*, vol. 62.

Simma B (ed) (2002) *The Charter of the United Nations: A Commentary*, 2nd edn, Oxford; Oxford University Press.

Simmons BA (2000) "Legalization of International Monetary Affairs", *International Organization*, vol. 54.

Simmons BA (2000) "Money and the Law: Why Comply with the Public International Law of Money?", *The Yale Journal of International Law*, vol. 25.

Smellie A (2004) "Prosecutorial Challenges in Freezing and Forfeiting Proceeds of Transnational Crime and the Use of International Asset Sharing to Promote International Cooperation", *Journal of Money Laundering Control*, vol.8, no.2.

Sproule DW, St. Denis P (1989) "The UN Drug Trafficking Convention: An Ambitious Step", *The Canadian Yearbook of International Law*, vol. 27.

Stern J (1999) *The Ultimate Terrorist*, Cambridge: Harvard University Press.

Stessens G (2000) *Money Laundering: A New International Law Enforcement Model*, Cambridge: Cambridge University Press.

Stewart D (1990) "Internationalizing the War on Drugs: The UN Convention Against Illicit Traffic in Narcotic Drugs and Psychotropic Substances", *Denver Journal of International Law and Policy*, vol. 18.

Tadeusz GW (1984) "A Framework for Understanding "Soft Law"", *McGill Law Journal*, vol. 30.

Tadros V, Tierney S (2004) "The Presumption of Innocence and the Human Rights Act", *Modern Law Review*, vol.67.

Talbot R (2002) "The Balancing Act: Counter-Terrorism and Civil Liberties in British Anti-Terrorism Law". In: Strawson J (ed) *Law After Ground Zero*, London: The Glass House Press.

Tanzi V (1998) "Macroeconomic aspects of offshore centres and the importance of money-laundering in offshore financial flows". In: UNODC, *Attacking the Profits of Crime: Drugs, Money and Laundering*, Vienna.

Thachuk KL (May 2002) "Terrorism's Financial Lifeline: Can It be Severed?", *Strategic Forum*, Institute for National Strategic Studies, National Defense University, no.191.

Thomas C (2002) "Trade-Related Labour and Environment Agreements?", *Journal of International Economic Law*, vol.5(4).

Tonry M (1997) "Forfeiture Laws, Practices and Controversies in the US", *European Journal of Crime, Criminal Law and Criminal Justice*, vol. 5.

United Nations Office for Drug Control and Crime Prevention (1998) *Financial Havens, Banking Secrecy and Money Laundering*, New York.

United Nation (1998) "Commentary on the United Nations Convention Against Illicit Traffic in Narcotic Drugs and Psychotropic Substances 1988", New York.

UNODC (November 2004) *Afghanistan Opium Survey 2004*.

Vera GD (1994) "The Relationship between the International Court of Justice and the Security Council in the light of the *Lockerbie* case", *The American Journal of International Law*, vol. 88.

Verbruggen F (1997) "Proceeds-oriented Criminal Justice in Belgium: Backbone or Wishbone of a Modern Approach to Organised Crime?", *European Journal of Crime, Criminal Law and Criminal Justice*, vol. 5.

Verbruggen F (2002) "On Containing Organised Crime Using "Container Offences": Some Reflections on Substantive Criminal Law Issues". In: Albrecht HJ, Fijnaut C (eds) *The Containment of Transnational Organised Crime: Comments on the UN Convention of December 2000*, Freiburg: Max-Planck-Institute.

Wai R (2003) "Countering, Branding, Dealing: Using Economic And Social Rights In and Around The International Trade Regime", *European Journal of International Law*, vol. 35.

Ward CA (2003) "Legal Imperatives for Implementation of Resolution 1373 (2001)". Paper presented at the 2003 Caribbean Regional Conference of the International Law Association, Barbados, West Indies, 26-29 March 2003 (typescript).

Ward CA (2003) "Building Capacity to Combat International Terrorism: The Role of the United Nations Security Council", (2003) *Journal of Conflict & Security*, vol. 8, no.2.

Wells C (2001) *Corporations and Criminal Responsibility*, 2nd edn, Oxford: Oxford University Press.

Wessel R (2004) "Debating the 'Smartness' of Anti-Terrorism Sanctions: The UN Security Council and the Individual Citizen". In: Fijnaut C, Wouters J, Naert F (eds) *Legal Instruments in the Fight against International Terrorism: A Transnational Dialogue*, Leiden and Boston: Martinus Nijhoff Publishers.

Wilkinson P (1979) "Terrorist Movements". In: Alexander Y, Carlton D, Wilkinson P (eds) *Terrorism: Theory and Practice*, Colorado, US: Westview Press, Inc.

Wilkinson P (1986) "Fighting the Hydra". In: O'Sullivan N (ed) *Terrorism, Ideology, and Revolution*, Sussex: Wheatsheaf Books Ltd.

Wilkinson P (2001) *Terrorism Versus Democracy: The Liberal State Response*, London: Frank Cass Publishers.

Williams P, Savona EU (eds) *The United Nations and Transnational Organised Crime*, London/Portland, Oregon: Frank Cass & Co.Ltd.

Wouters J, Naert F (2004) "Shockwaves through International Law after 11 September: Finding the Right Responses to the Challenges of International Terrorism". In: Fijnaut C, Wouters J, Naert F (eds) *Legal Instruments in the Fight against International Terrorism: A Transnational Dialogue*, Leiden and Boston: Martinus Nijhoff Publishers.

Zagaris B (2003) "FATF Gatekeepers Likely to Settle on a Modified Swiss Version of the Law", *International Enforcement Law Reporter*, vol.19, issue 7.

Zeidan S (2004) "Desperately Seeking Definition: The International Community's Quest for Identifying the Specter of Terrorism", *Cornell International Law Journal*, vol. 36.

Documents

<APG>

"Annual Report: 2000-2001", November 2001.
"Annual Report: 1 July 2001-30 June 2002", December 2002.
"APG Terms of Reference", as amended in 2002 Annual Meeting, December 2002.
"APG Terms of Reference", November 2004.
"First Annual Report: 1999-2000", April 2001.
"Revised Procedures for APG mutual evaluations", adopted at the Sixth APG Annual Meeting, Macau, China, September 2003.
"APG Typologies Report 2003-04", June 2004.
"Annual Report 1 October 2003-30 June 2004", November 2004.
"Explanatory Note on Membership", August 2002.

<FATF>

"Annual Report: 1989-1990", 7 February 1990.
"Annual Report: 1990-1991", 13 May 1991.
"Annual Report: 1994-1995", 8 June 1995.
"Annual Report: 1995-1996", 28 June 1996.
"Annual Report: 1996-1997", 19 June 1997.
"Annual Report: 1997-1998: Annex E—Providing Feedback to Reporting Financial Institutions and Other Persons: Best Practice Guidelines", June 1998.
"Annual Report: 1998-1999", 2 July 1999.
"Annual Report: 1999-2000; Annex A", 22 June 2000.
"Annual Report: 2001-2002", 21 June 2002.
"Annual Report: 2002-2003", 20 June 2003.
"Annual Report: 2003-2004", 2 July 2004.
"Annual Report: 2004-2005", 10 June 2005.

"Annual Review of Non-Cooperative Countries or Territories", 20 June 2003.

"Combating the Abuse of Non-Profit Organizations: International Best Practices", 11 October 2002.

"Combating the Abuse of Alternative Remittance System: International Best Practices", 20 June 2003.

"Freezing of Terrorist Assets: International Best Practice", 3 October 2003.

"Guidance notes for the Special Recommendations on Terrorist Financing and the Self-Assessment Questionnaire", 27 March 2002.

"Guidance for Financial Institutions in Detecting Terrorist Financing", 24 April 2002.

"Interpretative Note to Special Recommendation VII: Wire Transfer", 14 February 2003.

"Interpretative Note to Special Recommendation VI: Alternative Remittance", 14 February 2003.

"Interpretative Note to Special Recommendation III: Freezing and Confiscating Terrorist Assets", 3 October 2003.

"Interpretative Note to Special Recommendation II", 2 July 2004.

"Interpretative Note to Special Recommendation IX", 22 October 2004.

"Methodology for Assessing Compliance with Anti-Money Laundering and Combating the Financing of Terrorism Standards", 11 October 2002.

"Methodology for Assessing Compliance with the FATF 40 Recommendations and the FATF 8 Special Recommendations", 27 February 2004.

"Report on Money Laundering Typologies: 2000-2001", 1 February 2001.

"Report on Money Laundering Typologies: 2001-2002", 1 February 2002.

"Report on Money Laundering Typologies: 2002-2003", 14 February 2003.

"Report on Money Laundering and Terrorist Financing Typologies: 2003-2004", 14 February 2004.

"Review to Identify Non-Cooperative Countries or Territories: Increasing The Worldwide Effectiveness of Anti-Money Laundering Measures", 22 June 2000.

"Review of FATF Anti-Money Laundering Systems and Mutual Evaluation Procedures 1992-1999", 16 February 2001.

"Review to Identify Non-Cooperative Countries or Territories: Increasing The World-Wide Effectiveness of Anti-Money Laundering Measures", 22 June 2001.

"Review of the FATF Forty Recommendations: Consultation Paper", 30 May 2002.

"Review to Identify Non-Cooperative Countries or Territories: Increasing The World-Wide Effectiveness of Anti-Money Laundering Measures", 21 June 2002.

<IMF/World Bank>

IMF/World Bank, "Enhancing Contributions to Combating Money Laundering: Policy Paper", 26 April 2001.

IMF/World Bank, "Strengthening IMF-World Bank Collaboration on Country Programs and Conditionality", 23 August 2001.

IMF, "Intensified Fund Involvement in Anti-Money Laundering Work and Combating the Financing of Terrorism", 5 November 2001.

World Bank, "Proposed Action Plan for Enhancing the Bank's Ability to Respond to Clients in Combating Money Laundering and the Financing of Terrorism", 22 January 2002.

IMF/World Bank, "Intensified Work on Anti-Money Laundering and Combating Financing of Terrorism (AML/CFT): Joint Progress Report on the Work of the IMF and World Bank", April 2002.

IMF/World Bank, "Operationalizing Bank-Fund Collaboration in Country Programs and Conditionality", April 2002.

IMF/World Bank, "Anti-Money Laundering and Combating the Financing of Terrorism (AML/CFT): Materials Concerning Staff Progress Towards the Development of a Comprehensive AML/CFT Methodology and Assessment Process", 11 June 2002.

IMF, "Anti-Money Laundering and Combating the Financing of Terrorism (AML/CFT): Proposals To assess A Global Standard And To Prepare ROSCs", 17 July 2002.

IMF/World Bank, "Strengthening IMF-World Bank Collaboration on Country Programs and Conditionality-Progress Report", 19 August 2002.

IMF, "Intensified Work on Anti-Money Laundering and Combating the Financing of Terrorism (AML/CFT): Progress Report on Responses to the AML/CFT Questionnaire", 10 September 2002.

IMF/World Bank, "Implementation of the Basel Core Principles for Effective Banking Supervision, Experiences, Influences, and Perspectives", 23 September 2002.

IMF, "Report on the Outcome of the FATF Plenary Meeting and Proposal for the Endorsement of the Methodology for Assessing Compliance with Anti-Money Laundering and Combating the Financing of Terrorism (AML/CFT) Standard", 8 November 2002.

IMF/World Bank, "Financial Sector Assessment Program-Review, Lessons, and Issues Going Forward", 24 February 2003.

IMF, "Offshore Financial Center Reform: A Progress Report", 14 March 2003.

IMF/World Bank, "Twelve-Month Pilot Program of Anti-Money Laundering and Combating the Financing of Terrorism (AML/CFT) Assessments and Delivery of AML/CFT Technical Assistance: Joint Interim Progress Report of the Work of the IMF and the World Bank", 31 March 2003.

IMF/World Bank, "Status Report of the Work of the IMF and the World Bank on the Twelve-Month Pilot Program of AML/CFT assessments and Delivery of AML/CFT Technical Assistance", 5 September 2003.

IMF, "Issues paper for an evaluation of technical assistance provided by the IMF", 5 November 2003.

IMF, "Report of the Working Group of IMF Executive Directors on Enhancing Communication with National Legislators", 15 January 2004.

IMF/World Bank, "Strengthening IMF-World Bank Collaboration on Country Programs and Conditionality-Progress Report", 24 February 2004.

IMF, "IMF Executive Board Reviews and Enhances Efforts for Anti-Money Laundering and Combating the Financing of Terrorism", Public Information Notice (PIN) No.04/33, 2004.

IMF/World Bank, "Twelve Month Pilot Program of AML/CFT Assessments: Joint Report on the Review of the Pilot Program", 11 March 2004.

<UN>

"Analytical Study Prepared by the Secretariat in accordance with General Assembly Resolution 32/147", UN Doc., A/AC/160/4, 28 February 1979, para.16-39. In: Friedlander RA (1981) *Terrorism: Documents of International and Local Control*, vol. III, London: Oceana Publications, Inc.

"CTC Programme of Work for the first 90-day period", attached to the "Letter dated 19 October 2001 from the Chairman of the Counter-Terrorism Committee addressed to the President of the Security Council", UN Doc., S/2001/986, 19 October 2001.

"CTC Programme of Work for the second 90-day period", attached to the "Letter dated 15 January 2002 from the Chairman of the Counter-Terrorism Committee addressed to the President of the Security Council", UN Doc., S/2002/67, 15 January 2002.

"CTC Programme of Work for the third 90-day period", attached to the "Letter dated 27 March 2002 from the Chairman of the Counter-Terrorism Committee addressed to the President of the Security Council", UN Doc., S/2002/318, 27 March 2002.

"First Report of the Monitoring Group on Afghanistan Established Pursuant to Security Council Resolution 1363 (2001) attached to the "Letter dated 14 January 2002 from the Chairman of the Security Council Committee established pursuant to resolution 1267 (1999) concerning Afghanistan addressed to the President of the Security Council", UN Doc., S/2002/65, 15 January 2002.

"Fourth Report of the Monitoring Group established Pursuant to Security Council Resolution 1363 and extended by resolution 1390 (2002)" enclosed in "Letter dated 7 July 2003 from the Chairman of the Security Council Committee established pursuant to resolution 1267 (1999) addressed to the President of the Security Council", UN Doc., S/2003/669, 8 July 2003.

"Follow-up of the Counter-Terrorism Committee to resolution 1456 (2003) of the Security Council" attached to "Letter dated 14 February 2003 from the Chairman of the Security Council Committee established pursuant to resolution 1373 (2001) concerning counter-terrorism addressed to the President of the Security Council", UN Doc., S/2003/198, 19 February 2003.

"French Communiqué of 12/20/91", UN Doc., A/46/825-S/23306. In: Grant JP (2004) *The Lockerbie Trial: A Documentary History*, New York: Oceana Publication, Inc.

"Guidelines of the Committee for the Conduct of Its Work", UN Doc., S/AC.40/2001/CRP.1, 16 October 2001.

"Guidelines of the Committee for the Conduct of its Work", adopted on 7 November 2002 and amended on 10 April 2003.

"Information Note on Submissions to the CTC Directory", UN Doc., SCA /20/01(8), 27 November 2001.

"Joint US/UK Declaration of 27 November 1991", Annexed to UN Docs.A/46/826-S/23307 and A/46/827-S23308. In: Grant JP (2004) *The Lockerbie Trial: A Documentary History*, New York: Oceana Publication, Inc.

"Letter dated 3 November 1998 from the Permanent Representative of France to the United Nations addressed to the Secretary-General", UN Doc., A/C.6/53/9, 4 November 1998.

"Letter dated 20 June 2002 from the Chairman of the Security Council Committee established pursuant to resolution 1373 (2001) concerning counter- terrorism addressed to the President of the Security Council", UN Doc., S/2002/692, 20 June 2002.

"Letter dated 1 December 2003 from the Chairman of the Security Council Committee established pursuant to resolution 1267 (1999) addressed to the President of the Security Council containing the SECOND REPORT of the MONITORING GROUP pursuant to resolution 1455 (2003)", UN Doc., S/2003/1070, 2 December 2003.

"Letter dated 23 August 2004 from the Chairman of the Security Council Committee established pursuant to resolution 1267 (1999) concerning Al-Qaida and the Taliban and associated individuals and entities addressed to the President of the Security Council", UN Doc., S/2004/679, 25 August 2004.

"Letter dated 14 February 2005 from the Chairman of the Security Council Committee established pursuant to resolution 1267 (1999) concerning Al-Qaeda and the Taliban and associated individuals and entities addressed to the President of the Security Council", UN Doc., S/2005/83, 15 February 2005.

"List of International, Regional and Subregional Organizations with which the Counter-Terrorism Committee Will Deepen Contact" attached to "Special Meeting of the Counter-Terrorism Committee with International, Regional and Subregional Orgnaizations", UN Doc., S/AC.40/2003/SM.1/6/Rev.1, 3 April 2003.

"Measures to eliminate international terrorism", Report of the Working Group, UN Doc., A/C.6/54/L.2, 26 October 1999.

"Memorandum From the Russian Federation Submitted in accordance with Paragraph 12 of Security Council Resolution 1456 (2003) on the Issue of Combating International Terrorism", UN Doc., S/2003/191, 18 February 2003.

"Note by the President of the Security Council", UN Doc., S/2004/70, 26 January 2004.

"Outcome Document of the Special Meeting of the Counter-Terrorism Committee with International, Regional and Subregional Organizations", UN Doc., S/AC.40/2003/SM.1/4, 31 March 2003.

"Provisional Summary Record of the First Part of the 57th Meeting", Presentation by Ambassador Jeremy Greenstock, then Chairman of the CTC at the Symposium, UN Doc., S/AC.40/SR.57, 18 March 2003.

"Remarks of the Chairman at the Closing Session", UN Doc., S/AC.40/2003/SM.1/5, 26 March 2003.

"Report of the *Ad Hoc* Committee on International Terrorism", UN Doc., A/9028, 1973, para.26. In: Friedlander RA (1979) *Terrrosim: Documents of International and Local Control*, vol. I, New York: Oceana Publications, Inc.

"Report of the *Ad Hoc* Committee on International Terrorism", UN Doc., A/32/37, 1977, para.10. In: Friedlander RA (1979) *Terrrosim: Documents of International and Local Control*, vol.I, New York: Oceana Publications, Inc.

"Report of the Ad Hoc Committee established by General Assembly resolution 51/210 of 17 December 1996", UN Doc., A/52/37, 31 March 1997.

"Report of the Secretary-General to the Security Council on the Protection of Civilians in Armed Conflict", UN Doc., S/1997/957, 8 September 1997.

"Report of the Ad Hoc Committee on the Establishment of an International Criminal Court", UN Doc., A/50/22, 1995. In: Bassiouni MC (ed) *The Statute of the International Criminal Court: A Documentary History*, New York: Transnational Publishers, Inc.

"Report of the Preparatory Committee on the Establishment of an International Criminal Court", vol. I, UN Doc., A/51/22, 1996. In: Bassiouni MC (ed) *The Statute of the International Criminal Court: A Documentary History*, New York: Transnational Publishers, Inc.

"Report of the Ad Hoc Committee established by General Assembly resolution 51/210 of 17 December 1996", UN Doc., A/54/37, 5 May 1999.

"Report of the Secretary-General on the Humanitarian Implication of the Measures imposed by Security Council Resolution 1267(1999) and 1333(2000) on Afghanistan", UN Doc., S/2001/241, 20 March 2001.

"Report of the Committee of Experts appointed pursuant to Security Council resolution 1333(2000), paragraph 15(a), regarding monitoring of the arms embargo against the Taliban and the closure of terrorist training camps in the Taliban-held areas of Afghanistan" enclosed in "Letter dated 21 May 2001 from the Secretary-General addressed to the President of the Security Council", UN Doc., S/2001/511, 22 May 2001.

"Report of the Secretary-General on Prevention of armed conflict", UN Doc., A/55/985-S/2001/574, 7 June 2001.

"Report of the Secretary-General on the humanitarian implication of the Measures imposed by Security Council resolution 1267(1999) and 1333(2000) on Afghanistan", UN Doc., S/2001/695, 13 July 2001.

"Report to the Counter-Terrorism Committee pursuant to paragraph 6 of Security Council resolution 1373(2001) of 28 September 2001", enclosed in "Letter dated 19 December 2001 from the Chairman of the Security Council Committee established pursuant to resolution 1373(2001) concerning counter-terrorism addressed to the President of the Security Council", UN Doc., S/2001/1232, 24 December 2001.

"Report of the Ad Hoc Committee established by General Assembly resolution 51/210 of 17 December 1996: Sixth Session (28 January-1 February 2002)", UN Doc., A/57/37, 2002.

"Report of the Security Council Committee established pursuant to resolution 1267(1999) concerning Afghanistan" attached to "Letter dated 17 January 2002 from the Chairman of the Security Council Committee established pursuant to resolution 1267(1999) concerning Afghanistan addressed to the President of the Security Council", UN Doc., S/2002/101, 5 February 2002.

"Report of the Monitoring Group established pursuant to Security Council resolution 1363(2001) and extended by resolution 1390(2002)" enclosed in "Letter dated 13 May 2002 from the Chairman of the Security Council Committee established pursuant to resolution 1267(1999) concerning Afghanistan addressed to the President of the Security Council", UN Doc., S/2002/541, 15 May 2002.

"Report of the Policy Working Group on the United Nations and Terrorism", UN Doc., S/2002/875, 6 August 2002.

"Report of the Security Council Committee established pursuant to resolution 1267 (1999) attached to "Letter dated 20 December 2002 from the Chairman of the Security Council Committee established pursuant to resolution 1267 (1999) addressed to the President of the Security Council", UN Doc., S/2002/1423, 26 December 2002.

"Report of the Government of the United States called for under Security Council resolution 1455(2003)" attached to "Letter dated 17 April 2003 from the Permanent Representative of the United States of America to the United Nations addressed to the Chairman of the Committee", UN Doc., S/AC.37/2003/(1455)/26, 22 April 2003.

"Second report of the Monitoring Group established pursuant to Security Council resolution 1363 and extended by resolution 1390 (2002)" enclosed in "Letter dated 19 September 2002 from the Chairman of the Security Council established pursuant to resolution 1267 (1999) addressed to the President of the Security Council", UN Doc., S/2002/1050 and Corr.1, 27 September 2002.

"Secretary-General's Letter of 4/5/99", UN Doc., S/1999/378, 5 April 1999. In: Grant JP (2004) *The Lockerbie Trial: A Documentary History*, New York: Oceana Publication, Inc.

"Special Meeting of Security Council's Counter-Terrorism Committee Hears Calls for Systematic International, Regional Cooperation", Press Release, UN Doc., SC/7679, 6 March 2003.

"Statement of the Chairman of the 1267 Committee on De-listing Procedures", Press Release, UN Doc., SC/7487/AFG/203, 16 August 2002.

"Third report of the Monitoring Group established pursuant to Security Council resolution 1363 and extended by resolution 1390 (2002)" enclosed in "Letter dated 16 December 2002 from the Chairman of the Security Council Committee established pursuant to resolution 1267 (1999) addressed to the President of the Security Council", UN Doc., S/2002/1338, 17 December 2002.

United Nations Office on Drugs and Crime, "The Global Programme Against Terrorism", in "Global Programmes".

Index

ABM, 193
Abu Sayyaf, 12, 20
acquisitive crime, 26
acronym, 101
active personality principle, 57
   ICSFT, 76
ad hoc committee, 60
administrative asset-freezing, 209
administrative corporate liability, 140
Afghanistan, 9, 13, 99
   Security Council, 78
Ahmed Khalfan Ghailani, 18
Al-Qaida, 3, 11, 15, 98
   hawala, 28
   jihad, 11
alternative remittance system, 155
AML/CFT, 125, 127
ancillary harm, 43, 66
ancillary offence, 66
anonymity, 51
anti-terrorism convention, 59, 65
Anti-Terrorism, Crime and Security Act
   2001, 45
APG, 174, 178
   co-chair, 181
   Commonwealth, 179
   consensus, 181
   first round, 184
   joint Plenary, 186
   membership, 180
   mutual evaluation, 183
   NCCT, 187
   non-compliance policy, 184
   purpose, 179
   self-assessment, 183
   Steering Group, 181
   Strategic Plan, 181
   symposium, 179
   technical assistance, 185
   terrorist financing, 183
   Typologies Working Group, 186
   typology, 179
appeal procedure, 110
Arab, 8
armed conflict, 63
armed robbery, 13
arms embargo, 99
Article IV, 174
assessment, 170
asset sharing, 58
asset-freezing, 199
ASSP, 153
asylum-seeker, 96
attempt
   inchoate offence, 48
aut dedere aut judicare. *extradition*

backup plan, 188
Bali bombing, 29
bank secrecy rule, 55, 59, 143
   Convention against Corruption, 68
   ICSFT, 74
   Palermo Convention, 68
   the 1990 FATF Recommendation, 56
   the 2003 revised text, 56
   Vienna Convention, 56
banknote, 28
BCBS, 144
BCCI, 43

beneficial owner, 51. *risk-based
     approach. CDD*
beyond reasonable doubt, 43
bin Laden, 18
biological weapon, 109
bombing in Jakarta, 29
bona fide third party, 68
buffer zone, 136

Caliphate, 11
     Central and Southeast Asia, 11
     North Africa, 11
capital, 16
capital flight, 190
CAS, 175
cash, 13. *cross-border transportation*
cash courier, 29
cash smuggling, 133
casino, 126
CDD, 126, 131, 150
     cash transaction, 136
     correspondent banking, 126
     disclosure system, 134
     flexibility, 131, 134
     Interpretative Note, 135
     politically exposed person, 126
     Special Recommendation, 131
     suspicion, 132
     threshold, 132
     wire transfer, 132
cell, 17
     Mohamed Sadeek, 17
     operational funding, 18
     operational money, 17
     seed money, 17
CEMAC, 187
centralised coordination, 204
CFATF, 174, 178
Chapter VII, 83
charitable organisation, 13, 22
charity, 30
civil confiscation, 208. *terrorist
     financing*
civil law system, 70

civil liberty, 96
climate of trust, 56
Clinton, 8
coca, 13
co-chair, 181
     Australia, 181
Cold War, 6
Colombia, 12
Columbia, 19
Commonwealth Secretariat, 109
complicity, 47, 77
conditionality, 189
confidentiality, 56, 59
     Vienna Convention, 56
confiscate, 130
confiscation, 39, 44, 58, 130
     civil confiscation, 45
     Convention against Corruption, 67
     criminal confiscation, 45
     ICSFT, 67
     instrumentality, 45
     object confiscation, 44
     Palermo Convention, 67
     reformative approach, 58
     traditional approach, 58
     value confiscation, 44
     Vienna Convention, 46, 58
consensus, 100
conspiracy, 66. *inchoate offence*
     ICSFT, 70
constituency, 12
corporate criminal liability. *criminal law*
     FATF Forty Recommendations, 49
     ICSFT, 70
corporate liability, 70
correspondent banking, 134, 149
     Basel Committee, 134
     risk-based approach, 150
     Wolfsberg Group, 149
corruption. *symbiotic relationship*
Counter-Terrorism Committee, 84
Country Assistance Strategy, 170
crime of aggression, 112
crimes against humanity, 112

terrorism, 113
criminal activity
    kidnapper, 28
    kidnapping, 20
    narcotics trade, 19
Criminal activity, 19
criminal confiscation, 67
criminal corporate liability, 140
criminal finance, 199
criminal law, 47
criminalisation, 39
    all-inclusive approach, 129
    Al-Qaida, 66
    Convention against Corruption, 67
    distribution, 66
    ICSFT, 66
    is intentionally ignorant, 47
    know, 47
    list approach, 129
    money laundering, 42
    negligent money laundering, 47
    Palermo Convention, 67
    predicate offence, 66
    should have known, 47
    terrorist financing, 65
    threshold approach, 129
    Vienna Convention, 43
cross-border transportation, 51
cross-country review, 158
CTC, 84, 89
    Assistance Database, 93
    best practice, 93, 94
    contact point, 92
    database, 93
    dialogue, 92
    FATF, 116
    first programme, 92
    model legislation, 93
    permanent body, 89
    programme, 91
    revitalising, 95
    second programme, 92
CTED, 95, 117
custom, 119

customary international law, 112
customer due diligence, 126
customer identification, 51, 72
    ICSFT, 72
    Palermo Convention, 72
    the 1990 Forty Recommendations, 53
    the 1996 Forty Recommendations, 53
    the 2003 Forty Recommendations, 53

dealers in precious metals, 126
decentralised terrorist group, 17
decolonisation, 123
definition of money laundering, 26
definition of terrorism, 63
    ICSFT, 109
de-listing, 100, 101, 103, 112
diamond, 30
    Al-Qaida, 30
displacement effect, 50
distribution process, 26
domino theory, 6
    Saudi Arabia, 6
donation, 21
    Benevolence International
        Foundation, 22
    Holy Land Foundation, 22
    zakat, 21
double criminality rule, 44
double-edged sword, 116
drug, 13, 57
drug baron, 210
drug trafficker, 13
dual criminality, 97, 209
duplication, 115, 127, 201
    assessment, 201
    centralised coordination, 204
    confidentiality, 203
    database, 204
    on-site visit, 202
    pilot programme, 202
    research, 205
    sanction, 205
    technical assistance, 203
    typology, 205

EAG, 178
ECOWAS, 187
effects doctrine, 57
Egmont Group, 42, 54, 143
    function, 54
Egypt, 8
elite, 16
    Mullah Mohamed Omar, 16
enforcement body, 100
equal legal footing, 104
equality, 184
ESAAMLG, 178
ETA, 3, 20
ethno-nationalist, 5
Ethno-nationalist/separatist terrorism, 2
EU Money Laundering Directive, 133
evidence-taking, 58
exterior supervision, 53
extradition, 58, 59, 142
    Vienna Convention, 59

FARC, 3, 5, 15, 21, 66
FATF, 125
    awareness-raising, 179
    common methodology, 160
    graduated approach, 162
    mandate, 125
    membership, 167
    research, 167
FATF membership, 203
    China, 203
feedback, 141
financial assistance, 168
financial devastation, 208
financial institution of any kind, 50
Financial Intelligence Unit, 41
financial resource, 9
First World War, 8
fiscal offence, 78
fiscal offence exception, 142.
    extradition
FIU, 41, 127, 137, 141, 153
    administrative model, 54
    AML/CFT, 127

confidentiality, 154
Convention against Corruption, 75
definition, 154
ICSFT, 75
information filtering, 42
law-enforcement model, 54
Palermo Convention, 75
prosecutorial model, 54
specialty, 154
flexibility, 136, 139
    accountant, 137
    casino, 136
    duplication, 139
    lawyer, 136
    notary, 137
    professional secrecy, 138
    real estate agent, 136
    resistance, 138
    risk-based approach, 138
    trust, 136
flow of information, 55
    ICSFT, 76
food for thought, 156
Ford Foundation. *cell*
Forty Recommendation (1990), 40
Francis Fukuyama, 5
freezing, 96
freezing and seizing, 68
frontman, 42, 65
FSA, 173
FSAP, 172
FSRB, 161, 177
    alienated, 188

GABAC, 187
GAFISUD, 178
gate keeper, 50, 133
General Assembly, 32
generality, 155
genocide, 112
GIABA, 187
Golden Crescent, 178
Golden Triangle, 178
Goldstein, 3

government of residence, 101
grassroot, 7
GRECO, 192, 203
ground truth, 95

Hamas, 3, 14, 15, 22
hard enforcement, 188
hard law, 119, 120, 155
hawala, 28, 105
    ICSFT, 75
    IMF, 177
Hezbollah, 95
high-cost economy, 189
hijacking, 63
HIV/AIDS, 211
hostage-taking, 63
human right, 96, 103, 104, 212
    concession, 104
Human Rights Committee, 114
humanitarian exception, 104

IAIS, 150, 196
ICC, 112
    civilian population, 113
    extermination, 113
    jurisdiction, 112
    murder, 113
    referral, 113
    Resolution 1593, 114
    serious crime, 113
    terrorism, 113
    US, 113
ICC statute, 113
ICSFT, 60, 61, 87, 88, 127. *Resolution 1373*
    bank secrecy rule, 68
    nature, 61
    scope of application, 61
ICTR, 111
ICTY, 111
ideological terrorism, 2
imcomplete offence, 70
IMF, 160, 168
    common assessment tool, 171

consulting service, 207
financial assistance, 168
fire brigade, 168
Global Dialogue Series, 177
lending, 176
NCCT, 171, 187, 207
pilot programme, 171
soft enforcement, 175
Imperialist, 9
IMU, 12, 13, 16
in personam, 45
in rem, 45
inchoate offence, 47
incitement. *inchoate offence*
incomplete offence, 77
individual. *responsibilisation strategy*
inducement, 188
informal transfer system, 105
informal value transfer system, 139
insurance, 143
intelligence, 27, 103
intention, 69
Inter-American Convention against
    Terrorism, 127
intermediary, 133
    Basel Committee, 133
internal control, 75, 138
internal control and training, 53
internal policy, 54, 138
International Convention for the
    Suppression of the Financing of
    Terrorism, 35
International Court of Justice, 114
International Criminal Court, 34, 70
international criminal law, 30
international security, 99
intrusive legal tool, 212
inventory record, 158
IOSCO, 147, 152, 196
    membership, 152
IRA, 3, 20
Iranian Revolution, 5, 6
Islamist, 5, 6, 15
Israel, 8

Japanese Red Army, 4
Jemmah Islamiya, 29
Jordan, 8
jurisdiction, 56
    adjudicate, 56
    enforce, 56
    executive, 56
    ICSFT, 76
    judicial, 56
    legislative, 56
    prescribe, 56

kidnapping, 12
know-your-customer, 146
KYC, 146
    centralised approach, 146
Kyrgyzstan, 19

lawyer, 126
Lebanon, 9
legal person. *corporate criminal liability*
legitimate business, 22
    Al-Qaida, 23
    gum arabic, 23
    honey, 24
    intermediary, 22
    Sudan, 23
    Sweden, 23
    Usama bin Laden, 22, 23
legitimisation, 26, 199
lending, 170
level playing field, 147, 157, 197
    ratione materiae, 198
    ratione personae, 198
Libya, 85
Libyan government, 36
listed person, 104
    Resolution 1452, 104
listing, 100
listing approach, 109
Lockerbie, 35, 85
Lod airport, 32

M19, 13

Mafia, 179
mandate, 100
match-making, 204
Matrix of Assistance, 93
MENAFATF, 178
mens rea, 47
    ICSFT, 69
Middle East, 6
Middle Eastern states, 8
MILF, 16
militia, 13
Mindanao, 16
mini-definition, 63
model law, 109
Model Legislative Provisions on
    Measures to Combat Terrorism, 109
momentum, 208
money laundering
    technique, 128
money laundering case, 28
money-making stage, 30
MONEYVAL, 178
Monitoring Group, 98, 101
Monitoring Team, 102
Muslim, 9
mutual assistance, 59
mutual evaluation, 158, 182
    confidential nature, 191
    FATF, 159
    New Zealand, 184
    third round, 161
    Vanuatu, 184
mutual legal assistance, 58, 97, 142
    ICSFT, 77

Nairobi, 18
naming and shaming, 189
narcotics trade
    fatwas, 20
    IMU, 19
national indictment, 110
national liberation movement, 65
NCCT, 147, 157, 161
    Austria, 163

criteria, 161, 166
IMF, 162
list, 165
Myanmar, 165
Nauru, 165
Nigeria, 165
non-binding, 165
non-compliance policy, 163
non-member, 165
non-universal, 165
normative imperialism, 165
reprisal, 166
soft enforcement, 166
stigmatisation, 165
third round, 172
Turkey, 163
Netherlands, 37
Nicaragua Case. *soft law*
non-bank financial institution, 50
non-compliance policy, 185
non-payment, 185
Non-Cooperative Countries and
    Territories, 124
non-FATF member, 158
non-financial institution, 50, 126
ICSFT, 72
non-profit organisation, 140, 155
notary, 126
no-tipping off, 53, 127, 138
ICSFT, 74
nuclear terrorism, 108

OAS Model Regulation, 47
objective factual circumstance, 69
objective territorial principle
    Vienna Convention, 57
objective territoriality, 57
OFC, 172
OFC programme, 174
off-duty military personnel, 64
Office on Drugs and Crime, 116
OGBS, 161
OIC, 65
oil, 7

on-site visit, 95, 159
operational approach, 97, 209
    organised crime, 209, 211
    Resolution 1591, 210
opinio juris, 124
opium, 105
Organisation of the Islamic Conference,
    64
organised crime, 39, 207
    financial devastation, 39
other profession, 72, 73

Pakistan, 17
Palermo Convention, 61, 127
Palestine, 13
paper trail, 52
paper truth, 95
passive personality principle, 57
    ICSFT, 77
peer pressure, 162
PELP, 3
permanence, 84
perpetrator-oriented approach, 39
petition, 101
Philippines, 12
pilot programme
    common methodology, 171
    FATF, 174
    FSRB, 174
piracy, 57
Plenary meeting, 158, 160
PLO, 3
Policy Working Group on the United
    Nations and Terrorism, 113
political offence, 78
political offence exception, 142.
    extradition
politically exposed person, 133
    Basel Committee, 133
poppy
    Afghanistan, 20
    Karzai government, 20
post hoc investigation, 52
predicate offence, 43, 56, 128

serious offence, 129
   terrorist financing, 129
primary harm, 43, 66
principal offence, 65
principle of flag, 57
princple of protection, 57
princple of universality, 57
private sector, 49
procedural matter, 107
Proceeds of Crime Act 2002, 45
proceeds-oriented approach, 39
procurement, 16
professional secrecy, 127
prosecution office, 155
Prosecutor v. Tadic, 83, 111, 210
protective principle
   ICSFT, 77
provisional measure, 68

quasi-judicial function, 83
quasi-legislative function, 83
questionnaire, 158

RAF, 4
ratione personae, 126
real estate agent, 126
real-time screening, 150
reasonable ground, 137
reciprocity, 174
Recommendation 21, 164, 189
record keeping, 51
   ICSFT, 73
   the 1990 Forty Recommendations, 53
recruitment, 13
Red Army Faction, 4
Red Brigade, 3, 28
refugee, 96
religious terrorism, 2
religious terrorist, 12
reporting of (suspicious) transaction, 51
representation principle, 57
reputation, 189
research, 205
Resolution 1192, 37

Resolution 1267, 78
Resolution 1333, 78, 97
Resolution 1363, 98, 100
   Monitoring Group, 100
Resolution 1368, 82
Resolution 1373, 81, 127
   definition of terrorism, 95
   extradition, 96
   financing of terrorism, 86
   momentum, 97
   universal nature, 85
Resolution 1390, 81, 98
   individual, 98
   momentum, 106
   particular, 98
   temporary, 98
Resolution 1455, 102, 106
   momentum, 106
Resolution 1526, 102
Resolution 1535, 95
Resolution 1617, 196
   FATF, 196
Resolution 53/108, 60
Resolution 731, 36
Resolution 748, 37
Resolution 883, 37
responsibilisation, 49
   horizontal expansion, 50
   individual, 51
   the 1996 revised Recommendation
      20, 51
   vertical extension, 50
responsibilisation strategy, 40, 51, 133
   customer identification, 51
   individual, 72
retroactive search, 150
reversal of burden of proof, 208
reversed burden of proof, 68
revitalisation, 207
right of victim, 68
risk-based approach, 134, 161
   CDD, 135
risk-based transaction monitoring, 150
Rome statute, 113

ROSC, 173

safe harbour, 53
safe harbour provision, 53
  ICSFT, 74
SAM, 13
sanction, 205
Sanctions Committee, 98, 100, 110
  consensus, 101
  decision-making procedure, 100
  operating procedure, 100
sanctions regime, 98
Saudi Arabia, 7
SDI, 193
secular terrorist, 12
security, 143
Security Council, 35, 81
  Asia/Pacific Group on Money
    Laundering, 116
  chapter VII, 82
  Chapter VII power, 35
  charity, 107
  CTC, 117
  definition of terrorism, 108
  duplication, 107, 115
  fair trial, 111
  FATF, 116
  humanitarian exception, 111
  IMF, 116
  informal value transfer system, 107
  judicial review procedure, 111
  momentum, 107, 117
  operational approach, 81
  rule of law, 107
  soft law, 108
  special meeting, 116
  structural approach, 81
  subsidiary body, 112
  transnational crime, 107, 118
  window of opportunity, 118
  World Bank, 116
self-assessment, 158, 182
  FATF, 159
self-defence, 7

self-determination, 64. *soft law*
self-regulatory organisation, 152
separate harm, 43
shell bank, 134
Six-Day war, 8
Sixth Committee, 116
smart sanction, 99
social welfare service, 15
soft enforcement, 119, 122, 188
  enforcement, 191
  inducement, 208
  market economy, 191
  monitoring, 191
  Montreal Protocol, 122
  naming and shaming, 190
  non-compliance policy, 189
  on-site examination, 192
  Ozone Convention, 122
  peer pressure, 191
  political pressure, 190
  reputation, 190
  self-assessment, 191
  technical assistance, 188
  universal membership, 192
  value deprivation, 208
soft law, 120, 154
  all or nothing situation, 123
  BCBS, 196
  binding force, 120
  corruption, 123
  declaration, 121
  definition, 120
  detailed content, 122
  dispute settlement, 121
  FATF, 121
  General Assembly Resolution 1514,
    123
  guideline, 121
  ICSFT, 121
  non-profit charity organisation, 123
  OECD, 123
  opinio juris, 123
  Outer Space, 123
  precision, 121

ratification, 122
realm of soft law, 122
resolution, 121
Security Council, 121
soft enforcement, 121
softening, 122
sovereignty, 122
Special Recommendation, 121
spectrum, 122
the 1982 UN Convention on the Law
  of the Sea, 121
transformation, 193
uncertainty, 193
Somalia, 9
source of international law, 212
specialist body, 119
  1390, 121
  Resolution 1373, 121
specialty, 56, 59, 156
  ICSFT, 76
sponsor, 13
state behaviour, 123
state of mind, 47
state practice, 123
Steering Group, 181
stigmatisation, 189
stock exchange, 152
stock market, 30
Strategic Plan, 181
subjective territoriality, 57
substantive matter, 107
Sudan, 17, 114
suicide bomber, 13
supervision, 75, 139
  BCBS, 144
  casino, 140
  Core Principle, 139
  hawala, 139
  ICSFT, 75
  non-profit organisation, 140
  risk-sensitive basis, 140
supply of weapon, 115
surveillance, 168
suspicion-based model, 53

suspicion-based reporting model
  ICSFT, 73
switchboard, 93
symbiotic relationship, 186
symptomatic treatment, 35
synergy effect, 106, 156
Syria, 8

Taliban, 98
tax evasion, 59
technical assistance, 168, 170, 204
  feedback, 204
temporariness, 99
terrorism, 62
  defining, 62
  mini-definition, 63
  universal definition, 64
terrorist financing, 24, 126
  cash smuggling, 29
  diamond, 29
  distribution, 25
  gold, 29
  hawala, 28
  lead line, 26
  money-making activity, 25
  stock market, 30
  wire transfer, 29
terrorist organisation, 10
Third World, 33
threat to international peace, 210
threshold, 52
threshold-based reporting model, 53
  ICSFT, 73
transformation, 157, 194
  customary law, 195
  opinio juris, 195
  Palermo Convention, 194
  state practice, 195
  treaty, 194
travel ban, 99
treaty, 119
  soft law, 123
Triad, 179
Trojan horse, 199

duplication, 201
  free ride, 200
trust, 126
Twin Tower, 79
typology, 177

UF, 17
UN Convention against Corruption, 61
unfreezing, 105
universality, 84
Usama bin Laden, 8, 11, 13, 16, 97, 112
UTA Flight 772, 35
Uzbekistan, 12

value confiscation. *terrorist financing*
value deprivation, 188
video conference, 177
Vienna Convention, 40, 47
  state of mind, 47
Vietnam War, 7

war crime, 57, 112
weaponry, 13
Western Sahara Advisory Opinion, 123
Western states, 4
wire transfer, 25, 29, 134
  9/11 hijacker, 29
  special recommendation, 134
WMD, 1, 7, 9, 14, 82, 115, 211
  nuclear weapon, 14
  Resolution 1540, 82
  WMD committee, 14
Wolfsberg Group of Banks, 147
World Bank, 168
  database, 176
  FIRST initiative, 175
  membership, 168
  technical assistance, 176

Yakuza, 179
Yemen, 17

zakat, 22